Management for Professionals

The Springer series "Management for Professionals" comprises high-level business and management books for executives, MBA students, and practice-oriented business researchers. The topics cover all themes relevant to businesses and the business ecosystem. The authors are experienced business professionals and renowned professors who combine scientific backgrounds, best practices, and entrepreneurial vision to provide powerful insights into achieving business excellence.

The Series is SCOPUS-indexed.

Shusong Ba · Yang Wang · Haifeng Bai ·
Haokang Thomas Zhu

RWA Tokenisation in Web 3.0 Era

Springer

Shusong Ba
HKU Business School
Hong Kong, China

Peking University
Beijing, China

Haifeng Bai
CMB International Asset Management Limited
Hong Kong, China

Yang Wang
Hong Kong University of Science and Technology
Hong Kong, China

Haokang Thomas Zhu
China Asset Management (Hong Kong) Limited
Hong Kong, China

ISSN 2192-8096 ISSN 2192-810X (electronic)
Management for Professionals
ISBN 978-981-96-7662-0 ISBN 978-981-96-7663-7 (eBook)
https://doi.org/10.1007/978-981-96-7663-7

This Springer imprint is published by the registered company Springer Nature Singapore Pte Ltd.
The registered company address is: 152 Beach Road, #21-01/04 Gateway East, Singapore 189721, Singapore

Preface I

The Financial Industry Is Confronting a Major Digital Migration and Transformation: Exploring Innovative Practices in Web 3.0 and Digital Virtual Assets in Hong Kong

At present, short-term market turmoil and changes in the international economic and trade pattern make it easy for the financial community to ignore the emerging deep, fundamental, and trending innovations and changes. In fact, in today's global economy, digitalization and Technological innovation has become a key factor in promoting economic development. Especially in the field of Web 3.0 and digital virtual assets, these technologies are redefining the operation of the capital market, bringing unprecedented possibilities and new challenges to the traditional financial service industry. It is against the background of this major change in the economic and financial landscape that the government of the Hong Kong Special Administrative Region of China has successively launched a series of forward-looking economic and financial policies to support the development of Web 3.0 and digital virtual assets, which established Hong Kong's strategic vision to seize the opportunities presented by the major changes and develop into a global financial technology hub. Based on this trend and combined with the specific practice of the Hong Kong Special Administrative Region, RWA, and Tokenization provides readers with an analytical perspective on how to promote financial innovation and transformation under the existing policy framework.

This book not only interprets the basic concepts and technical characteristics of Web 3.0 in detail but also shows how these theories are applied in practice through a large number of practical cases. The content of this book covers topics from the basic theory of Web 3.0 to the application of blockchain technology and artificial intelligence big data, to the practical cases of token economics, as well as stablecoins and real-world asset (RWA) Tokenization models.

At the same time, the cases and practices contained in this book focus on the background of Hong Kong's policies. Hong Kong has always been a "super contact" connecting East and West. With the rise of the digital economy, the Hong Kong Special Administrative Region government has launched a series of incentives, including tax incentives, optimization of regulatory frameworks, and investment in innovative technologies, in order to promote the development of Web 3.0 technology and digital virtual assets. The book introduces how Hong Kong can promote compliance with digital assets through these policies and improve the transparency and efficiency of financial markets.

As an innovative financial operation model, Tokenization can solve many limitations and problems in the traditional investment and financing model from a technical point of view. Through case analysis and theoretical discussion, the author shows how tokenization can promote the effective flow of capital, improve market transparency, and provide new investment opportunities for investors. Tokenization refers to the conversion of assets (such as equity, debt, real estate, etc.) into digital tokens, which are recorded and traded on the blockchain. This process not only improves transaction efficiency but also reduces transaction costs and participation thresholds. Through specific cases of Hong Kong, many chapters of this book show how tokenization is actually applied to various asset classes and explore how these technologies can help Hong Kong maintain its status as a global financial center.

While promoting the innovation of financial technology, how to effectively manage the accompanying risks is a major challenge that policymakers and industry participants must face. By summarizing Hong Kong's experience, this book explores how regulators can ensure the stability and security of the market by formulating reasonable policies and regulatory frameworks in the rapidly developing digital asset market. The book gives examples of how Hong Kong's financial regulators classify and manage stablecoins and other cryptocurrencies and formulate a series of regulatory measures, including capital requirements, liquidity management, and anti-money laundering and counter-terrorism financing policies, to ensure that these emerging products will not have a negative impact on the broader financial system.

In addition to Hong Kong's practice, this book also refers to the experience of many countries and regions around the world in the same field. It regulates the current global development trend of Web 3.0 and digital virtual assets and also shows innovative cases in different regulatory environments.

In short, RWA and Tokenization reveal the potential of digital assets and Web 3.0 technology to readers. More importantly, it also explores and provides a blueprint for how to innovate and practice under the existing policy and regulatory framework. Through rich case analysis and in-depth theoretical discussion, this book provides valuable references for scholars, policymakers, entrepreneurs, and investors in the field of financial technology. The case of Hong Kong, China, provides valuable experience and inspiration for other parts of the world, which is worthy of reference for readers interested in this topic.

Hong Kong, China
August 2024

Shusong Ba
Executive Dean of the HSBC Financial Research Institute, Vice President of the China Macroeconomics Association, Chief Economist of the China Banking Association, Expert Member of the Chief Executive's Policy Unit Expert Group, Hong Kong Special Administrative Region Government

Preface II

Embracing Web 3.0: Opening a New Era of Tokenization

In this era of rapid transformation, the continuous development and innovation of internet technologies have led to the rise of Web 3.0, the next generation of the internet. It has had a profound impact on various aspects of society. Particularly in the field of finance and investment, the core technologies of Web 3.0—blockchain and tokenization—are reshaping investment and financing models, bringing unprecedented changes to the industry.

In the Web 3.0 era, the tokenization of RWA is a quiet but rapidly evolving financial revolution. Its core concept is "Web 3.0 empowers the real economy." The development of Web 3.0's technical and financial infrastructure provides new solutions for improving the liquidity of global RWAs, enhancing transaction efficiency, reducing transaction costs, and optimizing the inclusiveness of financial services. Based on blockchain networks and smart contract technology, various RWAs such as bonds, stocks, currencies, funds, trusts, real estate, artworks, carbon credits, etc., are transformed into digital tokens that are easy to divide, quickly transfer, and can be traded globally in real-time at a low cost 24 hours a day, 7 days a week. This not only enables these assets to be traded and managed more efficiently, conveniently, and with a lower threshold but also allows them to better integrate into the digital economy ecosystem.

Although the concept of tokenization has been discussed in the technical field for many years, it has only truly entered the public eye recently with the maturity and popularization of blockchain technology. The core of tokenization lies in using the decentralized and non-tamperable characteristics of blockchain to issue tokens to represent certain assets or rights, realizing the circulation and exchange of value. Although tokenization brings many benefits, it also requires strong technical support and a high degree of security. The core features of blockchain technology—distributed ledgers, cryptographic security, and smart contracts—are the foundation for realizing tokenization. Distributed ledgers ensure the non-comparability and transparency of data; cryptographic technology protects users' privacy and transaction security; smart contracts automatically execute contract terms, reducing human intervention and errors. However, the complexity and novelty of the technology also bring challenges. For example, vulnerabilities in smart contracts may be exploited by hackers, resulting in financial losses; the scalability problem of blockchain networks may also lead to issues in transaction speed and cost. Therefore, continuous technical innovation and strict security measures are the keys to the success of Tokenization. In addition, tokenization also faces complex legal and regulatory issues globally. Different countries and regions have different attitudes and relevant regulations towards tokenization, which brings uncertainty to the promotion and application of tokenization and also poses legal risks to investors and participants.

RWA and Tokenization was born in such a transformative context. As scholars and practitioners who started researching Web 3.0 and Tokenization technology relatively early in China, we, with enthusiasm and a sense of mission for this field, decided to write this book to share our years of research results and practical experience with readers. We hope to deeply analyze the principles of Web 3.0 and Tokenization technology, combined with numerous cases, to clarify their applications in investment and financing and look ahead to future development trends, providing readers with a comprehensive and systematic understanding and helping them grasp the huge opportunities brought by Tokenization.

This book strives to comprehensively explain Web 3.0 and Tokenization technology from theory to practice, from concepts to cases, and from opportunities to challenges. Chapter 1 systematically introduces the definition, characteristics, and impacts on traditional investment and financing models of Web 3.0, helping readers quickly establish a basic understanding of Web 3.0. Chapters 2–4, as the theoretical cornerstone, deeply explore the blockchain technology principles on which Tokenization is based and the token economics theory contained therein, helping readers lay a solid knowledge foundation. At the practical level, Chaps. 5 and 6, as typical applications, focus on analyzing the two most core models in Tokenization—various types of RWAs and stablecoins. The RWA model innovatively proposes ways to digitize and tokenize RWAs, greatly broadening the application scenarios and boundaries of Tokenization. And stablecoins, as the bridge connecting the digital world and the real world, play a key role in promoting the prosperity of the Tokenization ecosystem. Through detailed cases and in-depth analysis, readers can clearly understand the operation mode and realization path of Tokenization.

However, the development of Tokenization is not smooth. It also faces many risks and challenges. Chapters 7 and 8, with a prudent attitude, discuss the potential problems of Tokenization in terms of supervision and social impacts, objectively analyze the resistance and limitations it faces, and propose coping strategies and development suggestions. Only in this way can the development of Tokenization be healthier and more sustainable.

We always uphold an open, innovative, and inclusive attitude and humbly accept the valuable insights of industry experts and scholars. We have specially invited many well-known domestic and foreign experts to write prefaces and recommendations for this book. From the academic and practical perspectives, they have highly evaluated the value of this book. Their participation undoubtedly adds important academic weight to this book and enhances its practical height. During the writing of this book, we received the help of many people. We especially thank our families, teachers, and friends for their support and encouragement during the writing process. Mr. Peng Liu, Dr. Wenzhou Yi, Dr. Wenzhi Ding, and Dr. Yuxiang Li participated in the writing. The editors of Cheers Publishing have made great efforts for the smooth publication of this book. Without the support and help of the above-mentioned people, this book would not have been able to come out. We express our sincere gratitude to everyone.

The wave of Web 3.0 is surging, and tokenization is evolving from a concept to a reality. As participants, contributors, and beneficiaries of this transformation, we deeply feel the mission on our shoulders and the huge opportunities ahead. We sincerely hope that this book can be a helpful assistant and guide for readers to understand tokenization and seize the opportunities of Web 3.0. We also hope that this book will not only be a carrier for the dissemination of knowledge but also a starting point for change, inspiring everyone to actively participate in this transformation and bravely become pioneers and forerunners.

Hong Kong, China
August 2024

Yang Wang
Vice President for University Advancement, Chief Scientist of the Hong Kong Web 3.0 Association

Haifeng Bai
Managing Director and Co-Head of CMB International Asset Management

Haokang Thomas Zhu
Head of Digital Asset Management and Family Wealth Management

Praise for *RWA Tokenisation in Web 3.0 Era*

"'RWA and Tokenization' provides a comprehensive analytical framework for tokenized assets. It offers foundational and essential information for understanding the complexities of this field, making it a highly valuable read."

—Hongbin Cai, *Dean of the Faculty of Business and Economics, The University of Hong Kong, Member of the Chief Executive's Policy Unit Expert Group, Hong Kong Special Administrative Region Government*

"This book expands the discussion of tokenization to the economic and social dimensions, delving into the profound impact of tokenization on economic systems. Through a unique perspective, it helps readers gain a deeper understanding of this emerging field."

—Hongping Cai, *Chairman and Founding Partner of Hand Capital, Former Chairman of Deutsche Bank Investment Banking, Asia-Pacific*

"This book provides us with a clear framework on how tokenization can bring revolutionary changes to the real economy. Through a wealth of case studies and in-depth analysis, readers are able to better understand this trend, making it highly suitable for industry professionals who wish to apply theory to practice."

—Delin Chen, *Chairman of the Board, Circle Coin Technology, Former Chief Executive, Hong Kong Monetary Authority*

"Through thorough research, this book not only elaborates on the theoretical foundations of tokenization, but more importantly, it provides practical pathways and case studies. It is highly suitable for industry professionals who wish to apply theory to practice."

—Jiaqiang Chen, *Chairman of the Board, Huili Bank, Former Secretary for Financial Services and the Treasury, Hong Kong*

"This book fully demonstrates the potential of tokenization technology and specifically explores its practical applications across various industries. For practitioners of tokenization, this is a must-read material."

—Zhongni Chen, *Member of the Legislative Council, Hong Kong*

"In the rapidly changing financial world, this book not only provides valuable insights and tools for understanding and utilizing tokenization, but also offers a precious reference for the potential evolution of investment and financing under the empowerment of technology."

—Fang Yuan, *Founding Managing Partner, Xingjie Capital, Chairman of the ESG Committee, Former President of LGT Capital, Greater China*

"This book provides an in-depth analysis of how Web 3.0 is leading the development of tokenized assets. It elaborates in detail on the technical principles and application cases of RWA tokenization, offering profound insights into the significance of financial innovation."

—Peifan Ge, *Member of the Legislative Council, Hong Kong, Vice Chairman of the Hong Kong Democratic Alliance for the Betterment and Progress of Hong Kong*

"Tokenization is becoming a new trend in the digital asset market. This book systematically organizes the technological foundations and application models, providing comprehensive guidance and reference for financial institutions in their digital asset strategies."

—Wei Guo, *Chairman of the Board, Digital China Holdings Limited*

"This book, through a wealth of data and case studies, showcases the immense potential of tokenization. Readers will gain a sense of the urgency and significance of this technology's future development."

—Xu Jin, *Chairman, Wealth and Asset Management, Manulife Investment, Greater China, Chairman, Manulife Funds*

"This book provides a timely dissemination of RWA knowledge. The practice of RWA is yet another example of the beneficial combination of centralized trust and digital technology, which broadens financing channels."

—Mei Luo, *Director, Digital Financial Asset Research Center, School of Economics and Management, Tsinghua University*

"This book, with a wealth of practical examples, vividly illustrates the operating mechanisms and real-world value of the tokenization model. Both academic researchers and practitioners in the field can draw inspiration from it."

—Yuan Qi, *Dean, Institute for Artificial Intelligence Innovation and Industry, Fudan University, Former Vice President, Alibaba (China) Ltd., Former Executive Dean, Alibaba Data Science and Technology Institute, Former Chief AI Scientist and Chairman of the Data Intelligence Committee, Ant Group*

"*'RWA and Tokenization'* provides an authoritative analytical framework for tokenized assets. It offers an important reference for understanding the complexities of this field, making it an exceptionally valuable read."

—Dagen Qiu, *Member of the Legislative Council, Hong Kong*

"This book explains the complex concepts of tokenization in a clear and accessible manner. It is not only suitable for professionals but also for general readers interested in financial technology."

—Hailong Shang, *Member of the Legislative Council, Hong Kong*

"This book not only contributes significantly to popularizing Web 3.0 knowledge in Hong Kong, but also plays a positive role in helping Hong Kong embrace the era of tokenization and in the development of its position as an international financial center."

—Jianguang Shen, *Chief Economist, JD Group*

"This book provides us with a clear framework on how tokenization can bring revolutionary changes to the real economy. Through a wealth of case studies and in-depth analysis, readers are able to better understand this trend."

—Guangshao Tu, *Chairman, Shanghai Institute of New Finance, Former Vice Chairman, China Securities Regulatory Commission, Former Standing Committee Member of the Shanghai Municipal Party Committee and Executive Vice Mayor of Shanghai, Former General Manager, China Investment Corporation*

"This book provides us with the logical and theoretical framework on how tokenization can support the real economy. It serves as both a foundational read and a guide. Through the examination of cases and in-depth analysis, readers will gain a better understanding of the theory and practice of tokenization and RWA. Additionally, this book is beneficial for the expansion and penetration of digital asset tokenization, as well as its positive practices and implementation in society."

—Zhongmin Wang, *Chairman, Shenzhen Institute for Financial Stability and Development, Former Vice Chairman, National Social Security Fund Council*

"*'RWA and Tokenization'* provides a cutting-edge analytical framework for asset tokenization, deeply revealing the complexities of this field and laying the foundation for its further development. This is a work of significant reference value."

—Xiangdong Wei, *Associate Director, PhD Program in Financial Technology, School of Business, The Hong Kong Polytechnic University*

"Why has innovation been successful in China? Because of China's large economic scale, the cost of trial and error is relatively low, and once successful, the overall economic impact of innovation is significant. As a professional accountant, I support the construction of innovative systems. When the productivity of an innovation-driven economy is formed, the marginal cost of utilizing that productivity is very low. This is not only a characteristic of the digital economy but also a concrete manifestation of new types of productivity.

"*RWA and Tokenization*" makes a professional effort in how digital assets and the digital economy can bring innovation and change to society. It extends the discussion of tokenization to the economic and social dimensions and delves into the profound impact of tokenization on the economic system. From the unique perspective of tokenization, this book helps readers better understand this emerging field. I sincerely recommend everyone to read this book."

—Weijun Wu, *Vice Chairman, Deloitte China*

"This book helps readers deeply understand the operation principle of Tokenization technology through a comprehensive analysis. At the same time, its cautious attitude towards potential risks also increases the credibility of this book."

—Lina Xu, *Professor and Chair of the Actuarial Department, Columbia University*

"Tokenization is becoming a new trend in the evolution of digital finance. This book provides us with a clear framework and a wealth of case studies for understanding and utilizing tokenization. It is an essential reference book for practitioners on the eve of rapid changes in the financial markets."

—Xiaofeng Zhong, *Chairman, Greater China, Groupama Asset Management*

Test yourself. How can Tokenization transform the financial world?

- Tokenization is regarded as a limited implementation of RWA. Is this statement correct? (Multiple choice)
  - A. true
  - B. False
- The main sectors for future tokenized investment and financing will primarily revolve around standardization, transparency ( ), and creative applications. (multiple choice)
  - A. Profitability
  - B. Safety
  - C. Low risky
  - D. Participation
- The Hong Kong Monetary Authority held the ( ) Project Sandbox launch ceremony in 2024.8.28. This marks an important step in the practical application of Tokenization technology in the financial industry. (multiple choice)
  - A. Ensemble
  - B. Ubin
  - C. Ethena
  - D. Ondo finance

Scan the code to join the bookshelf and claim your reading rewards.

Scan the code to access all test questions and answers, and explore the financial world of RWA and tokenization together.

Scan the QR code on the left to view more test questions from this book.

Contents

Web3.0: The Third Generation of the Internet

1

1.1 Web 3.0: The New Internet Economy with Ownership

As an emerging internet technology, Web 3.0 is built on blockchain technology and aims to create a more open and decentralized network environment. This new generation of internet technology enables users to be not only content consumers but also content creators and owners. In Web 3.0, users directly control their personal data and assets through blockchain technology, which is in sharp contrast to the current Web 2.0, where data and user interactions are mainly controlled by centralized service providers. In the development history of the internet, Web 3.0, like a rising star, is gradually reshaping our understanding and imagination of the digital world.

The term "Web 3.0" was first proposed by Gavin Wood, a co-founder of Ethereum, in 2014. It opened a new era of internet development and indicated a new direction of social development. As shown in Table 1.1, in the Web 1.0 era, network activities were limited to the display of static web pages; in the Web 2.0 era, we witnessed the rise of centralized platforms of technology giants such as Google, Meta, and Amazon; the Web 3.0 era, however, proposes a completely different vision-breaking this centralized control model. Under the framework of Web 3.0, a decentralized online ecosystem is constructed based on blockchain technology. In this ecosystem, platforms and applications are no longer controlled by a few giants but are jointly owned and maintained by all users. Users obtain corresponding ownership and control rights by participating in the development and maintenance of services.

To turn this vision into reality, Wood proposed the concept of Web 3.0 and established the Web 3.0 Foundation, which is dedicated to supporting the development of "decentralized" technology projects. The company Parity Technologies, led by him, focuses on building blockchain infrastructure for Web 3.0 (such as the Polkadot project, etc.). It provides solid technical support for decentralized applications.

S. Ba et al., *RWA Tokenisation in Web 3.0 Era*, Management for Professionals,
https://doi.org/10.1007/978-981-96-7663-7_1

Table 1.1 Comparison of the web development process

Development dimension	Web 1.0	Web 2.0	Web 3.0
Interactive mode	Clean culture	Reader-writer	Reader-writer and ownership
Creativity	Simply test	Multiple contents	Interactive economy
Economic model	Company	Platform	Network
Structural pattern	Personal computer	Cloud and mobile devices	blockchain technology
Control mode	Decentration	Centration	Decentration

In a recent interview, Wood, from the perspective of both a proponent and practitioner of Web 3.0, deeply discussed the core values and future development blueprint of Web 3.0. He firmly believes that with continuous technological advancements and the widespread expansion of its applications, Web 3.0 will become the new cornerstone of the digital world, leading human society toward a more equitable, transparent, and sustainable development path.

1.1.1 The Blueprint of Web 3.0: Constructing a Decentralized Digital Future

As a new stage in the development of the Internet, Web 3.0 is reshaping our perception and imagination of the digital world. It is built on innovative technologies such as blockchain, smart contracts, encryption technology, and decentralized storage, aiming to create a more open, transparent, secure, and autonomous new network ecosystem. The vision of Web 3.0 is not only a technological upgrade and iteration but also a transformation and reconstruction of various aspects, such as the digital economy, social governance, and cultural communication.

1.1.2 Decentralization: Reshaping the Power Structure of the Digital World

Decentralization is a core feature of Web 3.0. Through a distributed network architecture and consensus mechanism, it weakens centralized authority and empowers users with autonomy. In the Web 3.0 world, every user is an equal node. Without relying on centralized institutions or platforms, users can freely create, store, exchange, and manage their digital assets and data. This decentralized design not only improves the stability and security of the system but also provides users with more privacy protection and decision-making freedom.

Another important significance of decentralization lies in its ability to break the monopoly of data and wealth and realize the redistribution of value. In the

Web 2.0 era, a few tech giants accumulated a large amount of user data and traffic through centralized platforms, forming an oligopolistic pattern in the digital economy. However, under the Web 3.0 framework, users can directly participate in the creation and exchange of data and value through encryption technology and economic incentive mechanisms, thus obtaining a more equitable distribution of benefits. This decentralized economic model will greatly stimulate the creativity of individuals and communities and promote the prosperity and development of the digital economy.

1.1.3 Smart Contracts: Encoding Trust and Reconstructing Business Logic

Smart contracts are a key technology in Web 3.0. By converting contract terms into self-executing code, they reconstruct and optimize traditional business logic. Smart contracts run on the blockchain. Once reached and deployed, they cannot be tampered with or revoked, thus providing a new trust mechanism. This characteristic of "code is law" not only improves the efficiency and transparency of contract execution but also reduces the risks of fraud and breach of contract.

The application scenarios of smart contracts are very extensive, covering various fields such as financial services, supply chain management, intellectual property protection, and social governance. For example, in the decentralized finance (DeFi) field, smart contracts can automatically execute financial services such as lending, trading, and insurance without the participation of intermediary institutions, thus reducing costs and risks. In terms of copyright protection, smart contracts can help creators achieve automatic content authorization and charging, safeguarding the rights and interests of creators. As smart contract technology continues to mature, we will see more and more innovative applications emerging, reshaping the way our business and society operate.

1.1.4 Privacy and Security: Protecting Digital Sovereignty with Technology

In the Web 3.0 world, privacy and security are no longer luxuries but the basic rights of every user. Through encryption technology and decentralized storage, Web 3.0 provides solid protection for users' data sovereignty. Users can independently control their digital identities and data assets without worrying about privacy leakage or data abuse. At the same time, the decentralized network architecture also greatly improves the security of the system, avoiding single-point failures and external attacks.

The privacy and security protection of Web 3.0 is not only a technological advancement but also an advocacy and practice of digital rights. In the era when data has become the new "oil," how to protect personal privacy and maintain data sovereignty is a major challenge faced by the digital society. This design concept of "privacy-centric and security-based" is bound to become an important direction for the future development of the Internet. Web 3.0 provides an innovative solution to this problem. Through technological means, it gives users control over their own data and reshapes the power structure of the digital world, mainly reflected in the following three aspects:

- In the financial field, Web 3.0 completely changes our perception of financial services through DeFi.Users can directly conduct cryptocurrency trading, lending, and other businesses on the blockchain without the need for traditional financial institutions as intermediaries. This not only improves efficiency but also significantly reduces costs.
- In the fields of art and media, the rise of non-fungible tokens (NFT) has provided a new economic model for artists and creators. Artworks and digital content can be bought and sold as NFT on the blockchain, ensuring the ownership of copyrights and the transparency of transactions. This enables creators to directly profit from their works without going through third-party platforms.
- In the field of supply chain management, blockchain technology has increased supply chain transparency, reduced fraud and errors, and improved the efficiency of the entire system.

1.1.5 Applications and Challenges: The Path to the Future

The application prospects of Web 3.0 are extremely broad, covering various fields such as finance, social networking, gaming, and art. Emerging concepts and models such as DeFi, NFT, and decentralized autonomous organizations (DAO) are reshaping the boundaries and imagination of traditional industries. More and more entrepreneurs and developers are engaging in the ecological construction of Web 3.0, exploring the infinite possibilities of the future Internet.

However, the development of Web 3.0 also faces many challenges. Firstly, there are issues regarding technological complexity and usability. For ordinary users, the barriers to blockchain and encryption technology are relatively high. Designing more user-friendly and easy-to-use interfaces and providing more human-centric interactive experiences are crucial for the large-scale popularization of Web 3.0. Secondly, there are regulatory and legal issues. The decentralized nature of Web 3.0 conflicts to a certain extent with the existing legal framework. How to establish a sound regulatory system while protecting innovation is an issue that requires continuous exploration. Finally, the decentralized network of Web 3.0 also faces new security challenges. Whether it can prevent and address risks such as smart contract vulnerabilities and 51% attacks requires the joint efforts of developers and the community. Despite these challenges, the technological innovation and value concepts represented by Web 3.0 are opening up new horizons for the digital age. As technology continues to evolve and the ecosystem matures, Web 3.0 has the potential to become the core driving force shaping the future digital economy and digital society.

1.1.6 Analysis of the Underlying Logic of Web 3.0: Reconstruction of Accounting Methods

In the long history of human civilization, written records have a history of more than 5000 years and the evolution of accounting methods has also undergone three significant changes, which have had a profound impact on the economic systems of human society. The earliest form of accounting, single-entry bookkeeping, can be traced back to 3,500 BC. Early accounts were recorded on clay tablets unearthed in the Sumerian region. This accounting method only involved records of income and expenditure. In the fourteenth century, with the rise of oceanic trade, city-states in the northern part of the Mediterranean in Italy saw the further development of accounting methods-double-entry bookkeeping emerged. The complexity of oceanic trade, including partnership operations, lending relationships, and tax handling, required accounting methods to be more detailed and comprehensive, and single-entry bookkeeping could no longer meet these needs. Further innovations in accounting methods occurred in the digital age. Since the birth of Bitcoin in 2009, distributed ledger technology (DLT) has come into being. This accounting method not only records the value of digital assets and network assets but is also a product of humanity's adaptation to digital lifestyles. The book *Being Digital* foresaw the trend of the digital migration of human society, and distributed ledger technology was born to adapt to this trend.

Accounting methods are the cornerstone of economic transactions and a key factor in the progress of social civilization. They have had a wide-ranging impact on many fields, such as the economy, society, and politics. For example, double-entry bookkeeping is regarded as the cornerstone of capitalist economic and political systems. In a distributed accounting system, accounting methods, account systems, and accounting units form three basic levels. With the advent of the Web 3.0 era, the accounting system has shifted from traditional bank accounts to encrypted accounts, and the accounting unit has changed from legal tender (hereinafter referred to as "fiat currency") to digital currency.

Against the backdrop of Web 3.0, the operation models of capital and finance have undergone significant changes. Crypto-capital plays an increasingly important role in the global financial market. From the initial coin offering (ICO) in 2017 to the currently discussed security token offering (STO), initial exchange offering (IEO), as well as the issuance of RWA and stablecoins, these are all specific manifestations of crypto-capital.

Blockchain technology, as the cornerstone of Web 3.0, has the core principle of distributed ledger technology. Compared with traditional accounting methods, blockchain technology provides a decentralized, transparent, and immutable record-keeping system. In this system, information and transactions are jointly verified by all nodes and are stored on each node through encryption, ensuring the security and integrity of data.

The innovation of Web 3.0 should start from the periphery and gradually expand to core areas to form core competitiveness. On this basis, the innovative development of Web 3.0 should evolve from digital native to digital twin, which marks the starting point of disruptive innovation. At the same time, true innovation should meet the innate needs of humanity rather than simply imitating existing products so as to better serve society. In addition, the innovation of Web 3.0 should rely on an open and transparent global ledger to build business models that match new values. Finally, with the development of Web 3.0, we need to develop user-friendly terminal tools similar to the "browser" and "graphical operating system" in the Internet era. In the future, these tools may become operating systems based on natural language to promote the popularization and application of the technology.

1.1.7 Detailed Explanation of Web 3.0 Application Innovations and Economic Models

The economic models of blockchain applications differ significantly from those of blockchain infrastructure. For example, blockchain infrastructure such as Bitcoin and Ethereum usually adopt a single-token economic model because they represent basic protocols. However, when application protocols are developed, they can design more diverse and rich economic models and tools than the basic protocols.

Economic models are mainly divided into functional tokens, security tokens, and NFT. Functional tokens represent the tokenization of usage rights, security tokens represent the tokenization of ownership rights, and NFT represent the tokenization of digital goods and digital services. Application innovations in Web 3.0 can utilize one, two, or all three of these tokens to build their economic models, thus creating more and greater innovation space than the technical protocols themselves. The integration and interoperability of Web 3.0 application innovations is an important trend for the future. The bridge between traditional finance and Crypto finance is not only a prerequisite for Web 3.0 technological innovation but also a result of its application innovation. Currently, at least five bridges are helping the traditional financial market and the Web 3.0 financial market/Crypto financial market achieve interoperability, jointly forming the overall framework for Web 3.0 application innovation in the next decade. These bridges include:

- **Crypto Asset Exchange-Traded Funds**

  This provides a way for traditional investors to invest in crypto assets.
- **Fiat—Collateralized Stablecoins**

  Regions such as Hong Kong, China, and Singapore have started to introduce compliant fiat-collateralized stablecoins, which helps stabilize the cryptocurrency market.
- **STO (Security Token Offering)**

  Compliant and legal tokenized equity provides new possibilities for connecting the traditional financial market and the crypto market.

- **RWA**

  Examples include HSBC in Hong Kong and China, tokenizing gold, and BlackRock in the United States, tokenizing US Treasury bond funds. These are instances of tokenizing physical assets and helping build a bridge between traditional finance and crypto finance.
- **Licensed Exchanges**

  Compliant and regulated exchanges are the key to the interoperability between traditional finance and the crypto market. They not only provide investment and trading services for crypto assets but also offer fiat-to-digital-currency exchange services. For example, on platforms like Coinbase, a large number of stablecoins such as USDC are issued through the trading platform. This not only promotes investment and trading in crypto assets but also enables the exchange between fiat currency and digital currency.

1.2 Web 3.0: The New Internet Era Driven by Artificial Intelligence

1.2.1 The Booming Development of AI

With the rapid evolution of AI technology, we have entered the Web 3.0 era with AI at its core. This marks a revolutionary advancement in technology and profound changes in education, ethics, global policies, and daily life. From GPT-3 to ChatGPT and then to Sora, the evolution of AI technology has far exceeded our imagination.

Although Sora's current performance has not yet met human expectations, the iteration of the model is a gradual process, which makes us full of anticipation for its future. Sora's potential in complex creative tasks (such as movie production) especially demonstrates significant progress in AI's ability to handle high-level cognitive tasks. The development of this technology not only improves task-processing efficiency but also triggers extensive discussions about the future development direction of AI and its impact on human society.

Meanwhile, although the concept of artificial general intelligence (AGI) is eye-catching, vertical application-oriented robots currently have greater market potential due to their ability to address specific needs. I believe that with the maturation of technology, the reduction of costs, and the increase in market demand, AGI will eventually become a reality and may completely transform the way we work and live.

Overall, we can divide the "capabilities" of AI that bring about productivity changes into two aspects: improving production efficiency and realizing content production transformation.

1.2.2 Improving Production Efficiency

It is easy to notice that as an advanced productivity tool, AI is gradually taking over some tasks that originally required human labor. Take the content generated by ChatGPT as an example. Simply inputting a few keywords can generate articles and planning outlines that basically meet the requirements. Although AI currently does not possess true creativity, its ability to handle repetitive tasks and fixed-logic tasks is impeccable. This may herald the advent of a new productivity revolution.

1.2.3 Realizing Content Production Transformation

In the field of content production, generative AI, digital avatars, and other technologies are bringing about a transformation, which is known as AI-generated content (AIGC). The new-generation AIGC technology can not only handle text and voice but also create code, images, videos, and even robotic movements. These technological advancements make future Internet applications such as VR/AR and the metaverse more promising.

For this reason, the development of AI technology has transcended national boundaries, and its impact extends to all of humanity. Relying on past technological-based wars to contain other countries is clearly no longer applicable. Currently, the international landscape is influenced by important factors such as politics and the economy. In the process of the global development of AI technology and the exploration of its true value, countries need to seek more cooperation rather than confrontation, which will help promote global peace and development. Although the United States has an advantage in some AI fields, China also has its own advantages and the necessary conditions for achieving breakthroughs. Facing a severely competitive international environment, China needs to strengthen independent technological innovation, including the research and development of hardware (such as chips), software, and AI algorithms, collect more comprehensive data, and focus on the development of vertical fields. These strategies can gradually help China reduce its dependence on external technologies and enhance its position in international technological competition.

1.2.4 The Combination of AI and Web 3.0

In the wave of digital technology, the combination of AI and Web 3.0 is leading a new technological revolution. The rapid development of AI coincides with the new bull market in the Web 3.0 market, making "AI + Web 3.0" a highly-concerned field today. The relationship between AI and Web 3.0 is subtle and profound. On the one hand, AI has set off a revolutionary wave in traditional productivity, while the blockchain in Web 3.0 has changed traditional production relations, being more in line with human nature. Therefore, people are full of expectations for the combination of these two technologies, hoping that it will give birth to amazing projects.

On the other hand, the focuses of AI and Web 3.0 do not completely overlap. AI requires a large amount of computing power and data to train models, while Web 3.0 emphasizes the use of a decentralized, fair, and transparent public ledger to transmit information and value more securely and efficiently.

Currently, AI, with its ability to improve production efficiency and stimulate innovation, is changing the way we handle data and make decisions. From data collection and pre-processing to model iteration, review, reasoning, and finally to deployment and monitoring, every step of AI is precise and efficient. The core of Web 3.0—decentralization of data rights confirmation, new token economies, and the construction of public trust-provides an ideal platform to ensure data transparency and security. It can be seen that the influence of "AI + Web 3.0" on the economic system and financial market has already begun to emerge.

When AI meets Web 3.0, the two technologies complement each other's advantages, jointly solving each other's technical pain points and achieving their respective development. This integration not only brings new business models and values but also indicates the future development direction of technology.

Specifically, the combination of the two can be divided into three layers: the infrastructure layer, the middle layer, and the application layer. At the infrastructure layer, AI's big-data processing capabilities can optimize Web 3.0's decentralized network, making data storage and distribution more efficient. In the middle layer, AI's analysis capabilities can deeply explore the potential value of scattered data and automatically and intelligently handle many complex situations in Web 3.0, promoting the business extension and development of the latter. At the application layer, AI enables global users to access Web 3.0 more smoothly, promotes breakthroughs in data processing and analysis, and helps design financial products that are more in line with market demands and user preferences by analyzing market trends and interpreting user behavior.

Next, we will explain the ways in which AI and Web 3.0 are combined from the infrastructure layer, the middle layer, and the application layer respectively.

1.2.5 Infrastructure Layer

The combination of Web 3.0 and AI shows amazing potential at the infrastructure layer. Just imagine: Web 3.0 provides AI with decentralized computing resources, datasets, storage resource networks, algorithm models, and computing power. The explosive growth of AI applications has put forward higher-performance and lower-cost requirements for computing power, and Web 3.0 can just pool idle and scattered infrastructure resources to meet AI's needs for storage and computing services.

In AI model training, personal privacy and data security are of utmost importance. In the Web 3.0 environment, data privacy and security are particularly crucial. Web 3.0's encryption technologies (such as data encryption, cryptographic computing, secure parameter sharing, and encrypted result processing) can ensure that data is not leaked during use. These decentralized encryption technologies are developed and hosted on permissionless peer-to-peer networks, providing strong support for AI's privacy protection.

In addition, the transparency of blockchain provides a safe and verifiable solution while protecting privacy. This ensures the trustworthiness and transparency of the AI development system and promotes its continuous development. Through blockchain technology, all data operations can be verified and traced, making the data processing process more transparent and secure.

1.2.6 Middle Layer

The core of the combination of AI and Web 3.0 at the middle layer lies in improving production efficiency and optimizing resource allocation.

Just imagine a world driven by Web 3.0, where token incentives, governance mechanisms, and decentralized identities jointly create an open data network and trading platform. Through user and data rights confirmation, as well as more reasonable value exchange, more and more people are attracted to participate in AI's data contribution and construction. Resources and talents flow freely on this platform, and cooperation and sharing reach an unprecedented height.

For the development of Web 3.0, AI is undoubtedly a powerful booster. AI can help collect and analyze on-chain data, detect abnormal activities in Web 3.0, and at the same time, support the development, deployment, and maintenance of smart contracts, enriching and accelerating Web 3.0 businesses. AI can optimize Web 3.0's businesses through automated and intelligent operations, improving the flexibility, application scope, and operation efficiency of Web 3.0. For example, for smart contracts, an important part of Web 3.0, AI algorithms can dynamically adjust the execution conditions of smart contracts according to real-time data, improving their flexibility and application scope. This automated and intelligent processing method not only improves efficiency but also reduces the possibility of human errors.

What's more remarkable is that by analyzing on-chain data, activities, and behaviors, AI can not only accurately identify and target the audience, optimizing the business development of Web 3.0, but also help members in DAO governance better understand the needs and opinions of the community, providing decision-making support and promoting the prosperity of the community.

Through the token incentive mechanism, more and more people are encouraged to participate in this ecosystem, which promotes the joint development of Web 3.0 and AI. This combination shows how to achieve efficient and fair resource allocation in a decentralized environment, providing new ideas for future technological innovation.

1.2.7 Application Layer

At the layer where it directly interacts with users, AI can inject vitality into Web 3.0 and lower the usage threshold. Compared with Web 2.0 projects, Web 3.0 projects generally have a higher understanding threshold, which invisibly hinders the public from using Web 3.0 and affects its popularity. The integration of AI can create a user-friendly interface for Web 3.0. Vertical AI models adapted through knowledge bases and fine-tuned with data can also perform tasks such as information interpretation and reply analysis, building a bridge between the general public and Web 3.0, enabling users to operate and interact more intuitively and conveniently without having to deeply understand the technical details of Web 3.0.

In addition, AI's creative content generation can bring more possibilities to Web 3.0. In terms of content generation, AI is completely transforming the creative industry and helping to build a decentralized content market. Using blockchain technology to record the creative process and copyright information ensures the rights and interests of creators. This transparent and reliable market environment will attract more creators and other users, jointly promoting the prosperity and development of the Web 3.0 ecosystem. With the help of AI, creators can generate high-quality text, images, music, and other content and directly publish and trade it through the Web 3.0 platform. This model not only greatly reduces the cost of creation but also ensures that creators receive appropriate rewards. Content generated by AI can be traded as NFTs on the Web 3.0 platform, and users can also use AI to create content more easily. This helps to activate those "silent" users on traditional platforms. In addition, AI can provide personalized experiences based on user information, further enhancing user interaction with the Web 3.0 platform.

1.3 Web 3.0: A New Internet Model Breaking the Limitations of Traditional Investment and Financing

The development of Web 3.0 technology has brought revolutionary changes to the investment and financing field. Traditional investment and financing models have many limitations. For example, in financing, there are issues like high thresholds, high financial costs, and long approval cycles. In investment, problems include information asymmetry and uneven risk diversification. The tokenized investment and financing model based on Web 3.0 uses blockchain technology to achieve the digital representation and trading of assets, showing the potential to reduce financing costs and enhance liquidity. Web 3.0 offers new financing and investment channels to market participants through peer-to-peer transactions, reduced intermediary involvement, and instant settlement.The advantages of the tokenized investment and financing model lie in enhancing asset liquidity, allowing assets to be traded globally, thus reducing transaction costs and time. Meanwhile, blockchain technology improves the security and transparency of transactions.

Additionally, the decentralized feature of this model reduces the reliance on traditional financial intermediaries, and the use of smart contracts decreases the likelihood of legal disputes.

However, this emerging model also faces challenges such as regulatory uncertainty, technical security issues, and market acceptance. The current infrastructure is not perfect, which means that most token products are only accessible to qualified investors and institutional investors. Looking ahead to the future of tokenized investment and financing, its development will focus on improving standardization, transparency, and security, as well as expanding innovative applications. Therefore, it is urgent to address issues related to law, regulation, security, and trust.

1.3.1 Analysis and Dilemmas of Traditional Investment and Financing Models

Investment and financing have always been essential for enterprise growth. For a long time, traditional investment and financing models have been regarded as one of the main ways for enterprises to obtain funds. However, with the continuous development of the economy and technology, traditional investment and financing models have exposed a series of problems. In terms of financing, there are problems such as high thresholds, difficult financing, and limited financing amounts. In terms of investment, issues include information asymmetry, uneven risk diversification, and fluctuations in collateral value. Against this backdrop, a brand-new investment and financing model based on Web 3.0 is gradually coming into the spotlight.

1.3.2 Types and Characteristics of Traditional Financing Models

The financial market is an important part of the modern economic system and a key factor in improving resource allocation efficiency and promoting the integration of industry and finance. Traditional financing models mainly include the following types:

- **Bank Loans**

  This is one of the most common and traditional financing methods. Enterprises can apply for loans from banks and repay them according to a certain interest rate and term. This financing method usually requires enterprises to provide collateral or pledges to reduce the bank's risks. The approval cycle for bank loans is relatively long, and the interest rates are relatively low.
- **Bond Financing**

  This is a way for enterprises to borrow money from investors by issuing bonds. Enterprises promise to pay interest according to a certain interest rate and term and finally repay the principal. The characteristic of bond financing is that the financing cost is relatively low, making it suitable for financing long-term projects or assets. However, it requires the payment of fixed interest, which increases the financial burden on enterprises.

- **Equity Financing**

  This is a way for enterprises to raise funds by issuing stocks or private equities. Enterprises use this to attract investors and share their future earnings with them. The advantage of equity financing is that it can quickly obtain a large amount of funds. However, it will erode the interests of the original shareholders of the enterprise and may weaken the control of the enterprise's management.

- **Self-Financing**

  This refers to enterprises financing through internal accumulation, self-owned funds, etc. The advantage of this financing method is that there is no need to pay interest or dividends. However, the financing scale is usually small, making it difficult to meet the capital needs of large-scale projects or expansion plans.

1.3.3 Problems and Challenges Faced by Traditional Financing Models

Based on the above analysis, traditional financing mainly faces three types of problems and challenges. First, the threshold is high, and financing is difficult. In traditional financing models, the financing threshold for enterprises is often high. Bank loans and bond financing usually require enterprise to provide sufficient collateral or guarantees, and equity financing may weaken the control of the enterprise's management, all of which increases the difficulty of financing. Second, the financial cost is high. The financial costs such as handling fees, interest, and dividends required for financing are relatively high, thus increasing the financial burden on enterprises. Third, the approval cycle is long. The cumbersome approval procedures lead to a long financing cycle.

1.3.4 Types and Characteristics of Traditional Investment Models

Traditional investment models are mainly divided into the following types according to different characteristics and risk-return profiles, which can meet the needs of different investors:

- **Stock Investment**

  This is a common investment method. Investors become partial owners of an enterprise by purchasing its stocks. This investment method allows investors to obtain returns through stock price increases and corporate dividends. Stock investment can be long-term or short-term. Long-term investors usually focus more on the fundamentals of the enterprise, while short-term investors may place more emphasis on market sentiment and technical analysis.

- **Bond Investment**

  This is a relatively stable investment method. Investors provide loans to bond issuers by purchasing bonds, expecting to receive regular interest income and principal repayment in the future. There are many types of bonds, including government bonds, corporate bonds, and municipal bonds.
- **Bank Deposits**

  This is one of the investment methods with the lowest risk, including savings accounts and fixed-term deposits. By depositing money, investors can obtain fixed interest income. Although the returns of this method are relatively low, the safety is high.
- **Real Estate Investment**

  This type of investment involves the purchase of land, residential or commercial properties, etc. Investors mainly obtain profits through rental income and property appreciation. This type of investment usually requires a large initial capital investment and has relatively low liquidity.
- **Fund Investment**

  This involves pooling the funds of multiple investors and investing in a variety of assets, including mutual funds, index funds, and exchange-traded funds (ETFs). Fund investment can provide investors with professional asset management and risk diversification.
- **Precious Metals and Commodity Investment**

  Such as gold, silver, crude oil, agricultural products, etc., are usually regarded as hedges against inflation or risk-diversification strategies. This type of investment is subject to global market fluctuations and is suitable for investors with an in-depth understanding of the market.
- **Insurance Products**

  Annuity insurance and life insurance can provide protection and investment value. Investors can obtain the returns specified in the insurance contract in the future by paying premiums.

1.3.5 Problems and Challenges Faced by Traditional Investment Models

Although traditional investment models have a long history and are widely accepted, they face various problems and challenges, mainly including:

- **Liquidity Risk**

  Some traditional investments (such as real estate and certain private equities) have low liquidity, which means that investors may face difficulties when they need to liquidate their investments.
- **Interest Rate Risk**

  Bond investments are particularly affected by changes in interest rates. When interest rates rise, the prices of existing bonds usually fall because newly issued bonds may offer higher returns.
- **Inflation Risk**

  An increase in inflation may erode investment returns, especially for fixed-income investments such as bonds and bank deposits, whose actual returns may decline in a high-inflation environment.
- **Regulatory Risk**

  Changes in regulations and policies may affect the investment environment, such as changes in tax policies, modifications to investment and trading rules, etc., which may all affect the attractiveness and returns of investments.
- **Management and Expense Issues**

  For investments made through funds and other managed investment methods, management fees and performance fees may significantly affect the overall rate of return.

1.3.6 A Solution Superior to Traditional Investment and Financing Models: Tokenized Investment and Financing Based on Web 3.0

Improving the direct financing system has long been a focus of domestic and foreign theories and practices. Difficult issues include high financing costs, insufficient liquidity, etc. In recent years, some innovative financing methods have emerged in international practice, proposing new solutions to these problems in terms of systems or technologies. However, this may also bring new problems such as rampant speculation and poor actual liquidity. The rise of STO has attracted widespread attention in the international community. Token products are an innovative direct financing method that emerged in overseas practice since 2017. The issuance/trading structure of tokens features peer-to-peer transactions, few intermediaries, and instant settlement, which is expected to reduce issuance and trading costs.

1.3.7 The Development History of Tokenized Investment and Financing

Currently, there is no unified definition of tokens. It can be understood as the public issuance of legal and compliant digital securities within relevant laws, regulations, and regulatory frameworks. Specifically, a token is a cryptographic digital rights and interests certificate that transforms physical assets (such as artworks) and financial assets (such as real-estate investment trusts, equities, debts, etc.) into blockchain-based digital assets by using blockchain technology to record various assets, rights, and services in reality on the blockchain.

The Tokenization solution originated in the United States. Although the concept of "tokens", the origin of digital securities, emerged relatively early, data shows that the world's first digital security was issued by Block Chain Capital, a blockchain venture-capital firm in the United States, on April 10, 2017. In July 2019, the U.S. Securities and Exchange Commission (SEC) successively approved two applications for the issuance of digital securities based on the RegA + exemption provisions. After that, other countries also followed suit. For example, after rejecting the prospectuses of digital securities submitted by more than 130 companies, the German securities regulatory agency finally approved the issuance applications of multiple digital securities in 2019. The world's major stock exchanges (such as the New York Stock Exchange, NASDAQ, the London Stock Exchange, the Australian Securities Exchange, the Singapore Stock Exchange, etc.) attach great importance to blockchain technology, digital assets, and digital securities, and actively participate in cultivation and promotion in various forms. Since 2012, the United States, Japan, Singapore, and other countries have successively established digital asset exchanges. In January 2022, the SEC approved the Boston Securities Token Exchange (BSTX) to use blockchain for settlement and provide blockchain market data products.

The investment and financing solution based on Web 3.0 is an inevitable product of the development of blockchain technology and its deep integration into finance. It is an innovative product of the integrated development of traditional finance and digital technology. With the rise of digitization, against the backdrop of the rapid development of DeFi and NFT, the ownership rights and interests of various types of assets no longer need to rely on off-chain securities forms, but can be represented digitally. These assets cover investment contracts, company shares, specific bills, debt mortgages, sub-rights, real estate, venture capital, private equity, real property, and hedge funds, etc. Digital securities have the same legal relationships as off-chain securities and the characteristics of matching returns and risks. However, due to the use of blockchain as the underlying technology and infrastructure, their design and operation deviate from the issuance, trading, and registration and settlement mechanisms stipulated by current securities laws.

The process of tokenizing digital assets is to use the digital signatures, consensus mechanisms, smart contracts, time-stamps and other technologies of the blockchain to confirm the rights of digital assets. It incorporates asset owners, producers, and users as important nodes into the blockchain network, and records and traces the entire lifecycle of the transmission, use, trading, and revenue of digital assets.

After Tokenization is completed, digital rights and interests are formed, which are recorded, distributed, functioned or triggered for various related activities on a distributed ledger based on smart contracts. These rights and interests can be sold, issued, and traded in cyberspace. The blockchain stores tokens in a chain-like structure and adds time-stamps to the data. Investors become owners of digital securities by purchasing tokens and possess relevant rights such as ownership, use rights, management rights, trading rights, and revenue rights of digital assets in the form of tokens. Issuers tokenize related digital assets to raise funds and issue them to investors through private or public offerings. Although these tokens are digital, they fully conform to the characteristics of financial investment products, being profitable, risky, and tradable, with no return of principal.

1.3.8 Comparative Analysis of the Advantages of Tokenized Investment and Financing Over Traditional Investment and Financing

Table 1.2 details the main differences and interrelationships among equity investment and financing, debt investment and financing, and tokenized investment and financing. The main differences and interconnections of these three types of investment and financing projects are reflected in five aspects: cost, liquidity, operation/strategic pressure, location, and regulatory uncertainty.

In terms of cost, equity investment and financing usually have higher costs because investors and financiers require higher returns to compensate for risks; debt investment and financing have relatively lower costs, and interest expenses are tax-deductible; tokenized investment and financing, conducted on the chain with low initial legal and marketing costs, has the lowest overall issuance cost. In terms of liquidity, tokenized investment and financing has the highest liquidity, followed by equity, and the lowest is debt. Tokenized investment and financing, due to its divisibility, can divide asset shares, thus enhancing liquidity. In terms of

Table 1.2 The comparison of equity, debt, and tokenized investment and financing

Project	Equity investment and financing	Bond investment and financing	Tokenized investment and financing
Cost	High	Medium	Low
Mobility	Low-medium	Low	Medium–high
Operational/strategic pressures	Low	High	Low
Place	Locally oriented	Locally oriented	Global
Regulatory uncertainty	Low	Low	Medium

operation/strategic pressure, since debt investment and financing require relatively rigid principal and interest repayment, equity and tokenized investment and financing are superior to debt investment and financing. In terms of location, tokenized investment and financing, conducted on the chain and publicly transparent and traceable, is not restricted by geographical location. In terms of regulatory uncertainty, as blockchain technology is relatively new, it faces more uncertainties. In general, each of the three types of investment and financing has its own advantages and disadvantages. As a new investment and financing method, tokenized investment and financing has huge development potential in the future.

Tokenized investment and financing based on Web 3.0 is an emerging investment and financing model that uses blockchain technology and Tokenization to reform traditional investment and financing methods. This model provides a variety of advantages that traditional investment and financing models do not have by digitizing assets and building a DeFi ecosystem, as follows:

- Enhanced Liquidity

  Tokenization can convert assets with traditionally low liquidity, such as real estate and artworks, into digital tokens that can be traded globally. This process of segmentation and digitization significantly improves asset liquidity, enabling investors to buy and sell small-value asset shares more conveniently.
- Access to Global Markets

  Through Tokenization, assets can be traded across national borders easily, allowing global investors to access markets that were previously difficult to reach due to geographical or political restrictions. This not only increases the number of potential buyers and sellers of assets but also helps improve the transparency of asset prices.
- Reduced Transaction Costs and Time

  Blockchain technology can automate many steps that require manual processing in traditional financing, such as the clearing and settlement processes. This automated process not only reduces transaction costs but also significantly shortens transaction time.
- Enhanced Security and Transparency

  Using blockchain technology means that all transaction records are immutable and visible to all network participants. This improves the transparency of the entire financing process and helps prevent fraud and misrepresentation.
- Decentralization

  DeFi reduces the reliance on traditional financial intermediaries (such as banks and investment companies), lowering the risk of a single point of failure. At the same time, it may lower the participation threshold, allowing more small-scale investors to participate in investment.

- Use of Smart Contracts

  Smart contracts allow for the automatic execution of contract terms when pre-set conditions are met. This automated contract execution mechanism reduces the possibility of legal disputes and ensures that all parties operate according to pre-set rules.
- New Financing Channels

  For start-ups and small enterprises, raising funds directly from global investors through the STO (Security Token Offering) method is a faster and lower-threshold way to obtain capital compared to traditional financing channels.

In summary, the tokenized investment and financing model based on Web 3.0 provides an efficient, transparent, and globally accessible investment method, injecting new impetus into the flow of assets and capital. However, this model also faces challenges such as regulatory uncertainty, technical security issues, and market acceptance, which require careful consideration and planning during implementation.

1.3.9 The Dilemmas Faced by Tokenization and Its Future Trajectories

1.3.9.1 The Dilemmas Faced by Tokenization

Except for a few projects that issue tokens to retail investors within certain limitations by complying with specific local laws, issuing special prospectuses, and registering specific securities, most tokens in the current market are only available to qualified investors. Regulations in most regions require investors to prove they have a certain amount of financial assets to be considered qualified investors. The reason why most token products (including those related to US Treasuries) are only accessible to qualified or institutional investors is that the compliant issuance to retail investors incurs high costs. These costs stem from the lack of correlation between the underlying assets and the finally issued tokens. Relevant securities laws have strict requirements for issuing securities to retail investors, including the preparation and registration of prospectuses. In addition, the laws in most judicial jurisdictions stipulate that the ownership of assets such as stocks and bonds needs to be recorded in a specific way (such as in the register maintained by the issuer).

Currently, authoritative institutions do not accept tokens and blockchain as tools for direct ownership registration. This means that token ownership cannot directly represent the ownership of underlying assets under these laws and regulations. For tokens issued using an asset-backed model (such as tokens with US Treasuries as underlying assets), a "bridge" is needed between the underlying assets and the expected tokens. Since the token is a new type of security, this "bridge" can be established by treating the token as an independent security. However, this also means that the token needs to independently comply with all relevant securities laws. That is, the issuer needs to prepare and register an additional prospectus that regards the token as a security.

To understand this, we can look at the traditional model of issuing securities to retail users. Whether issuing stocks or bonds, the following eight steps are required:

- Internal Preparation by the Company: Determine the characteristics of the company's securities, and select and hire investment banks (underwriters) and other financial professionals (such as lawyers and accountants) to assist in the IPO (Initial Public Offering) process.
- Selection of Underwriters: Underwriters will assist the company in preparing and executing the bond issuance.
- Due Diligence, Audit, and Rating (for Bonds): Review internal controls and governance structures to ensure compliance; for bonds, ratings will affect their credit quality.
- Preparation of Prospectus: If it is for retail investors, the prospectus must be approved by the regulatory authorities to ensure that investors receive sufficient information.
- Pricing Determination: Determine valuation, issuance price, and other conditions together with the underwriters.
- Marketing: Conduct roadshows, interact with potential investors, and explain the company's business situation, etc.
- Issuance and Listing: Need to meet the listing requirements and standards of the stock exchange.
- Post-transaction Management: Such as financial information disclosure, announcements, etc.

It can be seen that if one hopes to sell security-type assets to retail investors, a complex process is required. In these processes, there are two reasons why tokens are difficult to be directly offered to retail investors:

- **High Costs and Insufficient Returns**

  The entire process of issuing securities to retail investors can cost millions of dollars and requires regulatory approval. The size of the crypto market is relatively smaller than the traditional market, unable to meet large-scale financing needs. Therefore, the cost of compliant issuance is too high, and the returns are insufficient.
- **Incomplete Infrastructure**

  For example, there are no compliant securities exchanges to provide trading services for tokens, and securities registration institutions do not currently support tokens as a means of ownership registration, and so on.

If issuers do not want to incur such high costs and transaction frictions, they can only issue products to qualified investors and institutional investors. Currently, the mainstream tokenized assets in the digital asset market are issued by special purpose vehicles (SPV) established by start-up companies as issuers, with traditional capital-market securities (such as US Treasuries) as the underlying assets, using an asset-backed model. In this case, the bonds purchased by investors are not actually US Treasuries but corporate bonds issued by the SPV with US Treasuries as the underlying assets. This actually has a very high counterparty risk, which can downgrade US Treasuries originally rated AA + to BBB - rated corporate bonds through this structure.

Other directly issued corporate bonds are basically issued by smaller companies without going through a complete issuance process for retail investors. To save costs, they can only be offered to qualified investors.

1.3.9.2 The Future Trajectories of Tokenization

In the future, tokenized investment and financing can be specifically divided into the following four main trajectories:

- **Tokenized VC Funds**

  These funds issue tokens, giving holders a direct claim on fund shares, thus enhancing the flexibility and liquidity of investment.
- **Share-like Tokens**

  These tokens possess some of the attributes of traditional stocks, such as ownership shares in a specific entity, limited partner (LP) shares, voting rights, dividend—distribution rights, profit-sharing rights, and potential interests in the future success of the enterprise.
- **Asset-backed Tokens**

  These tokens represent rights to a series of substitute or non-substitute assets, similar to the process of converting a portfolio of real-estate mortgages into securities. Asset-backed tokens combine asset rights with digital tokens, providing investors with a new type of asset class.
- **Crypto-bonds**

  By eliminating the involvement of intermediaries and registration institutions, crypto-bonds can significantly shorten the settlement cycle and reduce operational risks, thereby improving the efficiency of the bond market.

The future development of these four token trajectories will focus on standardization, transparency, security, and innovative applications, as follows:

- **Standardization**

  Standardization will promote the interoperability and mutual trust among different projects, enhancing market participation and liquidity. The standardization and compliance of tokens have become an indispensable development path, enabling various tokenized assets to circulate and trade in a wider market.

- **Transparency**

  Improving transparency is crucial for investors to understand the true value and risks. Blockchain technology can make the token trajectories transparent, publicly and clearly presenting transaction records and asset information, enabling investors to have a clearer understanding of project situations and increasing market credibility.

- **Security**

  Ensuring project security is key. Strengthening the protection measures for smart contracts and wallets, and establishing a more secure technical and regulatory framework to safeguard the safety of investors' assets. Through multi-level security measures, risks can be reduced, and the overall security level of the market can be improved.

- **Innovative Applications**

  Token trajectories will continuously explore innovative application fields, such as green energy, real estate, artworks, bonds, etc. The exploration of these emerging fields will bring more opportunities to token trajectories, unleash more potential, and expand the application scope and influence of tokenized assets. At the same time, issues related to law, regulation, security, and trust need to be addressed to ensure the legality and sustainability of these applications.

As the token trajectories continue to develop, market participation will gradually increase, attracting more and more institutions and investors. This will promote the growth and development of token trajectories. In general, token trajectories have great development potential. In the future, emphasis will be placed on improving standardization, transparency, security, and innovative applications. However, risks and challenges in law, regulation, security, and trust also need to be carefully addressed. Investors and industry participants should pay close attention to these development trends and risks, and make investment and participation decisions based on their individual needs and risk-tolerance.

1.4 Web 3.0: The New Internet Technology Leading Tokenized Assets

The innovation of RWA (Real-World Assets) Tokenization not only brings a leap in asset transaction efficiency. More importantly, it presents unprecedented possibilities for transformation in aspects such as the granularity, liquidity, digitization, and scope for financial innovation of RWA. Through Tokenization, the allocation thresholds and transaction costs of assets that were previously out of reach for ordinary investors due to high costs and complex procedures can be significantly reduced. This means that both ordinary investors and large-scale financial institutions can more flexibly allocate their asset portfolios, further unlocking the potential of capital.

Of course, RWA Tokenization is not without risks and challenges. There are a series of issues, including unclear global regulatory policies, immature technology, and incomplete infrastructure and ecosystem enterprises. In the article *"Hong Kong Should Become the Leader of the Future RWA Ecosystem"*, published in the *"Hong Kong Ta Kung Pao"* on October 11, 2023, by the book's authors Zhu Haokang and Professor Wang Yang, a unique *"RWA 2 + 4 research framework"* was proposed. This framework takes the two types of tokens for RWA Tokenization and the four core elements as the starting point for the feasibility study of RWA Tokenization. This methodology conducts research and practice around two types of tokens (security-type tokens and utility-type tokens) and four core elements (legal foundation, financial framework, technical tools, and data-driven) to find opportunities amidst challenges and promote the healthy development of RWA.

However, there is no doubt that RWA Tokenization represents a global digital finance evolution direction that combines modern financial engineering and Web 3.0 frontier technologies. It holds the promise of being a historic opportunity to redefine asset value and wealth management methods.

1.4.1 Global Financial Institutions Are Actively Engaging in the New Track of RWA Tokenization

In September 2022, a report released by the Boston Consulting Group predicted that by 2030, the global scale of RWA Tokenization would reach $16 trillion. Similarly, in March 2023, Citibank in the United States released a 162—page research report titled *"Money, Tokens, and Games" (Blockchain's Next Billion Users and Trillions in Value)*, which comprehensively expounded on the specific paths for Web 3.0 to reach 1 billion users and for digital assets to reach a scale of trillions of dollars. Citibank believes that by 2030, $4 – 5 trillion of RWA will be tokenized, and the trade finance transaction volume based on blockchain technology will reach $1 trillion. Almost everything of value can be tokenized, and the Tokenization of digital finance and RWA may be the "killer - application" for the breakthrough of blockchain technology.

In addition, major global mainstream financial institutions are also stepping up their efforts in the Tokenization of RWA. In January 2023, Goldman Sachs Group announced the official launch of its digital asset platform GS DAP. This platform had successfully helped the European Investment Bank[1] issue 100 million euros of two-year digital bonds as early as 2021. In February 2023, Hamilton Lane, a giant in the US private equity industry with a management scale of over $100

[1] The European Investment Bank is a non-profit long-term lending bank of the European Union. It aims to support projects within Europe and globally by providing loans and guarantees, so as to boost the economic development and integration of Europe.

billion, tokenized and sold part of the shares of its flagship equity opportunities fund (equity opportunities fund V) on the blockchain network Polygon. In the same month, Siemens AG in Germany also issued 60 million euros of digital bonds on the blockchain for the first time.

It can be seen that more and more financial institutions have realized that directly issuing tokenized financial products on the blockchain can effectively solve the problem of asset liquidity and achieve transparent transactions. In particular, heavy-weight private equity institutions and asset management companies such as KKR, Apollo, and Hamilton Lane have begun to try selling tokenized fund shares on digital asset trading platforms like Securitize, Provenance, and ADDX to save intermediate channel costs and directly reach a wider range of investors.

On September 7, 2023, several leading digital asset enterprises, including Coinbase, Circle, and Aave, jointly launched the Tokenized Asset Coalition (TAC). Other members of the coalition include Base, Centrifuge, CREDIX, Goldfinch, and rwa.xyz, etc. The coalition believes that RWA Tokenization will become the development direction of the digital asset field. It hopes to take on the responsibilities of promoting industry education, standardization, and the development of innovative companies, and jointly build the infrastructure suitable for the adoption of RWA.

On September 8, 2023, the Federal Reserve System of the United States (hereinafter referred to as the "Fed") released a working paper titled *"Tokenization: Overview and Financial Stability Implications"*. From three dimensions of scale, advantages, and risks, it clearly depicted the full picture of RWA Tokenization and how it will become an important part of the future financial system. The paper pointed out that Tokenization has opened up a new path, enabling investors to access markets that were previously inaccessible due to high investment thresholds. At the same time, the programmability of tokens and the application of smart contracts allow for the embedding of more complex functions, greatly enriching the diversity and flexibility of assets. In addition, Tokenization has also greatly promoted the development of the lending and credit markets by using tokens as collateral.

Larry Fink, CEO of BlackRock, the world's largest asset management company, publicly stated in November 2022 that "the next generation of the market and the next generation of securities will be the Tokenization of securities" and "if we can create more tokenized assets and securities, it may completely transform the financial industry." In March 2024, BlackRock announced a partnership with Securitize, a blockchain technology company focused on RWA Tokenization, to launch a tokenized private equity fund on the Ethereum blockchain. This is BlackRock's first asset-tokenized fund, officially named "blackRock USD institutional digital liquidity, BUIDL". BUIDL aims to provide a stable value of $1 for each token and directly pay the daily-accumulated dividends to investors' wallets in the form of new tokens every month. The fund will invest 100% of its total assets in cash, US Treasuries, and repurchase agreements, allowing investors to earn returns while holding tokens on the blockchain. In addition, investors can transfer their tokens to other pre-approved investors throughout the year. Fund participants will also have flexible custody options and can choose how to hold their tokens. The initial ecosystem participants of BUIDL include Anchorage Digital Bank NA, BitGo, Coinbase, and Fireblocks, as well as other market participants and infrastructure providers in the crypto industry. Just one month after its launch, on April 30, 2024, the total scale of BUIDL reached $350 million.

Tyrone Lobban, head of digital assets at Onyx, a blockchain subsidiary of JPMorgan Chase, a giant in the US investment banking industry, pointed out: "We believe that tokenizing assets such as US Treasuries or money market fund shares means that these assets can potentially be used as collateral in DeFi liquidity pools. By introducing these trillion-dollar-scale institutional assets into DeFi, we can use new (DeFi-based) mechanisms for trading, borrowing, and lending."

The ambitions of BlackRock and JPMorgan Chase in the digital asset field also indicate that traditional financial giants on Wall Street are accelerating their embrace of blockchain technology. With the participation of more institutional investors, RWA is expected to become an important part of the digital asset ecosystem, bringing transformation to a wider range of the real economy.

In Asia, the government and financial institutions of the Hong Kong Special Administrative Region of China are also stepping up their efforts in the RWA Tokenization track. In October 2022, the government of the Hong Kong Special Administrative Region released the *"Policy Statement on the Development of Virtual Assets in Hong Kong"*, indicating that it would promote the issuance of tokenized green bonds in Hong Kong and explore the "Digital Harbour" to achieve the Tokenization of the Hong Kong dollar. In February 2023, under the government green bond program, the government of the Hong Kong Special Administrative Region successfully issued 800 million Hong Kong dollars of tokenized green bonds, which was the world's first government—issued tokenized green bonds. In June 2023, Bank of China International issued 200 million yuan of fully digital structured notes for the Hong Kong market through UBS Group, becoming the first Chinese-funded financial institution to issue tokenized securities in Hong Kong. UBS Group stated that this was the first such product in the Asia–Pacific region that complied with Hong Kong and Swiss laws and was tokenized on the Ethereum blockchain.

In February 2024, the government of the Hong Kong Special Administrative Region announced the successful issuance of approximately 6 billion Hong Kong dollars of digital green.

bonds, including multiple currencies such as the Hong Kong dollar, the yuan, the US dollar, and the euro. This became the world's first multi-currency digital bond issuance. The Financial Secretary of the Hong Kong Special Administrative Region said that the issuance of these digital green bonds demonstrated Hong Kong's leadership and advantages in integrating the bond market, green sustainable finance, and financial technology. The Secretary for Financial Services and the Treasury of the Hong Kong Special Administrative Region pointed out that the issuance of digital green bonds again highlighted the continuous support of the Hong Kong Special Administrative Region government for promoting innovative bond forms and green transformation, which is conducive to deepening society's understanding of the combination of financial technology and sustainable development and consolidating Hong Kong's leading position as a green and sustainable financial center. The Chief Executive of the Hong Kong Monetary Authority (HKMA) was pleased with the launch of these landmark digital green bonds following the successful issuance of the first batch of digital bonds in 2023. He emphasized that the multiple innovations introduced in this issuance would increase investor participation and interoperability, enhance transparency and efficiency, and is expected to promote the further development of the digital securities market. Lin Huihong, Chief Executive of HSBC Hong Kong, and Sun Ye, Vice-Chairman and Chief Executive of Bank of China (Hong Kong), also supported this issuance, believing that it would further strengthen Hong Kong's global leading position in green finance, the capital market, and financial technology innovation. The digital green bonds issued this time used the Central Moneymarkets Unit (CMU) for debt instruments and were integrated with HSBC's digital asset platform HSBC Orion, reflecting Hong Kong's determination and ability to promote financial technology innovation and the development of green sustainable finance.

In Singapore, Marketnode, a digital asset infrastructure company jointly established by Temasek Holdings and the Singapore Exchange, worked with HSBC and United Overseas Bank in September 2022 to create an end-to-end tokenized wealth management product infrastructure from issuance to distribution. As part of the RWA Tokenization collaboration project—Project Guardian led by the Monetary Authority of Singapore (MAS), Marketnode aims to serve Singapore's asset management industry, which has a scale of 5.4 trillion Singapore dollars.

RWA Tokenization not only opens up a new dimension for the capital market but also brings revolutionary changes to the global financial ecosystem. Tokenization is not just a simple technical application but a complex system integrating multiple aspects such as technology, economy, law, and society. It breaks through the limitations of traditional finance, greatly increasing asset liquidity and providing more ordinary people with the opportunity to participate in the financial market. RWA Tokenization is the result of the convergence of financial innovation and technological progress. It has the potential to redefine asset management and investment methods, making them more efficient, transparent, and inclusive. However, this innovation also brings many challenges and problems, which require the joint efforts of the industry, the government, and society to solve. Precisely for this reason, RWA Tokenization is becoming an indispensable part of financial institutions' layout for the future financial system. It is an active effort to bridge the real world and the digital economy, a firm investment in the huge potential of Web 3.0 in the future, and an inevitable choice for the development of digital globalization.

1.4.2 The Development Potential of RWA Tokenization

RWA refers to tangible or intangible assets that exist in the real world and do not rely on the Internet, including but not limited to bonds, stocks, currencies, funds, trusts, commercial bills, real estate, commodities, intellectual property rights, carbon credits, and other types. These assets are ubiquitous in our daily lives and form the foundation of the global economy.

RWA Tokenization, on the other hand, refers to converting the above-mentioned various assets into digital tokens existing in the blockchain network. The vast majority of RWA can be tokenized. Essentially, RWA Tokenization is a new way of issuing, managing, and investing in financial assets. It combines global mainstream assets with the digital finance market, achieving a paradigm upgrade of the financial ecosystem. For example, traditional real-estate investment requires a relatively large amount of capital, and the investment process involves complex legal and financial procedures, with a high investment threshold and relatively poor liquidity of real estate, making it difficult for investors to liquidate quickly. However, once real-estate shares or income rights are tokenized, they can be split into several small-value shares with low unit prices, and can be traded and circulated globally. They can also achieve low-cost and rapid mortgage lending based on DeFi. Another example is that if a YouTube blogger earns $50,000 in advertising revenue per month, this income right can also be tokenized. Maple Finance has already tokenized the income rights of YouTube channels and then converted them into collateral to help YouTube bloggers obtain low-cost financing.

According to research by the Boston Consulting Group, the global scale of RWA Tokenization is expected to grow to $16 trillion by 2030 (accounting for approximately 10% of the global GDP in 2030). It is estimated to include $3.2 trillion of real-estate tokens, $3.9 trillion of equity tokens, $1.2 trillion of bond and investment fund tokens, $3 trillion of alternative financial asset tokens, and $4.8 trillion of other tokenized assets (see Figs. 1.1 and 1.2).

As shown in Fig. 1.3, Citibank believes that by 2030, the scale of global RWA (the digital securities part) Tokenization will reach $510 billion. Specifically, it includes $190 billion in tokenized corporate bonds and quasi-sovereign bonds, $150 billion in tokenized real-estate funds, $70 billion in tokenized private equity and venture capital funds, and $100 billion in tokenized securities financing and collateral. In addition to digital securities, Citibank also predicts that by 2030, the global trade market based on blockchain technology may reach a trading volume of $1 trillion, accounting for approximately 8 to 10% of the total global trade financing.

1.4.3 Uncovering the Key Advantages of RWA Tokenization

RWA Tokenization will bring a series of benefits, which specifically include the following aspects:

First, enhancing asset liquidity. Based on the characteristics of Web 3.0 technical infrastructure and trading infrastructure, after RWA is tokenized, it can achieve real-time and rapid settlement, uninterrupted trading throughout the year, and access to a vast number of qualified investors globally. As a result, it can obtain extremely high liquidity, ensuring that the value of high-quality assets is no longer

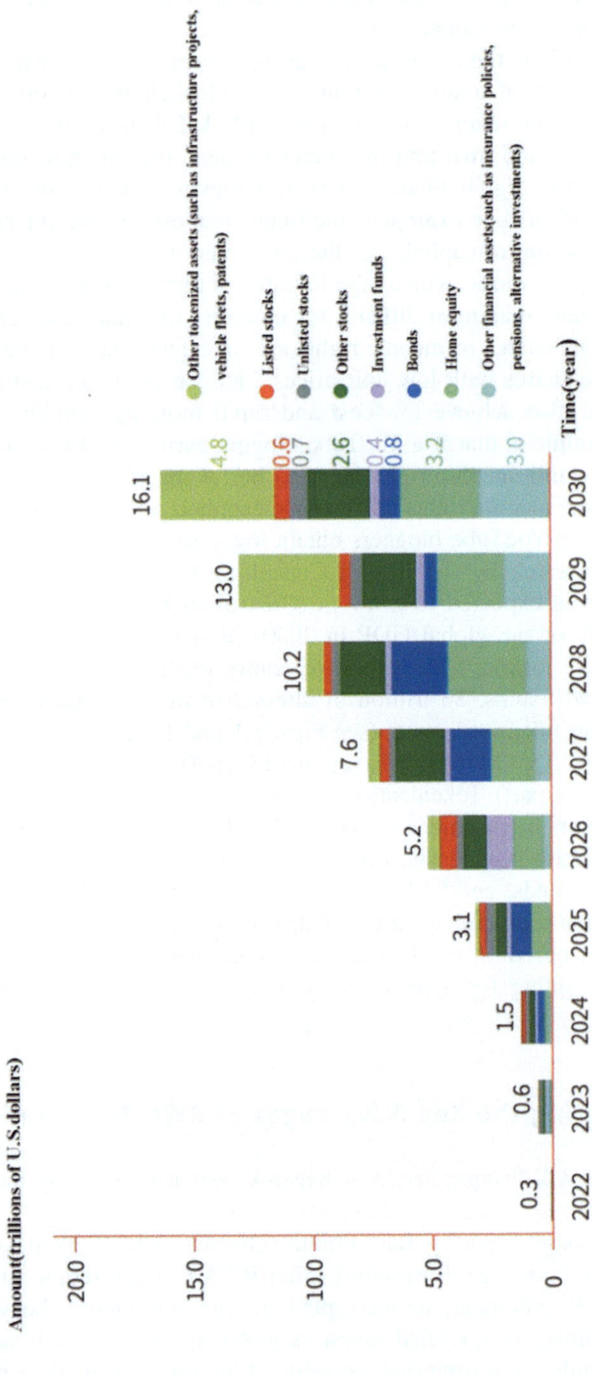

Fig. 1.1 The scale of the RWA token is expected to exceed $1.6 trillion in 2030 (*Source* Boston consulting group)

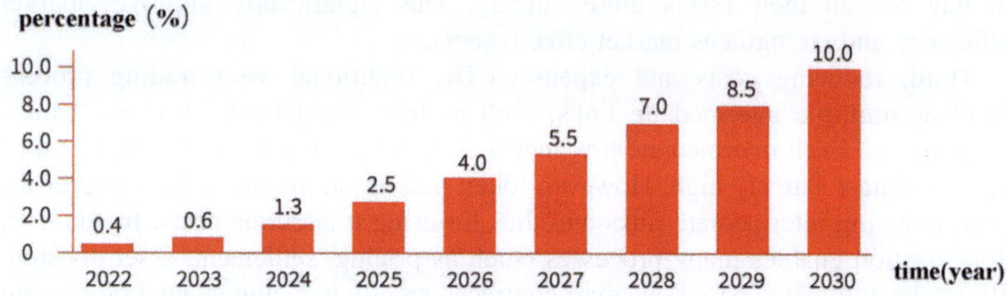

Fig. 1.2 The percentage of the tokenized market in the global GDP (*Source* Boston consulting group)

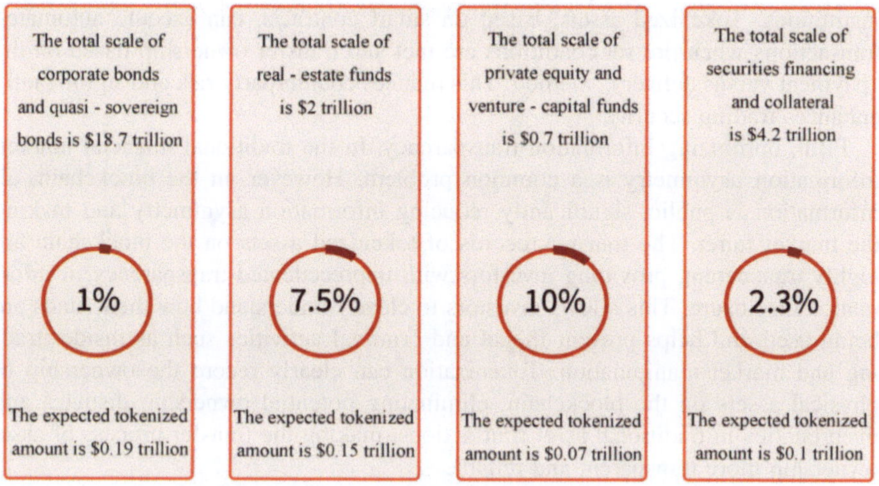

Fig. 1.3 Trillions of dollars' worth of financial assets are expected to be tokenized in 2030

underestimated. In addition, tokenized assets can be divided into smaller shares for trading, significantly reducing the investment and financing thresholds for high-quality assets. High-quality assets that were previously only accessible to wealthy investors are no longer out of reach. Moreover, investors can more flexibly split and sell part of their assets to optimize asset allocation. Assets with high value but low liquidity, such as luxury houses and famous paintings, are restricted by factors such as geographical location, laws and regulations, market scale, and trading methods. Their trading processes are often extremely complex, time-consuming, and labor-intensive. However, after Tokenization, these assets can be divided and traded on the blockchain network, reducing trading thresholds and greatly enhancing their liquidity.

Second, improving trading efficiency. Based on blockchain technology, tokenized assets can enable almost real-time trading and settlement, allowing investors to buy or sell their assets more quickly. This significantly improves market efficiency and strengthens market effectiveness.

Third, reducing costs and expenses. The traditional asset trading process involves multiple intermediate links, such as investment banks, brokers, banks, lawyers, etc. Each intermediate link incurs certain fees, making the overall cost of asset trading relatively high. However, token trading on the blockchain is peer-to-peer, reducing intermediate links and thus lowering transaction costs. In addition, Tokenization enables many processes (such as pricing, settlement, asset division, etc.) to be automated based on smart contracts, greatly reducing manual processing costs. The transparency and immutability of the blockchain also make fraud and errors less likely to occur, reducing additional costs caused by fraud and errors.

Fourth, enhancing trading security. In the traditional asset trading process, a high level of trust is usually required among the buyer, the seller, and intermediary institutions. Tokenized assets, based on smart contracts, can execute automated transactions when pre-set conditions are met and transfer ownership based on the "payment versus delivery" method. This reduces counterparty risk and significantly enhances trading security.

Fifth, optimizing information transparency. In the traditional financial market, information asymmetry is a common problem. However, in the blockchain, all information is public, significantly reducing information asymmetry and making the market fairer. The transfer records of tokenized assets on the blockchain are highly transparent, providing investors with unprecedented transparency in information disclosure. This allows investors to clearly understand how their funds are being used and helps prevent illegal and criminal activities such as insider trading and market manipulation. Tokenization can clearly record the ownership of physical assets on the blockchain, eliminating potential ownership disputes and uncertainties in traditional asset transactions, making the transfer process of asset ownership more transparent and reliable.

Sixth, enhancing financial inclusivity. After Tokenization, a large-value asset can be split into multiple small-value tokens, lowering the investment threshold and enabling ordinary people to participate in the financial market. Tokenization allows more people to invest in assets that were previously only available to wealthy investors, greatly increasing the inclusivity of the financial market.

Seventh, being more environmentally sustainable. Traditional financial transactions and asset management usually generate a large number of paper documents (including contracts, reports, invoices, etc.). This not only consumes a large amount of paper but also requires processes such as transportation and storage, imposing a certain environmental burden. After RWA is tokenized, all information is stored on the blockchain, fully digitalized, eliminating the need for paper documents. This greatly reduces the environmental resource consumption of asset transactions. In addition, the traditional financial system requires a large number of data centers and servers to process and store data, consuming a significant amount of energy. In the past, the blockchain mining process might have consumed a large amount of energy, but the application of technologies such as proof-of-stake and sharding has gradually addressed this issue. New-type blockchain systems do not need to build large-scale data centers, further reducing energy consumption.

1.4.4 Challenges of RWA Tokenization

Like any new thing, RWA Tokenization also faces a series of challenges and problems that may hinder its large-scale development.

First, legal and compliance challenges. The legal supervision of digital assets varies greatly among different judicial jurisdictions globally, and compliance standards also differ. The legal issues involved in the Tokenization of physical assets are complex and diverse, covering multiple fields such as contract law, securities law, trust law, commercial law, and tax law. It often needs to meet different and even conflicting legal requirements of multiple countries or regions simultaneously, making the global trading of RWA tokens complex and difficult. For example, a token may be regarded as a security in one country, but as a commodity or currency in another. This requires issuers to conduct detailed research on the compliance requirements of various countries and regions. This not only consumes a large amount of time and resources but also poses significant risks, as even a small oversight can lead to serious legal consequences. In addition, the uncertainty of the regulatory environment is also a major challenge. Many countries and regions have not yet clearly defined regulatory policies for digital assets, or are in the process of formulating or amending relevant regulations. This requires issuers to closely monitor regulatory dynamics in various countries to prevent sudden policy changes from affecting the compliance of projects. This uncertainty may also affect investors' confidence, leading to undervalued token prices or reduced liquidity.

Second, technical and security challenges. When tokens need to be issued and circulated on multiple blockchains, or need to interact with systems outside the blockchain ecosystem, interoperability issues may arise. Although blockchain technology provides a high level of transparency, it also brings additional risks to network security. Hackers may use the information on the blockchain to attack smart contracts or wallets, resulting in the theft of tokens or the invalidation of smart contracts.

Third, ecological shortcomings are also important challenges. Currently, the number of professional third-party digital asset custody institutions is limited, especially those with limited experience in custody of RWA tokens, which may have a negative impact on asset security and stability. Although the blockchain has good transparency, without sufficient supervision and practical standards, repeated or unauthorized Tokenization activities may still occur. In addition, for issuers of RWA tokens, they must consider a series of procedures such as KYC (Know Your Customer), KYT (Know Your Transaction), and AML (Anti-Money Laundering). Even during the circulation of tokens in the secondary market, in some cases, a whitelist[2]system may be required. However, currently, relatively few companies can provide such complete solutions, and the prices are relatively high.

Overall, RWA Tokenization represents an important exploration direction for new Internet technologies in the financial field. It provides a brand-new digital trading and circulation channel for RWA, with the potential to greatly improve asset liquidity and investment efficiency. Currently, there are significant differences in the attitudes and regulatory policies towards Tokenization among countries. Some countries (such as the United States, Singapore, etc.) have already introduced relatively clear regulatory frameworks to regulate and guide Tokenization activities. These countries usually classify tokens into different categories (such as security-type tokens, utility-type tokens, etc.) and formulate targeted regulatory rules based on different categories. The author believes that regulatory authorities need to strike a balance between encouraging innovation and preventing risks. On the one hand, they should create a favorable development environment for Tokenization, reduce unnecessary regulatory barriers, and promote technological innovation and the implementation of applications. On the other hand, they should also strengthen the supervision of Tokenization activities, prevent illegal activities such as fraud and money laundering, and protect the rights and interests of investors. This requires close cooperation between regulatory authorities and industry participants to jointly explore Tokenization paths that meet market demands and regulatory requirements. Although there are still many challenges in terms of technology, regulation, etc. at present, with the joint efforts of all parties, RWA Tokenization is expected to become an important driving force for future financial innovation and inject new vitality into economic development.

[2] Refers to a list of approved blockchain addresses. Only by logging in to such addresses can one participate in the trading of specific tokens

Technical Principle of RWA and Tokenized Blockchain

2

2.1 Technical Principles of RWA Tokenization Based on Blockchain

The technology of RWA (Real-World Assets) Tokenization leverages the unique properties of blockchain, such as immutability, decentralization, and transparency, to address some challenges in the traditional asset market. The advancement of blockchain technology signals a fundamental transformation of market structures and is likely to have far-reaching impacts on the global financial market. By enabling decentralized recording of assets and increasing market transparency, the application of blockchain in RWA Tokenization not only optimizes transaction processes but also enhances the overall security and efficiency of the system, demonstrating profound potential for change.

The Tokenization of RWA will be propelled by traditional financial institutions, regulatory bodies, and authoritative entities like central banks. It is a brand-new financial system built on a permission chain. The realization of this system requires collaborative efforts in multiple aspects, including computational systems (such as blockchain technology) and non-computational systems (such as legal systems), as well as on-chain identity systems and privacy-protection technologies. Firstly, the computational system serves as the foundation. Blockchain technology provides a secure, transparent, and efficient trading environment for this system. On this basis, a sound non-computational system (such as a robust legal system) is needed to ensure the legality and compliance of transactions. Meanwhile, the combination of on-chain identity systems and privacy-protection technologies can safeguard the security of user identities and privacy data. Secondly, on-chain legal tender (such as the Central Bank Digital Currency CBDC, tokenized deposits, and legal stablecoins) is a crucial component of this system. It will serve as the main circulating currency in the new financial system, ensuring the stability and reliability of transactions. Finally, well-developed infrastructure is the key to the success of this system. For example, wallets with low entry barriers and easy usability

S. Ba et al., *RWA Tokenisation in Web 3.0 Era*, Management for Professionals,
https://doi.org/10.1007/978-981-96-7663-7_2

enable more users to participate conveniently. Oracle technology ensures the accurate transmission of data both on and off the chain, and cross-chain technology guarantees the interoperability between different blockchains.

When understanding from the perspective of first-principle thinking, blockchain has become a hot technology in the financial and economic industries because it is an ideal infrastructure for asset Tokenization. Blockchain can offer a brand-new solution for information transmission, contract processing, and instruction systems. It can not only transmit information quickly and widely but also address issues such as untrustworthy information on the Internet, potential concentration and abuse of power due to centralized power structures, as well as information opacity and unfairness through its decentralized, transparent, and immutable distributed ledger.

It can be said that blockchain is a technology that can truly and effectively support the digitization of contracts. Therefore, at its core, blockchain is a digital contract platform. Smart contracts are an important form of asset expression, and tokens are the digital carriers of assets after the formation of contracts. They empower assets with complex information based on trust and enable decentralized and automated operations. The three core technologies supporting these features of blockchain are cryptography, consensus mechanisms, and networks.

2.1.1 Cryptography

Blockchain's direct need for cryptography mainly stems from two considerations: determining ownership and protecting data privacy. On the traditional Web 2.0 Internet, electronic data is easily replicated, and it's not as straightforward as physical assets to prove ownership. Thus, the digital signature technology in cryptography, which is used to prove the ownership of digital assets, meets this requirement. Since the blockchain ledger is maintained jointly by nodes in the network and data is transparent, data privacy needs protection. The anonymization of transaction information through cryptography technology can achieve this goal, and it can also be used as a cryptographic tool for generating random numbers in consensus schemes.

In a decentralized system, users need to prove their identities to the nodes maintaining the network to gain common recognition, ensuring the validity of their identities. However, this would undoubtedly lead to high costs. Digital signatures offer a solution with public-key and private-key concepts: the private key is kept by the user, and the public key is published to network nodes. Users can generate signatures with their private keys, and nodes can verify these signatures with public keys.

Blockchain contains associations and data between accounts. To maintain transparency while protecting user privacy, blockchain employs a series of cryptographic tools (such as asymmetric encryption, zero-knowledge proof, ring signatures, etc.) to anonymize some information in transactions.

2.1.2 Consensus Mechanisms

The core of the blockchain system is the maintenance of blockchain ledger data. As a data structure stored in chronological order, the essence of consensus is the process of nodes validating and ledger updating. The final result is that the blockchain system provides a unified ledger externally. This distributed system consensus includes the self-processing of node data and the interaction between nodes.

2.1.3 Blockchain Networks

Blockchain utilizes a P2P network architecture based on the Internet. Each participating node in the network contributes computing power, storage space, and network connectivity. Through the network, these capabilities can be shared resources, not managed by intermediate entities but directly accessible by other peer nodes. Therefore, each node is both a user and a provider, and nodes are interconnected with a flat topology.

In addition to the basic communication protocols that ensure network connectivity, the network layer can include mining protocols, file-transfer protocols, etc., depending on different application requirements. Although nodes in the blockchain network have no hierarchy, based on different scenario needs, nodes are designed as full nodes, SPV nodes, miner nodes, and client-side nodes, corresponding to the four functions of node routing communication, ledger storage, consensus participation, and wallet on the blockchain.

The three core technologies of blockchain run through the entire blockchain architecture, laying the foundation for various business implementations. So, what is the blockchain hierarchy like in terms of the actual operation and construction of blockchain?

2.1.4 Blockchain Hierarchy

Regarding blockchain, we often hear the term "Layer 1". Although this technical term may seem complex or ambiguous, its meaning is actually quite simple. Layer 1 refers to the sovereign blockchain, such as the Ethereum and Bitcoin networks. We can imagine blockchain technology as a pyramid composed of several layers, where each layer depends on the layer below it, but not vice versa.

Layer 0 is the foundation of the entire pyramid, including network protocols, Internet protocols, and all miners, validators, and nodes. Therefore, Layer 0 is not the blockchain itself but the infrastructure of blockchain.

Layer 1 is the first entity independent of any other blockchain. For example, Layer 2 blockchains like Arbitrum or StarkNet rely on Layer 1 (Ethereum) to operate. Ethereum and Bitcoin both belong to Layer 1.

Layer 1 (including the Bitcoin network and Ethereum) is decentralized in design and not controlled by any central institution. Layer 1 scaling solutions (also known as "on - chain scaling") refer to scaling solutions implemented in the blockchain's underlying protocol.

Layer 1 is responsible for processing and completing transactions on its own blockchain. This involves technical details such as consensus mechanisms (e.g., Proof-of-Work (PoW), Proof-of-Stake (PoS)), block time, and dispute resolution. Specifically, Layer 1 has five main functions: blockchain consensus (such as PoW, PoS, etc., ensuring data consistency among nodes), blockchain data (including transaction data, chain structure, timestamp, Merkle tree, etc.), blockchain network layer (enabling communication between nodes through the P2P network and ensuring data transmission and synchronization), blockchain incentives (encouraging nodes to participate in blockchain operation through reward mechanisms like issuing digital currencies), and blockchain contracts (supporting the execution of smart contracts and enabling decentralized applications).

Layer 2 is an overlapping network above the basic layer, commonly known as Layer 2 solutions. The protocol utilizes Layer 2 by removing some interactions from the basic layer to increase scalability. Therefore, smart contracts in the main blockchain protocol only handle deposits and withdrawals and ensure that off-chain transactions comply with regulations. The Lightning Network of Bitcoin is an example of a Layer 2 blockchain. Layer 2 is a third-party integration used in conjunction with Layer 1, aiming to increase the number of nodes and thus improve system throughput.

Layer 2 scaling solutions, also known as off-chain scaling, refer to methods that improve transaction processing speed through state channels, sidechains, Rollups, etc., without changing the underlying blockchain protocol and basic rules. They specifically include:

- State Channels: Allow users to conduct multiple transactions off-chain and only submit the final state to the chain.
- Sidechains: As blockchains independent of the main chain, they can interact with the main chain. Sidechains can adopt consensus algorithms different from the main chain to provide higher performance or specific functions, and data bridges are used to transmit data and state information between the main chain and sidechains.
- Rollups: A solution that submits a large number of off-chain transactions to the chain after packaging them, improving throughput. It includes Zero-Knowledge Rollups (ZK Rollup) and Optimistic Rollup.

By packaging multiple transactions for batch processing, the number of on-chain transactions and associated fees are reduced. In addition to the above common solutions, Layer 2 also has hybrid solutions such as Plasma, off-chain computing, and sharding. These technologies enable Layer 2 to improve on-chain throughput and transaction efficiency.

The scalability solutions for the Ethereum blockchain aim to alleviate network congestion, but after adopting these solutions, the congestion issues they originally intended to solve often resurface. To address the problem of soaring costs, developers have created a three-level network (Layer 3), which inherits the security of the parent blockchain through recursion.

Unlike Layer 1 and Layer 2, Layer 3 is often referred to as the "special - purpose layer". In other words, each Layer 3 blockchain is constructed according to specific purposes and optimized for these purposes. Thus, Layer 3 not only benefits from fractal expansion but also performs extremely efficiently in specific application scenarios.

In the RWA field, blockchain technology mainly revolves around virtual machines (VM), smart contracts, and oracles.

2.1.5 Virtual Machines

A virtual machine is the computing environment for executing smart contracts on the blockchain. It provides a secure and isolated sandbox environment to ensure that the execution of smart contracts does not affect other parts. Different blockchain platforms use different virtual machines. For example, Ethereum uses the Ethereum Virtual Machine (EVM), and Polkadot and EOS use WebAssembly (WASM). Currently, Ethereum's EVM is a relatively mature virtual machine. It allows the deployment and execution of code and can execute complex control logic. Users only need to install the necessary client-side software to access the EVM and use it to execute programs on Ethereum while also supporting the deployment of smart contracts. Essentially, the EVM acts as a "world settlement computer", executing software operations in a decentralized environment. The EVM is maintained by different individuals/companies, and it provides computing power to the system in exchange for rewards. Since there is no centralized control, it cannot be shut down by any single party. The EVM is also described as a "distributed state machine", where "state" refers to the address, account balance, and smart contract code that exist at a specific moment. Therefore, in Ethereum, each transaction causes a change in the Ethereum state, and this change is reflected across the entire network.

During operation, the EVM is the execution environment when Ethereum is running. It is responsible for executing the bytecode of smart contracts and maintaining and reading the state. It maintains the state of smart contracts by reading and updating external data. When executing smart contracts, the EVM can update the state according to the execution results of smart contracts.

2.1.6 Smart Contracts

Smart contracts are self-executing codes deployed on the blockchain. Ideally, smart contracts can be regarded as Turing machines, automatically executing according to pre-set conditions without human interference. Currently, the completeness of the Ethereum Turing machine provides a means to express various asset types for smart contracts. As a result, token standards such as homogeneous tokens, non-homogeneous tokens, and semi-homogeneous tokens have emerged.

In the blockchain system, decentralization provides a trustworthy environment, enabling smart contracts to play their role. They are processed in the form of transactions and events through the modularization of smart contracts and remain a set of transactions and events after execution. Their mission is to ensure that a set of complex digital commitments with specific logic and triggering conditions are correctly executed according to the regulations of participants. In RWA, they are used to create RWA tokens, establish transaction logic to ensure compliance with predefined rules, interact with oracle data, and automatically adjust the state and attributes of assets based on the data provided by oracles. Smart contracts can establish different accounts, relationships, permissions, functions, and operating conditions according to the specific content and logic of the business. They are used to automatically handle various businesses such as rent payment, dividend distribution, and equity conversion, simplifying the management process, reducing operating costs, increasing business combinability, and ensuring the accuracy and timeliness of transactions.

2.1.7 Oracles

Although the application of blockchain and Tokenization technologies has revolutionary potential, due to the operating mechanism of blockchain, each node must perform deterministic operations. For the same input data, all nodes will obtain the same output result. When nodes acquire and process external data, they will face non-deterministic operations. This non-deterministic operation may lead to data discrepancies between nodes, affecting the consensus process. Therefore, blockchain itself cannot actively obtain external data, which is also known as the "oracle problem".

The vast majority of potential application scenarios for smart contracts can only be realized by connecting off-chain data and systems. For example, in the financial field, smart contracts rely on external market price data when executed. In the insurance industry, smart contracts make judgments based on IoT and network data when handling claims. Smart contracts in trade finance require the connection of relevant documents and digital signatures to confirm and execute payment operations. Additionally, many smart contracts need to interact with traditional payment networks for fiat currency transactions during settlement, and a large amount of necessary data is generated off-chain and cannot be directly transmitted to the chain.

Moreover, since blockchain is essentially an "island", users, assets, liquidity, applications, and data are fragmented. To achieve the large-scale application of RWA Tokenization, blockchains need to be connected to each other. Only by reconnecting the "islands" into a "continent" can the true potential of blockchain be unleashed and the inter-connectivity of blockchains be realized. Therefore, the essence of an oracle is to be responsible for the information transmission between the blockchain and the outside world.

An oracle is an important part of blockchain technology. It provides a mechanism to bring off-chain data onto the chain. Since the smart contracts of blockchain cannot directly access external data, the oracle serves as a bridge to ensure that smart contracts can be executed based on external events or data. In the RWA field, decentralized oracles are usually used to increase data reliability and credibility, adapting to high-value assets. The working process of an oracle can be divided into: data request, creation of request contracts, task allocation, data acquisition, data verification and consensus, data aggregation, and data transmission. The data acquired by the oracle is transmitted to the smart contracts on blockchain Layer 1 to trigger contract execution. When the data volume is too large, some oracles also seek expansion solutions on Layer 2 to improve data processing speed and scalability.

Under the combined action of these core blockchain technologies and components, blockchain can well meet people's demand for the "computability" of asset value and rights. Blockchain can record transaction information without being manipulated and achieve repeatable processes and verifiable results while ensuring privacy. This forms a unified standard and measurement, eliminating the interference of human subjective consciousness on contracts. Taking the traditional financial system as an example, financial derivatives occupy a crucial position in the traditional financial market. With an estimated nominal value exceeding hundreds of billions of dollars, they have great leverage potential and have created an asset scale dozens of times the value of underlying assets. There is a wide variety of financial derivatives, which are complex and diverse, covering multiple fields such as stocks, fixed income, foreign exchange, credit, interest rates, and commodities. In these fields, derivatives also come in various forms, including options (such as ordinary call options, put options, and exotic options), warrants, futures, forward contracts, and swaps. Against the backdrop of high leverage and high risk, transparency is of utmost importance.

These contracts are like toolkits in the financial market, providing investors with a wealth of choices and strategies. Whether it is hedging risks or speculating for profits, the derivatives market offers a broad space for participants with different needs. Although these complex financial tools may seem esoteric, they play an indispensable role in the operation of the financial market, contributing to market liquidity and stability.

2.2 The Concept and Development History of RWA

RWA Tokenization refers to the process of converting the equity value of tangible or intangible assets into digital tokens. This technology records asset information (including attributes, status, transaction history, and ownership) on the blockchain, enabling assets to be traded and circulated within the blockchain network. RWAs include tangible assets (such as real estate and precious metals) and intangible assets (such as stocks and bonds). Tokenization technology successfully connects physical assets with the digital currency domain, breaking down the barriers between them, providing broader liquidity, and enriching the types of digital assets. RWA Tokenization is not only a form of asset digitization but also a technical means to achieve on-chain transactions by mapping RWAs onto the blockchain. This technical approach promotes the integration and innovation of different asset classes in the financial market, offering new opportunities and challenges for investors, while also posing challenges to the operational models of traditional financial markets.

As shown in Table 2.1, whether tangible assets like real estate and precious metals, or intangible assets such as intellectual property rights and investment funds, can enter the digital market through Tokenization. Among the tangible asset categories of RWAs, we can observe Tokenization practices for assets such as real estate, precious collectibles, precious metals, vehicles, industrial machinery, and raw materials. PAX Gold, as a representative of assets backed by gold, demonstrates how tangible assets can enter the digital asset market through Tokenization. Additionally, projects like RealT and LABS Group have further promoted the application and development of the RWA model by integrating real-estate assets into Real Estate Investment Trusts (REITs) and enabling on-chain transactions.

The intangible assets of RWA include stocks, bonds, intellectual property rights, investment funds, derivative assets, revenue-sharing contracts, cash assets, accounts receivable, and credit scores, etc. The Tokenization of these assets is also of great significance. In particular, bond-type assets (such as short-term US Treasury bonds or bond ETFs) account for a relatively large proportion in the Tokenization of intangible assets, indicating that bond assets play an important role in the digital asset market.

2.2.1 The Operational Mechanism of RWA Tokenization in the Financial Market

RWA Tokenization represents a technical means of mapping RWAs onto the blockchain, with its core being the on-chain transfer of real-world transactions. This process involves the accurate valuation of real-world assets and introducing them as tradable tokenized objects into the blockchain. The implementation of RWA Tokenization projects includes three key steps: the financialization of assets, the credibility of financial data, and the Tokenization of credible data.

Firstly, asset financialization. This is a prerequisite for introducing off-chain assets into the blockchain ecosystem. It involves defining the economic value, ownership, and legality of assets. At the technical level, the challenge is how to accurately reflect the ownership of assets in the form of Tokenization and design the asset-transfer process. At the legal level, it is necessary to establish a clear regulatory framework to ensure asset liquidity, safeguard transaction security, and properly handle asset liquidation and dispute resolution.

Table 2.1 Asset categories and overviews of RWA

RWA asset category	Advantages	Risks/Challenges
Fixed-income	Currently, it is the most popular asset with growth potential, solving issues such as high entry barriers, information asymmetry, and low liquidity.	Regulatory compliance
SME financing	Solves the liquidity dilemma of enterprises and provides above-market returns for on-chain investors.	Challenges in supervision, corporate credit, audit, and legal traceability
Rare metals	The market has inherent stability, cost-effectiveness, global liquidity, and transparency, and has initially taken shape.	Regulatory uncertainties, technical risks, and market application and liquidity issues
Real estate	Tangible assets, and financial products like REITs have relevant experience in the traditional market that can be borrowed.	The compliance complexity of asset Tokenization
Artworks	Facilitates mortgage loans and explores untapped markets.	As an emerging market, it may not necessarily become the main area for RWA development
Infrastructure	Finances infrastructure development in less-developed regions.	The legal frameworks for the ownership of related assets vary greatly in different regions
Digital rights of commodities with financial attributes	Rich in commodity types and highly demanded in the market, with collection or value-preservation functions, especially during economic fluctuations.	Affected by supervision and trade policies, and commodity prices are greatly influenced by supply-demand relationships, market sentiment, and the economic environment
AI computing power	The demand for AI computing power continues to grow, and it can flexibly adapt to different scales of application needs, with technological innovation, especially the distributed computing and edge computing combined with DePIN.	Issues related to data privacy and network security

(continued)

Table 2.1 (continued)

RWA asset category	Advantages	Risks/Challenges
Green energy	Many countries provide policy support and subsidies, in line with environmental protection trends, such as the photovoltaics-energy storage ecosystem and carbon credits combined with DePIN.	Risks of policy changes, technological replacements, and equipment aging
Fan ecosystems in music and sports	Has a fan economy and diverse income sources (such as streaming media ticket sales, peripheral product sales, concert and event ticket sales, etc.), and brand-effect advantages.	Greatly affected by market and fashion trends, and there are copyright risks
New content platform model	Has global market potential, rich and diverse content, and can spread across borders, such as the content distribution of cultural and media IP franchises and Watch2Earn.	Affected by policies and regulations in different countries and regions, with compliance risks

Secondly, the credibility of financial data. This step involves storing the determined asset data in a distributed ledger. After converting RWAs into data, token issuers need to provide data containing asset value and ownership information to smart contracts to ensure data accessibility and transparency. However, complete transparency may not be conducive to financial privacy. Therefore, RWA Tokenization technically uses zero-knowledge proof to protect transaction privacy. At the legal level, more explicit rules need to be formulated to balance the needs of transaction security and privacy protection.

Thirdly, the Tokenization of credible data. The final step is to issue fungible tokens or NFTs to the market or specific investors through the RWA protocol, aiming to endow RWAs with liquidity and enable them to circulate in the market. Throughout the entire process of RWA Tokenization, the transparency and credibility of blockchain data are of utmost importance. The valuation, liquidation, and other aspects of off-chain assets must be strictly controlled to ensure the accuracy and legality of data and prevent fraud, which is the key to the success of RWA projects.

2.2.2 The Core Characteristics of RWA

The core characteristics of RWA include asset correlation, asset transparency, enhanced liquidity, cost-effectiveness, and smart contracts. Their roles in promoting large-scale application are as follows:

- Asset Correlation ensures that blockchain projects are closely related to actual physical assets. This not only provides higher credibility but also adds value assurance to assets. This correlation is particularly important for traditional investors because it helps enhance the reputation of the entire field, making blockchain projects more acceptable and trustworthy in the traditional financial market.
- Asset Transparency significantly improves the convenience of audit and compliance management by ensuring that all transactions are recorded and publicly disclosed on the blockchain. This transparency is crucial for building investor trust as it reduces investment risks and attracts more institutional investors to participate.
- Enhanced Liquidity significantly improves asset liquidity by converting traditional assets into tokens that can be freely traded on the blockchain. This transformation not only makes assets more tradable but also helps attract more users and developers, thus promoting the development of a healthy ecosystem.
- Cost-effectiveness by using blockchain technology to reduce transaction costs, especially in cross-border transactions and complex asset-structure operations, it makes it easier for small-and medium-sized investors and enterprises to participate in the market. This cost reduction expands the user base and increases the overall activity and participation in the market.
- Smart Contracts the application of smart contracts enables asset-related operations (such as dividend payments and ownership transfers) to be executed automatically, significantly reducing the need for human intervention and minimizing operating costs and transaction risks. The advantages of smart contracts are particularly suitable for complex financial transactions and asset management, providing possibilities for broader financial applications.

Through the analysis of these core characteristics, it can be seen that the application of blockchain technology in physical asset management can not only improve efficiency and transparency but also reduce costs and enhance the overall liquidity and participation in the market. These characteristics work together to promote the large-scale application of blockchain technology in a broader financial and investment field, especially showing great potential in enhancing the integration of traditional assets and emerging technologies.

2.2.3 The Current Situation of the RWA Market

In terms of total volume, the scale of the RWA market has grown significantly since 2023. As of July 31, 2024, statistical data shows that the total value locked (TVL) of RWA market protocols has reached $6 billion, involving 57 contract products, with a scale increase of over 60 times compared to 2022.

Currently, the RWA market shows a prominent head effect. The top 4 projects in terms of market scale are stUSDT ($706 million), Ondo Finance ($154 million), Matrix Dock ($124 million), and RealT Tokens ($83 million), with a cumulative market share of approximately 86% (see Fig. 2.1). According to data from the

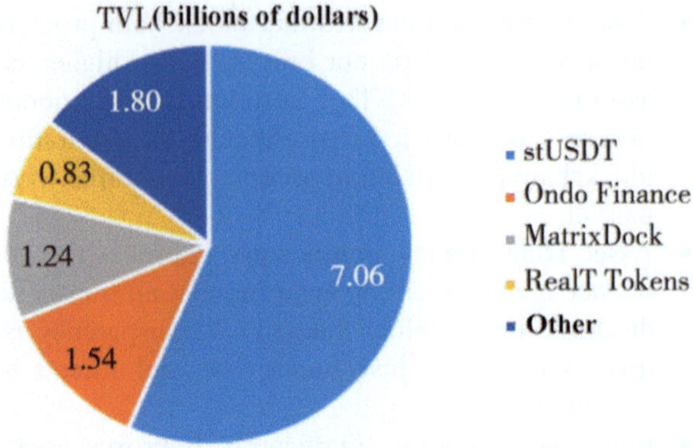

Fig. 2.1 The prominent head effect in the RWA market (*Source* DeFiLlama)

RWA track monitoring platform DeFiLlama, as of July 31, 2024, the value of the tokenized government bond market has increased from approximately $496 million a year ago to $1.284 billion, with an average annualized yield of about 5%.

In the current market environment, the growth of RWA-type assets such as tokenized government bonds reflects an increased preference among investors for asset categories with stable and more predictable expected returns. Especially for investors seeking a balance between the traditional financial market and the cryptocurrency market, they are increasingly inclined to choose products like tokenized government bonds that combine the characteristics of both.

In the short term, under the wave of interest-rate hikes, the risk-free interest rates of major economies have risen to 4% or even higher, which is highly attractive to cryptocurrency market investors. As a result, more and more projects are attempting to introduce RWAs into the cryptocurrency industry.

In the long term, the integrated development of encrypted assets and traditional assets is an inevitable trend. With the continuous reform and innovation in the traditional financial market, RWAs can bring more opportunities and competitiveness. Moreover, blockchain technology is being accepted and adopted by more people. By digitizing RWAs, transaction costs can be effectively reduced, and the liquidity and transparency of assets can be improved, thus providing new impetus for the development of the world economy.

According to a report by the Boston Consulting Group, it is predicted that by 2030, the global market scale of Tokenization of illiquid assets is expected to reach $16 trillion, accounting for 10% of the global GDP. This includes two parts: on-chain asset Tokenization and the fractionalization of existing traditional assets (such as ETFs and real-estate investment trust funds). For the cryptocurrency industry, even obtaining a small share of this huge market represents significant growth opportunities.

2.2.4 The Future of RWA: Deep Integration with DeFi

DeFi is a financial service system based on blockchain technology, especially leveraging smart-contract platforms like Ethereum. The goal of this financial model is to eliminate centralized institutions (such as banks and insurance companies) in traditional financial services, making financial services more open, transparent, and accessible. The core characteristics of DeFi include permission-less access, high decentralization, complete transparency, high programmability, and good interoperability. This means that anyone can use these services without approval, all transaction information is publicly transparent, and complex financial operations can be automatically executed through smart contracts. The applications of DeFi are very extensive, including lending platforms, decentralized exchanges (DEX), stablecoins, asset management, and decentralized insurance, etc. For example, on DeFi lending platforms, users can borrow or lend assets relatively freely without the complex approval processes of traditional banks, and the interest rates are often more competitive. DEX allows users to directly exchange assets without intermediaries, providing higher privacy protection and security.

RWA is tokenized by mapping the rights and interests of its underlying assets onto DeFi through Tokenization on-chain. The combined application of RWA and DeFi protocols can connect centralized and decentralized systems, making RWA "DeFi - ized".

As shown in Fig. 2.2, introducing RWAs and integrating DeFi into the real world is an inevitable trend. RWA and DeFi will promote each other and develop jointly. On the one hand, compared with DeFi native assets, RWA injects asset diversity into DeFi. Native on-chain assets, due to their high homogeneity, high correlation, and high volatility, cannot meet the development needs of DeFi protocols. In contrast, RWAs inject assets with low correlation to on-chain assets, stable and observable returns, and good liquidity into DeFi. Therefore, injecting RWAs can not only build a more diverse investment portfolio strategy but also provide diversified collateral, enhancing the security and effectiveness of DeFi, which is in line with the regulatory requirements on the chain. On the other hand, the on-chain of RWA provides fragmented entry barriers for RWA investors, as well as investment options with higher fees, security, information transparency, and asset liquidity. The optimization that DeFi brings to the financial market will be realized through RWA Tokenization. In other words, RWA is a trend of DeFi "swallowing" the traditional economic world. For RWAs to be tokenized, it is first necessary to standardize and clarify external information from off-chain, including the economic value of RWAs, ownership, and legal protection of asset rights and interests. Then, after the standardized external information is digitized, it is introduced into the blockchain through an oracle and becomes on-chain data that can be directly accessed by DeFi protocols, and corresponding digital tokens are generated. After the external data is on-chain, it will be stored in a distributed ledger as the metadata of digital tokens to ensure data transparency and accessibility. Different categories of RWAs are incorporated into DeFi through legal and compliant means, corresponding to different DeFi protocol standards. Finally, the

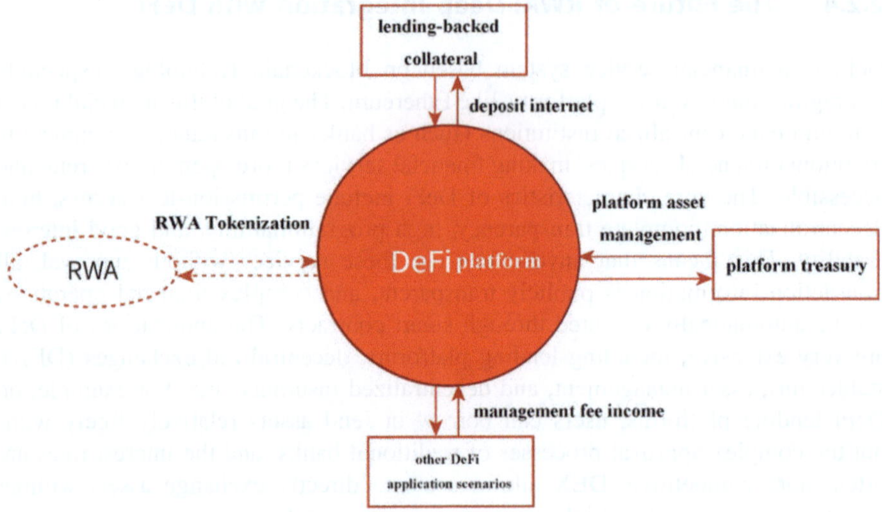

Fig. 2.2 Schematic diagram of the asset flow of RWA entering DeFi

generated RWAs can serve as the underlying assets of DeFi protocols, integrate with DeFi protocols, participate in the activities of the DeFi ecosystem, and meet investors' demand for RWAs.

The Tokenization process of RWA reveals that the improvement of asset transparency benefits from all off-chain information and transaction history being stored in a distributed ledger for access. The increase in asset security due to the on-chain of RWA not only benefits from this but also from fragmented risk-exposure allocation, decentralized management, and smart-contract guarantees. Finally, the improvement of asset liquidity is not only because Tokenization successfully reduces the costs and barriers of asset investment, attracting more on-chain and even off-chain investors, but also because of the automatic market maker (AMM) in DeFi protocols, which allows asset holders to complete transactions in a timely manner and obtain liquidity. As the feasibility of DeFi protocols introduced by RWA is proven, the value "depression" of the RWA market will attract a large number of investors.

2.3 The Differences and Connections Between RWA and Tokenization

This section first provides an overview of the development history of RWA, from the initial stablecoin stage to the introduction of STO, and then to the broader RWA stage. Secondly, it conducts a comparative analysis of IPO, STO, and RWA, highlighting the main differences among them in terms of security types, underlying assets, and regulatory compliance. Finally, it analyzes the differences and connections between tokens and RWAs in terms of trust assumptions, regulatory frameworks, and market applications.

2.3.1 The Development History of RWA

Tokenization is an STO activity based on blockchain technology, representing a process of converting traditional financial assets into digital assets through blockchain technology. This conversion makes assets easier to trade globally and improves liquidity and transparency.

Against this backdrop, the concept of RWA can be regarded as a broader application of STO. RWA is not limited to traditional securities but also includes all RWAs and their attached rights and interests, such as tangible assets like real estate, artworks, and precious metals, as well as intangible assets like equity and creditor's rights. Through Tokenization, these assets are converted into digital tokens on the blockchain, enabling them to be traded and managed more efficiently and transparently on a global scale.

By expanding the concept of STO, RWA Tokenization not only provides new investment opportunities for investors but also offers more flexibility and security for asset ownership and transactions. Additionally, the application of blockchain technology can ensure the immutability and traceability of transaction records, enhancing market trust.

Therefore, RWA Tokenization can be understood as an expansion and deepening of STO in application. It introduces the advantages of blockchain technology to a broader range of asset categories, providing a new perspective and tools for asset management and investment. The promotion and application of this technology indicate the future development direction of the financial market and may have a profound impact on global asset allocation and the operation mode of the financial market.

From the broad definition of RWA, its development can be traced back to the emergence of stablecoins, with a relatively long history that can be roughly divided into three stages.

2.3.2 Stablecoin Stage

A stablecoin is a digital currency pegged to reserve assets such as fiat currencies and gold. It is also a type of cryptocurrency that can freely circulate, be extended onto the blockchain, and is linked to reserve assets. Take fiat-pegged stablecoins as an example. When a unit of stablecoin is minted, the stablecoin issuer backs it with a corresponding unit of fiat currency. In this way, holders of stablecoins can own a virtual asset with a "stable price" and can also quickly trade cryptocurrencies represented by Bitcoin (BTC). It can be said that stablecoins provide a stable-priced asset target for participants in the blockchain ecosystem.

The representative of this stage is USDT, which was issued by Tether, a company under Bitfinex, in 2014. It is pegged to the US dollar at a 1:1 ratio and claims to have sufficient US-dollar reserves as collateral. USDT tokenizes the real-world asset of the US dollar, and by borrowing from the gold standard system and pegging it 1:1, it becomes a very special RWA.

2.3.3 STO Stage

STO has the legal attributes and rights of traditional securities, such as equity, creditor's rights, revenue rights, and voting rights. STO can be generally understood as the evolution of securities vouchers from "paper vouchers → electronic vouchers → token vouchers".

The development history of STO can be traced back to 2017. After ICO was regulated due to its negative impacts, the concept of STO was proposed within the industry, that is, linking tokens to actual assets or rights and complying with corresponding securities regulations. At that time, the main objects of STO were the equity shares of blockchain projects. Typical cases include Polymath, which completed an STO in 2018, raising $59 million and launching its security-type token standard ERC - 1400; tZERO completed an STO in 2018, raising $134 million and officially launching a security-type token trading platform in January 2019.

2.3.4 RWA Tokenization Stage

RWA can be regarded as an extension of STO, a broader concept whose tokenized objects include all real-world assets and their attached rights and interests.

In terms of market discussion, RWA Tokenization gained momentum in 2022. As the Federal Reserve raised interest rates, DeFi declined, while risk-free returns represented by US Treasury bonds in TradFi increased significantly, leading to a large-scale outflow of funds from the DeFi market. According to statistical data from DeFiLlama, at the beginning of May 2022, the TVL of the DeFi market was approximately $136.67 billion, which dropped to $52.62 billion at the end of June 2022, a decrease of approximately 61.5% in less than two months. Against this backdrop, an important narrative for the heated discussion of RWA is "staying on - chain and investing in the real world."

2.3.5 Comparison of IPO, STO, and RWA Tokenization

Compared with STO, the underlying assets of RWA Tokenization are tangible valuable assets, and the financing scale is relatively larger. It is under regulatory supervision, with more transparent operations, higher security, greater compliance, designated exchanges, and relatively higher investment thresholds. Compared with

IPO, STO and RWA Tokenization break the traditional stock T + 1 method and adopt the T + 0 method, enabling more convenient real-time trading around the clock, opening up the global financial market, effectively shortening the investment cycle, reducing transaction frictions in the process, and thus lowering financing costs and improving the efficiency of resource allocation (see Table 2.2). Due to the limited number of countries that recognize them, the investment risks are relatively higher. STO and RWA Tokenization can be understood as the financialization of "blockchain + projects" that can be actually implemented under strict supervision.

RWA Tokenization is the process of digitally representing physical assets on a distributed ledger. The economic value and rights of these assets are embedded in digital tokens on the blockchain to ensure that the value of the tokens is supported by these assets. Tangible assets usually need to be held in custody to ensure the physical backing of the tokens. The integration of Web 3.0 and the real economy is an inevitable trend in industry development. STO and RWA Tokenization

Table 2.2 Comparison of STO, IPO, and RWA tokenization

Item/type	IPO	STO	RWA Tokenization
Security type	Securities	Tokens	Tokens
Underlying assets	Tangible Valuable Assets	On-chain assets	Tangible Valuable Assets
Enterprise type	Varies according to exchange regulations, generally large - and medium-sized companies	Almost all are concept-type small companies or decentralized organizations	Mostly start-up companies based on physical entities
Enterprise risk	Relatively low	Extremely high	Relatively high
Financing scale	Large	Medium-and Small-sized	Large
Supervision	Strong	Weak	Strong
Centralization	Yes	No	Yes
Operational transparency	Yes	No	Yes
Recognized countries	Global	Extremely few	Extremely few
Investment risk	Medium	High	High
Investment risk	Medium	High	High
Accredited investors	Yes	No	Yes
Investor protection	Yes	No	General
24-hour trading	No	Yes	Yes
Designated exchanges	Yes	No	No

represent two different integration paths. STO promotes the DeFi-ization of traditional financial assets from a compliance perspective, while RWA Tokenization integrates RWA into DeFi from the perspective of DeFi, leveraging the advantages and financial logic of DeFi.

The development of DeFi needs to be wary of the risk of "financial circularity". DeFi must serve economic development and achieve commercial circulation. The homogeneity and high volatility of native on-chain assets limit the development of DeFi protocols, causing DeFi projects to often serve themselves or financial arbitrageurs, forming a closed-loop financial cycle. Therefore, DeFi projects must incorporate RWA into their systems and participate in the economic development of the real world to build a more stable decentralized financial system. As a bridge between the real world and the cryptocurrency world, synthetic assets of RWA play an important role in the Tokenization process, promoting the communication and integration between RWA and the Web 3.0 world.

2.3.6 The Limited Implementation of Tokenization for RWA

In the trust assumption of RWA, since tokenized RWAs are off-chain after all, they cannot be liquidated through the enforcement of smart contracts and still rely on the endorsement of traditional financial institutions. The trust attributes of these RWAs may never reach the same level as crypto-native assets. At the same time, due to the existence of RWA trust assumptions, completely permission-less DeFi protocols also have difficulty supporting RWA. Therefore, in the processing of RWA assets in current RWA Tokenization projects, the role and influence of a centralized entity are generally still present.

Tokenization has always been regarded as a limited implementation of RWA. Tokens are usually traded only on compliant platforms approved by regulators. Therefore, it is one of the few asset-Tokenization solutions recognized by regulators in the blockchain industry. RWA refers to a type of assets that tokenize real-world assets through blockchain technology. Tokens are a form of RWA, but the concept of RWA is broader. RWA can include various real-world assets such as real estate, artworks, commodities, and even intellectual property rights, while tokens are often limited to more traditional financial assets such as stocks, bonds, or the rights and interests of specific projects.

In terms of regulation, RWA may face a more complex environment. Since it involves various types of assets, each asset may have its specific regulatory requirements, making the compliance issues of RWA more complicated. In contrast, tokens usually follow established securities regulations, and their regulatory framework is relatively clearer and more straightforward.

In terms of liquidity, the liquidity of tokens is superior to that of RWA. RWAs representing unique or large-scale assets (such as real estate) may have relatively low liquidity, while tokens are usually designed to be more easily traded and thus generally have higher liquidity. This difference also affects their valuation methods. RWA may require more complex valuation methods, especially for non-standardized assets, while the valuation of tokens is usually more straightforward, especially when they represent traditional financial assets.

In terms of technical implementation, RWA may require more complex solutions to ensure the authenticity of assets and ownership, while the technical implementation of tokens is relatively standardized, mainly focusing on issuance and trading mechanisms. This also affects their usage scenarios: RWA is commonly used in asset securitization, cross-border trade financing, and partial ownership of high-value assets, etc.; tokens are mostly used in crowdfunding, representing corporate equity, and equity distribution, etc.

For example, if stocks are the main part of RWA, then stocks can appear on-chain in two forms. One is that stocks already traded in the stock market are directly put on-chain through some centralized institutions. The other is tokens. That is, this stock may not be traded in a traditional exchange from the beginning. Instead, the enterprise directly issues it publicly after tokenizing the equity, similar to native on-chain stocks, which do not need to be mapped through existing exchanges. In fact, from a legal and compliant perspective, since a large number of enterprises are listed in Hong Kong, China, and the United States through the variable interest entity (VIE) structure, tokens are actually a form of contractual control, and this contract is feasible either on paper or in a smart contract.

2.3.7 Comparison of the Issuance Processes of RWA and Tokenization

As of the end of 2022, the SEC had approved 39 token projects. Commercial implementation is an important criterion for measuring the quality of a project. Therefore, the more commercially viable a project is, the more likely it is to obtain token approval. For example, the successfully tokenized tZERO company has a business model with practical application scenarios. tZERO currently provides services including securities brokerage services, human-goods and storage management system services, and smart-contract routing solutions for 24-hour trading platforms.

The issuance of tokens is unevenly distributed among countries and regions, mainly in the United States, Switzerland, and EU countries. The United States is the country with the largest number of token issuances globally, accounting for 40%. The legal framework in the United States provides a basis for token issuance, and tokens can be issued in accordance with Regulation D and Regulation S. The top 5 security-type tokens in terms of actual financing are all located in the United States. The two security-type token exchanges with the largest trading volumes, Open Finance and tZERO, are both established in the United States. The second-ranked country in terms of issuance quantity is Switzerland. Switzerland's neutral status and high degree of internationalization provide a favorable development environment for tokens. The third-ranked country is Estonia in Northern Europe.

Estonia has a good entrepreneurial atmosphere and environment for Internet products, giving birth to globally-known Internet application products such as Skype and Hotmail. Except for the United States and Switzerland, the remaining token projects are mainly distributed in EU countries.

2.3.8 The Issuance Process of Token STO (Narrow Sense)

Tokens are written on the blockchain through smart contracts. Securities tokens are not only a digital representation of ownership but also can automatically complete many post-issuance business operations. From the perspective of the issuance process of securities tokens, tokens are usually issued in three steps: preparation for issuance, issuance, and full- cycle management.

Step 1: Preparation for Issuance. This step mainly involves establishing an SPV and preparing an issuance memorandum. The main contents of the token issuance memorandum include the overall situation, issuance details, special considerations, the market, etc.

Step 2: Issuance. The issuance process includes the following three aspects: (1) KYC/AML verification: Tokens should verify investors. After the issuing company completes the verification work, it creates investor accounts on the platform; (2) Token issuance: Use standard smart contracts and confirm that these contracts include all necessary global compliance requirements, such as restrictions on investor accounts, lock-up periods, and repurchase restrictions; (3) Financing: Raise funds from intended investors according to the previously announced standards and requirements, transfer tokens to investors' wallets, and also have the option to use third-party custody services.

Step 3: Full-Cycle Management. This part includes continuous communication with investors, secondary-market trading, etc. The details of communication are clearly stated in the issuance memorandum, including regular reports and exchanges on ad-hoc events. Restricted stocks have certain restrictions on secondary-market trading (such as lock-up periods and upper limits on the number of investors in different regions) to ensure compliance.

Tables 2.3 and 2.4 list the overall process of tokens for a certain real-estate project, including the main matters included in each step, the estimated time required, the responsible departments, and the roles played in the tokens.

2.3.9 The Issuance Process of Token RWA (Broad Sense)

The essence of RWA product design lies in avoiding direct linkage with physical assets or rights and interests. Although the supported assets can be physical objects or rights and interests, the object of Tokenization is not the rights and interests themselves but tokens with platform characteristics or the utility of similar rights and interests.

Table 2.3 Main contents of the token issuance memorandum for a certain real-estate project

Matters	Main contents
Overall situation	Company overview, risk, and financial reports
Issuance details	Exemption from registration rules, such as whether the company is allowed to advertise Determine the minimum investment scale to better attract value investors Determine the maximum investment scale The company has the right to reclaim tokens under certain conditions, such as when investors have not completed the KYC/AML verification process or have not signed the subscription terms Secondary-market trading is restricted by current securities regulations Investors can freely choose to invest in US dollars, euros, Bitcoin, Ethereum, etc Deadline Use of funds raised The company hires external legal and other experts to draft private-placement issuance documents
Special considerations	Such as taxes, continuous reporting, etc
Market	The company formulates a marketing plan

Table 2.4 Main process of token issuance for a certain real-estate project

Project process	Task items	Estimated time required	Role in STO
Preparation for issuance	Articles of association	1 week	Advice/knowledge sharing
	Issuance documents	1 month	Advice/knowledge sharing
	Special Preparation (Exclusive to Real-Estate Projects)	0-4 weeks	Support
	Market	3 months	—
Issuance	Know Your Customer (KYC)/Anti-Money Laundering (AML)/ Certification	Continuous	Main
	Token issuance	1 day	Main
	Fundraising	1 day	Main
Lifecycle management	Continuous communication	Continuous	Execution
	Secondary trading	Continuous	Main

The key to the retail-token native model is to combine non-security-type RWA tokens with alternative investment exchanges and rely on the support of Crypto Funds (such as early-stage crypto capital and later-stage creator agreements). Taking the licensed exchange HashKey as an example, although its compliant RWA products have not been widely promoted, the RWA market of its retail-token model can adopt a combined strategy of offshore international-station listing, Tokenization departments, crypto capital, and fund creators.

Through the DAO, community, or node model, encourage retail investors and institutions in the physical-asset industry chain to participate. Participation in this model is not limited to after token listing but starts from the initial stages of community building, product discussion, and node consensus-building, ensuring that all participants become part of the consensus, realizing the digitization and on-chain transformation of assets, and at the same time forming a hedge with the physical world.

Combine traditional financial stocks with virtual assets. Listed companies invest in virtual assets (such as Bitcoin spot ETF) or lay out Web 3.0. When the value of virtual assets rises, it drives the growth of the value of their stocks in the physical world. If the main business of a listed company is closely related to the layout of Web 3.0 and Crypto investment, the increase in its value will be more significant.

Adopt a combined strategy of NFT + functional tokens (FT) + meme coins. NFT serves as a carrier for retail-investor identities and digital-rights vouchers and also as an underlying asset for airdropping liquidity tokens. FT is used to provide liquidity or governance functions and becomes a functional token for RWA application scenarios. Meme coins, combined with the RWA narrative, brand, or IP franchise in the physical world, serve as the brand leader for NFT and FT. The three interact with each other to build a complete token ecosystem.

Cash in the physical world enters the liquidity pool through structured design instead of adopting a revenue-distribution model. Use smart contracts to achieve continuous injection of cash flow, forming a special creator fund or liquidity-exchange pool to achieve predictable and continuous liquidity management. This is an advanced version of the stock-coin linkage model. Listed companies issue compliant RWA tokens based on their main business or basic asset packages. RWA tokens can be purchased through convertible bonds, and at the same time, RWA tokens can airdrop physical financial assets. This model combines the stocks of listed companies, virtual-asset investment, and RWA token issuance, realizes the underwriting of RWA products through convertible bonds, and uses the operating cash flow of the company to establish a liquidity pool for RWA tokens, providing airdrops or allocations of the company's stocks or options to RWA-token holders to achieve mutual value-driving and user growth.

2.4 Implementation Methods of RWA and Tokenization on the Blockchain

The emergence and development of blockchain technology have provided a solid foundation for the Tokenization of RWA. In the first section of this chapter, blockchain is introduced in detail. As a distributed ledger technology, it ensures the immutability and traceability of data through cryptography. This technical feature endows the digital representation of assets on the blockchain with extremely high security and credibility.

The implementation of RWA Tokenization first begins with the digitization of real-world assets. This is a complex and precise process, and it is also an important stage before asset Tokenization is carried out on the chain. It involves the identification and verification of RWA, the establishment of a legal framework and ownership, as well as the creation of security tokens representing RWA. This process requires the participation of various parties (such as asset owners, token issuers, regulatory agencies, lawyers, and auditors), and includes three key steps: asset evaluation, asset registration, and asset certification:

- In the asset evaluation stage, professional evaluation institutions will conduct a comprehensive analysis and value assessment of the assets to ensure the fairness and accuracy of the evaluation results.
- The asset registration stage involves legal and administrative procedures to confirm and record the ownership of assets. This step is crucial for ensuring the legal status of assets.
- In the asset certification stage, regulatory agencies will verify the authenticity and legality of assets through various means to prevent fraud and illegal transactions.

Only after these three major steps can an asset be accurately converted into a digital form, laying the foundation for subsequent Tokenization.

Transferring and synchronizing RWA data and documents from the off-chain world to the on-chain world requires the use of decentralized oracles. Decentralized oracles provide safe and reliable real-world data (such as the price, quality, and status of RWA) services for the blockchain (see Fig. 2.3). Decentralized oracles are of great significance for the Tokenization of RWA because they enable the information connection between the off-chain world and the on-chain world.

Decentralized oracles can ensure the accuracy of real-world data used for RWA Tokenization, such as the source, valuation, and ownership of RWA. Decentralized oracles use various mechanisms and incentive measures to verify and confirm data sources and providers, such as reputation, staking, and voting. Oracle networks can process a large amount of data and requests and provide faster and cheaper data transmission, which improves the scalability and efficiency of RWA Tokenization. Oracle networks can use multiple data sources and providers and cross-check and compare data, which can increase the diversity and redundancy of real-world data.

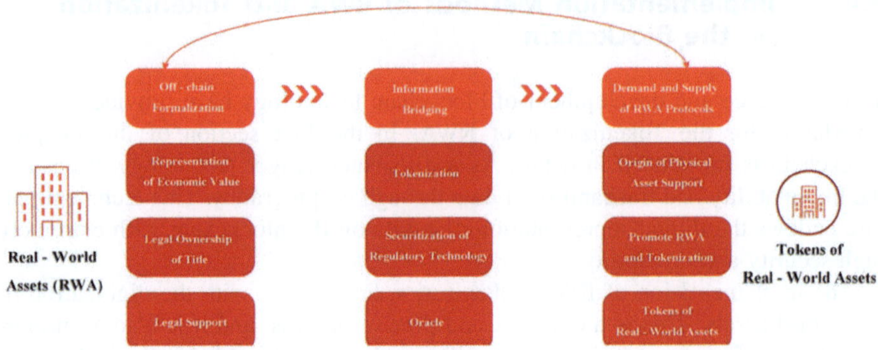

Fig. 2.3 The process of RWA tokens becoming legal assets

After the digitization of assets is completed, the key to the Tokenization process lies in the design and implementation of smart contracts. A smart contract is an automatically executing program stored on the blockchain that can automatically execute contract terms when pre-set conditions are met. Asset issuers can precisely set the issuance details of tokens, trading rules, and the distribution method of returns generated by assets by writing and deploying smart contracts. In the process of RWA Tokenization, smart contracts are mainly used to define the attributes of tokens, issuance rules, trading mechanisms, and return distribution methods, etc. A well-designed smart contract can ensure the transparency, fairness, and efficiency of the token issuance and trading process, and at the same time, it can also protect the rights and interests of investors to the greatest extent.

Writing smart contracts requires knowledge of blockchain development and finance. To ensure quality and security, smart contracts usually need to go through strict testing and auditing to identify and fix potential loopholes and errors. At the same time, to improve the scalability and interoperability of smart contracts, it is also necessary to follow some common industry standards and protocols, such as ERC - 20 and ERC - 721. Only smart contracts that have been carefully designed and strictly tested can provide reliable technical support for RWA Tokenization.

The introduction of smart contracts makes the RWA Tokenization process more automated and efficient. Traditional asset transactions usually require a large number of manual operations and paper documents, while smart contracts can automatically execute these operations, reducing the need for human intervention and improving transaction efficiency. At the same time, the execution results of smart contracts will also be automatically recorded on the blockchain, forming permanent and immutable transaction records. This transparent and immutable feature can enhance the trust of all parties in the transaction and reduce the risks of fraud and disputes.

Although smart contracts provide strong technical support for RWA Tokenization, there are still some issues that need to be noted in practical applications. The first is the security issue of smart contracts. Since smart contracts cannot be modified once deployed, any loopholes or errors in the contract code may be exploited by attackers, leading to significant losses. Therefore, sufficient security audits and testing are required before deploying smart contracts. The second is the legal validity issue of smart contracts. Currently, countries have not clearly defined the legal status of smart contracts. When contract disputes occur, the legal validity of the execution results of smart contracts is still uncertain. This requires further clarification and improvement by legal and regulatory agencies.

With the support of smart contracts, digitized assets will be converted into a series of blockchain tokens (see Fig. 2.4). Blockchain tokens are the core elements of RWA Tokenization, which map real-world assets into the digital world of the blockchain. Through Tokenization, originally indivisible assets can be divided into smaller units, which greatly reduces the investment threshold and enables more investors to participate in asset investment. Different types of assets require different Tokenization standards. Homogeneous assets such as bonds are usually suitable for the ERC - 20 standard. ERC - 20 defines a set of standard token interfaces and specifications, including functions such as token transfer, balance query, and authorization. Tokens that comply with the ERC - 20 standard are compatible with most blockchain wallets and exchanges and have good interoperability. Non-homogeneous assets such as artworks are more suitable for the ERC - 721 standard. ERC - 721 defines the standard interface for NFTs. Each NFT is unique and has its own identification and metadata. This uniqueness makes NFTs particularly suitable for unique assets such as artworks and collectibles.

The last important link in Tokenization is the management, trading, and return distribution of assets. Using the automatic execution function of smart contracts, assets can be efficiently managed and returns can be distributed. For example, the rental income in real-estate investment can be automatically distributed to token

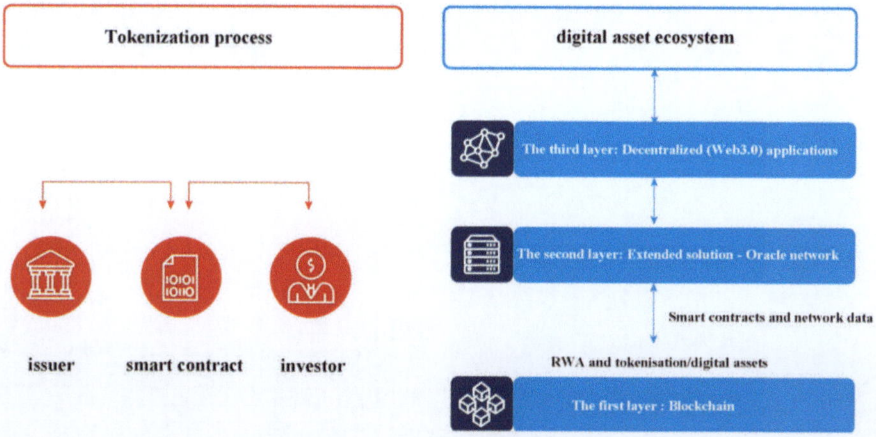

Fig. 2.4 Tokenization process of the digital asset ecosystem

holders through smart contracts without the involvement of any intermediary institutions; the sales proceeds of assets such as artworks can also be automatically distributed to token holders according to the shareholding ratio through smart contracts. This automated asset management and return distribution method not only improves operational efficiency and reduces management costs but also increases the transparency of investment, enabling ordinary investors to easily participate in high-end asset investments that are usually difficult to access.

After tokens are distributed to investors, they can be traded on decentralized exchanges or through secondary markets such as DeFi. This step is crucial because it introduces liquidity to assets that are traditionally less liquid, simplifies the transfer of ownership, and makes broader participation possible. Tokenization makes asset trading more convenient and efficient. Investors can buy and sell tokens at any time without going through cumbersome and time-consuming settlement processes.

In addition, the continuous management and governance of these assets are achieved through blockchain-based systems. Token holders can exercise their rights and influence decision-making through the voting mechanism integrated into smart contracts. This decentralized governance method improves the transparency of decision-making, allows all token holders to participate in asset management, and avoids the control and manipulation of a single centralized institution.

Types and Core Elements of RWA Tokens

3

RWA Tokenization is a complex system involving knowledge from multiple disciplines, including law, finance, technology, and data. To help readers gain a more comprehensive understanding of the underlying mechanisms and intrinsic value of real-world asset Tokenization, this chapter will delve into the "RWA 2 + 4 framework" originally proposed by Zhu Haokang. This framework refers to the two types of tokens and four core elements in RWA Tokenization.

Firstly, RWA Tokenization gives rise to two different types of tokens: security tokens and utility tokens. Security tokens typically represent the ownership or revenue rights of underlying assets. Investors who purchase such tokens expect to receive returns through asset appreciation or revenue distribution. In contrast, utility tokens represent the right to use specific services or resources, and their value mainly depends on the supply–demand relationship of the related services or resources. Understanding the differences and characteristics of these two types of tokens is of great significance to investors and market participants.

Secondly, the implementation of RWA Tokenization relies on the support of four core elements: legal supervision, financial architecture, technical support, and data application. As the foundation of RWA Tokenization, legal supervision determines which assets can be tokenized and the rules and regulations that Tokenization needs to follow. This provides the necessary legal framework and guarantee for RWA Tokenization. The financial architecture offers a complete system for RWA Tokenization, including asset evaluation, auditing, verification, token issuance and trading, as well as relevant risk-management mechanisms, etc., to ensure the transparency, reliability, and stability of RWA Tokenization. Technical support is an important tool and means for realizing RWA Tokenization, including cutting-edge technologies such as blockchain, smart contracts, big data, artificial intelligence, privacy-preserving computing, and oracles. The application of these technologies

S. Ba et al., *RWA Tokenisation in Web 3.0 Era*, Management for Professionals,
https://doi.org/10.1007/978-981-96-7663-7_3

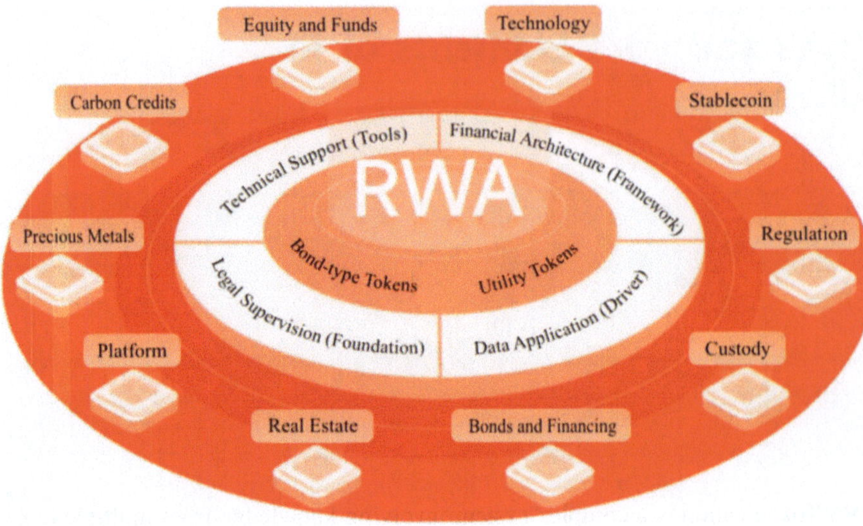

Fig. 3.1 RWA 2 + 4 framework

can greatly improve the efficiency, security, and scalability of RWA Tokenization, providing a solid technical foundation for the digital transformation of assets.

Finally, data application is an important driving force for RWA Tokenization, including asset transaction data, market behavior data, as well as macro-economic and social data, etc. By analyzing and applying this data, market participants can better understand the value and risks of tokens and the assets behind them, and make more informed investment decisions.

As shown in Fig. 3.1, the "RWA2 + 4 framework" provides a comprehensive and systematic perspective for understanding RWA Tokenization. Through in-depth analysis and discussion of the two types of tokens and the four core elements, readers can better grasp the important components and operational mechanisms of RWA Tokenization, and be well-prepared to participate in this emerging field.

3.1 Type 1 of RWA Tokens: Security Tokens

In July 2017, the SEC pointed out that digital assets generated based on the ICO model may constitute financial securities and are required to comply with securities regulations. Subsequently, the SEC launched an investigation and imposed fines on illegal ICO projects, forcing some ICO projects to pay fines and return funds to investors. On October 18, 2018, the SEC announced the establishment of the Strategic Hub for Innovation and Financial Technology (FinHub), which serves as a communication window with financial technology companies and legislative bodies. Its purpose is to prevent new ICO activities from violating the law again and to strengthen the protection of investors' rights and interests.

Many people consider STO as an upgraded version of ICO after it became compliant. The latter was once the mainstream fundraising and issuance method in the cryptocurrency-asset field but was suspended by regulatory authorities in various countries due to excessive risks. In contrast, STO provides a more compliant and risk-controllable solution. The following are the fundamental differences between STO and ICO:

- **Different Token Attributes**

ICO usually involves early-stage blockchain projects issuing native tokens to raise funds, while STO focuses on issuing security tokens. In addition to on-chain tokens, it can also include tokens supported by RWAs (such as company equity or physical assets).

3.1.1 Investor Rights Differ

When purchasing tokens through Initial Coin Offerings (ICO), investors do not receive ownership or management rights over the project. Instead, they only gain value returns from the token itself. However, Security Token Offerings (STO) issue security tokens, which grant investors ownership rights over assets, making their rights similar to those of traditional securities.

3.1.2 Differences in Regulatory Environment and Risks

ICOs lack underlying asset value support. While they improve fundraising efficiency, they also increase investment risks, leading to bans by multiple regulatory agencies. In contrast, STOs comply with existing securities regulations, meaning the tokens inherently have certain asset values, making risk exposure more manageable.

In April 2019, FinHub released a framework guideline further clarifying the distinction between security tokens and utility tokens. The document explicitly states:

- Security tokens are primarily used for investment purposes, typically promising future profits, and are regulated as securities.
- Utility tokens are used in specific use cases, such as allowing holders to access blockchain-based services. These tokens are not considered securities.

Security tokens generally possess the following features:

1. Ownership Rights: Security tokens represent ownership of underlying assets or companies.

2. Dividend Rights: Some security tokens provide dividends or profit-sharing rights, similar to stocks.
3. Voting Rights: Certain security tokens grant voting rights to holders.
4. Regulated Transactions: Security tokens are subject to securities law regulations, which must be strictly followed.

Each country or regulatory region has its own specific criteria for determining whether a token is classified as a security token (Fig. 3.1, Table 3.1).

Across the globe, there have already been several successful cases of security token issuance, providing valuable experience and insights for the future development of security tokens. One notable example is Aspen Digital, which issued $18 million worth of Aspen Coin real estate security tokens in August 2018. The underlying asset for Aspen Coin is a portion of ownership in a luxury ski resort in Aspen, Colorado, USA. This ski resort is one of the most prestigious ski destinations in the world, featuring 179 luxury residences, serving as a high-end vacation retreat for ultra-high-net-worth individuals. Aspen Coin security tokens comply with the *U.S. Securities Act of 1933, specifically Regulation D Rule 506(c)*, meaning that only accredited investors meeting specific qualification criteria are allowed to participate. Investors in Aspen Coin security tokens own a share of the Swiss-style ski resort, allowing them to earn rental income and benefit from the appreciation in real estate value. This provides investors with a new form of asset allocation and investment strategy.

Table 3.1 Regulations for determining whether a token is a security token in different countries or regions

Country/Region	Regulation
United States	According to the *Securities Act of 1933*, the SEC determines whether a token is classified as a security. The Howey Test (see Fig. 3.2) is used to assess this, or a four-factor analysis is applied: (1) Whether investors expect profits; (2) Whether the token represents common enterprise interests; (3) Whether profits come from others' efforts; (4) Whether the investment requires the actions of others to generate returns. A token is considered a security only if all four conditions are met
European Union	In October 2020, the EU issued the *Digital Finance Package*, which includes two key legislative proposals: *Proposal for Markets in Crypto-assets* and *Proposal for Digital Operational Resilience*. These regulations define classification, risk management, and investor protection measures for security tokens. In April 2023, the EU Parliament officially adopted *MiCA*, which provides clear rules on token classification, information disclosure, marketing, and regulatory requirements
Hong Kong, China	In 2018, the Hong Kong Securities and Futures Commission (SFC) stated that some security tokens fall under traditional securities regulations. In 2019, the SFC ruled that token exchanges handling security tokens must be licensed. These sandbox-style regulatory measures evolved into formal licensing frameworks in October 2023, when the SFC allowed licensed firms to issue and trade security tokens (STO). The Stock Exchange of Hong Kong and regulated banks can now apply for STO-related licenses. On November 2, 2023, the SFC released updated *guidance on digital asset regulation*, tightening rules on token issuance and exchange operations
Singapore	In 2017, MAS issued the *Guide to Digital Token Offerings*, stating that security tokens are classified as financial products and subject to securities law supervision. The guide provides six case studies illustrating the differences between utility tokens and security tokens
Australia	In 2019, the Australian Securities and Investments Commission (ASIC) released a report emphasizing that the classification of tokens depends on their nature. If a token functions like shares or investment products, it is classified as a security token and subject to securities law oversight

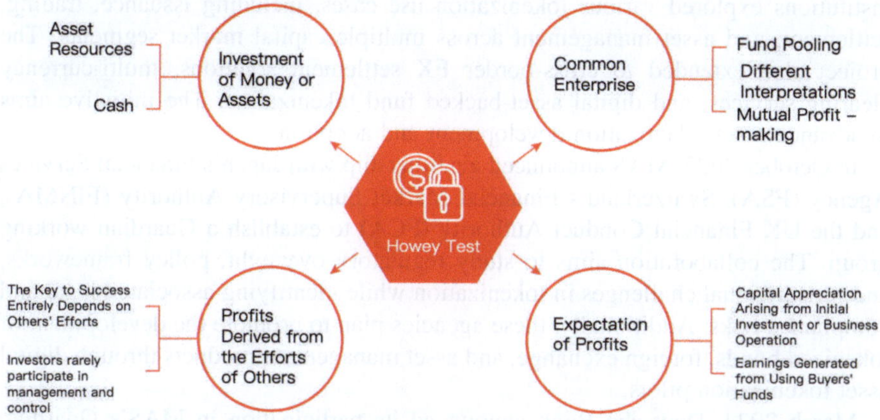

Fig. 3.2 The four key elements of the Howey test

With the continuous development of the digital asset market, more financial institutions are beginning to explore the issuance of security tokens. In July 2022, OSL, a subsidiary of Hong Kong-listed company BC Technology Group, became the first digital asset brokerage in Hong Kong to issue security tokens through a private placement. This marked a pioneering move in Hong Kong's security token issuance. Each token issued by OSL represents a U.S. dollar bond with a face value of $10,000, pegged to Bitcoin's price. The tokens were issued on the Ethereum blockchain, ensuring security and transparency. BC Technology Group acted as the guarantor and issued the bonds through private placement to qualified institutional investors, ensuring compliance with regulatory standards. The bond had a maturity of three months, offering investors a fixed interest rate coupon along with an additional return linked to Bitcoin's price movements. In addition to the fixed coupon, investors also received an extra yield bonus when Bitcoin's price surpassed a certain threshold. This innovative design allows investors to share in the appreciation of digital assets while also providing a degree of downside protection.

In May 2022, Monetary Authority of Singapore (MAS) launched an industry pilot program called the "Guardian" project. The initiative focuses on deep collaboration with financial institutions to explore the economic potential and value proposition of asset tokenization. Additionally, the project aims to test the feasibility of applying tokenization in DeFi (Decentralized Finance) while managing financial stability and regulatory risks. The first phase of the Guardian project was led by JPMorgan, DBS Bank, and Marketnode, focusing on establishing a tokenized bond and foreign exchange (FX) liquidity pool, with transactions secured on blockchain networks. Following this, the Guardian project expanded, bringing together 17 financial institutions across 5 asset tokenization industry pilots. Participants included Standard Chartered, Franklin Templeton, New York Mellon Bank, Citi Bank, and HSBC, among other international financial institutions. These institutions explored various tokenization use cases, including issuance, trading, settlement, and asset management across multiple capital market segments. The project also extended to cross-border FX settlement solutions, multi-currency clearing services, and digital asset-backed fund tokenization. The initiative aims to advance asset tokenization development and adoption.

In October 2023, MAS announced a partnership with Japan's Financial Services Agency (FSA), Switzerland's Financial Market Supervisory Authority (FINMA), and the UK Financial Conduct Authority (FCA) to establish a Guardian working group. The collaboration aims to study regulatory oversight, policy frameworks, and jurisdictional challenges in tokenization while identifying associated legal and compliance risks. Additionally, these agencies plan to promote the development of tokenized bonds, foreign exchange, and asset management products through digital asset tokenization pilots.

March 2024, Deutsche Bank announced its participation in MAS's Guardian Initiative as part of advancing bilateral tokenization technology cooperation. According to the statement, Deutsche Bank will assist in designing and testing an open-architecture, interoperable blockchain platform, aiming to provide services for security tokens and digital funds, as well as establish relevant industry standards to drive innovation. The initiative emphasized that participation in the Guardian Initiative contributes to shaping financial services innovation and better meeting evolving customer demands. Deutsche Bank will collaborate closely with the digital asset management platform Memento Blockchain. The two parties had previously cooperated on the development of digital funds.

Regarding regulatory collaboration, Deutsche Bank launched the DAMA project. Anand Rengarajan, Head of Securities Services for Asia–Pacific and Global Head of Sales for Securities Services at Deutsche Bank, stated: "*We will continue striving to promote the development and application of digital assets in Singapore and the Asia–Pacific region, aiming to be an industry leader.*"

In addition to promoting industry pilot projects, MAS has also launched several new infrastructure initiatives, including the "Global Layer One" (GL1) and the Interlinked Network Model (INM) to support the development of cross-border asset tokenization. GL1 is an open digital infrastructure jointly developed by MAS, JPMorgan, DBS Bank, MUFG, and Standard Chartered. It aims to facilitate cross-border exchange and ensure that tokenized assets can be seamlessly traded within a global liquidity pool. Meanwhile, the Interlinked Network Model (INM) provides a universal framework for independently operated networks to exchange digital assets, allowing financial institutions to transact without requiring all institutions to be on the same network. This significantly enhances the flexibility and scalability of asset tokenization.

With the rapid growth of the digital asset market, more innovative projects are emerging. On May 3, 2024, Fasanara Capital-backed tokenization platform RWA collaborated with Swiss fintech lender Karmen to launch the first private credit pool on the Celo network. This pool applies automated risk-based pricing to structure tokenized loan assets, setting an initial loan cap of $6 million and allowing accredited investors[1] to invest in USDC-denominated tokenized loans. This project offers institutional investors a new investment channel. On May 7, 2024, the Hong Kong Monetary Authority (HKMA) announced the establishment of an "Ensemble Project" framework working group to collaborate with international organizations in setting standards and policy frameworks to support the development of Hong Kong's tokenization market infrastructure. The working group will formulate policy standards to support the issuance of wholesale digital currencies (wCBDC) and improve interoperability between tokenized currencies and tokenized assets. The first working group meeting will focus on infrastructure development and initial discussions on creating a tokenized asset exchange mechanism. The group will also explore using wCBDC as a bridge for cross-border tokenized deposits and bank settlement systems. The working group plans to launch the Ensemble Project sandbox in mid-2024, advancing research on tokenized asset models.

3.2 RWA Token Type II: Utility Tokens

Utility tokens are essential tools in the blockchain and digital economy sector. They can serve as access permissions for products or services, act as a carrier for on-chain data, or enable specific functionalities within a network platform. The value of a utility token is primarily determined by its functional use case within its ecosystem, closely tied to the level of network participation and transaction demand. For example, Ethereum's native token (ETH) is a typical utility token. Users must pay ETH as gas fees to execute transactions and smart contracts on the Ethereum network, ensuring computational and operational efficiency. The value of such tokens is largely determined by network activity and utility demand—as transaction volume increases, demand for ETH rises, and its value appreciates accordingly.

A crucial distinction between utility tokens and security tokens is that utility tokens do not represent ownership or equity in a project. Holders do not receive dividends or profit-sharing returns. Instead, utility tokens are designed for accessing specific applications, services, or functionalities within an ecosystem. Their value stems from their functional utility rather than being a tradable investment asset. In contrast, security tokens are directly tied to asset ownership and typically provide financial returns to holders. This fundamental difference means utility tokens are not designed as investment instruments but rather as functional enablers within their respective ecosystems.

Utility tokens can be further classified into four categories: reward tokens, which are used to incentivize users for participating in specific activities, such as tokens distributed by exchanges as trading rewards or DeFi protocols providing

[1] According to SEC definitions, an accredited investor must meet at least one of the following conditions: (1) An individual must have earned over $200,000 in each of the past two years (or $300,000 jointly with a spouse) and reasonably expect the same for the current year; or (2) An individual must have a net worth exceeding $1 million, excluding their primary residence.

yield incentives; usage tokens, which serve as access rights for specific products or services, such as tokens for cloud storage payments or NFTs used to purchase in-game items in blockchain-based games; governance tokens, which allow holders to participate in governance decisions on a platform or protocol, such as voting on proposals or influencing protocol upgrades; and data tokens, which represent access rights to specific datasets, such as tokens that grant permission to view personal health records or IoT device-generated data.

It is worth noting that these different types of utility tokens are not mutually exclusive. A single token, in its design and implementation, may possess multiple attributes, integrating different functionalities and use cases. For example, a reward token might also serve as a payment tool for products, allowing users to use their reward tokens to purchase goods or services on a platform. Similarly, a governance token may be combined with a reward token, enabling users to earn governance tokens by participating in platform activities, thus granting them the right to engage in decision-making processes. Furthermore, a data token may be linked to a product or service token, allowing users to obtain access rights to specific services while simultaneously providing their own data.

This combination of interactivity and multi-functionality makes utility tokens increasingly important in the blockchain and digital economy sectors. They are not just simple payment tools but serve as connectors between users, developers, data providers, and other participants, encouraging collaboration, promoting sharing, and facilitating autonomy. As blockchain technology continues to develop and mature, utility tokens will also keep evolving, giving rise to more innovations and possibilities. They have opened new doors for exploring economic models and organizational structures, potentially shaping a more open, transparent, and shared digital economy era in the future.

3.2.1 Reward Tokens

The main purpose of reward tokens is to incentivize users for their participation and contributions to a platform or service. By distributing reward tokens, projects can effectively encourage users to maintain close engagement with the platform over a certain period and motivate them to contribute more actively. For example, when users engage in transactions on a platform, participate in community governance, contribute resources and time, or complete specific tasks, they can earn a certain amount of reward tokens. These tokens can often be used on the corresponding platform to purchase goods and services, enjoy specific privileges, or exchange for other assets in the market, thus holding tangible economic value. For businesses or project developers, reward tokens provide a new and effective means of attracting and retaining users, stimulating their ownership and creativity, thereby fostering the healthy growth and sustainable prosperity of the platform.

Ethereum Name Service (ENS) airdrop strategy is a typical case of reward tokens successfully applied in the blockchain field. ENS is a decentralized domain name system designed to convert long and difficult-to-remember Ethereum addresses into simple and user-friendly domain names. To promote ENS adoption, attract more users, and reward early supporters, the ENS project officially announced a large-scale airdrop plan on November 9, 2021. A total of 100 million ENS tokens were issued, with 25% (i.e., 25 million tokens) distributed for free to eligible users. Any user who had registered an ENS.eth subdomain before November 1, 2021, was able to claim the corresponding ENS token rewards. Notably, the ENS project team also designed a series of refined airdrop strategies, where the number of tokens a user received was proportional to the duration they had held an ENS domain name and how close the domain was to its expiration date. This strategy not only encouraged users to establish a long-term and stable relationship with the platform but also motivated them to continue contributing to the growth of ENS. In practice, the ENS airdrop campaign achieved remarkable success, significantly increasing the platform's user base and domain registrations. Moreover, ENS tokens quickly gained value and liquidity across multiple exchanges, providing substantial economic returns to early supporters.

This case fully demonstrates the potential of reward tokens in attracting users, promoting ecosystem development, and realizing the value of the network. It provides valuable reference and inspiration for other blockchain projects on how to design and implement reward tokens. The ENS airdrop successfully attracted users, incentivized contributions, and promoted long-term engagement. By integrating reward token distribution rules with project growth strategies, the project team effectively linked user benefits with platform development, forming a positive cycle of profit-sharing and win–win outcomes. Reward tokens offer users a new form of incentive and a way to realize value appreciation, allowing them to participate in the construction of the platform while sharing the benefits of its growth.

Another noteworthy case of reward tokens is the Optimism (OP) airdrop event. Optimism is a Layer 2 scaling solution built on Ethereum, using optimistic rollup technology to improve transaction throughput and scalability. To reward early users and encourage more participation in the Optimism ecosystem, the project team launched a large-scale OP token airdrop on May 31, 2022. According to the airdrop rules, early users who engaged with the Optimism network—such as transacting on Optimism, deploying smart contracts, or participating in on-chain governance—were eligible to receive OP tokens. Additionally, Optimism also rewarded users who contributed to broader Ethereum activities, including DAO governance, multisig wallet usage, and Gitcoin donations. This multi-dimensional reward mechanism not only recognized direct contributions to Optimism but also considered users' broader involvement in the Ethereum ecosystem, ensuring a fair and comprehensive distribution across different user groups. Similar to ENS, the OP airdrop achieved great success. A large number of users participated in the development of the Optimism network and its ecosystem, leading to a significant increase in user engagement and network adoption. Following the OP token launch, the market responded enthusiastically, with the token price experiencing a sharp rise in the short term, providing substantial returns to early participants. More importantly, through the OP token, Optimism established an ecosystem that aligns the interests of users, developers, project teams, and supporters. By holding and using OP tokens, participants can share in the growth of the Optimism network, forming a self-sustaining incentive and collaboration mechanism.

ENS and Optimism cases fully illustrate the immense potential and broad application prospects of reward tokens in the blockchain sector. Through well-designed issuance and distribution strategies, project teams can effectively incentivize user participation, promote ecosystem development, and achieve shared network value. For users, reward tokens also provide a new form of incentive and wealth creation opportunity, enabling them to gain returns while participating in the platform's development.

3.2.2 Product or Service Tokens

The primary function of product or service tokens is to serve as usage rights or priority access to specific services or products. Holding such tokens allows users to access corresponding platform networks and obtain certain services or products. Typically, users need to use these tokens for payments within the platform network to purchase required services or products. This token model provides a new economic driver for platform or network operations while offering users a more convenient way to access these services or products.

Basic Attention Token (BAT) is a classic example of a successfully applied product or service token. BAT is a utility token designed for the digital advertising and content sector, aiming to address a series of challenges in the current online advertising industry, such as user privacy invasion, ad fraud, and revenue distribution issues. BAT tokens are primarily used within the Brave browser, a web browser equipped with built-in privacy protection and ad-blocking functionalities. When users browse the internet using the Brave browser, they can choose to view privacy-protected ads and, in return, receive a certain amount of BAT tokens as rewards. At the same time, users can also use BAT tokens to support their favorite content creators, such as websites and blogs. Content creators, in turn, can receive direct economic returns through BAT tips, eliminating the need for traditional advertising models. For advertisers, they can purchase ad placements on the Brave platform using BAT and leverage Brave's privacy protection and precise ad-targeting capabilities to reach genuinely interested audiences. The design of BAT tokens within the Brave browser ecosystem creates a multi-stakeholder model, where users gain access to premium content services, protect their privacy, and earn rewards for engaging with ads. Content creators receive fair and direct economic compensation, incentivizing the creation of more high-quality content. Advertisers benefit from more precise and effective ad placements, improving ad engagement rates and return on investment. BAT tokens eliminate unnecessary intermediaries, ensuring that user attention, content value, and advertising revenue are transformed into tangible economic incentives, thereby driving the healthy development of the entire ecosystem. The BAT case study fully illustrates the enormous potential of product or service tokens in reshaping business models, encouraging broader participation, and enhancing value flow efficiency. It provides us with a perspective to rethink how blockchain technology and tokenized economies can solve inefficiencies in traditional industries and business models, creating a more fair, efficient, and sustainable value exchange and distribution system.

In summary, product or service tokens have broad application prospects in the blockchain sector. Through reasonable design and implementation, these tokens can build a new economic incentive and value circulation system for specific products or services, effectively linking users, providers, developers, and various stakeholders to form a mutually beneficial and shared ecosystem network. The case of BAT fully demonstrates how product or service tokens can drive collaboration, stimulate innovation, and reshape business models. With the continuous development and maturity of blockchain technology, we have reason to believe that product or service tokens will be increasingly applied across more scenarios and industries, helping to establish a more efficient, transparent, and trustworthy digital economy.

3.2.3 Governance Token

The core function of governance tokens is to provide holders with voting rights and governance authority within a specific platform or network. By holding and using governance tokens, users can actively participate in the platform's decision-making processes, including development direction, rule formulation, and parameter adjustments for major matters. This participation mechanism creates a true sense of "platform ownership" for users, enabling them to exert tangible influence over the services they use and making governance an integral part of platform management. The introduction of governance tokens not only enhances users' engagement and sense of belonging but also provides project teams with a highly interactive and collaborative pathway to promote the platform's progressive development more effectively.

In numerous DeFi projects, governance tokens play a crucial role, serving as the cornerstone of platform decentralization. Take the decentralized lending platform Compound as an example. In February 2020, Compound introduced COMP governance tokens, marking a major upgrade to its governance mechanism. Prior to this, governance rights on the Compound platform were primarily concentrated in the hands of its core team, which posed certain limitations to its decentralization principles. With the introduction of COMP tokens, governance power was distributed among all token holders. COMP holders could vote on key platform decisions, such as liquidity allocation and fee adjustments, and also engage in discussions and proposals on community forums. To enhance user participation in governance, Compound introduced an innovative gas-free voting and delegation mechanism, allowing users to sign transactions on-chain and delegate their votes to third parties without incurring gas fees. This significantly lowered the barrier to governance participation, encouraging more users to actively exercise their governance rights.

Thus, the COMP token laid a solid foundation for Compound's decentralization, enabling users to become true platform owners and decision-makers.

Another successful application of governance tokens is found in the decentralized exchange Uniswap. As a globally leading DeFi platform, Uniswap launched the UNI governance token in September 2020, officially transferring control of the platform to its community. The UNI token serves as both a governance tool within the Uniswap ecosystem and a means of value acquisition and distribution. Uniswap allocated 60% of UNI tokens to platform users, liquidity providers, and community members as a reward for their contributions to the platform's development. UNI holders could participate in governance by voting on various proposals through Uniswap's governance platform, deciding on matters such as platform fee structures and liquidity mining programs. Additionally, UNI holders could stake their tokens to receive a share of platform revenue, providing them with long-term economic incentives. Uniswap effectively linked user interests with platform profits, creating an inclusive, mutually beneficial ecosystem. The UNI token not only empowered users with governance rights but also transformed them into stakeholders in the platform's revenue, significantly boosting user engagement and loyalty.

MakerDAO is another project that fully utilizes the function of governance tokens to an extreme. As one of the earliest DeFi projects, MakerDAO is built around its innovative collateralized debt vault mechanism and its stablecoin, DAI. Supporting it all is MakerDAO's unique governance token, MKR. The MKR token represents governance rights over the MakerDAO system, meaning that MKR holders have governance and decision-making power over the system. MKR holders are required to participate in voting on a series of system parameters, such as collateral types, collateralization rates, stability fees, and DAI deposit interest rates. The adjustments of these parameters directly impact the stability of DAI and the security of the system, affecting the overall operation of the platform. As a result, MKR holders must carefully exercise their voting rights and take responsibility for the decisions they make. For example, if the system faces uncollateralized debt, MKR holders will need to sell MKR through auctions to cover system deficits. In essence, the MKR token is not only at the core of MakerDAO's governance but also a key component in maintaining the overall stability and operation of the system. It delegates the platform's management and risk responsibilities to MKR holders, forming a decentralized and autonomous operational mechanism. MakerDAO's success fully demonstrates the important role of governance tokens in constructing complex DeFi projects and provides valuable experience for future projects.

In recent years, governance tokens have become an essential tool for blockchain projects to achieve decentralized governance. They connect project teams, users, and communities, forming an ecosystem of aligned interests and shared responsibilities. Through governance tokens, users can directly participate in platform decision-making, contributing to platform development and governance. Project teams, on the other hand, can use staking and vote delegation mechanisms to gain partial control while ensuring more transparent and credible governance. The success of projects like Compound, Uniswap, and MakerDAO fully demonstrates the vast potential of governance tokens. As more projects begin to adopt and implement governance tokens, it is reasonable to believe that decentralized governance will become a crucial development direction for future blockchain projects. Governance tokens will play an increasingly important role in advancing the blockchain industry toward maturity and completeness.

3.2.4 Data Tokens

In the digital economy era, the volume of data generated by human economic and social activities has reached unprecedented levels. Faced with this massive amount of data, we must find a secure and efficient way to store, manage, and utilize these valuable data resources, turning them into a true "data asset" that drives social progress and economic growth. However, to achieve this goal, we must address two key issues: first, how to ensure data security and privacy protection; and second, how to promote data sharing and circulation. Traditional data management models often struggle to balance these two seemingly contradictory demands, whereas data tokenization provides us with a new solution. Data tokenization refers to converting data sets into tokenized assets, which can then be circulated and traded on blockchain platforms. This approach ensures data security and privacy while maximizing data value, enabling optimal allocation and efficient utilization of data resources.

GoodData Foundation (hereinafter referred to as GoodData) is a typical example of data tokenization applications. As a blockchain platform dedicated to strengthening data protection and realizing data value, GoodData's core objective is to achieve a balance between security and efficiency throughout the entire lifecycle of data storage, usage, and sharing. This ensures that data is "available but not visible," thereby fully unlocking data value. On the GoodData platform, data transaction parties must not transfer data to a centralized platform where it could be lost or leaked. Instead, data transactions and exchanges are realized through data tokenization. This decentralized data trading mechanism not only maximizes the protection of data ownership rights but also provides data consumers with a secure and reliable data access channel.

More importantly, GoodData has designed a comprehensive incentive mechanism to encourage participation in data transactions, creating a dynamic data economy ecosystem. In this ecosystem, data tokenization plays a crucial role by significantly increasing data liquidity while ensuring that all participants benefit from the platform. Specifically, data owners can issue their data assets on GoodData's proprietary blockchain platform and receive corresponding data tokens (Good) as compensation. Resource providers can obtain Good tokens by contributing data sets, models, or computing power, while data consumers can purchase Good tokens to access and utilize specific data sets. Moreover, even ordinary users can earn passive income by holding Good tokens and participating in platform liquidity activities. This multi-party participation drives the data economy model, not only stimulating the enthusiasm of all participants but also achieving efficient allocation and value realization of data resources, creating an ideal platform.

Another noteworthy data tokenization project is Ocean Protocol. Similar to GoodData, Ocean Protocol is committed to building a decentralized data trading and sharing ecosystem to address the current challenges faced by the data economy, such as privacy protection and data silos. On the Ocean Protocol platform, data providers can issue data assets and tokenize them, enabling the secure sharing and exchange of data. Data tokens not only represent ownership of data assets but can also be used for data transactions and access control. Through data tokenization, data providers can flexibly set data pricing, usage conditions, and access rights, ensuring their rights and interests are fully protected. Meanwhile, data consumers can acquire and utilize data tokens to access the required data resources for analysis, mining, and application.

A major innovation of Ocean Protocol lies in its integration of a Balancer-based AMM (Automated Market Maker) mechanism to enhance the liquidity and price discovery of data tokens. Each data asset corresponds to an independent liquidity pool, where data tokens can be freely exchanged with other tokens (such as Ocean platform tokens). This mechanism not only provides liquidity support for data tokens but also offers market-based pricing benchmarks for data valuation. Additionally, Ocean Protocol has designed an incentive-based data governance model, where data governance tokens (Ocean DAO Token) enable holders to participate in critical platform decisions, such as the formulation of data usage rules and evaluation of data quality. This decentralized governance mechanism helps establish a fair, transparent, and trustworthy data trading environment, attracting more participants to join the data economy ecosystem.

In conclusion, data tokenization has become a crucial trend and innovation in the digital economy era. By converting data assets into tokenized forms within incentive structures, data tokenization opens new opportunities for data verification, valuation, liquidity, and application.

3.3 Core Element of RWA—Legal and Regulatory Compliance

As an innovative financial tool, RWA tokenization must first ensure compliance within the legal framework before entering the market. For financial innovations in this field, compliance is not an optional feature but a necessary prerequisite. To maintain the stability of financial markets and protect consumers' legal rights, regulatory bodies worldwide are gradually establishing detailed and strict legal frameworks to standardize and guide the real-world asset (RWA) tokenization process. In many countries and regions, RWA tokenization may be classified as a form of securities issuance, which means it is subject to relevant securities laws. This requirement dictates that issuers must obtain appropriate regulatory approvals or relevant financial licenses before launching tokenized asset offerings. Therefore, conducting an in-depth study of strict regulatory compliance is not only a necessary condition for ensuring the legality of the tokenization process and outcomes but also a crucial foundation for the success of RWA tokenization (Table 3.2).

On November 2, 2023, the Securities and Futures Commission (SFC) issued the *Circular on Virtual Asset-Related Securities Activities Conducted by Intermediaries* (hereinafter referred to as the "*Circular*") to provide clear policy guidance for the implementation of RWA tokenization in Hong Kong. Firstly, regarding the definition of tokenized securities, the SFC provided a clear interpretation. According to regulatory definitions, tokenized securities fall under "*securities and structured products*" as defined in Schedule 1, Part 1, Section 1 of the Securities and Futures Ordinance (SFO). They are considered traditional financial instruments (such as bonds or funds) that undergo fractionalization through blockchain technology or other digital techniques. From a categorization perspective, the SFC classifies tokenized securities as a form of digital securities. However, in essence, tokenized securities are simply traditional securities wrapped in a tokenized format. Consequently, existing legal and regulatory requirements for traditional financial markets fully apply to tokenized securities. Thus, intermediaries involved in tokenized securities activities must adhere to relevant regulatory requirements, including: Distributing tokenized securities or managing tokenized securities investments, Managing tokenized securities funds, Managing investments in tokenized securities, Conducting secondary market trading of tokenized securities through regulated asset trading platforms.

On one hand, the SFC believes that if all applicable requirements are met and appropriate risk mitigation measures are in place, allowing primary market trading of tokenized products is reasonable. On the other hand, the SFC adopts a more cautious stance toward secondary market trading of tokenized products, considering it necessary to provide protections similar to those available for non-tokenized product investors. Overall, the SFC supports intermediaries in taking measures to tokenize traditional securities. The focus of the *Circular* is to provide guidance to intermediaries to help them manage and address the new risks arising from the use of this innovative tokenization technology, thereby promoting a stable, responsible, and sustainable development of the tokenization market.

Since tokenized securities are essentially traditional securities in tokenized form, the SFC adheres to the principle of "same business, same risk, same regulation" when it comes to risk control. However, the SFC recognizes that tokenized securities differ from traditional securities in certain aspects, posing some new risks. Firstly, the transfer and settlement processes of tokenized securities may differ from traditional securities, potentially introducing additional risks. Secondly, tokenized securities are susceptible to disruptions in blockchain networks and security concerns related to network attacks. Additionally, different forms of blockchain technology can be categorized into three types: private, permissioned, and public blockchains. The SFC believes that different types should be subject to varying levels of regulatory measures:

Table 3.2 Licenses/qualifications related to the issuance of tokenized assets in various countries/regions

Country/Region	Activity	License/Qualification
United States	Operating a trading platform for securities-type tokenized digital assets	Entities facilitating the buying and selling of securities-type tokenized assets require registration with the SEC as an Alternative Trading System (ATS) and must obtain a securities trading license
	Broker-dealer registration	Intermediaries facilitating transactions involving securities-type tokenized assets must register with the SEC and comply with U.S. financial regulations. Registration with the Financial Crimes Enforcement Network (FinCEN) is required, designating the intermediary as a money services business or another type of financial entity
	Custody services	Handling investor funds or digital asset custody may require FinCEN registration, as well as licensing by state regulators or financial institutions overseeing money transmission services
	Issuing securities tokens	Companies must obtain MAS (Monetary Authority of Singapore) approval before issuing tokens and must comply with the Securities and Futures Act (SFA) and the Financial Advisers Act (FAA) during the issuance and trading process. A public offering prospectus is generally required unless an exemption applies

(continued)

Table 3.2 (continued)

Country/Region	Activity	License/Qualification
Singapore	Issuing securities tokens and prospectus exemptions	To support innovative enterprises and facilitate capital raising, Singapore has established certain prospectus exemptions, including: 1. Small Offerings: If an offering raises less than SGD 500,000 within a 12-month period, the company may be exempt from full securities registration. 2. Private Placements: If an offering targets fewer than 50 investors within 12 months, it may not require full securities registration. 3. Offers to Institutional Investors: If a tokenized security is only marketed to institutional investors, full securities registration may not be required. 4. Offers to Accredited Investors: If a tokenized security is marketed exclusively to accredited investors, a full prospectus filing may not be necessary
	Providing a range of capital market services, including securities tokenization, asset management, and investment advisory	Requires a Capital Markets Services (CMS) license
	Operating a securities-type token trading platform	Requires a Recognized Market Operator (RMO) license
Hong Kong (China, Special Administrative Region)	Licensed Virtual Asset Service Provider (VASP)	Any individual or entity conducting virtual asset trading or investment services in Hong Kong must be regulated by the Hong Kong Securities and Futures Commission (SFC). This includes securities-type token trading services, which must obtain SFC approval and adhere to regulatory oversight. Licensed investment advisors and brokers may provide tokenized investment products, but must meet traditional financial standards or use highly liquid tokenized assets for investment purposes

- For private blockchains: Since participation nodes are typically more controllable, the associated risks are relatively lower, allowing for moderate regulatory adjustments.
- For permissioned blockchains: While public participation and transaction validation are possible, issuers and nodes still need to obtain specific credentials and adhere to necessary licensing, reporting, and information disclosure requirements.
- For public blockchains: Due to their fully open and decentralized nature, the regulatory challenges are the greatest. Risk management may require strict investment restrictions and enhanced investor protection measures.

According to the requirements of the *Circular*, the provision of tokenized investment products must meet several key requirements. For example, providers must fully disclose all material terms of the tokenized contract to ensure investor protection and operational transparency. Additionally, governance rights and records of all asset transactions—whether related to on-chain or off-chain businesses—should be properly maintained. Service providers for tokenized products must also comply with due diligence requirements, manage network security, data privacy, and system downtime risks, and implement business continuity plans. Unauthorized measures should not be adopted in public blockchain environments. Furthermore, providers should clarify the security and integrity of tokenized contracts to the SFC and conduct third-party audits to meet legal compliance requirements. In addition, tokenized product providers must appoint at least one financial expert with practical industry experience and an adequate risk management framework before launching tokenized securities offerings. For new tokenized assets under regulatory consideration, detailed discussions with the SFC are required. Moreover, issuers of tokenized products must seek approval before their launch, and associated entities may also need to obtain specific licenses.

The *Circular* explicitly states that intermediaries handling tokenized products recognized by the securities regulator must be regulated entities, such as licensed corporations or registered institutions. These intermediaries must adhere to existing rules and guidelines, including conducting KYC (Know Your Customer) procedures and suitability assessments. In terms of information disclosure, the *Circular* outlines a series of requirements. For example, the issuance documents for tokenized products must clearly disclose the detailed arrangements for tokenization, particularly specifying whether blockchain-based settlement or off-chain settlement will serve as the final settlement method. The documents must also disclose the ownership or rights represented by the tokenization, including legal ownership and beneficial ownership of the tokenized securities, as well as ownership and entitlements associated with the product. Additionally, risks associated with tokenization must be fully disclosed, including network security risks, system downtime risks, technical vulnerability risks, regulatory environment risks, and legal challenges posed by current regulations.

Apart from Hong Kong, Singapore is also a major global hub for digital assets and tokenization innovation. The Monetary Authority of Singapore (MAS) applies a regulatory approach to security tokens similar to traditional securities. According to Singapore's Securities and Futures Act (SFA), any "capital market product" must comply with SFA requirements, including registration, licensing, and disclosure obligations. If a digital token meets the definition of a "capital market product", such as representing equity, debt, or investment interests, then its issuance and trading fall under the SFA. However, MAS provides exemptions for certain token issuances, such as "small offerings" (exemptions for amounts not exceeding SGD 5 million), "private placements" (exemptions for offerings to fewer than 50 investors within 12 months, without public solicitation), and "institutional investors" (exemptions for sales exclusively to institutional investors).

On August 1, 2017, MAS issued its first statement on ICO regulation, indicating that ICOs without security attributes would not be regulated. In November 2017, MAS published the *Guide to Digital Token Offerings* (referred to as the "*Guide*"), which did not explicitly introduce the STO (Security Token Offering) concept, but provided detailed descriptions of the regulatory principles for digital token issuances. According to the *Guide*, if a digital token qualifies as a "capital market product" under the SFA, it falls under MAS regulation. Under the SFA, capital market products include any securities, units in collective investment schemes, derivative contracts, and non-currency spot contracts traded in margin form. This implies that digital tokens are not a single product category but may represent equity, debt, business trust units, or function as units in a collective investment scheme. Therefore, the specific regulatory framework for digital tokens depends on their nature, and different legal frameworks may apply, such as the *SFA or the Payment Services Act (PSA).*

Additionally, MAS recognizes the important role of intermediaries in the issuance of digital tokens. According to the *Guide* to Digital Token Offerings, intermediaries not only include entities that issue and trade digital tokens but also those that provide investment advice on digital tokens. Therefore, entities providing investment advice must comply with the *Financial Advisers Act (FAA).* Notably, even if a regulated entity is located overseas or entirely offshore, but actively solicits or provides advisory services to the public in Singapore, it may still be subject to Singaporean regulations. To clarify the legal applicability of specific cases, MAS has included a series of case studies in the *Guide*, offering clearer regulatory guidance for market participants. In summary, Singapore has adopted a cautious yet innovation-friendly approach to regulating digital token issuance. While mitigating risks, it also leaves room for the healthy development of the digital token market.

MAS stated in the *Guide* that any company providing financial services using innovative technologies can apply to participate in the MAS regulatory sandbox. The sandbox provides a safe environment for financial technology innovation, allowing companies to test innovative products and services within controlled conditions while mitigating risks to financial systems and consumers. For companies applying for the regulatory sandbox, MAS will conduct evaluations based on the *FinTech Regulatory Sandbox Guidelines,* which include criteria such as innovation, customer benefits, and risk management measures. Through the sandbox,

MAS can better balance financial innovation with risk regulation, ensuring that financial technology experiments are conducted within a structured framework. In the final section of the *Guide*, MAS emphasized that relevant entities should refer to the guidelines and use listed case studies to better understand the overall regulatory landscape for digital token issuance. Additionally, if market participants have any uncertainties, they should consult MAS for further clarification. This reflects MAS's commitment to regulatory openness and transparency, fostering active communication between industry stakeholders and regulators, and promoting the orderly development of the digital token market.

In the United States, the issuance of security tokens mainly follows two regulatory pathways:

1. Registration with the SEC under the *Securities Act of 1933.*
2. Exempted offerings, which allow the issuance of security tokens without full registration, subject to regulatory exemptions. Specific exemptions include:
   - Regulation A+: Allows small-scale IPOs, enabling companies to raise funds publicly within a certain limit while also allowing sales to non-accredited investors.
   - Regulation CF (Crowdfunding Exemption): Allows companies to raise funds through crowdfunding, but with limits on the total amount raised.
   - Regulation D (Private Placement Exemption): Allows companies to issue securities to accredited investors without SEC registration.
   - Regulation S (Offshore Securities Offering Exemption): If a security offering is conducted entirely outside the United States, it may not be subject to certain requirements under the *Securities Act of 1933.*

In addition to establishing new RWA tokenization regulatory policies, many countries have opted to apply existing financial and securities law frameworks to provide guidance and regulations for tokenization and related transactions, ensuring fast adaptation to the RWA sector's development. The advantage of this approach is that it provides market participants with a familiar and predictable regulatory environment while ensuring transparency, fairness, and security in RWA tokenization activities. This means that many traditional financial institutions and trading platforms can utilize their existing licenses and qualifications to explore innovations in the tokenization space without having to apply for entirely new approvals or adapt to newly established regulations. For example, Deutsche Börse has developed the D7 digital securities settlement platform, which operates under Germany and the EU's existing regulatory frameworks. This platform, based on Germany's existing trading and clearing licenses, provides real-time[2] settlement

[2] This means that security tokens can be issued and start trading on the same day, greatly improving the flexibility and efficiency of the market.

support for tokenized securities, automated straight-through processing (STP),[3] and decentralized and automated clearing and custody systems.

Apart from financial licenses and qualifications, the advancement of RWA tokenization also requires consideration of various compliance factors, including AML (Anti-Money Laundering), KYC (Know Your Customer), taxation, information disclosure, judicial regulation, intellectual property protection, and real estate laws (Table 3.3).

Overall, RWA tokenization is a new form of asset management and trading, offering huge potential for value creation. However, each jurisdiction must develop tokenization policies based on its unique legal and blockchain technology landscape to ensure regulatory compliance and industry stability. At the same time, market participants must fully understand and comply with these legal frameworks to facilitate the effective implementation of tokenized assets.

3.4 Core Element of RWA: Financial Framework

The successful implementation of RWA tokenization relies on a robust financial framework. This framework must ensure proper risk assessment for underlying RWA assets while maintaining sufficient transparency. Therefore, designing a sound financial service structure and risk management strategy is crucial for effectively carrying out tokenization activities. In practice, RWA tokenization involves various legal entities and complex transactional structures, requiring considerations of compliance, accounting, and tax regulations from multiple perspectives.

One commonly adopted approach is to establish a group of SPVs (Special Purpose Vehicles). This structure typically includes two key entities: Special Purpose Company (SPC) Special Purpose Trust (SPT) The SPC serves as the primary issuer of RWA tokens, facilitating debt issuance while aggregating investor funds to acquire underlying assets or provide asset-backed support. The SPT, acting as the trustee, holds the legal rights to the tokenized assets on behalf of the token holders and represents their interests, while the SPC handles management and administration. Through this intermediary structure, the SPC and SPT create a governance mechanism that helps protect token holders' rights. In this framework, SPCs typically establish multiple independent companies, with each company corresponding to a specific asset pool or investment strategy. This type of arrangement is often referred to as a segregated portfolio (SP) or protected cell structure. Each segregated portfolio operates as an independent accounting entity, maintaining separate liability. In certain jurisdictions with robust legal protections, this structural separation helps shield investors from cross-liability risks, meaning that the failure of one portfolio does not impact other portfolios or the parent company.

---

[3] Refers to the fact that the entire process from the initiation of a transaction to its settlement is automated and requires no human intervention. This not only improves the processing speed but also reduces the possibility of errors.

Table 3.3 Main consideration factors and cases of RWA tokenization legal regulation

Regulatory requirement	Explanation	Case example
AML and KYC	Tokenization must comply with AML (Anti-Money Laundering) and KYC (Know Your Customer) regulations	In October 2022, the U.S. Treasury Department took enforcement actions against Bittrex, a digital asset exchange, resulting in a total fine of $53 million due to violations of sanctions regulations and anti-money laundering laws
Taxation	RWA tokenization impacts the tax obligations of both investors and issuers	According to U.S. tax reporting rules, income from digital assets is subject to capital gains tax. This applies to DeFi lending returns, blockchain-based trading, and tokenized digital asset transactions. Reporting requirements determine whether capital gains tax should apply to token holders and how taxes should be levied when digital asset tokens are used for payments or exchanged for fiat currency
Information Disclosure	Token issuers must be truthful and transparent in disclosing project information	BUSD stablecoin faced regulatory scrutiny due to lack of transparency in asset backing, leading to a ban on new issuance by the New York Department of Financial Services (NYDFS)
Judicial and Cross-border Supervision	Tokenization can introduce cross-border legal challenges, especially when different jurisdictions enforce different compliance requirements. Regulatory clarity is needed to define which country's laws apply when a token is issued or traded	Facebook (now Meta) attempted to launch Libra (later rebranded as Diem Coin), but faced regulatory pushback from multiple governments due to concerns about its monetary policy implications. Governments ultimately blocked Libra from being launched globally

(continued)

Table 3.3 (continued)

Regulatory requirement	Explanation	Case example
Custody and Trustee Management	Custodian obligations for tokenized assets must be clearly defined	Zurich-based banks and other financial institutions are developing specialized digital asset custody services, providing secure management of tokenized assets
Intellectual Property Protection	If tokenization involves intellectual property (IP) assets, legal protections must be established	Planetary Tokenized Energy seeks to use blockchain to tokenize renewable energy, but faces intellectual property challenges in data ownership and licensing rights. Some legal experts argue that new laws are needed to protect tokenized data assets
Real Estate	When tokenizing real estate, full property title disclosures must be provided. In some jurisdictions, selling tokenized real estate may require specific legal approvals due to concerns about private property transactions	In 2019, St. George's Barracks in the UK underwent tokenized asset restructuring, allowing Knight Dragon, a real estate company, to raise funds through tokenized property investment

Another common approach is to set up a group of limited partnership funds. Under this model: The fund manager acts as the general partner (GP), responsible for fund operations and investment decisions. Investors serve as limited partners (LPs), contributing capital to the fund while enjoying limited liability protection. The fund manager can then issue tokens representing fund shares. By tokenizing fund shares, the fund can access broader investment markets and attract a wider range of investors through secondary market transactions.

Although these structural approaches offer advantages, various challenges remain in real-world implementation.

A key issue is how to ensure the alignment between tokenized assets and their underlying assets while maintaining synchronization. This requires advanced technological and regulatory mechanisms such as smart contracts to ensure accurate asset transfers, clearing, and reconciliation across different layers of the asset structure. Additionally, a robust information disclosure mechanism must be established to ensure token holders can fully, accurately, and comprehensively understand the status and risks of the underlying assets.

Another key issue is how to manage various risks in the tokenization process, such as legal risks, operational risks, and technical risks. This requires establishing a comprehensive risk management framework and governance strategy to identify, assess, monitor, and mitigate risks. For example, in terms of legal risks, tokenization projects must comply with applicable legal and regulatory requirements and conduct preventive legal risk assessments and compliance reviews. In terms of operational risks, strong internal control mechanisms and business processes must be established to ensure transactions are compliant, efficient, and effective. In terms of technical risks, mature and reliable technologies must be selected, and security audits, stability assessments, and scalability stress tests must be conducted.

Additionally, the design of tokenization solutions must balance investor protection and regulatory policy objectives. For example, investor protection mechanisms can be borrowed from fiduciary trust models, ensuring investors' suitability and dispute resolution mechanisms to safeguard investor rights. From a regulatory perspective, enhanced engagement with regulators is necessary to align tokenization activities with compliance requirements and obtain regulatory guidance and approvals.

In September 2023, the Federal Reserve released a report titled *Tokenization: Overview and Financial Stability Implications*, stating that tokenization is a financial innovation that could accelerate the growth of digital asset markets. The report defined tokenization as a broad concept, recognizing that tokens can have different characteristics based on design choices. Typically, tokenization structures fall into multiple categories, including blockchain-based models, underlying asset-backed models, models capturing the economic value of underlying assets, settlement/payment mechanisms, and hybrid structures combining multiple elements. The valuation of underlying assets, such as real-world assets, commodities, or intellectual property rights, remains central to tokenization. Proper valuation, verification, and monitoring through trusted intermediaries, such as banks, are essential to maintaining asset authenticity and market stability. Choosing appropriate institutional and governance models ensures asset reliability and financial stability.

When designing RWA tokenization solutions, multiple key factors must be considered, including the choice of underlying blockchain, the type of underlying assets being tokenized, and redemption mechanisms, to ensure feasibility, compliance, and sustainability of the solution.

First, one of the key considerations in tokenization design is the selection of the underlying blockchain. Blockchains provide the infrastructure for issuing, storing, and trading tokens. Some projects choose to issue tokens on permissioned private blockchains, where these blockchains operate under a more centralized model, with predefined participants joining a private ecosystem. Other projects opt to issue tokens on permissionless public blockchains, such as Ethereum. Compared to private blockchains, public blockchains allow for broader participation and accessibility, but they offer weaker control mechanisms over token issuers. Project teams need to evaluate their business characteristics, target users, and compliance requirements before selecting the most suitable blockchain type based on its advantages and limitations.

Secondly, the type of underlying assets being tokenized is another critical factor. Underlying assets can take various forms, such as real-world assets (RWAs), digital-native assets, or synthetic assets. RWAs represent tangible assets mapped to the digital asset market and can take forms such as real estate, commodities, or traditional financial securities. Tokenization of RWAs typically requires trusted intermediaries (such as banks) to assess asset value and provide custodial services. Tokenization of digital-native assets usually involves smart contracts, automating governance and valuation. Different types of underlying assets face distinct challenges and risks during the tokenization process, requiring appropriately designed technological and regulatory frameworks.

The redemption mechanism is another essential factor in designing RWA tokenization solutions. Some tokenization projects (such as stablecoins) allow token holders to redeem tokens for corresponding underlying assets, establishing a direct link between the digital asset market and the RWA market. Beyond redemption mechanisms, tokenized assets can also be traded on secondary markets, such as digital asset exchanges or DeFi platforms. However, some tokenized securities (such as those representing debt or equity rights) may not include redemption rights, and token holders may instead receive other benefits, such as revenue-sharing from the underlying asset. Depending on the nature of the underlying asset and relevant regulatory frameworks, tokenization projects must carefully design redemption mechanisms and secondary market transaction structures accordingly.

Additionally, since securities-type RWA tokens have clear security attributes and represent ownership or equity rights over physical assets, their structural design must incorporate regulatory compliance considerations and traditional financial securitization experience. For instance, these tokens can be structured in the form of equity, granting holders fractional ownership and dividend rights, while also allowing trading on secondary markets or securities exchanges. From an information disclosure and regulatory perspective, security tokens must consider relevant market regulations, such as periodic reporting mechanisms, compliance with disclosure rules, and investor protection measures. The concept and rules of tokenized securities often integrate elements from traditional securities markets, making them more aligned with regulatory frameworks. When designing RWA securities-type tokens, special attention should be given to financial frameworks, compliance risk management, and related issues.

A key step in RWA tokenization is conducting thorough due diligence on the underlying asset before issuance. Taking real estate tokenization as an example, professional appraisal institutions must conduct in-depth assessments of property location, building quality, surrounding market demand, and perform comparative analyses to determine market valuation. Additionally, obtaining legal and contractual rights to the asset requires multiple layers of verification. Another essential step is obtaining independent opinions from third-party professionals to ensure fairness and credibility. Similarly, accounting firms and rating agencies often provide due diligence reports, verifying asset ownership, issuer solvency, and compliance with regulatory frameworks, ensuring transparent, accurate, and complete information disclosure. Rigorous due diligence and audits serve as a crucial prerequisite and foundation for RWA tokenization.

For instance, Aspen Coin is a typical real estate tokenization project. Its underlying asset is a luxury hotel in Aspen, Colorado, USA. Before issuance, the project engaged professional real estate appraisal agencies to conduct asset evaluations, assessing the pricing of similar properties in the Aspen market, historical transaction trends, and occupancy rates. This process ultimately determined the public offering price of the tokenized property and ensured compliance with token issuance regulations. Additionally, accounting firms conducted audits on all ownership rights, financial status, and post-issuance fund management, providing validation and assurance. The U.S. Securities and Exchange Commission's *Statement on Digital Asset Securities Issuance and Trading* also provided critical guidance and policy references for investor information and regulatory compliance.

RWA tokenization faces unique risk factors, and issuers and investors must pay close attention to and actively manage these risks, particularly in two key areas: risks associated with underlying assets and counterparty risks.

Underlying asset risks mainly concern the standardization of assets, liquidity levels, and pricing mechanisms. Generally, standardized assets with higher standardization levels, better liquidity, and well-established pricing mechanisms—such as government bonds—are relatively easier to tokenize, with risks that are more manageable. In contrast, non-standardized assets, such as real estate and intellectual property, have greater uncertainty in pricing, ownership, and transaction structures, making the tokenization process more complex and challenging. Due to differences in legal systems and financial infrastructure across different countries and regions, cross-border assets face additional risks related to legal compliance, market access, and settlement mechanisms. In markets where financial information is less transparent, challenges such as data integrity and valuation consistency can further complicate the tokenization process. Therefore, issuers must ensure the existence of reliable credit guarantees or risk mitigation measures during the tokenization process to reduce the risk of under-collateralization or forced liquidation.

3.5 Core Element of RWA: Technological Tools

In the traditional financial sector, asset transactions and management are subject to various restrictions and constraints, which limit the availability of many financial services. The rise of new financial technologies and the development of digital assets have opened up new possibilities. Blockchain technology and smart contracts play a crucial role in enabling RWA tokenization. To successfully implement RWA tokenization, a range of advanced technical tools is required, including foundational blockchain infrastructure, smart contracts, digital identity, security, prediction mechanisms, and cross-chain technologies. These technologies establish the fundamental framework for RWA tokenization, ensuring a secure, transparent, and efficient transaction process.

3.5.1 Blockchain Infrastructure and Layer 2 Network Upgrades

Selecting the appropriate blockchain infrastructure for asset tokenization requires careful evaluation of multiple factors. Projects must consider their own operational needs, business characteristics, and regulatory requirements when selecting a blockchain network as the underlying technical framework for tokenization.

On one hand, projects must assess whether the transparency of transactions and the openness of public information are crucial, or if privacy protection is a priority. If a project's main goal is to increase information transparency and enhance investor confidence, a fully public blockchain is more suitable. Conversely, if the project involves highly sensitive data or requires identity protection, then a blockchain with strong privacy features or permissioned access may be a better choice.

On the other hand, projects must evaluate transaction performance requirements. If the project requires high-frequency, low-cost transactions, such as liquid financial assets, it must assess the blockchain's transaction processing speed (TPS) and scalability while maintaining a balance between asset liquidity and decentralization. Conversely, if the project has lower transaction frequency and real-time processing demands, such as real estate or artwork tokenization, a more decentralized but relatively lower-performance blockchain may be suitable. Additionally, projects must evaluate the regulatory compliance of different blockchain networks, including aspects such as governance, security, and ecosystem maturity. Compliance is a key consideration in RWA tokenization. Projects must determine whether a blockchain network aligns with the regulatory requirements of its jurisdiction, including whether it supports necessary attributes such as KYC/AML compliance. Selecting a blockchain with a strong security track record and widespread adoption can enhance the reliability of the system. To minimize security risks and improve system resilience, it is essential to choose a robust blockchain network with rich functionality. This not only reduces development costs but also increases service flexibility. Cross-chain interoperability is another critical factor for projects to consider. As tokenization adoption grows, different blockchains must accommodate increased interoperability and communication between networks. If an RWA tokenization project requires integration with multiple blockchains for real-world asset transactions and settlement, the project must carefully evaluate the cross-chain technologies and user experience. Choosing a cross-chain framework with lower interoperability costs can significantly improve token liquidity and usability.

Currently, RWA tokenization primarily relies on public chains and consortium chains as underlying infrastructures. As an open and transparent distributed network, public chains provide distinct advantages in terms of RWA tokenization's liquidity and security. However, public chains still face scalability challenges. For example, during market surges, network congestion on public chains can lead to serious delays in transaction confirmation times, increased transaction fees, and overall inefficiencies. During the DeFi boom of 2020 and the NFT surge of 2021, network congestion caused significant disruptions, leading to intense debates over transaction speed and Gas fee disputes. It can be said that network scalability issues have, to some extent, hindered the widespread adoption of public chains for RWA tokenization, particularly in large-scale projects and high-frequency trading applications.

Consortium chains serve as an alternative technology path for many financial institutions in RWA tokenization. By establishing multi-center networks, consortium chains offer greater control over privacy protection, identity verification, and transaction security while improving transaction efficiency. They also help address regulatory concerns such as compliance risks, ownership verification, and governance standards. However, the drawback of consortium chains is that their semi-closed nature may impose strict access restrictions, which could create barriers to broader adoption and limit the liquidity benefits of RWA tokenization.

A small number of RWA tokens are issued on private chains. Private chain networks allow independent operation, maximizing customization needs. They generally offer higher transaction efficiency and can integrate traditional KYC/AML procedures more easily. However, private chains lack openness and inclusivity, making it difficult to attract external participants and limiting the development of a thriving token economy.

Public chains, consortium chains, and private chains represent different infrastructure models for RWA tokenization, each with unique technical pathways and functional positioning. Public chains emphasize openness, transparency, and transaction liquidity, making them the preferred choice for most RWA tokenization applications. In contrast, consortium chains and private chains focus on controllability, regulatory compliance, and operational efficiency, making them better suited for specific RWA tokenization use cases.

It is worth noting that, with the innovative development of blockchain infrastructure, some emerging blockchain networks are beginning to experiment with more flexible "hybrid architectures" to achieve differentiated customization across aspects such as identity, access, and scalability. This has opened up even broader possibilities for RWA tokenization.

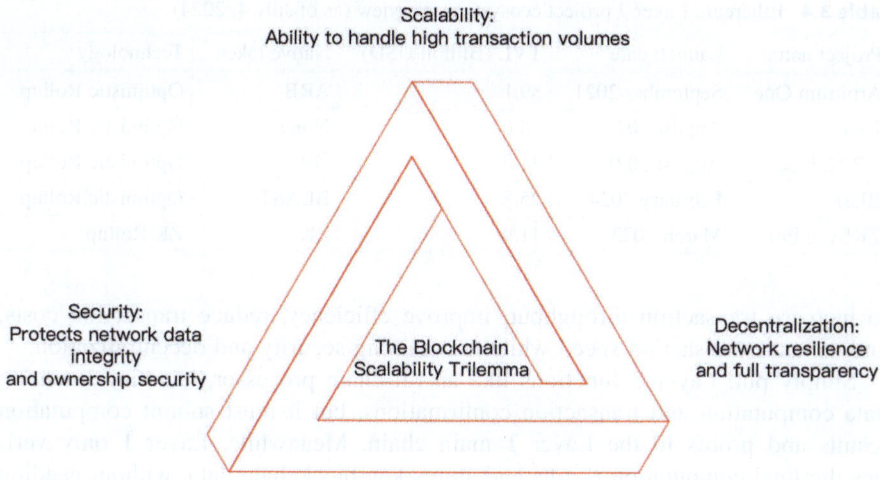

Fig. 3.3 The blockchain scalability trilemma

At its core, the aforementioned issues stem from the "blockchain trilemma,"[4] which presents trade-offs among decentralization, scalability, and security (Fig. 3.3). That is, it is theoretically impossible to achieve optimal performance in all three aspects simultaneously, necessitating trade-offs. Most public blockchains prioritize decentralization and security, which often results in constraints on scalability. However, for RWA tokenization, achieving high asset liquidity and transaction speed is crucial, requiring additional mechanisms to optimize scalability and resolve these inherent limitations to meet the advanced demands of the Web 3.0 era.

Currently, many blockchain technology developers are focusing on Layer 2 solutions, which involve building additional expansion layers on top of blockchains

[4] The "Blockchain Impossible Triangle" originated from an article titled On Sharding Blockchains created by James Ray, a member of the Ethereum community, on GitHub. The wide spread of this article was due to the promotion by Vitalik Buterin, the founder of Ethereum. The "Blockchain Impossible Triangle" refers to the fact that a blockchain system cannot simultaneously achieve decentralization and scalability, and developers must make trade - offs. Among them, decentralization means that a certain blockchain has a large number of nodes participating in block production and verification. Usually, the more nodes there are, the higher the degree of decentralization of the blockchain. Decentralization and the fairness it brings are the core values of blockchain technology. Security refers to the cost required to obtain control of the network. Scalability refers to the TPS (Transactions Per Second) of the blockchain. Faced with this dilemma, each public blockchain has chosen different directions for optimization and trade-offs. For example, one of the reasons for the poor scalability of a certain blockchain is that every transaction has to reach an agreement on all nodes. If there are many and scattered nodes, it will restrict the speed increase. Therefore, some blockchains will improve scalability by reducing the degree of decentralization.

Table 3.4 Ethereum Layer 2 project ecosystem overview (as of July 4, 2024)

Project name	Launch date	TVL (Billion USD)	Native token	Technology
Arbitrum One	September 2021	89.1	ARB	Optimistic Rollup
Base	August 2023	68.0	None	Optimistic Rollup
OP Mainnet	August 2021	31.9	OP	Optimistic Rollup
Blast	February 2024	25.8	BLAST	Optimistic Rollup
ZKSync Era	March 2023	11.9	ZK	ZK Rollup

to increase transaction throughput, improve efficiency, reduce transaction costs, and enhance transaction speed while maintaining security and decentralization.

Simply put, Layer 2 functions like an off-chain processor, handling intensive data computation and transaction confirmations, but it must submit computation results and proofs to the Layer 1 main chain. Meanwhile, Layer 1 only verifies the final computation results and stores key blockchain data, without needing to process complete data calculations or store all transaction data. This mechanism allows the main chain to efficiently process transactions at a higher speed, thereby improving scalability. As shown in Table 3.4, there are various Layer 2 technological implementations. Currently, Rollup solutions are widely supported and explored by developers, and they are considered one of the most promising Layer 2 technologies. Rollups execute transactions on Layer 2, batch and compress transaction data, and submit them in aggregate to Layer 1 for final validation. This process significantly enhances transaction processing speed. Rollup solutions are further divided into Optimistic Rollup and ZK Rollup, which represent the two primary Layer 2 technology approaches.

Optimistic Rollup, as the name suggests, "optimistically assumes all transactions are valid.“ This means that the technology presumes the majority of transactions are honest and does not validate them unless fraud is suspected. However, to ensure transaction security, Optimistic Rollup networks introduce a 7-day fraud challenge period. During this period, validators on Layer 2 can submit fraud proofs to challenge transactions suspected of being invalid. If no one submits fraud proofs within the challenge period, the transactions are deemed valid, and their execution is finalized. This mechanism improves transaction efficiency but requires trust in the challenge period. On the other hand, ZK Rollup (Zero-Knowledge Rollup) utilizes "zero-knowledge proofs."[5] It bundles large volumes of transactions on Layer 2 and compresses them into a single proof, which is then submitted to Layer 1 for verification. Unlike Optimistic Rollups, ZK Rollup does not assume

[5] Zero-knowledge proofs (ZK-SNARKs) were introduced in the 1980s by Shafi Goldwasser, Silvio Micali, and Charles Rackoff. The idea behind zero-knowledge proofs is that a prover can demonstrate knowledge of a value without revealing the value itself. This allows verification to occur without disclosing any sensitive information. For example, a zero-knowledge proof could verify that a person has a valid password without revealing the actual password. This cryptographic breakthrough forms the foundation for ZK Rollup security and scalability.

transactions are valid but instead proves their validity using cryptographic proofs. These proofs, once verified by Layer 1, confirm that the bundled transactions are accurate and unaltered. Compared to Optimistic Rollup, ZK Rollup eliminates the need for a dispute challenge period and can instantly determine the validity of transactions. The proof process is based on advanced cryptographic calculations (such as zero-knowledge succinct non-interactive arguments of knowledge, or zk-SNARKs). While this method reduces risks, it requires significant computational power and complexity, making it more difficult to develop than Optimistic Rollups. ZK Rollup currently has lower general adoption but is expected to gain prominence in the future due to its higher security and efficiency.

With continuous advancements in blockchain technology, the future layered structure of blockchain networks is expected to become more diverse and sophisticated. In September 2022, Ethereum co-founder Vitalik Buterin published an article titled *What Kind of Layer 3 s Make Sense?* In this article, he pointed out that Layer 3 should not just be an extension of Layer 2 rollups but rather a separate architectural layer with distinct goals and functions. Layer 2 focuses on scalability Layer 3 is designed for customization Layer 2 enables trustless scaling, while Layer 3 provides weakly trusted expansion capabilities. This structured approach enhances flexibility and allows Layer 3 to provide application-specific solutions, further refining blockchain scalability.

Some developers further speculate that Layer 3 may increasingly emerge in the form of "application chains" in the future, meaning that each decentralized application (DApp) would correspond to a dedicated Layer 3 chain. This architectural design can provide more flexible and efficient solutions for different application scenarios, catering to the specific needs of various DApps.

With the explosion of RWA tokenization and the rapid development of the Web 3.0 ecosystem, the future digital world will not only require mainstream public chains like Ethereum as the "main highway" for high-speed transactions, but also more Layer X protocols to build auxiliary infrastructure similar to secondary roads, overpasses, and subways. This multi-layered and structured network architecture can support a wider variety of applications, enabling limitless combinatorial innovation and meeting the diverse needs of different application scenarios.

Take Polygon as an example. It is a Layer 2 scaling solution based on Ethereum, designed to enhance Ethereum's transaction throughput and processing speed while reducing transaction fees. Polygon utilizes a technology known as Plasma, which achieves scalability by distributing transaction processing tasks across multiple sidechains. These sidechains can process transactions in parallel and then submit the transaction results to the Ethereum main chain for final confirmation. Through this approach, Polygon is able to improve the overall performance of the Ethereum network while maintaining security and decentralization. Polygon has already attracted a large number of DApp developers and users, particularly in the fields of DeFi, NFTs, and gaming, where it has seen widespread adoption. The success of Polygon demonstrates the immense potential of Layer 2 scaling solutions in driving the widespread adoption of blockchain applications.

Beyond scalability, privacy is also emerging as a key bottleneck for enabling large-scale institutional-grade RWA transactions. Institutional investors and high-net-worth individuals increasingly demand enhanced privacy and data security when conducting large-scale RWA tokenization transactions. At the same time, open market transactions are constrained by transparency requirements. The balance between privacy protection and security on blockchain platforms may make privacy protection an increasingly critical factor.

Aleo is a blockchain platform specializing in privacy protection. It utilizes zero-knowledge proof technology to provide users with a transaction environment that is both private and programmable. On the Aleo platform, participants can execute transactions and smart contracts while ensuring that their personal information and transaction details remain fully confidential. This technology helps traders keep their trading strategies and asset conditions undisclosed, effectively preventing security risks and market manipulation.

From a technical perspective, Aleo integrates a range of innovative cryptographic and blockchain technologies, including but not limited to zero-knowledge proofs, decentralized network structures, and programmable privacy systems. With the assistance of these technologies, Aleo achieves high scalability and efficient large-scale transaction processing while ensuring privacy protection. Aleo's potential applications are extensive—not only can it meet the privacy needs of financial and secret transactions, but it can also play a crucial role in supply chain management, medical data sharing, identity verification, and other scenarios requiring data privacy. In the context of RWA transactions, privacy protection is critical: it is necessary to maintain transaction efficiency while ensuring that the entire transaction process adheres to privacy standards and regulatory compliance.

In conclusion, as RWA tokenization continues to develop, the demand for blockchain infrastructure is also increasing. On the one hand, blockchain networks require innovative Layer 2 technologies to continuously enhance scalability and expand capacity to support large-scale RWA issuance and transactions. On the other hand, as more institutional investors participate, the need for transaction privacy and security is becoming increasingly important. Privacy-focused blockchain platforms such as Aleo offer potential solutions to these challenges. In the future, as the RWA tokenization market flourishes, it will receive strong technical support. With the increasing specialization and institutionalization of blockchain infrastructure, RWA tokenization is bound to move toward broader adoption.

3.5.2 Digital Wallets and Token Custody

Unlike traditional securities, one of the key features of RWA tokens is that transactions and transfers can be executed based on blockchain addresses. While any individual can easily generate a blockchain address for themselves, this also introduces potential risks that could seriously threaten asset security, such as misoperations, address errors, private key leaks, or mnemonic phrase exposure.[6] It is precisely because of these issues that digital wallets have emerged as an essential tool, becoming an indispensable component of digital asset management.

Digital wallets are core tools for managing and securing blockchain assets, primarily responsible for storing private keys, generating transaction signatures, and managing addresses. Utilizing encryption technology, digital wallets ensure the security of user assets while providing a user-friendly interface that makes it easy for users to execute and track transactions. There are various types of digital wallets, which can be broadly categorized into custodial wallets and non-custodial wallets, depending on whether the private key is held by a third party.

Custodial wallets refer to wallets where the user's private key is managed by a third-party custodian, commonly seen in wallets provided by cryptocurrency exchanges. Under this model, the user's private key is stored on the exchange's servers, and the responsibility for asset security lies with the custodian. The advantage of custodial wallets is their ease of use, as users do not need to handle complex private key management. However, the downside is that users must trust the third-party institution; if an exchange suffers a hack or a security breach, user assets may be at risk of loss.

A non-custodial wallet, on the other hand, is a wallet where the user retains full control over their private key. Based on whether the wallet is connected to the internet, non-custodial wallets can be further classified into hot wallets and cold wallets.

A hot wallet is a wallet where the private key is stored on an internet-connected device, such as MetaMask, which operates as a browser extension. This type of wallet provides high convenience, as the user's private key is stored on a personal computer. With the increasing use of smartphones, many wallets have launched mobile app versions, allowing users to store their private keys on a smartphone. Other well-known mobile-based hot wallets include imToken, TokenPocket, and

[6] In the blockchain world, a wallet address, private key, public key, and mnemonic phrase constitute the core elements of digital identity. The private key controls access to the wallet's assets, while the public key is derived from the private key and is used to generate a blockchain address. A blockchain address is public and can be used by others to send assets to the user. However, an address alone does not indicate ownership of the assets associated with it. When a user creates a wallet, they generate a private key through mathematical encryption, from which the public key and address are derived. A mnemonic phrase is essentially a "human-readable" representation of the private key, typically consisting of 12 or 24 words. It allows users to restore their wallet and access assets in case of device loss. The private key and mnemonic phrase are crucial security elements; losing them means losing access to the wallet and its assets, while exposure to others could result in unauthorized access and asset theft. A digital signature is used to verify the ownership of assets during transactions. Since public keys are visible on the blockchain and signatures must be unique for each transaction, asymmetric cryptography ensures that assets cannot be transferred without authorization. This mechanism allows users to retain full control over their assets while maintaining security. Essentially, the private key acts as a digital signature tool for users, the public key serves as a verification reference, and the wallet address functions as a receiving identifier. The combination of these elements forms a fundamental layer of blockchain security.

Coinbase Wallet, which mainly offer wallet services through smartphone apps. Hot wallets provide high liquidity and real-time transaction capabilities, making them ideal for frequent transactions and Web 3.0 applications that require active user participation. However, the fact that hot wallets are always online introduces security risks, particularly against phishing attacks and malicious software, which could potentially lead to asset theft.

A cold wallet, also known as an offline wallet or hardware wallet, stores a user's private key in a device that is not connected to the internet. This design maximizes security by preventing hackers from stealing private keys, offering an advanced level of asset protection. To complete a blockchain transaction using a cold wallet, a user must sign the transaction with their private key on the device, then transfer the signed data using QR codes, USB connections, Bluetooth, or NFC to a connected device (such as a computer or mobile phone) for broadcasting. Ledger and Trezor are two of the most well-known hardware wallet brands. Their wallets store private keys on dedicated hardware and work with companion apps on computers or smartphones. In some cases, users may need to manually transfer data between devices to sign transactions. While cold wallets provide a high level of security, they can be cumbersome to use. Additionally, if users make mistakes, authorize malicious transactions, or fall for phishing scams, they can still lose their assets.

It is evident that digital wallets serve as the bridge between users and the Web 3.0 world. However, today's digital wallets are often complex and not user-friendly for mainstream users. Because blockchain technology is decentralized, there is no third-party institution that can recover user assets. If a private key is lost or stolen, the user completely loses access to their assets. This makes security and usability two major challenges in Web 3.0 wallet development.

Currently, the industry is exploring multiple technological pathways to improve security and usability in digital wallets. One area of focus is Multi-Party Computation (MPC)[7] wallets and smart contract wallets. MPC wallets are particularly notable for their decentralized approach to private key security. They eliminate single points of failure by splitting a user's private key into multiple independent cryptographic shares. In on-chain transaction signing, MPC wallets store private key fragments across multiple devices to improve security. For example, the ZenGo MPC wallet encrypts the user's private key into two mathematical secret shares. One share is stored on the user's device, while the other is kept on ZenGo's servers. This design ensures that even if one share is lost or compromised, the user's assets remain secure.

To further mitigate the risk of users losing access to their assets due to unexpected service disruptions, ZenGo introduces a key recovery mechanism that eliminates the risks associated with single points of failure. Custodial key recovery

[7] Multi-Party Computation (MPC) is a cryptographic technique that allows multiple parties to collaboratively compute a function without revealing their individual inputs. In MPC wallets, this technology is used to split private keys among multiple parties, enhancing security and preventing single points of failure.

services are a professional third-party solution that securely stores encrypted key fragments and user data, ensuring they can be safely retrieved in case of loss or emergency. Traditionally, a trusted third party, such as a legal or financial service provider, is appointed to execute key escrow or key recovery under predefined conditions. These entities act as intermediaries and enforce secure data decryption and execution processes only under specific legal conditions. For instance, ZenGo's recovery mechanism does not require a password. Instead, its custodian service pre-defines a recovery policy based on user consent and permissions, linking private key fragments to a secure, pre-approved recovery credential such as a GitHub account. When needed, an external legal entity verifies the legitimacy and security of the recovery request to ensure compliance with the predefined recovery procedure. Every time a ZenGo digital wallet is launched, it automatically checks whether the associated GitHub account is in recovery mode. If recovery mode has been activated, the service downloads the necessary key fragment and reconstructs the complete private key. When a user initiates a digital asset transaction, ZenGo's server and client app (the user's mobile phone) combine their cryptographic shares to sign the transaction without exposing the full private key. This ensures that even in cases of device compromise or data leaks, the user's digital assets remain secure.

In addition to cryptographic security, ZenGo provides a simple and user-friendly backup and recovery mechanism. Users do not need to manually store or remember complex private key backups. Instead, they can recover access simply by scanning their biometric 3D face ID. Even if a user mistakenly deletes the ZenGo app or loses their phone (which would result in losing the client-side key fragment), they can quickly restore their wallet using a biometric scan, retrieving the missing key fragment from ZenGo's server backup.

A smart contract wallet represents the next generation of digital wallets. In most public blockchain ecosystems, apart from the externally owned accounts (EOAs) controlled directly by users with private keys, there is another type of account known as a smart contract account. Unlike EOAs, smart contract accounts operate based on programmable code. For example, if you send 1 ETH to an EOA, the recipient can freely control the ETH using their private key. However, if you send 1 ETH to a smart contract account, the ETH is now managed by the contract's logic, which could require additional approval, multi-signature verification, or pre-set transaction rules before any further actions like transfers or withdrawals can occur. At present, the majority of blockchain transactions require EOAs to initiate transactions, meaning that smart contract accounts cannot autonomously trigger transactions.

Since 2015, Ethereum and other blockchain developers have been actively researching how to make these two account types more functional and efficient. This has led to the introduction of the account abstraction (AA) concept. In simple terms, account abstraction merges the strengths of EOAs and smart contract accounts, allowing the latter to independently initiate transactions.

Discussions around account abstraction gained traction in 2015, but one of the most well-known developments came from Ethereum founder Vitalik Buterin in

September 2021, when he and other developers proposed EIP-4337. This introduced the user operations concept, enabling smart contract accounts to initiate transactions and interact with the network without needing an EOA to trigger them. This eliminates issues such as losing access to wallets due to lost seed phrases. Unlike EOAs, which primarily handle basic transactions, fund transfers, and signature verification, smart contract wallets function as an advanced digital asset management system. They allow users to set up custom security mechanisms, automated transaction rules, and multi-party approvals, significantly enhancing digital wallet usability.

In the process of RWA tokenization, digital asset custody services play a critical role. These services enhance asset security (preventing unauthorized access and misuse) while facilitating safe storage and key management for issuers and investors. Custodial security services are a highly specialized field that demands strong security infrastructure and risk management protocols. Since digital asset custody is inherently decentralized and immutable, losing a private key or experiencing a security breach due to malicious insiders, cloud service failures, or internal sabotage can result in irreversible losses. Therefore, digital asset custody must ensure comprehensive private key management, including key generation, secure storage, encryption, transaction authorization, and key lifecycle management. It also involves secure asset movement and blockchain smart contract integration. While technology can provide a certain level of protection, human error remains one of the primary risks associated with key mismanagement, incorrect address inputs, or unauthorized withdrawals. As a result, custodians must establish strict risk control measures to prevent both internal fraud and external attacks.

In addition, digital asset custodians must maintain certain qualifications and resources to actively engage with financial regulators. In many countries, digital asset custody services are evolving into licensed financial services, which requires custodians to meet various compliance and risk management standards. These include having adequate reserves, implementing information disclosure mechanisms, ensuring private key management security, performing security audits, and offering insurance coverage.

Currently, the market already has a range of professional digital asset custody service providers, such as Coinbase Custody and Safeheron. These institutions implement secure storage solutions, including cold storage, multi-signature (multi-sig)[8] protection, and multi-layered security protocols, to ensure asset safety. For example, Safeheron utilizes multi-party computation (MPC), trusted execution

[8] Multi-signature (Multi-Sig)—A security mechanism that requires multiple independent private key holders to authorize a transaction. In a blockchain context, multi-signature wallets enhance security by ensuring that multiple parties must jointly approve transactions, reducing risks of fraud or key compromise.

environments (TEE),[9] and zero-trust[10] security frameworks to enhance private key security. To mitigate internal threats, Safeheron safeguards assets against external cyberattacks, internal employee misconduct, and third-party software vulnerabilities. Additionally, Safeheron develops customized security solutions for institutional clients, helping businesses establish appropriate risk control measures tailored to their operational needs. If an extreme risk event occurs, Safeheron offers insurance protection[11] services, providing a final layer of security. Moreover, since regulatory requirements differ by region, Safeheron also provides customized compliance solutions.

Blockchain and Layer 2 Infrastructure, Smart Contract Design, Digital Identity, Digital Wallets, Secure Custody, Oracles, and Cross-Chain Technologies are all critical components of the RWA tokenization process. Each element must be selected and designed based on specific business requirements, market conditions, and regulatory demands. Moreover, these components must work together to create a secure, efficient, and compliant RWA tokenization solution. Therefore, understanding and mastering these technologies is essential for both RWA tokenization project teams and investors.

3.6 Core Element of RWA: Data Applications

Through RWA tokenization, asset issuance data, transaction data, and user behavior data become key structured data recorded on the blockchain. This ensures transparency, significantly improving the ability of asset operators and investors to track market dynamics, predict market trends, and manage risk. However, this shift also introduces challenges in data management. Traditional data processing and analysis methods often struggle to handle this new environment, creating demand for data analytics and AI-driven forecasting tools. Consequently, a wave of Web 3.0 financial platforms and analytics tools has rapidly emerged.

Due to the immutable and decentralized nature of blockchain design, external systems face barriers when interacting with on-chain data. Smart contracts cannot directly access off-chain data, so they rely on a mechanism called oracles to securely introduce external data sources. These external data sources may include

[9] Trusted Execution Environment (TEE)—A secure enclave within a hardware system that protects the confidentiality and integrity of executed code. Even if the underlying operating system is compromised, the processing environment remains secure, making TEE ideal for handling private key operations.

[10] Zero-Trust Security Model—A cybersecurity approach where no entity is inherently trusted, whether inside or outside a system. Every access request must be strictly verified, ensuring that unauthorized users cannot bypass authentication or gain direct access to protected resources.

[11] Digital Asset Insurance Services—These are insurance products provided by insurance companies to digital asset holders, offering protection against cyberattacks, hacking incidents, and smart contract failures. Traditional insurers like Lloyd's of London have begun offering coverage for such risks, while specialized providers such as Nexus Mutual and Evertas are.

transaction prices of digital assets,[12] securities exchange rates, national foreign exchange rates, commodity prices, index data, real estate prices, and weather data.

An oracle acts as a bridge between the blockchain and the external world, providing smart contracts with essential off-chain data to automate decision-making. This process is commonly referred to as "data feeding." Oracles play a critical role in many DeFi applications, particularly those requiring external data inputs in decentralized lending, stablecoins, cross-chain transactions, and logistics tracking.[13] For example, DeFi lending services require real-time price feeds from oracles to automate liquidation mechanisms and ensure the integrity of financial protocols.

Ensuring the accuracy and security of data from external sources is a key challenge for oracle systems. Data reliability is typically maintained through the following verification methods:

- **Diversity of Data Sources**

  Oracle systems do not rely on a single data source but instead collect information from multiple independent data providers. The system then aggregates and processes these sources to ensure accuracy and consistency. Even if one data source is compromised or manipulated, the system can cross-verify with others to obtain corrected information.
- **Decentralized Execution Mechanism**

  Oracle networks operate using a decentralized model, where multiple independent nodes fetch and verify data simultaneously. This redundancy ensures that even if one node is compromised or attacked, the system can continue functioning normally by relying on other operational nodes to maintain data integrity.
- **Incentive and Penalty Mechanism**

  Oracle systems integrate incentive structures that reward nodes for providing accurate data. Conversely, if a node submits incorrect or manipulated data, it may be subject to various penalties, such as losing staked tokens or facing reputation-based slashing.
- **Data Validation**

[12] This is a typical type of external data. The prices of centralized exchanges are formed outside the blockchain, usually based on the supply - demand relationships and trading activities within these exchanges. These exchanges operate on centralized servers, and their trading data is not automatically synchronized with the blockchain.

[13] A prediction market is a type of DeFi service that allows users to bet on various possible outcomes of future events. Users can place bets on the possible results of various public events such as election results, sports competitions, or market behaviors. If the prediction is correct, they can get a return based on the market odds. This kind of service is usually built on the blockchain to ensure transparent transactions, non - tamperable information, and automated result execution.

In addition to the above mechanisms, oracle networks also perform multi-step validation processes to ensure data accuracy and consistency before transmitting it to blockchain smart contracts.

Oracles play a crucial role in the RWA tokenization process, especially in ensuring price accuracy, asset valuation, and stable conversion between physical and digital assets. Traditional finance requires timely and accurate valuation of assets subject to price fluctuations (such as stocks, bonds, and real estate funds). The underlying asset data must be accurately reflected on-chain. Oracles facilitate real-time data feeds, allowing RWA token prices to remain consistent with their real-world asset values.

For example, if a bond is tokenized, the system must track its real-time value, transactions, and investor activities. Oracles connect external financial data to blockchain networks, ensuring that RWA token holders have access to real-time valuation information, allowing investors to make informed decisions.

With the development of RWA tokenization, a large volume of asset issuance, transactions, and user behavior data is being aggregated on blockchain networks. This provides a broad space for the application of data analysis and artificial intelligence technologies. Emerging Web 3.0 financial data platforms and analytics tools are rapidly emerging, helping asset operators and investors gain a better understanding of market dynamics, predict market trends, and manage investment risks. At the same time, oracles play a key role as bridges between blockchain and the external world in RWA tokenization. They retrieve real-time asset information from reliable external data sources and securely transmit it to blockchain smart contracts, ensuring that RWA tokens remain synchronized with their underlying asset values. As oracle technology continues to develop and improve, RWA tokenization is becoming more efficient, transparent, and reliable, providing strong technical support for the digital transformation of RWA.

Against the backdrop of rapid Web 3.0 development, oracle technology is increasingly recognized as a critical bridge between real-world data and blockchain smart contracts, attracting growing market attention. As of May 31, 2024, the oracle market is dominated by Chainlink, WINLink, and Chronicle Labs, collectively accounting for 75% of the global oracle market share. Chainlink, with its unique decentralized architecture and high-security design, has emerged as the industry leader in the oracle sector. The project, developed by SmartContract.com, was officially launched in September 2017, attracting partnerships with major enterprises such as Google and Oracle, along with numerous prominent investors. Chainlink was the first project to provide decentralized oracle services for Ethereum, utilizing on-chain smart contracts and off-chain data nodes to facilitate data requests and verification through delegation mechanisms and aggregation models.

To enhance data reliability and security, Chainlink has implemented a validation mechanism requiring participating nodes to cross-verify the same data source before aggregating and transmitting the final results to smart contracts. This design ensures data quality while improving the system's decentralization and resistance to attacks. Chainlink's oracle framework consists of a multi-layered data aggregation process, where key layers collaborate closely to protect oracle price feeds from manipulation and cyberattacks, ensuring the stable operation of DeFi applications.

The first layer is data source aggregation. In this layer, Chainlink collects raw market data from leading data providers, including traditional DeFi platforms and decentralized exchanges (e.g., Uniswap). After initial processing by data providers, raw data is aggregated into authoritative datasets. This includes volume-weighted price calculations adjusted for trading activity and time factors, as well as corrections for abnormal price fluctuations and fraudulent transactions. This ensures that oracle prices reflect overall market averages, rather than individual market distortions.

Secondly, node aggregation occurs. After the data source layer aggregates information, multiple node operators within the Chainlink network use this data for a second round of aggregation. Node operators form the backbone of the Chainlink network, responsible for extracting data from designated sources and transmitting it to smart contracts requesting data. Chainlink node operators can be classified into three categories: DevOps nodes, enterprise nodes, and community nodes. DevOps nodes are professional institutions specializing in blockchain infrastructure, with extensive experience in maintaining on-chain 3.0 facilities, managing cryptographic keys, and providing digital asset services. Enterprise nodes are operated by global corporations, including major telecommunications giants and large enterprises, such as T-Systems (a subsidiary of Deutsche Telekom), Swisscom, and LexisNexis. Community nodes originate directly from the Chainlink community, including winners of the Chainlink Oracle Olympics and other community contributors. This layer of aggregation enhances data reliability and redundancy across nodes, reducing reliance on a single data source and thereby mitigating single points of failure.

The final layer is oracle network aggregation. At the Chainlink oracle network layer, all participating nodes aggregate their data responses and reach a final data output through a consensus mechanism. Typically, this process requires a certain number of nodes to participate, and the median value of all node responses is used as the final result. This design further strengthens the overall integrity and security of the data, ensuring that even in extreme cases (e.g., computational attacks or data source outages), the entire network remains stable and continues to provide reliable price feed information.

Each data source within the Chainlink network has a unique on-chain address, allowing smart contracts to query specific data by calling predefined functions on these addresses. This design enables smart contracts to access off-chain data automatically and transparently, without compromising decentralization. As of September 2023, over 1700 Web 3.0 projects have integrated Chainlink oracles. Chainlink operates on more than 15 blockchains, delivering over 7.4 billion data points reliably, and connecting with more than 900 decentralized oracle networks.

The workflow of the Chainlink oracle system consists of six main steps:

3.6.1 Data Request

First, a smart contract sends a request to the oracle, indicating that it requires specific off-chain data, such as stock prices or weather information.

3.6.2 Oracle Node Selection

Within the Chainlink network, some oracle nodes are selected to respond to the data request. The selection of these nodes is based on multiple factors, including security, pricing, and historical performance.

3.6.3 Data Retrieval

The selected oracle nodes will retrieve data from designated sources. These sources may include:

- Open API[14] (Application Programming Interfaces), allowing direct access to data.
- Proprietary databases or other data providers, offering private or commercial data services.

3.6.4 Data Reporting

Once data retrieval is complete, the oracle node will submit the data report to the smart contract on the blockchain. Additionally, it will use digital signatures to verify the source and integrity of the data, ensuring its authenticity and reliability.

3.6.5 Data Aggregation

If multiple oracle nodes are selected, the Chainlink network will aggregate and process the collected data, providing a final, reliable, and consistent data input.

3.6.6 Data Usage

After receiving the final data input, the smart contract will execute its pre-programmed logic. For example, If the smart contract is a weather insurance

[14] API stands for some pre-defined functions. An application encapsulates its own service capabilities into APIs and exposes them to users for invocation through an API gateway.

contract, it may detect rainfall data at a specific location and automatically trigger an insurance payout to the affected users.

In 2021, Chainlink introduced the Cross-Chain Interoperability Protocol (CCIP). This is an open-source standard designed to enable standardized information transmission and security mechanisms across blockchain networks, allowing data exchange and message transfers between different blockchains. The core advantage of CCIP lies in its decentralized design, which can ensure the security and reliability of cross-chain communication. By using CCIP, smart contracts can request and receive data stored on other blockchain networks, and at the same time send transactions and messages to other blockchain networks without relying on a single centralized service. The launch of CCIP marks that Chainlink is evolving from a project focusing on oracle services to a more comprehensive cross-chain infrastructure provider.

Since 2023, Chainlink has been collaborating on multiple projects to promote RWA tokenization. In July 2023, Chainlink began supporting Backed Finance[15] in its RWA tokenization efforts, providing tokenized U.S. Treasury Bonds ETF IB01, tokenized European Bonds ETF IBTA, and tokenized S&P 500 index ETF CSPX.

In September 2023, Chainlink partnered with the Depository Trust & Clearing Corporation (DTCC) to integrate Swift's interbank financial messaging network for tokenized RWA transactions. Swift is a global financial messaging system that provides secure and standardized communication for banks and financial institutions, facilitating cross-border financial transactions. In this initiative, Swift utilized Chainlink's Cross-Chain Interoperability Protocol (CCIP) to enable secure cross-chain messaging and token transfers, while DTCC simulated the issuance and custodial management of tokenized securities (CSD). Specifically, DTCC experimented with BondTokens, representing traditional fixed-income securities, ensuring cross-chain asset migration and interoperability via Chainlink CCIP.

This project demonstrated how blockchain technology and decentralized oracle networks can be used to digitize traditional financial assets. By tokenizing bonds and other fixed-income assets, Chainlink's CCIP enabled cross-chain messaging and asset migration, significantly improving liquidity and reducing settlement costs and time. This has important implications for integrating traditional finance with DeFi.

In May 2024, Chainlink announced that it would provide oracle solutions for Aave's RWA initiative. Aave is a leading DeFi lending protocol that allows users to borrow funds using tokenized RWAs as collateral. As part of the RWA plan, Aave aimed to introduce more tokenized RWAs, such as real estate-backed bonds or securities, as loan collateral.

To support this plan, Chainlink worked with Aave to provide customized data transmission services, offering DeFi lending rate visibility to help Aave better

[15] Backed Finance is a regulated asset management institution that utilizes structured financial engineering to bridge the world of traditional securities with tokenized assets. It enables the tokenization of financial instruments such as bonds and ETFs, ensuring compliance with financial regulations while facilitating the trading and settlement of these assets on blockchain networks.

understand and manage its platform-wide lending rates. Additionally, Chainlink announced support for Aave V4, which introduced modular interest rate models, allowing Aave to dynamically adjust lending rates based on market conditions, ensuring platform stability and efficiency.

Apart from oracles, blockchain data platforms play an important role in the Web 3.0 financial ecosystem, such as Chainalysis[16] and Dune Analytics, which extract key government and market transaction data through on-chain data analysis. Dune Analytics is a powerful blockchain data aggregation and analysis platform specializing in processing and mining vast amounts of data from major blockchain ecosystems. The world's largest blockchain networks generate a massive amount of transaction data daily, including on-chain transfers, smart contract interactions, and token transactions. However, much of this data is difficult for the average user to access and analyze due to the limitations of data structures and blockchain storage complexity. Dune Analytics addresses this gap by offering users a customizable database where blockchain data can be easily converted and queried using SQL database queries. For example, users can analyze Ethereum transactions by tracking wallet addresses and transaction histories, aggregating data over time to gain valuable insights. Through SQL queries, users can directly access and organize structured data without writing complex scripts, significantly lowering the barriers to blockchain data analysis and enabling broader participation in blockchain research and applications.

Beyond providing data query services, Dune Analytics also fosters an active user community, where users can share their data analysis results on the platform. The main page of Dune Analytics highlights user-generated data sets, presenting a variety of statistical data related to major blockchain ecosystems. This includes DeFi project transactions, fluctuations in GAS fees, and aggregated NFT platform statistics, providing valuable insights into blockchain activity trends. Dune Analytics serves as a reference and inspiration hub for users across different domains. Users can explore, copy, and modify datasets and customize their own analytical models based on their specific needs. The platform provides robust query and visualization tools, allowing users to extract and structure complex data. Through advanced SQL queries, users can analyze data at multiple levels, identify relationships between indicators, and gain insights into the correlation between user growth and trading volume in specific DeFi projects. Users can also analyze the trends of NFT trading volumes in different markets. Additionally, Dune Analytics offers rich charting and visualization tools, helping users convert complex datasets into intuitive and digestible visual representations. These features enable

[16] Chainalysis is a leading blockchain data tracking and compliance platform. Currently, it provides regulatory and compliance services for regulatory agencies, exchanges, financial institutions, law enforcement, and security companies in over 70 countries. Its services include monitoring blockchain data flows, risk management and compliance evaluation, as well as developing security solutions for digital assets. It is also actively involved in research on stablecoins, cryptocurrency wallets, and digital payment systems.

researchers and industry analysts in the digital asset space to quickly monitor market trends, detect financial risks, and refine investment strategies. By leveraging on-chain data analytics, users can anticipate potential investment opportunities and market risks, and financial institutions can improve risk models and data-driven decision-making processes for more accurate asset management.

Artificial intelligence technology, particularly machine learning and deep learning, is playing an increasingly important role in modern financial research. These technologies can autonomously learn from complex datasets, predict market trends based on historical data, and significantly enhance the accuracy and efficiency of investment decision-making. In the case of RWA tokenization, artificial intelligence holds massive application potential, given the emergence of new digital asset classes.

Investors can leverage machine learning and deep learning algorithms to analyze real-time transaction data related to RWA tokenization, automatically identifying intrinsic speculative and influencing factors behind price movements. Through continuous training on historical data, AI models can accurately capture asset price fluctuations, assess potential risks and expected returns, and refine investment risk management strategies. These models not only allow for historical data backtesting and validation but also predict future price trends over a specified period, providing strong decision-making support for investors.

Beyond direct price forecasting, artificial intelligence can also integrate multi-source datasets for a more comprehensive evaluation of RWA token investment value and risks. For instance, by incorporating macroeconomic data, market network data, and social media sentiment data, AI models can assess the impact of various external factors on asset prices, identify potential risk events and opportunities, and generate early warning signals and investment recommendations. This multi-dimensional data analysis can help investors construct more stable and risk-managed investment strategies.

The application of artificial intelligence technology in the field of digital assets extends beyond price predictions—it also enables a deeper analysis of trading behaviors and market environments. Through detailed transaction analysis of RWA tokenization, machine learning algorithms can automatically detect irregular trading activities, identify potential fraud, wash trading, and market manipulation, and provide early warnings and alerts to investors and regulatory bodies. Additionally, analyzing relationships between trading clusters and market participants helps determine key market players, price stability, and liquidity conditions, offering comprehensive market intelligence for investment decision-making. Nansen.ai, as a specialized blockchain analytics firm, has integrated machine learning, mathematical modeling, and AI-driven behavioral analysis into its core tools. By identifying smart contract exchange patterns, fund flow trends, and behavioral key indicators, Nansen's analytics tools accurately assess and predict market trends, track the movements of "smart money", and monitor high-net-worth whale accounts. These insights allow investors to anticipate market sentiment and capitalize on emerging investment opportunities. In 2022, Nansen.ai launched its "Price Estimator" product, applying deep learning models to NFT price estimation. By analyzing over

800 NFT collections with detailed metadata and trading history, Price Estimator employs advanced algorithmic models to calculate fair values for NFTs, helping investors distinguish high-value NFTs with strong holding power from speculative assets. This tool significantly improves NFT investment accuracy and reduces decision-making costs for collectors.

A deeper exploration of RWA tokenization reveals not only technical innovations in blockchain infrastructure but also its real-world impact on the global financial system. This new asset class serves as a "bridge" between traditional economies and decentralized finance (DeFi), integrating legal, financial, technological, and data-driven elements. By facilitating precise investment targeting and increasing market efficiency, RWA tokenization presents innovative solutions to longstanding challenges in traditional finance. By applying "RWA 2.4 +" research methodologies, we gain a comprehensive understanding of RWA tokenization's mechanics, intrinsic value propositions, and risk structures. Discussions surrounding RWA token definitions and classifications not only contribute to theoretical frameworks but also shape the future digital economy's role in financial markets. The tokenization of RWAs is not merely about digitizing assets—it also leverages blockchain and smart contracts to ensure transparency, programmability, and auditability. This process is closely tied to legal compliance and regulatory alignment, ensuring that digital assets maintain their legal legitimacy and are widely accepted in financial markets.

In the future, RWA tokenization will be closely integrated with artificial intelligence, big data, and cutting-edge financial technology, further advancing the evolution of financial markets. For example, AI can analyze massive datasets to provide more precise market forecasts and risk assessments. Meanwhile, big data technology enables financial institutions to gain deeper insights into market dynamics and user demand, thereby optimizing financial products that better fit market needs. This fusion of AI and finance will significantly enhance financial product digitization and automation. As a result, RWA tokenization is expected to drive the expansion of financial inclusion, allowing a broader range of individuals and institutions to participate in global financial markets. By leveraging blockchain technology, capital transfers and asset transactions will become more efficient and transparent, reducing trading costs and settlement times. This transformation will help overcome geographic and institutional barriers that have traditionally limited financial services, promoting financial inclusion on a global scale and accelerating the diversification of international financial markets.

In summary, RWA tokenization is not just an important blockchain application—it also represents a fundamental shift in the global financial system. As technologies evolve and financial landscapes change, RWA tokenization will become an increasingly crucial innovation in global capital markets. Through further research and exploration, we can expect to see greater market efficiency, enhanced financial inclusion, and the emergence of new financial innovations that drive broader adoption and employment opportunities worldwide.

Principles of Token Economy and Ecological Development

4

4.1 Basic Theories of Token Economy

With the advancement of digital technology and the continuous growth of industry demand, the *14th Five-Year Plan for National Informatization* emphasizes the "increasing integration of the physical and digital worlds". In this context, the rapid development of the token economy based on blockchain technology is profoundly reshaping social relations and structures. The effective combination of the real world and the digital world has become the focus of research by governments and scholars at home and abroad. This chapter aims to explore the evolution and development of the token economy ecology and analyze the development model of the token economy from the perspective of new institutional economics. Theoretically, this chapter uses new institutional economics to provide a theoretical basis for the operation of the token economy. In practice, this chapter explores how to understand the interaction between the token economy and the social environment, and promote the integration and development of blockchain technology and the token economy, which is of great practical significance for the present and the future.

4.1.1 The Logic of Reality: The Evolution and Development of Token Economics

4.1.1.1 The Connotation and Development of Tokens

The practical application of the concept of token predates the concept itself, and its translation and understanding have evolved over time. Originally, token was translated as "substitute card" and was used to refer to various vouchers and chips as a means of reward to incentivize specific behaviors. In computer science, tokens are translated as "tokens" and are used to carry information such as logins and authentications. It wasn't until 2017 that token was translated as "token", although some scholars argued that this translation did not fully reflect its multifaceted

S. Ba et al., *RWA Tokenisation in Web 3.0 Era*, Management for Professionals,
https://doi.org/10.1007/978-981-96-7663-7_4

nature, and suggested that words such as "co-ticket" or "chain-bond" might be more appropriate. There is also a view that the word "token" combines the two meanings of "pass" and "proof", symbolizing the "pass" with integrity as the core.

Tokens play the role of virtual digital credentials in the blockchain world, representing identity, rights and value, with multiple attributes such as the right to use, the right to earn, the right to participate and the right to vote. Holding the token, individuals can participate in a variety of activities, use, process, and distribute resources.

The development of tokens has gone through three stages: initially, in the Internet era, tokens mainly referred to tokens used for login verification; Subsequently, with the advent of the Ethereum ERC-20 standard, the token evolved into an asset that could be traded directly on exchanges; Now, with the popularization of the term "token", we have ushered in the third phase, and the connotation of the token has been further expanded.

According to the book, a token is a "negotiable credential" or, more accurately, a "circulating cryptographic credential." It consists of three basic elements: first, "equity", which indicates that the token has inherent value, whether it is a tangible commodity, an intangible equity, or a credit or right, which comes from the society's recognition of the credit of the party that endorses its value; The second is "encryption", which guarantees the authenticity of the token by cryptography technology to ensure that it is recognizable and tamper-proof, which is the basis of token circulation; Finally, there is "circulation", which means that the token must be able to flow through the network, allowing for use, transfer, exchange, and trading. Together, these three elements define the essence of the token, making it a unified whole.

4.1.1.2 Blockchain-Based Token Economy Development

Blockchain technology was first introduced in Bitcoin and represents a decentralized, public, and immutable underlying data recording technology. The existence of a token does not change the essence of the blockchain; Conversely, the nature of the token will not change regardless of whether it relies on the blockchain or not. However, it is undeniable that blockchain and tokens constitute the most ideal ecological partners. If the token itself is a circulating certificate, then with the support of blockchain technology and the Internet platform, the existence of the token is no longer just a circulating certificate, but an existence based on its inherent and intrinsic value in the real economy.

Tokens are regarded as one of the most valuable applications of blockchain technology, and blockchain provides systematic security for the operation of the token economy. At present, blockchain-based tokens have been recognized and classified by financial institutions and scholars at home and abroad because of their wide application. For example, the Swiss Financial Market Supervisory Authority (FINMA) divides tokens into payment, application, and asset classes; Most scholars in China tend to accept the SEC's classification, i.e., product or service tokens, reward tokens, utility tokens, and security tokens; Some scholars have also proposed a classification method for payment tokens, utility tokens and security tokens.

Tokens play a central role in the construction of the token economy, and their effectiveness has promoted the gradual emergence of the token economic model. The combination of technology and economics led to a revolutionary change in operations and gave birth to a new economic model - the token economy. This economic model uses the token as an incentive mechanism, using the blockchain platform tool to complete a series of economic activities such as production, distribution, exchange, and consumption, in short, it uses the encrypted digital characteristics of the token to redefine the value-driven economic model of production relations through the incentive mechanism. The token economy is not only an extension of the market economy, but also the embodiment of the transformation of social production relations, which has formed a more advanced form of social production and exchange on the basis of the refinement and standardization of social division of labor. Melanie Swan, founder of the Institute of Blockchain Science, divided the development of blockchain technology into three eras, and found that the emergence of the token economy is closely linked to the development of blockchain technology. The concept of tokens is rooted in the blockchain 1.0 era, and Bitcoin is a payment token with high value and security in the blockchain system; The blockchain 2.0 era was marked by the emergence of the Ethereum network, which opened the era of token economy; The blockchain 3.0 era, on the other hand, will penetrate the token economy into all aspects of social life and lead a comprehensive transformation of the economy and society through the fair application of money, economy and market, as well as the application of efficiency and collaboration.

4.1.2 Theoretical Support of Token Economy: Based on the Theoretical Basis of New Institutional Economics

Token economics is an important concept in blockchain technology, which involves designing and utilizing digital tokens to incentivize and regulate the behavior of network participants. The theoretical foundation of this economic model can mainly be supported by new institutional economics, which emphasizes the impact of institutions on economic activities and the role of costs in economic decision-making.

The main distinction between institutional economics and classical economics lies in the exogenous nature of institutions. It focuses on the interaction between economic activities and institutions as its primary subject of study. Classical institutional economists argue that it is through defining a set of acceptable and unacceptable behaviors that institutions provide a structure for economic exchange, essentially setting the "rules of the game." In the 1960s, Oliver E. Williamson introduced the concept of new institutional economics. Unlike the old institutional school, new institutional economics introduced concepts such as transaction costs and institutional path dependence, more clearly defined key concepts in institutional economics such as property rights, costs, institutions, and agents, and brought about a series of theoretical shifts that gradually integrated it into mainstream economics and garnered widespread attention.

With these theories in place, token economics can be better designed and implemented to promote the healthy development of blockchain technology and its applications. New institutional economics offers a powerful toolkit and perspective to help explain and optimize various phenomena and issues within token economics.

4.1.3 Transaction Cost Theory

When consumers engage in transactions, their focus is often on the utility derived from the established costs rather than on transaction costs. Ronald H. Coase proposed the transaction cost theory in his 1937 paper *The Nature of the Firm.* He argued that "transaction costs should include the costs of measuring, defining, and safeguarding property rights, discovering transaction partners and prices, bargaining, negotiating contracts, and enforcing the strict performance of contract terms," among others. In short, transaction costs refer to the costs or expenses that are incurred but not considered by the transacting parties during the process of establishing commodity exchanges, such as time costs, insurance costs, and others, all of which can be considered as transaction costs. New institutional economics is a field of economic research that focuses on transaction costs, with transaction costs being its most fundamental concept.

So, why are transaction costs closely related to new institutional economics?

New institutional economics is the economic theory that studies the alternation of old and new institutions. The fundamental source of this alternation lies in the improvement of economic efficiency, while the existence of transaction costs can affect the efficiency of market operations. Due to the uncertainty of the real world, the proprietary nature of resource property rights, the bounded rationality of decision-making actors, and the opportunistic tendencies of enterprises, transaction in social operations requires a cost or expense. For example, political transaction costs incurred during the operation and adjustment of political systems, market-type transaction costs when participating in market operations, and management-type transaction costs arising within an organization. In the context of new institutional economics, these transaction costs are treated as sunk costs and incorporated into the traditional supply and demand analysis framework. Transaction costs are identified, calculated, and analyzed, and are incorporated into the decision-making process, thereby achieving efficient resource allocation.

In token economics, the design and application of tokens can significantly reduce transaction costs. This point is supported by new institutional economics, which emphasizes the central role of transaction costs in economic activities. Transaction costs in traditional markets include the costs of finding transaction partners, negotiating contract terms, ensuring contract execution, and supervising and adapting to contract changes. These costs are especially high in environments with information asymmetry and a lack of trust.

Tokenization reduces these costs in various ways, such as by automating contract execution, increasing transaction speed, reducing the involvement of intermediary institutions, and lowering information asymmetry and search costs. Smart contracts allow contract terms to be automatically executed, reducing the costs of supervision and enforcement while lowering the likelihood of breach. Blockchain technology accelerates transaction validation and increases market liquidity. Its decentralized nature allows the two parties to transact directly, without relying on intermediary institutions, thereby saving costs and time.

Blockchain technology is the core that enables token economics to achieve these advantages. Its decentralized characteristic not only enhances the system's security and resistance to interference but also strengthens the trust between market participants through transparency. Furthermore, blockchain simplifies cross-border transaction processes and reduces the complexity involving multiple banks and payment processing institutions, which is particularly important for global transactions.

In conclusion, the tokenization in token economics and the application of blockchain technology not only align with the theory of transaction costs in new institutional economics but also promote the practical application of economic theory. This signals the emergence of a more efficient, transparent, and fair economic operational model. The popularization and application of these technologies are reshaping the transaction structure and cost framework of the global economy.

4.1.4 Property Rights Theory

The essence of property rights is a social relationship. Human society is an organic whole in which people interact and communicate with one another. Only in such an organic whole is there a necessity for individuals to respect each other's property rights. From the perspective of new institutional economics, property rights are a type of right, and as a fundamental rule of society, they define the reciprocal relationships between individuals.

Property rights economist Armen A. Alchian stated, "Property rights are the rights to use an economic good, enforced by society." The essence of property rights is a series of incentive and constraint mechanisms, which further influence and motivate behavior. Different structures of property rights produce different incentives, leading to different efficiency outcomes. Property rights include ownership, income rights, usage rights, disposal rights, etc., and are a bundle of rights. The occurrence of a transaction means the exchange of two bundles of rights. New institutional economics believes that the differences in property rights bundles in transactions result in different exchange values for goods. Property arrangements directly affect resource allocation efficiency, and the incentives for individuals directly affect the economic efficiency of society.

Property rights theory is a core component of new institutional economics. It explores how property arrangements influence the effective allocation of economic resources. Property rights not only cover ownership of physical assets but also include the rights to use, control, and transfer assets. This theory emphasizes that the clear definition and protection of property rights are fundamental to ensuring smooth market transactions and efficient resource allocation.

In token economics, the concept of digital tokens provides a new practical domain for property rights theory. Digital tokens can be viewed as a special form of property rights, granting holders control and usage rights over network resources. These tokens are not only a medium of exchange but also represent a form of resource control. For instance, certain tokens may grant holders voting or governance rights on a blockchain platform, directly influencing the allocation and usage strategies of the platform's resources.

From the perspective of property rights theory, the rights of token holders in token economics share many similarities with the rights of traditional asset owners, but they also have unique features. Tokenized assets allow property rights to be divided into smaller units, enhancing asset liquidity while enabling more precise control and management. For example, governance tokens allow holders to vote on key decisions such as network upgrades and the use of funds. Essentially, this mechanism decentralizes economic decision-making power to multiple participants in the network.

With the help of blockchain technology, token economics ensures the clear definition and protection of property rights. The immutable and transparent nature of blockchain means that once ownership of a token is recorded on the chain, this ownership is difficult to alter illegally. This technology ensures clear and traceable asset ownership, reducing uncertainty and transaction costs for both parties involved in a transaction.

Additionally, the smart contract technology in token economics further strengthens the protection and enforcement of property rights. Smart contracts can automatically execute contract terms, meaning that once the conditions for the transfer or usage rights of property are met, the related actions will occur automatically without relying on third-party enforcement.

In summary, token economics, through blockchain and smart contract technologies, provides a new mechanism for the expression and protection of property rights. This not only changes the way asset ownership and usage rights are managed but also promotes improved resource allocation efficiency. Through these technologies, property rights theory in new institutional economics has found new application scenarios and practical opportunities in the modern economy.

4.1.5 Enterprise Theory

In neoclassical economic theory, the production system is a single market mechanism, with no analysis of the existence of firms or their internal organization. Coase, using the tool of transaction cost analysis, expanded the production system into a dual system comprising both firms and markets, which are in a substitute relationship with each other. This marked the beginning of new institutional economics' in-depth study of the existence and governance of firms. Currently, two major fields have emerged: from the perspective of the firm's transaction function, the transaction cost economics of firms, represented by Coase and Williamson, and the property rights economics of firms, represented by Sanford Grossman, Oliver Hart, and John Moore; from the perspective of the firm's function, the team production theory of firms, represented by Harold Demsetz and Alchian. The operation of the market mechanism requires cost support, and the emergence of firms created the preconditions for saving market operation costs.

As an organization, a firm allows entrepreneurs to act as authorities in controlling resources, which helps save transaction costs. Both market mechanisms and firms are means of resource allocation, and they can substitute for each other. Their fundamental driving force is derived from the savings in transaction costs. So, does this mean that firms can endlessly expand to save transaction costs? Certainly not. Firms also have management costs, and when the cost of organizing transactions within a firm equals the cost of market transactions, the firm's size reaches its optimal level.

Contract theory is an important branch of enterprise theory that delves into the operational mechanisms of the firm as a contractual structure. This theory posits that the relationships both within and between firms can essentially be viewed as a series of contracts aimed at coordinating the interests of all parties and alleviating potential conflicts of interest. In this way, contract theory provides a framework for understanding the structure, strategy, and behavior of firms.

In token economics, smart contract technology offers an innovative contract execution mechanism. Smart contracts are self-executing, immutable programs that run on blockchain platforms, ensuring the accurate execution of contract terms without the need for third-party intermediaries. These contracts typically involve the allocation, use, and governance of tokens, directly relating to the core activities of token economics. By encoding contract terms into transparent, self-executing code, smart contracts significantly improve the efficiency and credibility of contract execution, reducing supervision and enforcement costs.

Incentive compatibility theory, as another important branch of enterprise theory, focuses on how to design incentive mechanisms to ensure that the goals of all parties align with the overall goals of the organization. In token economics, the application of this theory is particularly crucial because the design and distribution of tokens directly influence participants' behavior and the overall function of the network. For example, by offering token rewards or dividends, users can be incentivized to participate in network maintenance, voting decisions, or other key activities, thus promoting the healthy and sustainable development of the ecosystem.

New institutional economics provides tools for analyzing and designing governance structures from a more macro perspective. It examines the impact of different governance forms (such as markets, hierarchies, and networks) on economic efficiency and resource allocation. In token economics, the application of governance tokens allows token holders to participate in the decision-making process through voting, thus influencing the direction of platform development collectively. This governance structure emphasizes transparency and participation, aiming to resolve potential conflicts of interest through a collective decision-making mechanism and improve the system's adaptability and responsiveness.

In conclusion, through the lens of contract theory and incentive compatibility theory, we can gain a deeper understanding of firm behavior and structure in token economics. The application of smart contracts not only demonstrates how technology can optimize the functions of traditional contracts but also highlights the innovation of token economics in designing effective incentive and governance mechanisms. The integration of these theories and technologies provides a more efficient, transparent, and participatory operational model for the modern economic system.

4.1.6 Theory of Institutional Change

The theory of institutional change is an important part of new institutional economics. Its representative figure, Douglass North, argues that long-term economic growth and social development are inseparable from the decisive role of institutions. While technological development and innovation drive economic growth, relying solely on technological innovation is insufficient for long-term economic development. It is only when people have an awareness of institutional innovation and change, and further consolidate the achievements of technological innovation through the establishment of institutions, that long-term economic and social development can be promoted. The three main pillars of the theory of institutional change are property rights theory, state theory, and ideology theory. The reasons for institutional change, the origin of institutions, and the dynamics, process, and forms of institutional change are all important aspects of the theory. Institutional change is a process where a relatively higher-yielding institution substitutes a lower-yielding institution, and thus, reducing transaction costs is one of the causes of institutional change.

New institutional economics posits that institutions are key factors influencing economic behavior and economic performance. Token economics, as an emerging economic model, can be seen as part of institutional change, as its development and popularization may impact existing economic systems and even trigger new institutional innovations.

New institutional economics emphasizes the profound influence of institutions (including laws, norms, policies, and cultural customs) on economic behavior and performance. Institutions provide behavioral norms and transaction frameworks, thus reducing uncertainty, lowering transaction costs, and facilitating effective economic activities. Token economics, as an emerging economic model based on blockchain technology, not only introduces tokens as a medium of exchange but also reshapes the fundamental rules of transactions and economic cooperation through smart contracts and decentralized operational models.

The development and popularization of token economics itself is a manifestation of institutional change. It challenges traditional financial and economic systems, providing an alternative way of economic interaction. For example, by using tokens, token economics allows value to be transferred rapidly and securely without traditional financial intermediaries. This mechanism reduces transaction costs and increases market inclusivity, enabling individuals and businesses anywhere in the world to directly participate in international markets.

Furthermore, token economics may also promote institutional innovation. Due to the transparency and immutability based on blockchain, token economics offers a new way to enhance trust and contract enforcement, which could stimulate the development of new legal and regulatory frameworks. For instance, as token economics expands, governments and international organizations may need to establish new laws to regulate token issuance, circulation, and its relationship with traditional currencies. At the same time, token economics raises new questions about power structures and asset distribution in society. Tokenization can enhance asset liquidity, potentially redistributing economic resources and affecting the economic structure of society. This possibility requires new social consensus and institutional design to ensure that the benefits brought by economic change are fairly distributed and to mitigate potential social tensions.

Token economics is not only a form of economic activity from the perspective of new institutional economics but also an example and catalyst of institutional change. Its development not only changes the way transactions and value storage occur but could also trigger broader changes in economic and social systems. This calls for policymakers, economists, and all sectors of society to closely monitor this transformation, understand its potential impact, and actively participate in the design and implementation of new institutions.

4.1.7 Asymmetric Information Problem Theory and Signaling Theory

Institutional economics is a discipline that studies how economic institutions affect economic behavior. Among its important components are the theories of asymmetric information and signaling. The theory of asymmetric information primarily focuses on the asymmetry of information held by the parties in an economic transaction. This information asymmetry can lead to market failure, such as the "lemon market" phenomenon, where lower-quality goods push higher-quality goods out of the market. To address the problems caused by information asymmetry, economic agents often adopt various signaling mechanisms to prove the quality of their products or services or their own reliability.

Signaling theory, developed by Michael Spence, arose from his study of how education can serve as a signal to help employers identify the abilities of potential employees. In this theoretical framework, individuals or firms with high-quality characteristics send signals through high-cost activities, such as obtaining higher education certificates or providing high-cost warranty services, to distinguish themselves from lower-quality competitors. This signaling helps reduce information asymmetry in the market and improves overall market efficiency.

In institutional economics, both asymmetric information and signaling theory jointly explain how institutions affect the decision-making of economic agents and market efficiency. Relevant departments can reduce information asymmetry by designing institutions (such as laws, regulations, and industry standards), and by mandating information disclosure or establishing quality certification systems to help consumers and investors make more informed decisions. At the same time, these institutions shape the cost and credibility of signals, further influencing market operations and resource allocation efficiency.

In token economics, the issuance and holding of tokens not only represent the medium of financial transactions but also carry important informational functions that are crucial for understanding and assessing a particular project or network. The design of the token itself—such as its total supply, issuance mechanism, distribution method, and how tokens can be acquired through various activities—reflects the creator's long-term vision and operational strategy for the project. For example, a token with a limited supply may aim to create scarcity, increasing the expected value for holders, while a token that can be earned through complex algorithms or community contributions may emphasize fairness and community participation.

In addition, the token distribution mechanism (i.e., how initial investors, developers, partners, or users are selected to receive tokens first) also conveys important signals. A fair and transparent distribution mechanism can enhance external confidence in the overall health and potential value of the project. If tokens are primarily concentrated in a few addresses, it may raise concerns in the market about manipulation or excessive centralization, thus affecting the project's credibility and attractiveness.

In practice, project teams often use various communication strategies to reinforce these signals. For example, they may release detailed white papers to describe the token's uses, technical details, and future roadmap. Through social media, community discussions, and the establishment of partnerships, project teams can further enhance the visibility and impact of their signals.

Ultimately, the effective transmission of these signals and the market's response together shapes the token's market performance. Investors and users are not only evaluating the market price of a token but also analyzing the deeper information embedded within these complex signals, such as the project's sustainability, the credibility of the team, and the overall health of the network ecosystem. Therefore, in the token economy, the issuance and holding of tokens become a key strategic tool, not only used for fundraising but also as a significant indicator of the project's success or failure.

4.1.8 Token Economic Efficiency Analysis

We apply contract theory from new institutional economics, combined with the working principles and model characteristics of token blockchain technology, to analyze the impact of tokens on economic efficiency. In new institutional economics, the concept of a contract refers to treating all market transactions (whether long-term or short-term, explicit or implicit) as a contractual relationship, which is a fundamental element of economic analysis.

4.1.9 Transaction Costs

One important method for measuring the efficiency of an economic model or transaction behavior is to examine the size of its transaction costs. Below, we apply transaction cost theory (TCT) from contract theory to analyze the impact of blockchain technology applications on transaction costs. Unlike incomplete contract theory (ICT), transaction cost theory posits that economic agents can make choices among different governance structures (market, hybrid forms, firms) during transactions, rather than making selections among a series of contracts. At the same time, a key condition for transactions is asset specificity (i.e., assets that are locked for specific purposes are difficult to repurpose; otherwise, their value would decrease or become worthless). To discuss the transaction costs of different governance structures (including blockchain), we will use the model developed by Riordan MH and Williamson. Specifically, it is as follows:

When there are transaction costs, the transaction costs for different governance structures are as follows: $TC_M = v(A)$, $TC_{Hy} = \beta_0 + w(A)$, $TC_F = \beta_1 + x(A)$. *The* subscripts M, Hy and F represent governance structures as market, hybrid form, and company. β_0 and β_1 are the fixed costs of the selected governance structure, with $\beta_1 > \beta_0 > 0$; *v(A)*,*w(A)* and *x (A)* is increasing functions of specific assets, and $\frac{\partial v(A)}{\partial A} > \frac{\partial w(A)}{\partial A} > \frac{\partial x(A)}{\partial A} > 0$.

From Fig. 4.1, it can be seen that assuming the uncertainty and frequency of transactions remain unchanged, v(A), w(A), and x(A) represent the governance structures of the market, the hybrid form of market and company, and the company, where A denotes the degree of asset specificity. Since blockchain is a decentralized system with no central node, and all nodes in the network are equal in transactions, its governance structure is similar to that of a market. On the one hand, compared with traditional economic models or transaction behaviors (which are primarily governed by hybrid forms of market and company or by companies), the market has the lowest transaction costs. Therefore, blockchain transaction costs are extremely low. On the other hand, since transactions in a blockchain system are open and free, when a node with transaction demand submits a transaction request in the network, other nodes willing to transact will immediately respond and complete the transaction. As a result, asset specificity is almost nonexistent, and transaction costs approach zero.

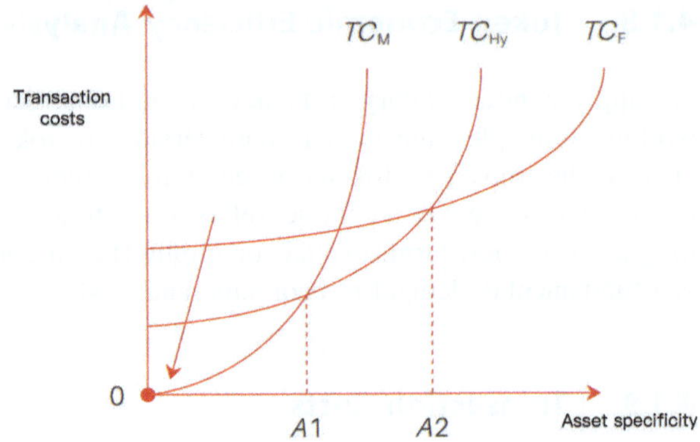

Fig. 4.1 Analysis of transaction costs and asset specificity

4.1.10 Contract Fulfillment

Transaction efficiency is also reflected in the fulfillment of transaction contracts, that is, whether the relevant rights and obligations are fully performed in accordance with the terms of the contract in a timely manner. Next, we use Benjamin Klein's self-enforcing contract model to analyze the impact of blockchain technology on contract fulfillment in transactions.

In a transaction, traders will compare the short-term benefits (*W1*) gained from violating the transaction contract with the present value (*W2*) of the future profit stream lost due to the termination of the business. When the condition $W1 < W2$ is met, contract fulfillment can be guaranteed. *W2* is the capital cost of the expected future profit stream that the other party may lose when sanctions for non-performance are applied, which is the reputation cost of the trader. The expression is as follows: $W_2 = \prod_0 + \prod_1 /(1+r) + \prod_2 /(1+r)^2 + \ldots$. It can be seen that the reputation capital of the parties to the transaction determines the effectiveness of the self-enforcing mechanism.

When applying blockchain technology to token transactions, on one hand, due to the immutability and transparency of the blockchain, once a trader engages in actions detrimental to the transaction or defaults, due to the data being unalterable, historical transactions being traceable, and information being publicly available across the network, people will avoid transacting with them in the future. Therefore, the trader's reputation cost is very high. On the other hand, because the current blockchain application of smart contract technology in different market transactions embeds the rights, obligations, and triggering conditions of the contract participants into both hardware and software, it allows the transaction contract to be automatically executed and terminated according to the computer program, thus making the cost of default high enough to deter such behavior. Therefore, transactions using blockchain technology possess a powerful self-enforcing mechanism. Additionally, using blockchain technology in transaction contracts further avoids the significant social costs associated with traditional transactions, such as filing lawsuits or enforcing court orders due to default.

4.1.11 Information Asymmetry

Another important factor affecting efficiency in economic models or transaction behaviors is information asymmetry. During the process of contract formation, some information is known to one party but unknown to the other, and even third parties cannot verify it (even if verification is possible, it would incur a high cost and be economically inefficient). However, this information can affect the efficiency of the transaction and the interests of both parties. Depending on when the information asymmetry occurs, it can be divided into adverse selection and moral hazard. Adverse selection occurs before the transaction, while moral hazard arises after the transaction.

Throughout history, to improve transaction efficiency and maximize their own benefits, people have been committed to solving the information asymmetry problem in transactions. This includes designing contract terms in advance to constrain the behavior of both parties, and manually verifying the true situation of the trading parties during contract execution. However, due to natural limitations and self-interest, the information asymmetry problem in transactions has always existed. Therefore, various methods should be used to address this issue.

Blockchain technology can effectively address the problem of information asymmetry. First, in a blockchain system, all network nodes are transparent and visible. The final confirmation of transactions is guaranteed by a consensus algorithm, ensuring consistency across all nodes. This makes the entire system fair, transparent, and trustworthy for all participants, maintaining information symmetry between transacting parties. Second, since every transaction on the blockchain is fully recorded, traders can easily review past transactions. This significantly reduces the risk of adverse selection and helps identify the most suitable counterparties. Additionally, blockchain data is immutable, meaning all transaction records—whether positive or negative—are permanently stored in each block. This increases the cost of malicious behavior, thereby reducing the moral hazard that may arise after transactions. As a result, blockchain serves as an ideal solution to mitigating information asymmetry in transactions.

4.1.12 DAO Organizations and Tokens

In the evolution of blockchain technology, smart currency (digital fiat currency) represents the 1.0 stage of the blockchain economy, marking the digitization of money. Smart contracts define the 2.0 stage, signifying the automation of contractual agreements. Further, the rise of smart communities represents the 3.0 stage of blockchain economy, surpassing traditional corporate models and aligning with the concept of Decentralized Autonomous Organizations (DAOs). This innovation in organizational structure represents a major breakthrough, much like how the corporate system significantly expanded human economic cooperation during the Industrial Revolution.

According to American economist J. Bradford DeLong, nearly 97% of human wealth has been created within just two to three centuries after the Industrial Revolution. The emergence of corporate systems coincided with the rise of the British Industrial Revolution and played a critical role in economic development. The invention of the limited liability company facilitated large-scale human collaboration, while the introduction of the joint-stock company transformed corporations into public platforms, enabling the transfer and circulation of equity. For instance, in large infrastructure projects such as highway construction, joint-stock companies provide an effective mechanism for raising capital. Investors can participate in development through equity investment and can also exit through stock transfers.

However, the core issue of the nature and boundaries of a company lies in transaction costs. Ronald Coase, the founder of institutional economics, once posed a question: If the market is so perfect, why do firms still exist? Why are organizational frameworks such as corporations and contracts necessary? In 1937, Coase introduced the concept of "transaction costs," which encompasses the costs required for market transactions or the price mechanism, such as bargaining, contract formation, and execution. The reason enterprises emerge is that internal management costs are lower than market transaction costs. However, the expansion of an enterprise's scale is not unlimited. When management costs exceed profits, the enterprise may face collapse, a concept known as Coase's ceiling theory. Therefore, when the marginal cost of internal coordination and management equals the marginal cost of market transactions, the enterprise has reached its limit in scale.

New institutional economists further extended Coase's theory of transaction costs to explain the existence of states and their boundaries with the market. According to this theory, the magnitude of transaction costs can be used to differentiate between state mechanisms, enterprise mechanisms, and market mechanisms. However, in reality, there exist economic organizational forms that transcend these three mechanisms, such as social enterprises in Western countries. These organizations are neither traditional enterprises nor state institutions but rather social entities that combine corporate characteristics, government mandates, and public interests. Additionally, institutions like the Federal Reserve function both as private enterprises and as public institutions. Some economic activities, such as currency issuance, financial transactions, internet infrastructure, and social security funds, are either linked to public interests, government interests, social welfare, or global concerns. If these activities are managed through state mechanisms, they may suffer from inefficient resource allocation. If handled through enterprise mechanisms, they may lack appeal due to high investment requirements, long cycles, and low returns. The complexity of these economic operations and the involvement of multiple stakeholders drive up transaction costs and reduce the effectiveness of macroeconomic regulation under enterprise, market, and state mechanisms.

DAO may be the fourth major institutional innovation following state mechanisms, market mechanisms, and enterprise mechanisms. By lowering transaction costs and optimizing resource allocation, DAOs help balance the conflict between the state and the market. A DAO is a self-operating organization based on a set of open and fair rules, requiring no external intervention. These rules typically exist in the form of open-source software, allowing individuals to become stakeholders by purchasing tokens or providing services. Stakeholders can participate in the organization's operations and development while sharing its benefits. Compared to traditional enterprises, DAOs operate with greater automation and flexibility, with equity represented in the form of tokens within the system. This simplifies corporate structures and reduces transaction costs. The tokens representing DAO equity can circulate rapidly, and their value is determined by the market, further reducing transaction costs.

Historically, double-entry bookkeeping, corporate systems, and the protection of private property laid the foundation for the rise of capitalism, becoming the cornerstone of modern commercial society. With the advent of cryptocurrencies, DLTs, and distributed autonomous organizations, they are bound to have a profound impact on the structure and operation of modern commercial society.

The relationship between tokens and DAOs is one of the key interactions in the blockchain space, and together they shape a new type of organizational and economic structure. In this structure, tokens are not only a tool for delivering value but also a key governance and incentive mechanism.

In a DAO, tokens are primarily used for the distribution of voting rights. Holding more tokens means having a greater voice and influence in the DAO's decision-making process. This token-based governance mechanism democratizes the distribution of power, allowing all community members to participate in making important decisions. Additionally, tokens serve as an incentive to reward members who contribute resources, complete tasks, or engage in governance for the DAO. This incentive mechanism not only enhances the vitality of the ecosystem but also promotes the long-term development of the organization.

DAO raise the capital needed for their launch and operations by issuing tokens, similar to stock offerings in traditional businesses. Token holders expect to receive returns upon the project's success, closely linking their interests to the project's outcome. In some DAO, tokens also function as internal currency for purchasing services or products or for trading among members, thereby enhancing the economic independence and circularity within the DAO.

However, the use of tokens in DAO also presents challenges. For instance, excessive concentration of token holdings may lead to a centralization of governance power, which contradicts the decentralized spirit of DAO. Moreover, the volatility of the token economy may impact the stability and predictability of the DAO. Despite these challenges, the deep integration between tokens and DAO signals a future of a more transparent, efficient, and decentralized economic system. As blockchain technology and smart contracts continue to evolve, we can foresee this relationship becoming even closer, jointly driving the innovation and evolution of economic models.

4.2 Model and Design of Token Economic Ecology

Tokenomics is an emerging field that integrates the concept of tokens with economic theory, with its core closely tied to economics. This discipline focuses on analyzing the interactions between individuals and tokens, particularly the processes of cryptocurrency issuance, distribution, and elimination. Economics is typically divided into microeconomics and macroeconomics; this book will primarily examine the internal mechanisms of Bitcoin and Ethereum—two specific blockchains—from a microeconomic perspective.

Just as central banks regulate the money supply through monetary policy, tokenomics applies similar principles to the cryptocurrency space. These policies form the cornerstone of a monetary system, which may face the risk of collapse if not carefully designed. In tokenomics, rules are enforced through code, and since any modifications require consensus among numerous network participants, changing these rules is extremely difficult. This decentralized protocol design makes cryptocurrencies, to some extent, more predictable than central bank-issued currencies. For example, the rate and schedule of currency issuance are predetermined, while the burn rate (i.e., the rate at which tokens are removed from circulation) is also somewhat predictable. Compared to fiat currencies, these characteristics provide cryptocurrency investors and holders with greater transparency.

The design of tokenomics encompasses various aspects, including token creation, introduction into circulation, and removal from circulation. Incentive mechanisms play a crucial role in this process. How can network participants be motivated to perform the desired actions? For instance, in order to record transactions on the blockchain, miners must be compensated with transaction fees. Similarly, in order to encourage people to stake their tokens to help validate the network, they must be rewarded accordingly. This design aims to guide user interactions within the network, ensuring its healthy operation and the active participation of stakeholders.

4.2.1 Model of the Token Economic Ecology

As a medium for transferring energy (value) within the token economic ecosystem, tokens represent a value system anchored in real-world assets. In a well-developed token economic ecosystem, tokens serve diverse roles, influencing various aspects of both economic and social structures. As an innovative economic model, the token economy quantifies rights, obligations, and responsibilities within the economic and social framework, enabling incentive mechanisms to extend to all participants within the ecosystem. By driving institutional reform, it compels the redistribution of production relations, ensures a sustainable cycle of energy within the system, and promotes the comprehensive and balanced development of the socio-economic ecosystem. To better understand the role of each component within this ecosystem, we categorize it into economic ecology and social ecology, which will be discussed separately.

4.2.2 Economic Ecology

Economic ecology represents the initial form of the token economic ecosystem. It is the economic drive that fuels the growth of token economies. The reason why economic ecology is considered the initial form is that the current viable and experimental approach to implementing token economies begins with projects issuing tokens on public blockchains. While we continue to explore the future directions of token economies, the pioneers of blockchain have taken the first bold step, bringing this emerging concept into the public eye.

As illustrated in Fig. 4.2, within the economic ecology of tokens, tokens continue to serve as a means of energy transmission, linking various business chains. Enterprises—specifically, the project teams that issue tokens—act as producers, leveraging blockchain as a technological infrastructure to integrate into the broader economic system through token issuance. By assuming different roles, tokens undergo continuous price discovery and value appreciation while also interacting with external value systems. This process of price discovery is also the mechanism through which consumers gradually engage with and contribute to the ecosystem. Through value exchanges with other consumers or producers, tokens achieve circulation within the economy.

In this process, tokenized goods or services exist on the blockchain in the form of tokens. The inherent security, immutability, and unique trust mechanisms of blockchain enable seamless and unrestricted exchanges of these assets, allowing the value network to transcend traditional boundaries. This facilitates the realization of the Pareto optimality effect across individuals, organizations, and even society at large—maximizing overall welfare.

In the economic ecology, consumers and producers simultaneously act as value decomposers—consumers spend tokens, thereby transferring value back to producers. Meanwhile, as token circulation expands and its application scenarios continue to evolve, the token's intrinsic value is continuously discovered and reflected in

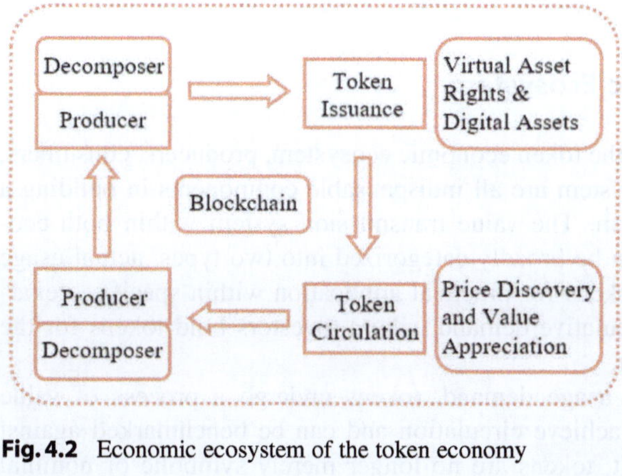

Fig. 4.2 Economic ecosystem of the token economy

its price. When enterprises gain additional resources due to the rising value of tokens, they can further expand their business operations, strengthen their capabilities, develop more ecosystem applications, and issue additional tokens, increasing the overall circulation and utility of their tokens.

4.2.3 Social Ecology

Compared to economic ecology, social ecology represents a more advanced stage of development. The primary reason for this distinction is that for the token economy to achieve widespread societal adoption, it must first gain broad public recognition and acceptance. A strong foundation of public awareness and understanding is essential for its successful integration into society.

At the same time, the endorsement of government authorities and the establishment of a well-structured token economic ecosystem are prerequisites for the development of social ecology. In a healthy token-based social ecology, producers are government entities or relevant institutions that issue tokens based on behavioral metrics or policy-driven initiatives. Unlike economic ecology, social ecology is not profit-driven, nor is a token's utility measured by its liquidity.

Governments issue tokens to maximize social welfare or promote social equity, and blockchain-based tokenomics provides the technological infrastructure to support this goal. The general public, as consumers of social tokens, typically utilize these tokens to access corresponding social benefits. Notably, in many cases, tokens also serve as behavioral incentives or regulatory tools—acting as a benchmark to encourage or discourage certain behaviors within society.

This concept can be compared to land division in nature—only when land is properly allocated and regulated can ecosystems thrive efficiently. As illustrated in Fig. 4.3, similar to economic ecology, energy within social ecology is either decomposed or accumulated through value exchanges between consumers and producers. This dynamic enables society to function more effectively, ultimately advancing towards a fairer and more prosperous state.

4.2.4 Token Economic Ecosystem

From a macro perspective of the token economic ecosystem, producers, consumers, and the value transmission system are all indispensable components in building a stable and evolving ecosystem. The value transmission system within both economic and social ecology can be broadly categorized into two types: actual usage demand, where users hold tokens for practical application within specific scenarios, and investment and speculative demand, where investors hold tokens for the purpose of asset appreciation.

At the level of fulfilling usage demand, tokens undergo a process of value creation, during which they achieve circulation and can be benchmarked against real-world assets. As a result, tokens are no longer merely symbolic or nominal

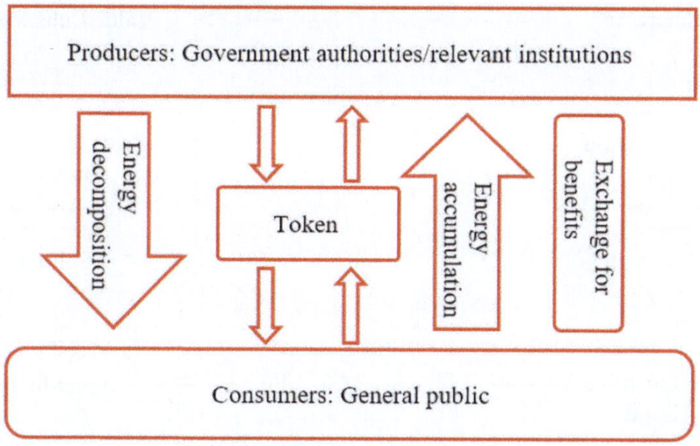

Fig. 4.3 Social ecosystem of the token economy

concepts. Users within the community reach a broad consensus on accepting the token, and the exchange process completes the cycle of value creation.

At the investment demand level, tokens facilitate the process of price discovery. Investors in this market dynamic only focus on whether their tokens will appreciate in value over time, rather than on the token's real-world applications. Investors seek capital preservation, while speculators enhance token liquidity through continuous trading.

By drawing an analogy to Irving Fisher's Quantity Theory of Money, there is a positive correlation between token liquidity and price levels. Thus, as the liquidity of a token increases, its price rises, boosting users' confidence in the token and creating positive incentives for greater holding and usage. Simultaneously, as more users adopt the token, issuers gain confidence, and the rising token price provides them with additional capital to build a more mature and extensive ecosystem, expanding the token's utility scenarios. As a result, the token's value appreciation further attracts investors and speculators, reinforcing a self-sustaining positive incentive cycle.

As shown in Fig. 4.4, the positive incentive self-reinforcing cycle of the token ecosystem is theoretically feasible. However, in practice, if the price of a token continues to rise, using it to offset transaction fees becomes less cost-effective for users. When users simultaneously have both investment and usage needs, the theoretical upward spiral of the ecosystem becomes internally contradictory. Economics suggests that human beings hold multi-dimensional value perspectives, and individuals have varying needs. Consequently, the motivations for holding tokens also differ. When individuals with diverse needs objectively exist, this diversity in choices helps explain the discrepancies between theoretical models and real-world outcomes.

In the future, there will be more forms of ecosystems waiting for us to explore to solve the various problems that exist in the world today. It may be that this form

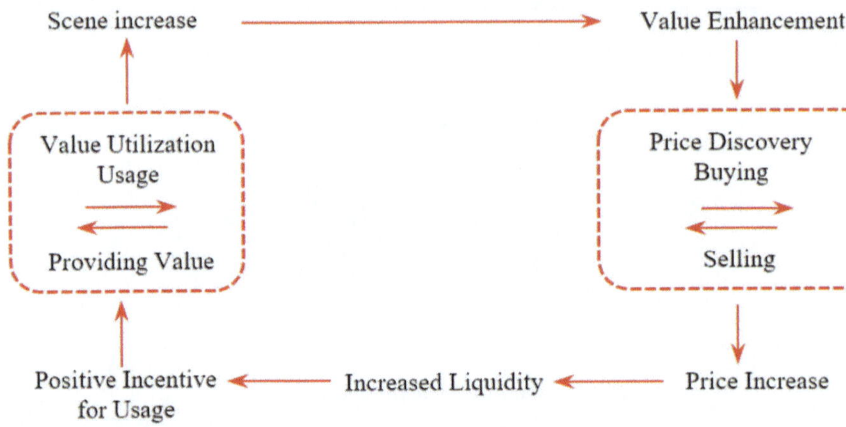

Fig. 4.4 Value transmission system of the token ecosystem

of token does not belong to the economic ecology, nor does it belong to the social ecology completely, and such tokens may carry profound significance in a broader global context. For example, there may be a "fan" group-based token structured as loyalty to an idol. Such tokens could ensure that fans with higher loyalty have a greater chance of purchasing concert tickets for their idols or participating in "fan" meetups. This form of token ensures fairness within the group to a certain extent, and also improves the efficiency of the group to a greater extent, thereby preventing the waste of resources caused by ticket scalpers inflating prices. While there are some aspects in common with socio-ecological roles, the significance of tokens is not entirely the same.

In short, although the form of tokens will become increasingly diversified and their significance more specialized, their fundamental purpose, in a broad sense, remains to uphold social fairness, enhance economic and social efficiency, and engage stakeholders to achieve a healthy and stable ecosystem. Furthermore, a well-developed token system fosters a virtuous cycle of community autonomy and serves as a foundation for community governance. Once a shared-interest community is established, its members will collectively bear risks and share benefits, making community decision-making and voting more efficient. The blockchain community facilitates value exchange between users and projects, while internet platforms provide an information exchange mechanism, and these two driving forces together form a well-structured token economic ecosystem. Therefore, the new applications of the token economy aim to integrate token exchange, platform functions, industrial roles, communities, and users within both economic and social ecosystems, enabling community self-governance and transactional oversight, ultimately forming a new token economic ecosystem (see Fig. 4.5).

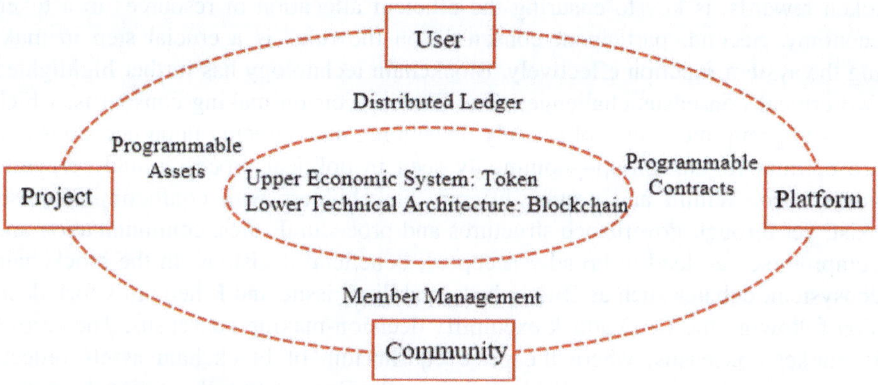

Fig. 4.5 Token economic ecosystem

4.2.5 The Design of the Token Economic Ecology

The design of the token economy is an emerging concept with vast development potential, poised to drive economic and social transformation. It is by no means merely "old wine in a new bottle." From the perspective of token utility, blockchain technology enables low-cost, high-efficiency, and low-transaction-fee rights verification, allowing individual ownership rights to be digitized. This, in turn, enhances transaction processes, making them more convenient, cost-effective, and efficient. Therefore, exploring the practical application and widespread adoption of tokens is an inherent pursuit of human progress. The fundamental requirement is to establish a well-structured and robust token economic system that fully leverages the utility of tokens.

4.2.6 Underlying System Design

The quality of a system's design is often evaluated based on whether it can achieve a Nash equilibrium. If a system enables participants to reach equilibrium through repeated interactions, it is considered a well-designed system. Conversely, if a system perpetually leads participants into conflict without ever achieving a stable equilibrium, it is deemed a poorly designed system. The design of a token economic system involves creating a small-scale regulatory ecosystem, where, under predetermined rules, the desired order—such as emphasizing freedom, incentives, exchange, and individuality—can be established. Therefore, the underlying system design is fundamental to the token economy.

For a local economy to function as a token economy, issuing tokens is essential. First, as a unit of behavioral measurement and a medium for incentives and penalties, tokens must have a tangible form; otherwise, they lose significance. Thus, the incentive mechanism, in which participants perform specific actions to earn token rewards, is key to ensuring the efficient allocation of resources in a token economy. Second, participant consensus on the rules is a crucial step in making the system function effectively. Blockchain technology has further highlighted two critical consensus challenges. The first is decision-making consensus, which refers to group members collectively developing and agreeing upon decisions that are optimal for the group—commonly seen in political processes and corporate governance. Within any group, different stakeholders with conflicting interests exist, yet through governance structures and procedural rules, communication and compromise can lead to broadly accepted, beneficial decisions. In the blockchain ecosystem, debates such as Bitcoin's "scalability" issue and Ethereum's fork decision following the DAO attack exemplify decision-making consensus. The second is market consensus, where the price equilibrium of blockchain assets reflects collective market sentiment. If blockchain technology is to fully realize the potential of tokenization and reshape economic structures, addressing decision-making consensus and market consensus is imperative.

4.2.7 Exchange Economy Core

The token economy is generally built around an exchange economy core, with other activities revolving around it. Exchange economy refers to an economic structure in which, under a given production framework, economic agents engage in trade by exchanging their respective goods or redistributing society's total resources and products among themselves to maximize overall social welfare.

The exchange economy exists due to differences in resource endowments and the division of labor among individuals. With the advent of the Internet era, the concept of the Internet exchange economy has emerged, driven by advancements in Internet technology. In this framework, the objects of exchange refer to the goods being traded, while the participants are the suppliers and demanders of these goods. The medium of exchange is typically fiat currency, but it can also be virtual currency or even a medium that lacks traditional monetary characteristics. The foundation of the exchange economy lies in the transfer of ownership of exchanged goods and the medium of exchange between suppliers and demanders, the information system governing exchange participants—including transaction purpose, counterparties, and quantities—and the resource allocation mechanism, which must account for participants' endowments and preferences to facilitate an efficient match between supply and demand.

The token economy, leveraging blockchain's decentralized and disintermediated nature, utilizes tokens as the medium of exchange. This allows individuals to transfer value in a trustless environment without relying on third-party intermediaries, eliminates information barriers between enterprises, and enhances information flow across organizations. These characteristics significantly reduce social transaction costs and address economic constraints such as information asymmetry and bounded rationality present in traditional economic models. Consequently, this structure has the potential to establish a new economic paradigm in the digital information era.

4.2.8 Tokenization of the Medium of Exchange

Tokenization refers to replacing the medium of exchange in the Internet exchange economy with a specific token, assuming that this token is issued and governed by a centralized entity. This token should exhibit the following six characteristics:

- Issued and managed by the network community on which the token economy relies.
- Exists in digital form.
- The network community has established an internal payment system.
- Widely accepted and used by members of the network community.
- Can be used to purchase data or physical goods within the network community.
- Can be used to price data or physical goods.

The two classifications of tokenization are as follows: First, when a price mechanism exists, the medium of exchange is either fiat currency or virtual electronic currency. In this case, the medium of exchange can be directly tokenized, as seen in e-commerce and the sharing economy. Second, when there is no price mechanism, the medium of exchange lacks monetary characteristics, requiring tokenization to introduce a price mechanism, such as in browsers and search engines. Before tokenization, internet users obtained information for free through portals and search engines, exchanging it for big data insights such as their personal preferences, while portal websites used this information to push targeted advertisements to users. However, in reality, users often do not know where their data is being used, how much of it is being utilized, or whether a fair transaction has taken place, effectively making them passive recipients of excessive advertising.

In the case of tokenization, if a portal website intends to utilize user data, it must compensate users with a certain amount of tokens. In turn, users can use these tokens to purchase the information they need on the portal. By introducing a price mechanism, this transaction becomes open and transparent, granting users control over their private data. At the same time, it effectively aggregates market information and enhances resource allocation efficiency.

4.2.9 Blockchain Overlay

Blockchain overlay refers to the implementation of tokens—issued and governed by a central entity—through blockchain technology. This involves recording relevant economic activities and transaction information on a blockchain-based distributed ledger while designing a reasonable incentive mechanism for each participant in the token economy ecosystem. These measures ensure the effective operation of the token economy, enabling a sustainable and self-reinforcing economic cycle. The blockchain overlay demonstrates three fundamental economic attributes of blockchain: a decentralized payment system, a distributed ledger, and an incentive mechanism. These features allow for the seamless transmission of energy and value within the future token economy ecosystem. However, its real-world implementation also presents challenges such as high transaction costs and complex governance structures.

A token is a tradeable asset, and with the support of blockchain technology, it is no longer merely a medium of exchange. Tokens and blockchain technology reinforce each other, ushering in a new era of the token economy. However, the token economy is still in its early stages, with developers continuously exploring and expanding its application scenarios. From the perspective of New Institutional Economics, the token economy represents a transformation in the modes of collaboration and production relationships within society. By leveraging blockchain technology, it significantly reduces transaction costs, facilitates the self-execution of contracts, and enables community co-governance and value sharing—marking a more advanced form of social production and exchange. The token economy is poised to drive the emergence of new business models, foster novel forms of community-driven governance, and ultimately lead to a comprehensive transformation of social production relationships. In summary, the token economy will serve as a bridge connecting the present with the future.

4.2.10 A Generalized Token Economy Model and Design: The Token-Based Value Internet

Blockchain technology, with its decentralized core nature, is gradually transforming our understanding of digital transactions and asset management. This technology enables value transfer without relying on traditional centralized institutions (such as banks), allowing assets to move directly between individuals. This fundamental shift enhances transaction transparency and significantly reduces fraud risk. The direct value transfer model improves efficiency while increasing system security, as all transactions are publicly recorded, verifiable, and maintained by multiple nodes across the network.

On the blockchain, value representation can take various forms, with digital tokens being the most common. These tokens can represent real-world assets such as currencies, shares, physical goods, and even voting rights. This characteristic of blockchain not only enables asset digitization but also ensures the security and uniqueness of digital assets through cryptographic techniques. The decentralized network facilitates the circulation and trading of digital tokens, greatly simplifying the complexities of traditional financial and commercial operations.

Bitcoin and Ethereum exemplify blockchain applications, each employing different technical models to manage transactions and account data. Bitcoin adopts the UTXO model, where each transaction output must be fully utilized in subsequent transactions to maintain a clear and consistent transaction record. In contrast, Ethereum's account model offers greater transaction flexibility and supports real-time state updates, which are essential for executing complex smart contracts. Smart contracts, essentially programs stored on the blockchain, automatically execute predefined actions once specific conditions are met. This extends the functionality of blockchains beyond simple monetary transactions.

Regarding token classification, blockchains define two primary types: fungible tokens and non-fungible tokens. Each unit of a fungible token (e.g., ERC-20) is uniform in value and function, making it ideal as a medium of exchange or a representation of stake. Non-fungible tokens (NFTs), such as ERC-721 tokens, are unique and used to represent non-replicable assets like artwork and collectibles. This classification expands blockchain applications and provides users with greater flexibility and choice to meet diverse needs.

The trustless nature of blockchain allows users to conduct secure transactions without relying on centralized trust authorities. This trust mechanism, based on algorithms and protocols, ensures that even completely unfamiliar parties can transact securely without requiring third-party guarantees. As a result, it not only lowers transaction costs but also reduces the likelihood of fraud and errors.

Looking ahead, the advancement of blockchain technology may give rise to a more extensive interconnected network composed of multiple blockchains, enabling seamless cross-chain exchange of assets and information. This vision of multi-chain interoperability will further drive the digital transformation of the global economy, unlocking limitless possibilities for the future of the digital economy.

4.2.11 A Narrow Definition of the Token Economy Model and Design: Token Economic Incentives

Having explored the significance of tokens in the digital economy, we now turn to their application in the real economy, commonly referred to as "token economic incentives." This incentive mechanism influences the behavior of participants in business activities by using blockchain-based tokens to provide rewards or impose penalties. Among various blockchain applications, token economic incentives represent a mainstream approach.

To answer the question "What is blockchain?" we typically summarize it in four points: Blockchain is a global ledger or distributed ledger; it serves as a fact-verification mechanism; it functions as a trust protocol; and it acts as a settlement platform. Similarly, the question "What is the use of blockchain?" can be addressed in four categories: Blockchain can be used as a tool for confirming rights; as a platform for record verification; as a mechanism for token economic incentives; and as a financial network.

Token economic incentives serve a dual purpose. Firstly, they leverage the reliability of blockchain tokens to expand the scope of participation. Trust is often a barrier to collaboration, but blockchain's trust mechanism enables even parties with conflicting interests to cooperate and transact. By broadening the trust framework, tokens facilitate the integration of industry supply chains and stakeholders into a thriving economic ecosystem, often referred to as a digital economy. Secondly, in trading markets or industry alliances, tokens act as a representation of value, incentivizing participants to act in their own interests. Through the strategic coordination of token distribution, economic welfare can be optimized.

Taking ride-hailing platforms such as Uber and Didi as examples, it is not only a marketplace for vehicles and passengers, but also an industrial ecosystem that includes ride-hailing platforms, vehicle rentals, drivers, passengers, financial institutions, and car manufacturers. In such a ride-hailing platform, a variety of tokens can be applied to incentivize and coordinate the behavior of all parties: provide tokens for managers and employees to motivate them to work for the growth of the company's market value; provide drivers with tokens to improve the quality of their services; provide customers with tokens to encourage them to use the platform more often. Together, these tokens promote the formation of a high-quality service and a long-term thriving ride-hailing service ecosystem. In a digital economy, there are usually multiple tokens that are suitable for different scenarios and people, and these tokens can be both interchangeable and non-interchangeable.

With the development of blockchain and token applications, we can gradually replace the traditional complex technical systems with tokens. One of the benefits of such an alternative is the use of a technology that has proven to be credible and unified. In addition, when various value representations exist in the form of tokens, they can be exchanged more conveniently, and can also be processed through complex programming and automation, for example, to realize the atomic operation of multiple tokens of a subject, that is, either all of them are completed, or all of them are revoked and restored. This illustrates the value that comes with applying tokens in the digital economy. From the perspective of multiple digital economic entities, we can also see the overall market efficiency improvement brought by tokens.

Tokens have explicit or implicit market prices, and price signals formed by free trading will make the market more efficient. The token economy practice model believes that the token supports the interaction between users and applications, and its large cycle of price signals and application scenarios will further promote the survival of the fittest in the market and make the market operate more efficiently.

4.2.12 Bitcoin's Token Economic Ecosystem Model and Design

Bitcoin's appeal is due in large part to the simplicity of its design. Let's take a closer look at its characteristics with the following points: the total supply of bitcoin is fixed at 21 million, a number that is hard-coded in the system. Approximately every 10 min, miners are rewarded with a new block that is successfully mined and rewarded with 6.25 BTC. It is worth noting that Bitcoin's initial block reward was 50 BTC, which has since undergone several halvings, including 25, 12.5, and the current 6.25. For every 210,000 blocks mined, the reward is halved,

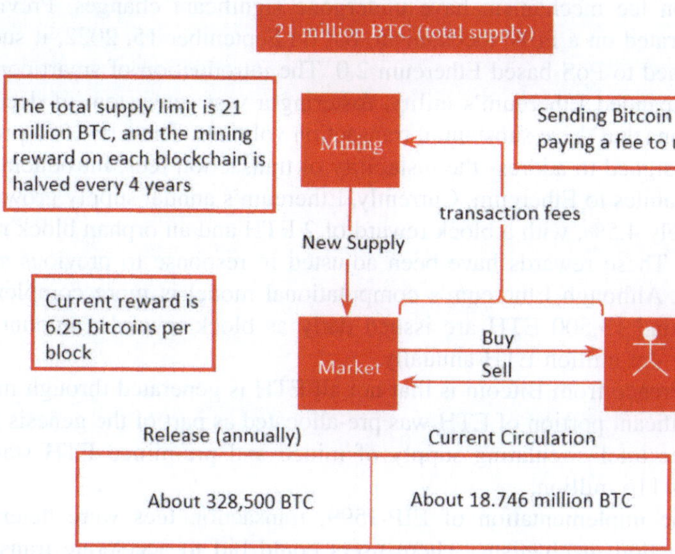

Fig. 4.6 Bitcoin token economic model and design

which means that approximately every 4 years, the reward is halved. If the protocol remains unchanged, it is expected that all bitcoins will be fully mined by around 2140.

Bitcoin's inflation rate follows a halving cycle every four years. Historically, after each halving, Bitcoin's price has risen significantly due to the expected reduction in supply. During the first two halving events, its value increased by approximately 9000% and 3000%, respectively. Currently, nearly 90% of Bitcoin's total supply is already in circulation, meaning that around 328,000 new bitcoins are generated annually.

Transaction fees are payments made by users to miners to ensure their transactions are included in the next block. The base fee is determined by the transaction size (measured in bytes), while users can increase the priority of their transactions by adding a tip, thereby expediting processing. Miners earn new bitcoins through mining and introduce them into circulation when selling them on the market.

Overall, Bitcoin's mechanism is predictable (see Fig. 4.6), and its simple yet elegant design makes it easy to understand and explain. While this does not directly aid in predicting price fluctuations, its transparency and clarity help reduce the uncertainty investors may face during analysis.

4.2.13 Ethereum's Token-Economic Model and Design

As shown in Fig. 4.7, Ethereum 1.0 shares design similarities with the Bitcoin network. However, with the introduction of EIP-1599, Ethereum's tokenomics and transaction fee mechanism have undergone significant changes. Previously, Ethereum operated on a PoW mechanism, but on September 15, 2022, it successfully transitioned to PoS-based Ethereum 2.0. The introduction of smart contracts has greatly expanded Ethereum's utility, fostering a vast ecosystem of decentralized applications that drive substantial transaction volumes. The EIP-1559 protocol update was designed to address the instability of transaction fees, introducing new economic dynamics to Ethereum. Currently, Ethereum's annual supply growth rate is approximately 4.5%, with a block reward of 2 ETH and an orphan block reward of 1.75 ETH. These rewards have been adjusted in response to previous system modifications. Although Ethereum's computational model is more complex than Bitcoin's, around 13,500 ETH are issued daily as block rewards, amounting to approximately 4.9 million ETH annually.

A key difference from Bitcoin is that not all ETH is generated through mining. In fact, a significant portion of ETH was pre-allocated as part of the genesis block. At present, the total circulating supply of mined and pre-mined ETH stands at approximately 116 million.

Prior to the implementation of EIP-1599, transaction fees were determined through an auction mechanism, where users could bid to accelerate transaction processing. This led miners to prioritize transactions with the highest bids, while users offering lower fees had to either wait or increase their bids. Since the implementation of EIP-1599 on August 4, 2021, transaction fees have been divided into a base fee and a small priority fee. The base fee dynamically adjusts based on network conditions, but its fluctuation is capped at 12.5% of the previous block's fee, effectively stabilizing transaction costs. The priority fee allows users to pay a tip for expedited transaction processing, though this tip is constrained by the

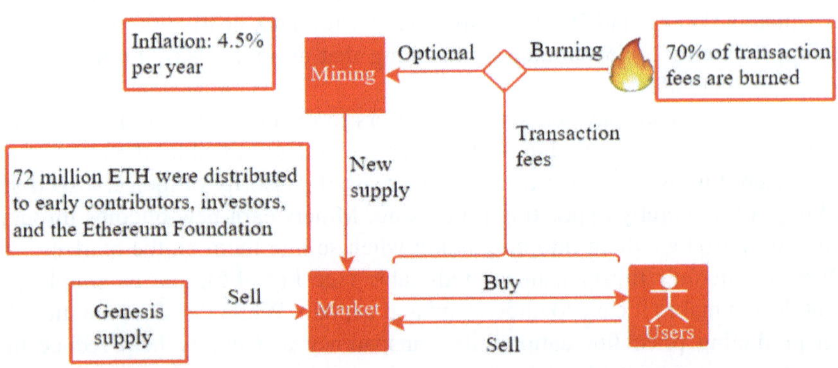

Issuance (per year)	Current circulation	Burning (per year)
About 4.9 million ETH	About 116 million ETH	Daily transaction fees: About 10,000 ETH Total annual fees: About 3.7 million ETH Total amount burned: About 2.6 million ETH

Fig. 4.7 Ethereum 1.0 token economic model and design

total gas limit of the block. One of the key innovations of EIP-1599 is that it not only establishes a base fee but also introduces a fee burn mechanism, permanently removing the base fee from circulation. If miners were paid the base fee without burning it, transaction fee volatility would persist, as off-chain protocols could still facilitate auction-like tipping mechanisms. Assuming approximately 70% of transaction fees are burned, this could result in an annual burn of around 2.6 million ETH. Given that approximately 4.9 million ETH are issued annually, this effectively reduces Ethereum's net supply. As Ethereum adoption grows, it may even transition toward a deflationary state.

By implementing EIP-1599, Ethereum not only optimizes its transaction fee mechanism but also significantly impacts token supply, introducing new variables to its future development.

The launch of Ethereum 2.0 marks a major network upgrade aimed at addressing the scalability challenges of version 1.0. This upgrade enhances network performance while introducing a new consensus mechanism and economic model. The core transformation of Ethereum 2.0 is the shift from a Proof-of-Work (PoW) to a Proof-of-Stake (PoS) system. This transition eliminates the need for traditional mining activities, replacing them with validators who secure the network by staking ETH. After the Merge, the supply of mined and pre-mined ETH remains in circulation, with no direct impact on users. Anyone willing to stake 32 ETH can become a validator. As the total amount of staked ETH increases, the issuance of new ETH also rises, but the annual percentage return (APR) for individual stakers decreases. Currently, approximately 6 million ETH have been staked, reducing the circulating supply to some extent.

At present, Ethereum 2.0's Beacon Chain is live, allowing users to stake their ETH. However, these staked funds remain locked until the official merger of Ethereum 1.0 and 2.0. This creates a potential supply shock, as staked ETH is temporarily removed from circulation. Becoming a validator entails responsibilities such as storing data, processing transactions, and adding new blocks. Validators who fail to fulfill their duties or engage in malicious behavior face penalties. The fee burn mechanism introduced by EIP-1559 will remain in place, potentially leading to slight inflation or deflation depending on transaction volume.

Tokenomics is a key factor in the success of a cryptocurrency project. A well-designed tokenomics model can drive adoption and growth, while a poorly structured model can lead to failure. Understanding how tokens flow through a protocol is crucial for evaluating a project's viability. The longevity of Bitcoin and Ethereum can largely be attributed to their incentive structures, which encourage user participation and transaction validation. Bitcoin's tokenomics derive value from digital scarcity, while Ethereum provides ETH with practical utility through smart contracts. Users can use ETH to pay for transaction fees in decentralized applications such as Uniswap, AAVE, and Maker. Tokenomics in the cryptocurrency space is an ongoing experiment. Blockchains and protocols continuously explore and refine token economic models to build more efficient and sustainable systems.

In conclusion, the Ethereum 2.0 upgrade is a positive step toward enhancing scalability and efficiency by introducing the PoS mechanism and an improved tokenomics model. These changes are expected to drive broader adoption and create a more stable network environment for Ethereum.

4.2.14 Application Scenarios of Token Economic Incentives in a Digital Economy

When token economies integrate closely with real-world business activities, they must navigate various legal and regulatory challenges. For instance, in the United States, if a token is classified as a security, it falls under the jurisdiction of the *Securities Act of 1933* and the *Securities Exchange Act of 1934*, as well as registration or exemption rules such as Reg D, Reg A, and Reg S, depending on the investor category. In China, if tokens function as pre-deposited customer funds, they are subject to corresponding financial regulations. Similarly, if a token is linked to user data and associated rights, it must comply with the *European Union's General Data Protection Regulation* (GDPR).

Ignoring legal constraints, we can explore the general application of tokenomics in a commercial economy. Economic incentives are typically categorized into three main types, using an internet-based ride-hailing platform as an example:

- **Equity or Option-Based Tokens**

  These tokens represent shares in the platform company or stock options for employees and are generally tied to the company's valuation.
- **Reward-Based Tokens**

  These tokens are designed to attract and retain users, including pre-deposited funds such as top-up bonuses or security deposits, loyalty points earned through spending and redeemable under specific conditions, user badges, ratings, tiers, and memberships often linked to exclusive benefits, and coupons issued either by the platform or third parties, subject to specific terms of use. Blockchain technology simplifies the creation and exchange of these tokens, allowing third-party service providers to offer additional exchange services within the digital economy.
- **Service Provider Equity Tokens**

  These tokens represent the rights of service providers (e.g., drivers), enabling them to share in the value generated by the network's growth. They may be earned as service rewards or through investment, similar to how miners in the Bitcoin network are rewarded for mining. In terms of value distribution, several models can be adopted, including traditional dividends, a growth-focused model without dividends, or the blockchain-specific burn model, where value is distributed by reducing the total token supply. The value of these tokens is closely tied to the performance of the digital economy—appreciating as the economy expands and depreciating in times of contraction. While a digital economy may have multiple tokens, there is typically one primary token that represents the overall value of the ecosystem.

Ideally, the main token in a digital economy should reflect the interests of service providers. Token-based economic incentives primarily influence the behavior of service providers, and businesses can gradually implement tokenomics—starting with a simple point system and eventually integrating all token types into a unified incentive model.

Token-based economic incentives apply across multiple aspects of the digital economy, leveraging principles from economics, game theory, and behavioral economics to encourage participation. Blockchain technology provides the essential infrastructure for such incentive mechanisms.

4.3 Logical Construction of Token Economy

At present, RWA tokenization has formed a complete on-chain economic ecology, attracting a large number of construction participants. Each of them plays a different role and together drives the development of this emerging field. We can broadly divide these construction participants into the following five categories:

- **Blockchain technology company**

  These companies develop and maintain the blockchain platforms (e.g., Ethereum, EOS, etc.) that asset tokenization relies on and provide underlying technical support for asset tokenization. They are committed to improving the performance, security, and scalability of blockchains, creating a better technical environment for asset tokenization.
- **Wallet and digital asset custody services company**

  These companies typically use technologies such as cold wallets and multi-sig to enhance security and provide a convenient user interface for asset management, secure digital asset storage and management services for users, and ensure that users' token assets are properly safeguarded.
- **Regulatory compliance services company**

  Tokenization involves complex legal and regulatory issues, and these companies provide legal advice and compliance review services for tokenization projects to ensure that they comply with relevant regulatory requirements. They help project parties develop compliance strategies and assist them in communicating with regulators to mitigate legal risks.
- **Platform-based tokenization company**

These platforms connect asset providers, investors, and other market participants, providing a unified venue for token issuance, subscription, and secondary market trading. Platform companies simplify tokenized operations and improve market efficiency through standardized processes and smart contract technology.

- **Professional tokenization company**

  Focuses on providing tokenization services for specific types of assets. These companies often have deep expertise in a vertical such as real estate, art, intellectual property, and more. They work closely with asset providers to design customized tokenization solutions and provide related valuation, due diligence, and promotion services to help assets achieve liquidity.

These five types of participants work together to build an economic ecology of RWA tokenization. Blockchain technology companies have laid a solid foundation for technology, wallet and digital asset custody service companies have ensured asset security, regulatory compliance service companies have ensured compliance, platform-based tokenization companies have provided the infrastructure for issuance and trading, and professional tokenization companies have introduced various high-quality assets.

Figure 4.8 illustrates the representative sectors and related companies in the RWA industry, and as more and more players join, the RWA tokenization ecosystem will be richer and more complete, injecting new vitality into the real economy.

4.3.1 Blockchain Technology Company

There are many types of blockchain technology, mainly including public chains, consortium chains, and private chains. Public blockchains (such as Ethereum, etc.) are open and decentralized, and anyone can participate in them. A consortium chain is an intermediate type of public and private chain that only allows specific organizations or entities to transact and verify, such as R3 Corda and Hyperledger Fabric. Private chains only allow transactions and verification by specific people or entities, and are usually used within a business or organization. Some blockchains are specifically designed to handle the special needs of RWA tokenization, such as:

- The Provenance blockchain enables financial institutions and fintech companies to issue, trade, and service tokenized financial assets at scale, seamlessly, and securely.
- Polymesh is an institutional-grade blockchain built specifically for regulated asset tokens, designed to solve some of the problems faced by traditional blockchains when dealing with regulated asset tokens, such as authentication, compliance, and governance.

Fig. 4.8 Overview of representative sectors of RWA tokenization and related companies

- Realio is a blockchain network built specifically for RWA that is compatible with the Ethereum Virtual Machine and offers a full suite of solutions for asset tokenization and subsequent transactions and management.
- MANTRA Chain is a protocol that powers regulated assets and real-world assets in the Cosmos ecosystem, aiming to provide a secure, transparent, and efficient environment to handle the issuance, trading of regulated assets and RWAs.

4.3.2 Wallet and Digital Asset Custody Services Company

While many wallets and digital asset custody companies support multiple types of digital assets, some have started to offer custody services specifically for RWA tokens, such as:

- Safeheron is a self-custody technology solution provider based on multi-party secure computing in a trusted execution environment, providing one-stop asset management security solutions for enterprise customers under the premise of private keys, including the security of private key management, the security of asset transfer, and the security of accessing decentralized financial platforms.
- Anchorage is a company that provides comprehensive digital asset custody services, including secure storage and trading services for RWA's tokens. As a U.S. federally regulated custodian bank, Anchorage provides secure, compliant digital custody services to corporate and institutional investors.
- Copper, a company that provides digital asset custody and clearing services to institutional investors, has ClearLoop technology that enables instant asset transfer and transaction settlement, including RWA's tokens.
- Trustology is a company that provides high-speed, secure digital asset custody services that support the custody of various types of digital assets, including RWA's tokens.

4.3.3 Regulatory Compliance Services Company

RWA tokenization needs to meet a variety of regulatory requirements, and regulatory compliance services companies can help issuers and investors ensure that their actions comply with relevant regulations and avoid potential legal risks. These companies mainly provide digital identity authentication services, such as:

- Quadrata Network provides blockchain-verified KYC, allowing users to invest in RWA tokens in a legal and compliant manner. This not only improves the security of transactions, but also facilitates the tokenization and trading of RWAs by enterprises, allowing businesses and investors to conduct secure and compliant transactions on a global scale.

- Verite is a standardized set of protocols for distributed digital identity. By using Verite, businesses and investors can securely and efficiently manage their identities on the blockchain, allowing them to better participate in the trading of RWA tokens. Verite's protocol can be applied to a variety of RWAs, such as real estate, financial assets, or goods.
- Spruce is a digital identity toolkit that can be used to measure investor and issuer compliance when trading RWAs. Spruce offers a range of tools and services to help businesses and investors manage their identities on the blockchain to meet a variety of regulatory requirements. By using Spruce, businesses and investors can enjoy the benefits of tokenization of RWA while ensuring that their actions are legal and compliant.

4.3.4 Platform-Based Tokenization Company

At present, there are a large number of technology companies that focus on offering tokens on the blockchain to help enterprises and institutions complete the tokenization of RWA, and we can divide these companies into platform and professional companies. The following are representative platform-based tokenization companies:

- DigiFT is the first and only decentralized digital asset exchange in the MAS Fintech Regulatory Sandbox. DigiFT provides a regulated decentralized finance solution on the Ethereum public chain, and improves the liquidity of security tokens backed by financial assets such as bonds and equities in the secondary market through the deployment of an automated market maker (AMM) mechanism. Asset-backed tokens issued by DigiFT are a new type of security that represents an economic interest in the underlying asset.
- Centrifuge provides a one-stop solution for the securitization and tokenization of structured credit assets, helping businesses convert various types of RWAs (such as invoices, real estate, or art) into tokens that can be traded on the open market.
- Securitize offers a suite of products designed to enhance tokenization compliance. The platform supports the entire lifecycle of tokens—from issuance and trading to management—providing enterprises with a comprehensive solution for asset tokenization.
- Tokeny, a Luxembourg-based platform, delivers institutional-grade services for issuing, transferring, and managing digital securities. It helps businesses and institutions transform various types of assets—such as equity, debt, or physical assets—into digital securities that can be traded globally.
- Curio Group facilitates asset tokenization and investor connections, increasing the liquidity of RWAs. It offers a one-stop solution covering asset valuation, tokenization design, token issuance, and trading.
- Securrency is a digital securities issuance and marketplace platform that provides businesses with a simple, secure way to convert various types of

assets—including equity, debt, and physical assets—into digital security tokens that can be traded globally.

4.3.5 Professional Tokenization Companies

Professional tokenization companies span various industries and categories.[1] Below is a key sector within professional tokenization:

- **Stablecoins**

  As pioneers in RWA digitization and one of the most successful applications, stablecoins seamlessly combine the convenience of digital assets with the stability of fiat currencies. They serve as a unit of value in digital asset transactions, providing investors with "entry channels" and "safe harbors," while playing an increasingly vital role in global payment systems. Moreover, stablecoins form a critical foundation for RWA tokenization, which in turn enhances their value backing and reserve diversity. As a result, stablecoins act as a bridge between digital assets and the mainstream financial system. Stablecoins can be categorized based on their issuance model: Centralized stablecoins (USDT, USDC, TUSD, PYUSD, etc.) , Decentralized stablecoins (DAI, etc.) , Algorithmic stablecoins (USDD, UST, FRAX, etc.)
- **Debt and Equity**

  The Ondo platform brings institutional-grade financial products, such as U.S. Treasury bonds and corporate bonds, into DeFi, enabling investors to trade and invest in these products on the blockchain. Goldfinch is a decentralized protocol that allows emerging market companies to obtain uncollateralized digital asset loans directly from global investors, bypassing traditional financial institutions. The TrueFi platform facilitates unsecured lending on the blockchain, allowing borrowers to access loans without providing collateral. Backed has developed ERC-20 tokens that represent ownership of structured financial products, with each token backed by different types of publicly issued securities, such as ABS, MBS, and CDOs. The Maple Finance platform digitizes all aspects of the lending business, enhancing the transparency and efficiency of both borrowing and investment processes.
- **Real Estate**

  RealT and Parcl enable investors to participate in the real estate market through tokenization. This allows investors to purchase tokens representing real estate value without having to buy entire properties, significantly lowering the entry barrier for real estate investment and enhancing asset liquidity. Robinland tokenizes institutional-grade commercial real estate in a legal and decentralized manner, providing retail investors access to high-quality commercial properties

[1] In the following chapters, the book will introduce the typical cases of related companies in detail

that were traditionally available only to large institutional investors, while also offering stable rental income opportunities.

- **Trade Finance**

  Some companies bring assets such as accounts receivable and warehouse receipts on-chain, making them tradable. This RWA tokenization addresses key challenges in traditional trade finance, improving asset liquidity, reducing risks, lowering cross-border financing costs, and enabling SMEs to obtain necessary cross-border financing more easily. For example, Polytrade is a decentralized trade finance platform specializing in accounts receivable financing. By leveraging tokenization, it enables the trading and circulation of invoices and receivables, enhancing trade finance efficiency and fostering a more equitable and efficient international trade system.

- **Precious Metals and Mining Rights**

  Precious metal tokens offer high divisibility, with each token representing a small fraction of gold or silver assets. This significantly lowers the investment threshold, enabling a broader range of investors to participate. Some tokens representing physical gold provide fiat-pegged stability and serve as an inflation hedge. For example, Paxos introduced Pax Gold (PAXG), a token backed by 1 ounce[2] of physical gold. Digix offers DGX, a gold token where each unit represents 1 gram of physical gold. Anthem Gold provides gold tokenization services, issuing AUG tokens, each backed by 1 gram of gold. Meanwhile, MetaBank is leading a tokenization project for rare earth mining rights in Laos, aiming to record the entire process of mineral exploration, extraction, inventory, and sales on the Lao national blockchain.

- **Environmental Assets**

  By tokenizing environmental assets, particularly carbon credits, these companies enable investors to engage in environmental and climate initiatives with lower costs and greater flexibility while also opening new financing avenues for sustainability projects. For example, Flowcarbon helps businesses and investors manage carbon credits more effectively by integrating the entire lifecycle of carbon credits into a unified system.

Asset tokenization is unlocking a new digital frontier for issuers and investors, allowing the global financial system to operate with lower costs, greater efficiency, enhanced inclusivity, and improved security. This transformation, driven by Web 3.0 technology, represents a fundamental shift in financial markets and a defining trend for the future of finance. As the Web 3.0 era unfolds, we anticipate the rapid expansion of the RWA tokenization ecosystem. However, the true value of this innovation lies not only in the development of specific technologies or strategies but also in how we leverage these tools to create a fair, transparent, and sustainable digital financial ecosystem. The tokenization of RWA could become a key driver

[2] 1 ounce =28.35g.—editor's note

of the future digital economy, placing us at the forefront of a historic transformation—witnessing the dawn of a new era and seizing the opportunities that come with it.

4.4 Token Economy Links Traditional Finance

The core value of the token economy lies in its role as a bridge to the traditional financial world, enabling the tokenization of financial assets such as equity and debt—converting them into a tradable digital form. The key to building RWA lies in intelligent supply and demand protocols. For blockchain protocols focused on RWA tokenization to be effective, both supply and demand sides must establish smart contract-based protocols. These protocols are implemented through code, requiring professional praisal bodies to conduct code reviews. Through this approach, RWA tokenization transitions from an abstract concept to an essential component of on-chain utility, bringing the credibility of real-world valuations and legal frameworks into the decentralized digital asset space.

DeFi allows users to interact directly with smart contracts through their cryptocurrency wallets. Smart contracts are self-executing agreements in which contractual terms are embedded in code. By automating contract execution, all participants can immediately determine outcomes without intermediaries or time delays. DeFi functions like Lego bricks, where fundamental financial modules and smart contracts can be combined to help investors achieve their financial goals. Smart contracts can also interact with one another to assemble more complex financial structures. Typically, DeFi operates on public blockchains, primarily Ethereum (ETH) and Solana, with RWA serving as a crucial component of its financial infrastructure. The integration of RWA and DeFi marks a milestone in the digitization of traditional financial and physical assets.

The significance of this integration is reflected in four key aspects:

First, RWA is closely integrated with DeFi, and the market potential is huge. RWA makes it easier for businesses or organizations to leverage the DeFi ecosystem to obtain financing, especially if they have physical and financial assets that cannot be quickly liquidated and need to replenish cash flow quickly. RWA not only provides an off-chain market for DeFi, driving DeFi's connection to the real world, but also providing a new opportunity for traditional financial customer groups to expand their investment reach.

Second, RWA optimizes the traditional financial asset trading model. Traditional financial and physical markets are usually labor-intensive, but blockchain technology, with its instant settlement and round-the-clock trading characteristics, significantly reduces the operating costs and entry barriers for market participants. Tokenization allows illiquid assets to be broken down into portfolios of smaller shares, which reduces the consumption of paperwork, money, and time for investors, resulting in fairer market conditions while giving rise to new business and social models such as shared property ownership.

Third, RWA tokenization enhances the liquidity of physical assets. Tokenization is a specialized form of securitization, with its core function being the conversion of illiquid assets into highly liquid ones. By integrating RWA into DeFi, not only does it enhance market efficiency, but it also provides investors with unique opportunities and levels of liquidity previously unimaginable. While tokenization cannot fundamentally increase liquidity for inherently illiquid asset classes—such as private equity, credit, infrastructure, real estate, and art—it can leverage direct interaction with investor communities and expanded DeFi applications to mitigate the high discounts typically associated with illiquid asset issuance. Additionally, tokenization enables asset fractionalization, breaking down unit assets into smaller denominations. This reduction in investment thresholds allows previously excluded investors to participate, thereby injecting additional liquidity into the market. The significance of these features has already been demonstrated in the cryptocurrency and DeFi sectors.

4.4.1 Implementation of Tokenized Equity: The Case of Inscriptions

Bitcoin was introduced in 2008 as a peer-to-peer electronic cash system designed to facilitate trustless transactions between parties over the network. Initially, Bitcoin was primarily used for micropayments, with popular applications including online gaming top-ups and small-value purchases. Over time, its application scope expanded. For instance, Layer 2 networks and Bitcoin inscriptions now enable more advanced decentralized applications and real-world asset tokenization.

The emergence of the BRC-20 inscription token ORDI catalyzed the development of Bitcoin's Layer 2 ecosystem. In March 2023, an anonymous developer, Domo, introduced the BRC-20 standard based on the Ordinals protocol. This standard utilizes specific JSON text files, known as inscriptions, for transactions. ORDI has a fixed supply of 21 million tokens. Following this, the SATS inscription was introduced. Derived from Satoshis, the smallest unit of Bitcoin, SATS serves as a tribute to Bitcoin's creator, Satoshi Nakamoto. Launched fairly on March 9, 2023, SATS became the 9th BRC-20 inscription on the Unisat wallet. The inscription process was completed on September 24, 2023, spanning six months, accumulating over $20 million in inscription costs, and engaging more than 36,000 participants. In October 2023, Unisat Wallet, a key player in the Bitcoin ecosystem, announced that SATS would be used as gas fees. Moving forward, all transaction fees and liquidity pool (LP) additions on Unisat will be conducted using SATS.

RWA-based Bitcoin inscriptions may become one of the important future directions. RWA enables Bitcoin inscriptions to be more than just a string of text or data simply recorded on the blockchain; instead, they transform into tokens with complex attributes and functionalities. RWA-based Bitcoin inscriptions create possibilities for developing new digital asset products. These products may possess unique attributes, such as revenue sharing, voting rights, or other financial derivative functions, to meet the diversified demands of the market. For instance, the

FUND inscription was a non-owned token fairly launched on March 10, 2023. At present, some real-world asset issuers have leveraged FUND to provide users with real-world empowerment and benefits. FUND can be regarded as the leading inscription in the RWA sector under the BRC-20 protocol.

4.4.2 Implementation Path of Tokenized Debt Applications: The Case of Digital Bonds

4.4.2.1 Definition and Characteristics of Digital Bonds

Tokenized bonds, also known as digital bonds, are debt instruments that the International Capital Market Association (ICMA) defines as those issued, traded, and managed using distributed ledger technology (DLT). Unlike traditional bonds, digital bonds do not rely on financial intermediaries for issuance and trading; instead, they operate through DLT systems, particularly blockchain technology. Blockchain, a subset of DLT, consists of a series of securely connected blocks, each containing transaction records.

From the perspective of market structure and key information embedding, digital bonds can be issued on both public and private blockchains. Public blockchains are decentralized and open to everyone, whereas private blockchains are controlled by a single entity and may require authorization for access. Within this infrastructure, key bond information—such as issuance amount, maturity date, and coupon rate—can be embedded through code-based identifiers, enhancing the bond's transparency and traceability.

From the perspective of traditional bonds, digital bonds are potentially transformative in five aspects. First, high transparency. As a type of bond contract, digital bonds utilize blockchain databases to provide cryptographically secure and publicly transparent ledger operations, in stark contrast to the traditional bond issuance process. Second, high market efficiency. The programmability of blockchain enables the automation of various stages in a bond's lifecycle, including coupon payments, which increases the speed of issuance and trading while reducing settlement times. Third, disintermediation. By creating unique digital assets, digital bonds have the potential to revolutionize financial capital markets, eliminating intermediaries and reducing transaction costs. Fourth, high market accessibility. Digital bonds can be fractionalized into smaller trading units, allowing a broader range of investors to buy and sell smaller bond portions, thereby enhancing market liquidity. Fifth, high security. The decentralized, private, and cryptographic nature of distributed ledgers reduces the risks of cyberattacks and financial fraud.

4.4.3 Market Size and Trends in the Digital Bond Market

According to DMI News, at least 17 tokenized bond issuance took place globally in 2023. As reported by the *Hong Kong Monetary Authority* (HKMA) in its August 2023 report, Tokenization of Hong Kong Bond Market, the total issuance of tokenized bonds worldwide had reached approximately $3.9 billion by the end of March 2023, highlighting the rapid growth of the digital bond market.

From an international perspective, many major financial institutions' fintech platforms are actively participating in the digital bond market and providing related technical services. Examples include HSBC's HSBC Orion platform in Hong Kong, Goldman Sachs' GS DAP™, and Société Générale's SG-Forge, all of which play significant roles in this field. Among them, SG-Forge stands out as the most prominent. As a fintech platform under Société Générale, SG-Forge has deeply engaged in the crypto market through tokenized financing on the DeFi protocol MakerDAO. In 2023, SG-Forge launched a euro-pegged stablecoin, which was used as the settlement medium for digital bonds issued by Société Générale. These bonds were issued on the Ethereum public blockchain and were fully subscribed via private placement by two top institutional investors, AXA and Generali, demonstrating market recognition of this issuance model.

Currently, the digital bond market is expanding rapidly, attracting widespread attention and participation from financial institutions and fintech platforms. The application of blockchain technology and central bank digital currencies (CBDCs) has introduced new opportunities to the bond market, signaling potential transformations in financial market operations. As technology continues to advance and the market matures, digital bonds are expected to play an increasingly significant role in the future.

4.4.4 Key Technologies in the Digital Bond Market: RWA and DeFi

RWA enables ownership of various financial and physical assets—including stocks, bonds, funds, revenue-sharing agreements, accounts receivable, real estate, artwork, and precious metals—to be recorded, managed, and traded on a globally accessible public blockchain. In theory, any asset, regardless of its value, can be digitized through tokenization, thereby enhancing its liquidity and tradability. The primary advantages of asset tokenization stem from blockchain's decentralized nature, which addresses certain inefficiencies in traditional finance—such as high intermediary costs and low transaction efficiency—by facilitating ecosystem-based applications.

The issuance and trading of digital bonds largely depend on the integration of RWA and DeFi technologies. First, their combination creates strong synergies. RWA digitizes real-world credit rights and obligations into blockchain-based digital bonds, while DeFi leverages smart contract execution environments to ensure automated transactions with enhanced security. Second, this integration significantly improves bond market efficiency. By utilizing automated smart contracts to process transactions, digital bonds minimize the need for intermediaries in traditional trading, thereby reducing both transaction time and costs. Furthermore, blockchain's transparency and immutability help mitigate operational risks, further enhancing overall market efficiency. Third, the combination of RWA and

DeFi streamlines risk management and market monitoring. Since all transactions recorded on the blockchain are publicly accessible, investors and regulators can more effectively track market dynamics, promptly identifying and addressing potential risks. Fourth, the integration of RWA and DeFi fosters global financial collaboration and facilitates cross-border investment. Since digital bonds are issued and traded on blockchain networks, they are globally accessible, allowing investors to participate in bond markets worldwide without geographical constraints.

4.4.5 Innovative Practices in Digital Bonds: The Case of Ondo Finance

Since 2021, in response to inflation, the Federal Reserve has implemented multiple interest rate hikes, prompting investors to turn to U.S. Treasury bonds as a means of securing stable, risk-free returns. However, high investment thresholds present a significant barrier for retail investors seeking to access U.S. Treasuries. Even for U.S. citizens, the complex KYC (Know Your Customer) and account opening procedures deter many from participating, while non-U.S. citizens face even greater difficulties. As a result, a key challenge for many RWA protocols is how to compliantly bring U.S. Treasuries onto the blockchain while lowering investment barriers.

One of Ondo's recent achievements is its preliminary resolution of compliance issues related to tokenizing U.S. debt within the existing legal framework of the United States. Ondo Finance is a financial protocol focused on the Real World Assets (RWA) sector, dedicated to leveraging blockchain technology to offer institutional-grade financial products and services, ultimately aiming to build an open, permissionless, and decentralized investment bank. Its core business revolves around bringing low- or no-risk, stable yield-generating, and scalable fund products—such as U.S. Treasury bonds and money market funds—onto the blockchain. This provides on-chain investors with an alternative to stablecoins, allowing holders, rather than issuers, to capture the majority of income derived from the underlying assets. Ondo Finance's business is primarily divided into three categories: the interest-bearing stablecoin Ondo US Dollar Yield Token ($USDY), the tokenized U.S. Treasury fund Short-Term US Government Treasuries ($OUSG), and Ondo US Money Markets ($OMMF), a tokenized money market fund currently in development. In 2023, the total value locked (TVL) within the RWA sector—where Ondo Finance operates—grew sixfold, positioning it as a key driver of the RWA industry.

4.4.6 Innovative Practices in Digital Bonds: A Case Study of Hong Kong's Digital Green Bonds

In 2022, the Financial Secretary of the *Hong Kong Special Administrative Region (HKSAR)* issued the Policy Statement on the Development of Virtual Assets in

Hong Kong. Since the release of this foundational document, the HKSAR Government has actively introduced policies to foster virtual asset development and has been making significant strides in advancing Web 3.0. In 2023, the Securities and Futures Commission (SFC) issued two key circulars: the *Circular and Appendices on Intermediaries Engaging in Activities Related to Tokenized Securities* and the *Circular on Tokenized SFC-Authorized Investment Products*. These circulars refined and further clarified the SFC's regulatory stance on tokenized securities, including adjustments and relaxations of certain existing policies.

As a traditional financial hub, Hong Kong has accumulated extensive practical experience in digital assets and has recently been advancing projects in three key areas to promote the development of digital virtual assets: fungible tokens, digital bonds, and digital stablecoins. All three initiatives have either been completed or achieved phased results. In 2023, as part of the digital bond initiative, the HKSAR Government issued HK$800 million in digital bonds with ESG characteristics, making them the world's first bonds that are both green and digital. In 2024, Hong Kong plans to issue approximately HK$6 billion in digital green bonds to solidify its position as an international center for green technology and finance. To ensure a prudent issuance process, a two-step approach was adopted: first, the bonds were deposited into Hong Kong's Central Moneymarkets Unit (CMU); second, the bonds were tokenized. Compared to the traditional bond issuance model, tokenized green bonds have significantly improved issuance efficiency, shortening the settlement process from five business days (T + 5) to just one day. The issuance of these digital bonds utilized Goldman Sachs' distributed ledger technology (DLT), with ownership recorded in GS DAP™'s tokenized securities accounts. Subscription registration, securities settlement, commission distribution, coupon payments, and other processes were conducted digitally on a private blockchain network, with legally enforceable on-chain records maintained.

From the perspective of Hong Kong's digital green bond practice, tokenized issuance can reduce the cost and time associated with the issuance process, while also enabling holders to clearly track the progress of fundraising projects and monitor daily carbon emission reductions. Furthermore, distributed ledger technology (DLT) can be utilized throughout the entire lifecycle of the bond. The primary advantages of this approach are reflected in three key aspects. First, it enhances asset liquidity. Tokenization transforms asset ownership into digital tokens that are stored, verified, and transferred on a blockchain network, enabling finer fractionalization and improving liquidity. Second, it allows for the inclusion of more information. Digital bonds can integrate a broader range of data, such as bond terms and ESG metrics, which are packaged and stored together with the digital bond, making them directly accessible via blockchain explorers. Third, it accelerates settlement speed. Tokens can be traded through blockchain infrastructure, expediting settlement processes, increasing liquidity, and reducing costs. The blockchain network operates 24/7 without time restrictions, enabling real-time settlement.

4.4.7 Implications for China from the Development of Overseas Digital Bonds

China has been an early mover in digital bond innovation. In 2019, Bank of China leveraged blockchain technology to establish a digital bond issuance system, testing the issuance of specialized bonds aimed at addressing the financing difficulties and high borrowing costs faced by small and micro enterprises. In 2020, China Construction Bank (CCB) partnered with Hong Kong-based fintech firm Fusang to issue digital bonds through CCB's Labuan branch in Malaysia, raising nearly USD 3 billion. The funds raised from this issuance were placed into fixed deposits with CCB, maturing in February 2021. These bonds were listed on the Fusang Exchange in the form of digital tokens, quoted in both USD and Bitcoin, and deployed on the Ethereum blockchain via the ERC-20 protocol.

As an integral part of China's financial infrastructure, China Central Depository & Clearing Co., Ltd. (CCDC) deeply understands and actively responds to national strategies, designating blockchain technology as a key development focus. Since 2018, CCDC has been researching and developing blockchain technology, amassing substantial technical expertise. In 2021, the company successfully developed a blockchain-based digital bond issuance prototype, marking a significant technological breakthrough in this field. Building on this, in 2022, CCDC was selected as a national pilot for blockchain innovation applications due to its technical strength and innovation capabilities. It also launched China's first public platform for blockchain-based digital bond issuance, providing a secure and efficient new channel for bond offerings. CCDC has successfully supported multiple bond issuances using blockchain technology, demonstrating the maturity and stability of its solutions. As the central custodian, CCDC leverages blockchain technology to offer digital bond services, with all participants being legally recognized members of the bond market. The types of bonds issued and their scale are subject to regulatory approval, and the business rules, operational logic, and regulatory oversight remain consistent with traditional bonds.

Unlike overseas digital bond issuance and trading, which emphasize decentralization via public blockchains, China's approach prioritizes operation within an institutional framework. It relies on standardized and compliant centralized management, with financial institutions collectively developing and sharing a digital bond issuance system. CCDC's digital bond infrastructure adopts private consortium blockchain technology, seamlessly integrating centralized governance, distributed ledger technology (DLT), and smart contracts.

Blockchain technology serves as the foundation for digital bond issuance, requiring market participants to connect to DLT nodes and become on-chain members to engage in the full bond issuance process. However, establishing and managing DLT nodes is both costly and technically demanding, necessitating significant investment in system infrastructure. Additionally, blockchain's underlying technology still lacks full maturity, presenting further challenges.

For digital bonds to gain wider adoption in China, the underlying blockchain technology must align with the unique characteristics and ecosystem of China's bond market. The focus is primarily on ensuring the secure storage of transaction data, enforcing smart contract execution in a regulated manner, and maintaining high network throughput to support large transaction volumes—rather than placing excessive emphasis on decentralization. However, blockchain security remains a concern, and improvements are still needed in core areas such as encryption algorithms, smart contracts, and consensus mechanisms. Moreover, blockchain's current transaction processing capacity falls short of the bond market's requirements, making it difficult to overcome computational bottlenecks in the short term. Lastly, the issuance of offshore digital bonds must carefully balance technological innovation with financial risk management.

Some international cases suggest that digital bond issuance may introduce compliance risks, performance risks, and regulatory arbitrage risks, posing new challenges for investor protection. For example, shortcomings in system infrastructure and regulatory compliance tracking may lead to delays in coupon and principal payments. Furthermore, given the varying regulatory frameworks governing bond issuance and trading across different countries and regions, directly replicating overseas models may not be suitable for China's specific market conditions.

Currently, the Hong Kong SAR government and regulatory authorities are proactively positioning Hong Kong as a global financial hub for virtual assets through a top-down approach. Official recognition underscores Hong Kong's competitive advantage in the global virtual asset landscape. According to the SFC, on April 29, 2024, six Hong Kong virtual asset spot ETFs were officially launched, all issued by Chinese-backed asset management companies. This development reflects the Hong Kong SAR government's active efforts to steer the virtual asset sector toward regulatory compliance.

In recent years, as China's financial markets continue to open in both directions, Hong Kong has emerged as a key offshore hub for Chinese bonds, with a thriving market for US dollar bonds and dim sum bonds issued by Chinese enterprises. Looking ahead, China's exploration of digital bonds should leverage offshore markets as a critical testing ground. By first piloting digital bonds offshore, China can accumulate valuable experience in assessing their performance and adaptability under different regulatory and market conditions. This pilot approach mitigates risks while laying a practical foundation and reference model for the digital transformation of the domestic bond market.

Digital offshore bonds are rapidly gaining traction among global investors due to their high investability and tradability. The application of DLT ensures that transaction data remains immutable and fully transparent, significantly enhancing international investors' trust in China's offshore bond market and increasing its appeal on the global stage. The integration of blockchain technology streamlines the entire bond lifecycle—from issuance and trading to final settlement—optimizing China's offshore bond market infrastructure and fostering the development of a cross-border digital bond circulation system. This, in turn, enhances the internationalization of China's bond market and strengthens its standing in the global financial system. Furthermore, the interoperability between compliant digital asset platforms and cross-border digital currency payment systems creates new opportunities for integrating digital bonds with digital stablecoins. This synergy not only diversifies investment options but also paves the way for the digital yuan's adoption in international settlements, further advancing the currency's internationalization.

Typical Case of RWA and Tokenization in Investment and Financing

5

5.1 Bonds

In February 2023, the Hong Kong Special Administrative Region (HKSAR) Government successfully issued HK$800 million in tokenized green bonds,[1] making it one of the first government-issued tokenized green bonds in the world. As of the end of March 2023, the total issuance of tokenized bonds worldwide had reached $3.9 billion, with 90% issued between 2021 and 2023. This was partly driven by the U.S. Federal Reserve's continued interest rate hikes since 2021, leading to higher bond yields and increasing the appeal of tokenized bonds.

U.S. Treasury securities are debt instruments issued by the U.S. Department of the Treasury to fund federal government expenditures. Fully backed by the U.S. federal government, U.S. Treasuries are considered among the safest investments globally. They are widely held by individuals, banks, financial institutions, as well as governments and central banks worldwide. During times of economic uncertainty, U.S. Treasuries are regarded as a safe-haven asset. As of July 4, 2024, the market size of tokenized U.S. Treasuries stood at approximately $1.8 billion, with an average yield of 4.95% (see Fig. 5.1, where FOBXX represents U.S. government money market funds).

Specifically, U.S. Treasury tokenization projects can be categorized into the following types: projects backed by U.S. Treasury ETFs[2] such as Backed Finance,

[1] A green bond is a fixed-income financial instrument specifically designed to support environmental and climate-related projects, such as renewable energy, energy efficiency improvements, pollution prevention, sustainable water and waste management, and biodiversity conservation. The use of funds raised through these bonds is strictly regulated to ensure a positive environmental impact.

[2] An ETF is a type of fund that allows investors to buy and sell shares on an exchange, functioning similarly to stocks but typically representing a specific asset or portfolio of assets. By investing in ETFs, investors can conveniently diversify their holdings and track the performance of a particular

S. Ba et al., *RWA Tokenisation in Web 3.0 Era*, Management for Professionals,
https://doi.org/10.1007/978-981-96-7663-7_5

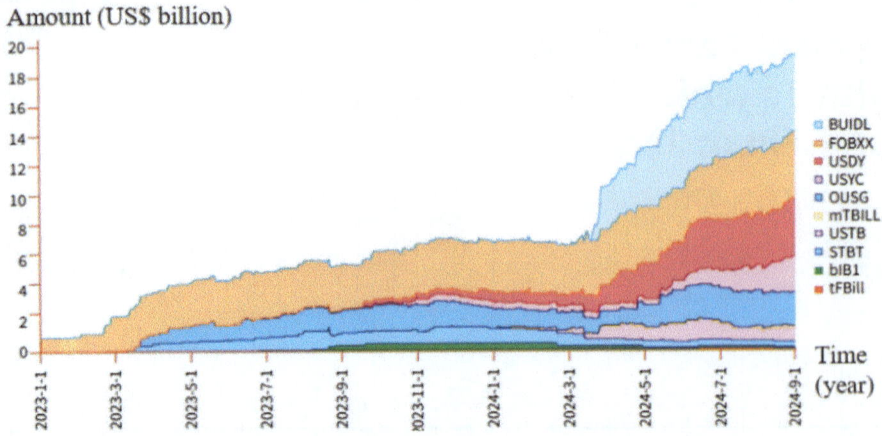

Fig. 5.1 Market size of tokenized U.S. treasury projects (*Source* rwa.xyz.com, as of July 4, 2024)

Swarm, MakerDAO, and ARKS Labs; projects backed by short-term U.S. Treasuries, including OpenEden, TrueFi, and Matrixdock; and projects backed by a diversified portfolio of assets, including U.S. Treasuries, U.S. government agency bonds, cash/reverse repos,[3] and corporate bonds, such as Franklin Templeton U.S. Government Money Fund Tokens, Superstate Trust, Ondo Finance, and Maple Finance. In this chapter, we will focus on two key projects: Ondo Finance's tokenization of U.S. government bonds and the Hong Kong Special Administrative Region Government's tokenized green bonds.

5.1.1 Case in Point: Ondo Finance's Tokenization of U.S. Government Bonds

Ondo Finance was founded in 2021 by Nathan Allman, a former Goldman Sachs digital asset executive, with a leadership team boasting experience at industry giants such as Goldman Sachs, Fortress, Bridgewater, and MakerDAO. As of August 2023, Ondo had raised $24 million in funding, with its Series A round led by Peter Thiel's Founders Fund, a prominent Silicon Valley angel investor, and Pantera Capital, a leading digital asset fund.

index. A U.S. Treasury ETF tracks the performance of a U.S. Treasury bond index. For example, the iShares 20+ Year Treasury Bond ETF (TLT) aims to track the performance of U.S. Treasury bonds with maturities exceeding 20 years.

[3] Cash/reverse repo refers to a form of short-term borrowing where an investor lends funds against securities as collateral and receives the principal plus agreed-upon interest upon maturity. Reverse repos are commonly used in financial markets to manage liquidity while providing investors holding cash with a short-term investment option.

As of September 2023, Ondo had issued four bond tokens: (1) OUSG, backed primarily by the BlackRock U.S. Treasury Bond ETF[4]; (2) OMMF, backed by U.S. money market funds,[5] which invest in highly rated U.S. government bonds and short-term debt instruments; (3) OSTB, backed by the PIMCO Enhanced Short Maturity Active ETF (MINT)[6]; (4) OHYG, backed by the iShares iBoxx High Yield Corporate Bond ETF.[7] As of July 2024, the latest iteration of Ondo's offerings has been streamlined to two bond tokens: OUSG, designed for accredited investors, and USDY, intended for retail investors.

5.1.2 Introduction to the 2023 Edition of OUSG Tokens

OUSG is Ondo's flagship product, with BlackRock, the world's largest asset manager, as its key partner. Before BlackRock launched the BlackRock USD Institutional Digital Liquidity Fund (BUIDL) in March 2024, the underlying asset of the 2023 edition of OUSG was the capital share of the Ondo Short-Term US Government Bond Fund ("Ondo Fund"). The primary asset held by the Ondo Fund was the fund share of the BlackRock Short-Term US Treasury Fund (SHV),[8] which itself exclusively holds U.S. short-term Treasury bonds. Thus, the underlying assets of OUSG can be considered U.S. short-term Treasury bonds.

The 2023 edition of the OUSG token was issued on the Ethereum blockchain. As of August 28, 2023, it had an issuance size of $156 million and an annualized yield of 5.06%. The token could be minted (i.e., subscribed) and redeemed on any U.S. business day at a price based on the "next daily NAV".[9] Investors were required to complete Know Your Customer (KYC) and Anti-Money Laundering (AML) verification before purchasing OUSG tokens on the Ondo platform. To qualify as an Ondo Finance investor, one had to meet both the Accredited

---

[4] The iShares Short Treasury Bond ETF (SHV) is designed to track the performance of an index composed of U.S. Treasury bonds with a remaining maturity of one year or less. It is an ETF listed and traded on the NASDAQ exchange, with approximately $20 billion in assets under management (as of September 2023) and an average daily trading volume of nearly $300 million.

[5] A money market fund (MMF) is a type of mutual fund that specializes in investing in money market instruments. In the U.S., money market funds primarily invest in government bonds, certificates of deposit, repurchase agreements, commercial paper, and other highly liquid, low-risk financial instruments. Additionally, money market funds serve as a major source of financing for large banks.

[6] The PIMCO Enhanced Short Maturity Active ETF (MINT) is a product of PIMCO (Pacific Investment Management Company) that focuses on short-duration, investment-grade debt securities.

[7] The iShares iBoxx $ High Yield Corporate Bond ETF (HYG) tracks the performance of high-yield corporate bonds, offering investors relatively high returns while carrying elevated risk.

[8] In addition to SHV holdings, a small portion of stablecoins and USD cash is maintained to facilitate subscription and redemption transactions.

[9] The NAV is calculated by the fund manager.

Investor[10] and Qualified Purchaser[11] criteria—an Accredited Investor is defined based on personal financial status or income, while a Qualified Purchaser is determined by the size of their investment portfolio.

Once an investor was verified, they were added to a whitelist and required to review and sign documents such as the limited partnership agreement and subscription documents. They could then submit a subscription request for OUSG tokens via the Ondo smart contract and transfer either USD or stablecoins (USDC or DAI) to Ondo's digital asset account at Coinbase.[12] Ondo would calculate the "next daily NAV" and approve subscription requests. Upon approval, investors would receive OUSG tokens, while Ondo would use escrowed USD to purchase SHV via its securities broker and custodian, Clear Street, ensuring that the underlying assets matched the issued tokens. OUSG tokens did not directly pay interest. Instead, when SHV distributed dividends, the Ondo Fund reinvested the proceeds into additional SHV holdings, thereby increasing the value of the tokens. Investors who wished to receive periodic interest could do so by setting up automatic partial token sales.

To redeem the 2023 edition of OUSG tokens, investors needed to submit a redemption request through the smart contract. Ondo would calculate the next daily NAV and confirm the request before proceeding with the redemption process. If Ondo lacked sufficient stablecoins or USD for immediate redemption, it would sell the required amount of SHV through Clear Street to fulfill the redemption request. The settlement process—during which investors would receive stablecoins or USD—typically took 2–3 business days.[13] Upon completion of the SHV sale, Clear Street would transfer USD proceeds to Coinbase, where the funds would be converted into USDC. Ondo would then transfer the USDC to the investor's wallet, completing the redemption.

The underlying structure of the 2023 edition of the OUSG token was relatively complex (see Fig. 5.2). Ondo employed a traditional fund structure, managing OUSG tokens through multiple entities wholly owned by its parent company.

[10] The concept of an accredited investor was previously discussed in the Centrifuge case.

[11] A Qualified Institutional Buyer (QIB) is a type of investor that, due to its sophisticated investment experience, is exempt from certain regulatory protections under the Securities Act's registration provisions. Typically, a QIB is an entity managing at least $100 million in securities investments independently or a registered broker-dealer investing at least $10 million in unaffiliated securities. On August 26, 2020, the SEC amended the definitions of QIB and Accredited Investor, expanding the list of eligible entities. This included institutions that were not explicitly listed as QIBs but qualified as Accredited Investors and met the $100 million securities ownership threshold. The amendments also allowed these entities to be formed solely for the purpose of acquiring offered securities.

[12] Coinbase was the first U.S.-based digital asset exchange to obtain a regulatory license and was listed on Nasdaq on April 14, 2021. On September 20, 2021, Coinbase launched Coinbase Prime, an institutional prime brokerage platform offering integrated trading, custody, and financing services for digital assets.

[13] The sale of ETFs requires two business days for settlement before USD or stablecoins become available.

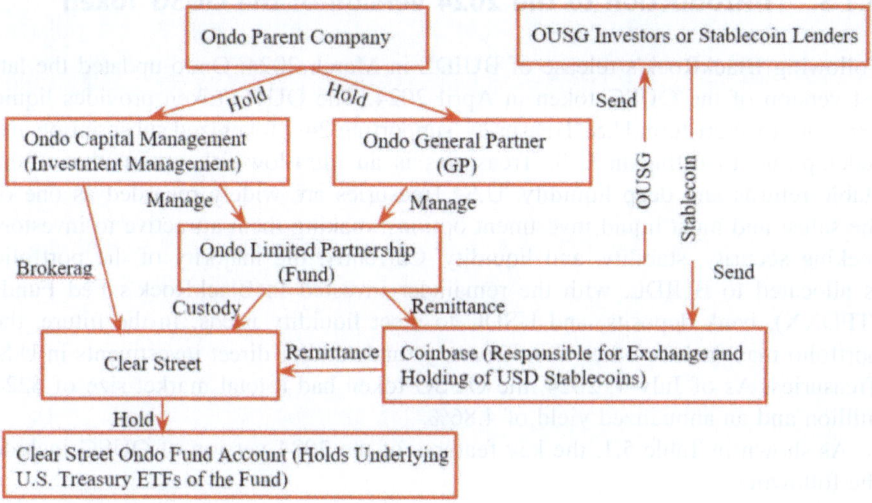

Fig. 5.2 The complex architecture behind Ondo's 2023 version of the OUSG token (*Source* Compiled based on information from the Ondo. Finance website)

At the same time, Ondo carefully selected third-party service providers that met regulatory requirements and ensured that the underlying assets were held at a bankruptcy-protected custodian. The structure was as follows: Ondo's parent company, Ondo Finance Inc., established a general partner entity, Ondo I GP, to manage the Ondo Fund and coordinate its operations. Ondo Finance Inc. also founded a wholly owned subsidiary, Ondo Capital Management LLC, to assist Ondo I GP in fund management. Additionally, Ondo created a limited partnership, Ondo I LP, which served as the issuer of the Ondo Fund. Ondo I LP was responsible for receiving investor funds in USD, issuing OUSG tokens, and purchasing or liquidating SHV, the underlying asset of the Ondo Fund.

Additionally, several companies provide key services to the Ondo Fund, including: • Clear Street, a broker-dealer and custodian, manages the SHV fund shares held in the Depository Trust & Clearing Corporation (DTCC)[14] accounts for Ondo Fund management. Coinbase Prime facilitates the receipt and custody of stablecoins for the Ondo Fund and enables conversions between stablecoins and U.S. dollars. • NAV Consulting provides third-party fund administration services, including daily net asset value (NAV) calculations. • Richey May serves as the tax advisor and auditor for the Ondo Fund.

[14] The Depository Trust & Clearing Corporation (DTCC) is the world's largest financial transaction clearing and settlement service provider. Through its subsidiaries, DTCC offers clearing, settlement, and various information services for transactions involving equities, corporate and municipal bonds, government and mortgage-backed securities, over-the-counter derivatives, and emerging market bonds.

5.1.3 Introduction to the 2024 Version of the OUSG Token

Following BlackRock's release of BUIDL in March 2024, Ondo updated the latest version of the OUSG token in April 2024. The OUSG token provides liquid exposure to short-term U.S. Treasuries, supporting 24/7 tokenized subscription and redemption. Investing in U.S. Treasuries is an ultra-low-risk option that offers stable returns and deep liquidity. U.S. Treasuries are widely regarded as one of the safest and most liquid investment options, making them attractive to investors seeking security, stability, and liquidity. Currently, the majority of the portfolio is allocated to BUIDL, with the remainder invested in BlackRock's Fed Funds (TFDXX), bank deposits, and USDC to meet liquidity needs. In the future, the portfolio may include other U.S. Treasury funds and/or direct investments in U.S. Treasuries. As of July 4, 2024, the OUSG token had a total market size of $224 million and an annualized yield of 4.86%.

As shown in Table 5.1, the key features of the 2024 version of OUSG include the following:

- **Instant 24/7/365 Minting and Redemption**

  By investing with USDC through the official website, investors immediately receive OUSG tokens at the same wallet address used for the investment. Investors can also instantly redeem OUSG tokens for USDC. For security reasons and due to service partner limitations, the amount available for instant minting or redemption within any given 24-hour period is capped at the amount displayed on the official website.
- **Lower Minimum Investment and Redemption Amounts**

  For instant transactions, the minimum investment and redemption amount is $10,000. For non-instant transactions, the minimum investment is $100,000, and the minimum redemption amount is $50,000

Table 5.1 Comparison of OUSG and rOUSG

Category	OUSG	rOUSG
Token type	Accumulating	Redistributing (Distribution)
Yield distribution overview	Reflecting by increasing the redemption price (Net Asset Value per Share)	Distributed daily in the form of additional rOUSG tokens
Token price	Increases as treasury yields grow	Maintained at $1.00
Scope of application	Buying and holding for cash management (some custodians only support accumulation tokens), collateral in smart contracts	Interest-bearing settlement or medium of exchange

- **Accumulation (OUSG Tokens) and Reset (rOUSG Tokens) Versions**

  OUSG tokens are available in two versions: the accumulation version (OUSG token) and the reset version (rOUSG token), which maintains a stable price of $1 (see Table 5.1). As the value of the underlying assets appreciates, the price of OUSG tokens increases over time. In contrast, rOUSG tokens distribute returns in the form of additional rOUSG tokens rather than price appreciation. For example, if an investor holds 100 rOUSG tokens and the OUSG token price rises from $1.00 to $1.01, the rOUSG token price remains fixed at $1.00, but the investor's wallet balance increases to 101 rOUSG tokens. This automatic "reset" occurs daily when Ondo updates the OUSG token price on business days.
- **Simple, instant conversion of OUSG and rOUSG tokens**

  Investors can easily and instantly switch between OUSG and rOUSG tokens at any time on Ondo's website.
- **Waiver of management fees**

  Ondo's management fee on OUSG tokens is maintained at a low rate of 0.15%. These fees have been waived until January 1, 2025.
- **How the 2024 version of the OUSG token works**

  Suppose an investor wants to use 100,000 USDC to make an instant investment in OUSG tokens. When the investor makes a deposit, the smart contract automatically performs two actions: first, it determines how many OUSG tokens the investor should receive. The amount of OUSG tokens received depends on converting the deposited stablecoin to its USD equivalent (1 USDC = 1.00 USD) and then dividing this amount by the current net asset value (NAV) of OUSG tokens. For example, if an investor deposits 100,000 USDC worth $100,000, and the NAV is $100 per token, the investor will receive $100,000/ $100 = 1,00 OUSG tokens. The deposited USDC is then transferred to the fund's Coinbase account, where it is used to purchase the underlying assets of the OUSG token.

At the end of each business day, Ondo updates the fund's net asset value (NAV) based on the performance of the underlying assets and any accrued fees and/ or expenses. The NAV of each OUSG token is then calculated by dividing the total NAV of the OUSG share class by the total number of OUSG tokens. Next, the on-chain OUSG token price is updated to reflect the new NAV. Finally, the OUSG token price update automatically triggers an rOUSG token reset, with the updated balance automatically reflected in the investor's wallet (if the investor holds rOUSG tokens).

When an investor requests an instant redemption of OUSG tokens, a similar process occurs in reverse. The amount of USDC the investor receives is determined by multiplying the number of OUSG tokens redeemed by the prevailing NAV (expressed in USD) and then transferring an equivalent amount of USDC at a fixed rate of $1.00 per USDC.

5.1.4 USDY Token Overview

The USDY token is a tokenized note backed by short-term U.S. Treasury securities and bank demand deposits. Available to non-U.S. individual and institutional investors, USDY is designed to combine the accessibility of stablecoins with high-quality, USD-denominated yields. Developing a product that meets these criteria while adhering to applicable U.S. laws and regulations does impose certain constraints. For instance, although investors begin accruing interest immediately upon Ondo's receipt of their deposit, USDY tokens can only be minted and made transferable after 40–50 days. Additionally, Ondo can only process redemptions via bank wire transfers to non-U.S. bank accounts. USDY is overcollateralized by a 3.29% principal-protected position partially funded by Ondo Finance, reinforcing the link between USDY and Ondo Finance. This overcollateralization also serves as a buffer against short-term price fluctuations in U.S. Treasuries. As of July 4, 2024, the total USDY token supply stands at $331 million, with an annualized yield of 5.30%.

- **USDY Token Subscription**

  Once investors complete the verification process, they will receive an email notification confirming their eligibility to invest. From that point onward, they can deposit USDC and USDT at any time. For deposits exceeding $100,000, bank wire transfers are also accepted. After Ondo processes the funds (typically within 2–3 business days), investors will begin earning interest.

  Investors' purchases are placed in a queue that determines the date on which Ondo can issue tokens to them. This approach ensures compliance with legal and regulatory requirements. Once Ondo has processed an investor's funds, the investor receives a temporary global certificate, which grants them the right to receive the tokens as soon as Ondo is permitted to issue them. This typically occurs 40–50 days after Ondo processes the investor's deposit. The issuance date will be specified in the investor's temporary global certificate. Upon maturity, the tokens will be delivered to the designated wallet, after which investors are free to transfer them to any eligible recipient within permitted jurisdictions.
- **USDY Token Redemption**

  To comply with applicable U.S. laws and regulations, Ondo can only process redemptions via bank wire transfers to non-U.S. bank accounts. Investors who wish to redeem must provide Ondo with the necessary banking details before their redemption request can be processed. Redemptions of temporary global certificates (i.e., prior to the issuance of USDY tokens) are only available for amounts exceeding $100,000. For smaller amounts, investors must wait until the tokens are minted before redeeming them.

Table 5.2 Comparison of OUSG and USDY

	OUSG	USDY
Collateral	Short-term U.S. Treasuries (SHV)	Short-term U.S. Treasuries and bank deposits, plus equity subordination
Return rate	Tracks BlackRock's SHV short-term treasury ETF, net of fees; slight interest rate risk	Floating rate determined by Ondo Finance; no principal fluctuation due to interest rate risk
Investor region	Global (U.S. and non-U.S.)	Non-U.S
Investor eligibility	Institutional (Qualified Purchasers)	Retail and Institutional
Issuer	Ondo I LP	Ondo USDY LLC
Legal structure	Limited Partnership Interest	Senior secured loan

5.1.5 Comparison of OUSG and USDY Tokens

As shown in Table 5.2, both OUSG and USDY tokens are institutional-grade tokenized cash equivalents, but they differ slightly in terms of target investors and use cases, as outlined in the following five aspects:

- OUSG provides tokenized exposure to short-term U.S. Treasury bonds, while USDY is backed by tokenized Treasury bonds and bank deposits.
- OUSG represents a membership/equity interest in a fund holding Treasury bonds and money market instruments, whereas USDY is an interest-bearing note.
- Both OUSG and USDY are total return instruments—any interest earned on the underlying assets is reinvested, causing the token value to appreciate over time.
- OUSG is available exclusively to accredited investors on a global scale, while USDY is accessible only in eligible jurisdictions but does not require investor accreditation.
- OUSG can be freely traded on the secondary market at any time but only among investors who have completed Ondo's verification process. USDY, on the other hand, is subject to a lock-up period during which it cannot be traded, but once this period ends, it can be freely transferred within eligible regions.

5.1.6 Introduction to the FluxFinance Protocol

In addition to issuing a series of tokens, the Ondo team developed the FluxFinance Protocol (Flux), a decentralized lending platform, which was later sold to Neptune Foundation. Flux operates on a peer-to-pool (p2pool) model, supporting overcollateralized lending with the following key features:

- Lenders can earn interest by supplying stablecoins to Flux. There are no restrictions for USDC lenders.

- Borrowers can take out stablecoin loans by depositing collateral. USDC borrowers using OUSG tokens as collateral must meet OUSG token eligibility requirements.
- Flux is governed by Ondo DAO.

Managed by a decentralized autonomous organization (DAO), the Flux protocol is designed to provide leveraged exposure to U.S. Treasury yields. It allows OUSG holders to use their tokens as collateral to borrow stablecoins from the platform. Retail investors who do not meet the eligibility criteria to purchase OUSG tokens can still gain indirect exposure to U.S. Treasury yields by lending USDC to OUSG holders on FluxFinance.

- **fTokens Tokens**

  Users can deposit assets into Flux to mint fTokens, which are ERC-20 tokens representing their balance within the protocol. Some of the deposited assets may be lent out by the protocol, generating interest as a return for users. For example, a user can deposit USDC into Flux to mint fUSDC. By doing so, the user's USDC becomes available for borrowers, and the user earns the USDC supply rate. Lenders earn interest by minting fTokens. The interest accrued by the protocol is not distributed; instead, the exchange rate of fTokens changes, allowing users to redeem their assets at any time. Borrowers use fTokens as collateral to borrow other assets. These collateralized fTokens also accrue interest, potentially offsetting part of the borrowing cost. fTokens are generally transferable. However, for permissioned assets, fTokens adhere to the transfer restrictions of the underlying asset, which may result in failed transfers if they would cause the borrower's account liquidity to become negative.
- **Lending**

  Lenders provide assets to the Flux market (by depositing them into a pool) and collectively earn interest on the supplied assets (i.e., the supply rate). The protocol then makes these assets available to borrowers, who deposit other assets as collateral. Users become lenders by depositing assets and minting fTokens. The interest accrued by the protocol is not distributed; instead, the exchange rate of fTokens increases over time, allowing users to redeem more assets as interest accumulates. The interest rate earned by lenders (the supply rate) fluctuates depending on market utilization (i.e., the percentage of deposited assets that have been borrowed). Although unlikely, in extreme cases, lenders may incur losses if the protocol accumulates bad debt.
- **Borrowing**

  Flux is an overcollateralized lending protocol. Borrowers must provide collateral worth more than their debt to demonstrate their ability to repay. Each asset has a specific collateral factor, determining the portion of its value that can be borrowed. Assets with a collateral factor of zero cannot be used as collateral.

Like lenders, borrowers mint fTokens and deposit them as collateral. When assets are used as collateral, the supplied assets continue to accrue interest (i.e., the supply rate), which may offset the borrower's cost of borrowing (i.e., the borrow rate).

The borrowing rate for an asset fluctuates based on its utilization rate (i.e., the percentage of the asset pool that has been borrowed). As utilization increases, the borrowing rate rises to balance the supply and demand of the asset. Once utilization surpasses a threshold (the "kink point"), the borrowing rate increases sharply, incentivizing borrowers to repay part of their debt to maintain sufficient liquidity for lenders.

Borrowers should monitor their positions to ensure their loan-to-value (LTV) ratio remains at a healthy level. If an account's liquidity (i.e., the aggregate collateral factor of its assets) turns negative, the borrower's account becomes subject to liquidation and may incur a small liquidation fee.

- **Liquidation**

  Flux operates as a self-sustaining overcollateralized lending protocol. Borrowers' collateral value must always exceed their debt balance to ensure that neither the protocol nor its lenders suffer losses. Liquidation events on Flux should be relatively rare. Supported markets, especially those with eligible collateral, are generally not highly volatile. However, in certain extreme cases, a borrower's equity may become insufficient, requiring liquidation—where a portion of their collateral is sold to repay the debt. Third-party liquidators (typically bots) are incentivized to perform this function, as they can purchase collateral at a slight discount relative to the oracle price. To avoid liquidation, investors should monitor their LTV ratio and ensure it remains at a healthy level.

- **Governance**

  Flux is governed by OndoDAO. Ondo issues the ONDO token, whose holders control the protocol through on-chain governance proposals, including decisions on economic parameters and smart contract upgrades. Initially, the ONDO token was non-transferable and used solely for governance. Flux Finance expands the use case for Ondo's tokenized bonds by allowing users to earn yields on U.S. Treasuries while leveraging repeated borrowing. This enables broader distribution of U.S. Treasury yields to decentralized platform users, lowers investment barriers, and maximizes returns generated from the tokenization of U.S. Treasury yields. The ONDO token was issued during Ondo Finance's early transition and publicly sold on CoinList. Following the sale, the tokens were subject to a one-year lock-up period, after which they were released linearly on a monthly basis. Through an on-chain community vote, ONDO was unlocked for circulation on January 18, 2024. While ONDO serves a governance role within both Ondo DAO and Flux Finance, it has not yet been officially linked to real-world asset (RWA) products. However, the community remains open to this possibility, and in the future, ONDO may be incorporated as part of the incentive mechanism for RWA products like USDY.

Flux enhances the use case of OUSG, increasing the investment value of its token. At the same time, Flux enables broader distribution of U.S. Treasury yields to decentralized platform users, lowering investment barriers and making U.S. Treasury yields more accessible.

5.1.7 Case Study: Santander Bank Becomes the First Institution to Issue Public Blockchain Bonds

In September 2019, Spain's largest bank, Santander, pioneered the issuance of the first-ever $20 million "end-to-end" blockchain bond, marking a new chapter in the financial sector. Unlike traditional bond issuance models, this bond was directly issued and stored on the blockchain, achieving full digitalization and automation of the entire process. By tokenizing key elements such as the bond, cash, and cryptographic keys and registering them on the blockchain, Santander ensured the security and compliance of the entire transaction process. This innovative approach leveraged the advantages of blockchain technology to streamline bond issuance and management. Through automation, Santander significantly reduced intermediaries, improved transaction efficiency, and shortened settlement times. Additionally, smart contracts and time-lock mechanisms on the blockchain effectively minimized counterparty risks, providing greater security for investors.

The issuance of this "end-to-end" blockchain bond utilized the Ethereum blockchain system, with professional support from fintech company Nivaura and law firm Allen & Overy. Nivaura provided technical solutions to ensure a smooth issuance process, while Allen & Overy safeguarded legal compliance and investor rights.

The bond issued by Santander had a one-year maturity and a quarterly coupon rate of 1.98%. Throughout its term, all relevant data and entitlements were recorded digitally on the blockchain and custodied by Santander Securities Services. This innovative storage method not only enhanced data security and immutability but also provided investors with convenient access to query and manage their holdings.

Through this groundbreaking initiative, Santander demonstrated the determination and courage of traditional financial institutions to embrace cutting-edge technology and lead industry transformation. The successful issuance of the "end-to-end" blockchain bond provided valuable insights and lessons for the digital transformation of the bond market and the broader financial sector. It not only showcased the immense potential of blockchain technology in improving efficiency, reducing costs, and optimizing processes but also offered regulators a reference for exploring compliance pathways for innovative financial products.

5.1.8 Case Study: UBS Issues the World's First Blockchain-Settled Bond by a Major Financial Institution

In November 2022, Swiss banking giant UBS introduced a groundbreaking innovation—the UBS Digital Bond. This was the world's first digital bond issued by a major financial institution and settled using blockchain technology, marking a significant step forward in the application of blockchain in traditional finance. The total issuance amount was 300 million Swiss francs, with a maturity of three years. Unlike traditional bonds, this digital bond was issued, traded, and settled entirely on the blockchain. The full digitalization of the process not only simplified operations and increased automation but also significantly shortened transaction times. Thanks to blockchain technology, the digital bond enabled 24-hours trading, offering a clear advantage over traditional bonds, which are restricted to limited trading hours.

The UBS Digital Bond attracted strong interest and participation from institutional investors, including asset management firms and banks across Europe and Asia. This demonstrated market confidence in innovative digital bond products and reflected investors' growing demand for more efficient and cost-effective digital financial services. Notably, the UBS Digital Bond was the first in the market to be publicly traded on both a blockchain platform and a traditional exchange. The blockchain trading platform was SIX Digital Exchange (SDX), while the traditional exchange was SIX Swiss Exchange. This dual-trading channel approach accommodated diverse investor preferences and trading habits, fostering integration between digital and traditional bond markets while enhancing market liquidity and trading activity.

In terms of structure, the UBS Digital Bond was issued as a senior unsecured digital bond with a three-year term. The total issuance amount was 375,000,000 Swiss francs, with a coupon rate of 2.33% and ISIN code CH1228837865. The issuance date was November 14, 2022, with a maturity date of November 14, 2025. These key design elements were carefully structured to align with investors' risk preferences and return expectations, ensuring the bond's attractiveness and competitiveness.

In terms of technology selection, the UBS Digital Bond adopted a blockchain framework based on a consortium chain. Unlike public blockchains, consortium chains require participant nodes to undergo identity verification, offering higher credibility and security. Additionally, the project was designed in strict compliance with Swiss financial regulations, ensuring that regulatory authorities could access and track full-process data in real time, maintaining the same level of compliance as traditional bonds. This balance between innovation and regulation provides a valuable reference for the development of digital financial products.

The successful issuance of the UBS Digital Bond fully demonstrated the immense potential of blockchain technology in enhancing efficiency, reducing costs, and optimizing processes. It proved that this emerging technology is profoundly transforming traditional financial markets. Not only has it opened new avenues for the digital transformation of the bond market, but it has also injected fresh momentum into financial innovation.

5.1.9 Case Study: BOCI Issues the First Tokenized Security by a Chinese Financial Institution

In June 2023, BOCI successfully issued RMB 200 million in fully digital structured notes in Hong Kong, becoming the first Chinese financial institution to issue tokenized securities in the region. This milestone marked the official entry of China's investment banking sector into the era of RWA tokenization, ushering in a new chapter in digital transformation.

The digital notes issued by BOCI leveraged blockchain technology throughout the entire process, achieving end-to-end digitalization—from issuance and trading to clearing and settlement—all conducted on the blockchain. This significantly enhanced efficiency and reduced costs. Investors could access real-time note information via the blockchain, improving transparency and trust. This innovative model not only provided a successful case study for the digitalization of investment banking but also pointed the way for the broader digital transformation of financial products and services.

Notably, this digital note issuance was the result of deep collaboration between BOCI and UBS in the field of digital structured notes. Originally pioneered by UBS and offered to clients across the Asia–Pacific region, the product involved innovative legal and blockchain framework explorations. It became the first such tokenized security in the Asia–Pacific region structured under both Hong Kong and Swiss law and tokenized on the Ethereum public blockchain. This groundbreaking initiative not only set a legal precedent but also expanded the application scenarios of blockchain technology, successfully bringing regulated securities onto a public blockchain.

In terms of technology selection, the digital structured notes were developed on the Ethereum public blockchain, with the entire process of issuance and circulation conducted via blockchain. As the world's largest open-source public blockchain platform, Ethereum offers a robust technological ecosystem and strong community support, providing a reliable infrastructure for the issuance and trading of digital notes. Furthermore, the transparency and traceability of public blockchains facilitate regulatory oversight and auditing.

Of course, introducing regulated financial products onto a public blockchain also imposes higher compliance requirements. BOCI operated strictly in accordance with regulatory requirements to ensure the legality and compliance of digital notes across issuance, trading, and settlement. This provides valuable experience and insights for other financial institutions looking to undertake similar initiatives.

BOCI's issuance of fully digital structured notes marks an important milestone in the digital transformation of China's investment banking sector. It not only pioneers an innovative path for the industry but also explores new possibilities for applying blockchain technology in finance. In the future, as more financial institutions embrace digital transformation, China's investment banking sector is expected to become more intelligent, efficient, and inclusive—creating greater value for clients and contributing more to economic growth.

5.1.10 Case Study: Evergreen Tokenized Green Bond in Hong Kong

To explore the opportunities and potential of blockchain-based tokenized bonds, the Hong Kong Monetary Authority (HKMA) and the Hong Kong Centre of the BIS Innovation Hub collaborated in 2021 to conduct a conceptual test on the issuance of tokenized green bonds in Hong Kong. In February 2023, the Hong Kong Special Administrative Region (HKSAR) Government successfully issued HKD 800 million in tokenized green bonds under the Evergreen project, making it one of the world's first government-issued tokenized green bonds.

Hong Kong's *Securities and Futures Ordinance* does not explicitly require debt securities to be in paper form, meaning that existing regulations on authorization and issuance are also applicable to digital bond issuance and circulation. For corporate issuers, the Companies Ordinance's prospectus requirements similarly apply to digital bonds. Under the Evergreen project, the tokenized green bond was issued exclusively to "professional investors" as defined by the *Securities and Futures Ordinance*.

In Hong Kong, digital bonds can be issued in a "non-native" manner, where they are first issued off-chain before being tokenized, or in a "native" manner, where they are issued directly on a blockchain platform. Current regulations do not mandate a specific issuance method, and tokenized bonds can be considered a compliant form. However, issuers must ensure adherence to relevant regulations such as the Companies Ordinance.

As shown in Fig. 5.3, the issuance and subscription process of the Evergreen project is strategically divided into off-chain and on-chain segments. Before the full tokenization of the bond, traditional processes such as book building and pricing are conducted off-chain to maintain conventionality and reliability. On the book-building and pricing date, the Hong Kong Central Money Markets Unit (CMU) creates smart contracts on-chain to represent the actual rights of the tokenized bonds and to execute smart contract instructions for tokenized Hong Kong dollar cash. At this stage, platform-certified participants (such as distributors) must transfer the corresponding funds to the CMU-managed Real-Time Gross Settlement (RTGS) account before they can participate in the subscription process via smart contracts on the platform.

Subsequently, all activities related to digital transactions are conducted on Goldman Sachs' blockchain-based digital platform, GSDAP.[15] These activities include,

[15] The GS DAP platform is built using the open-source Daml smart contract language and the privacy-focused Canton blockchain, both developed by the U.S.-based blockchain technology

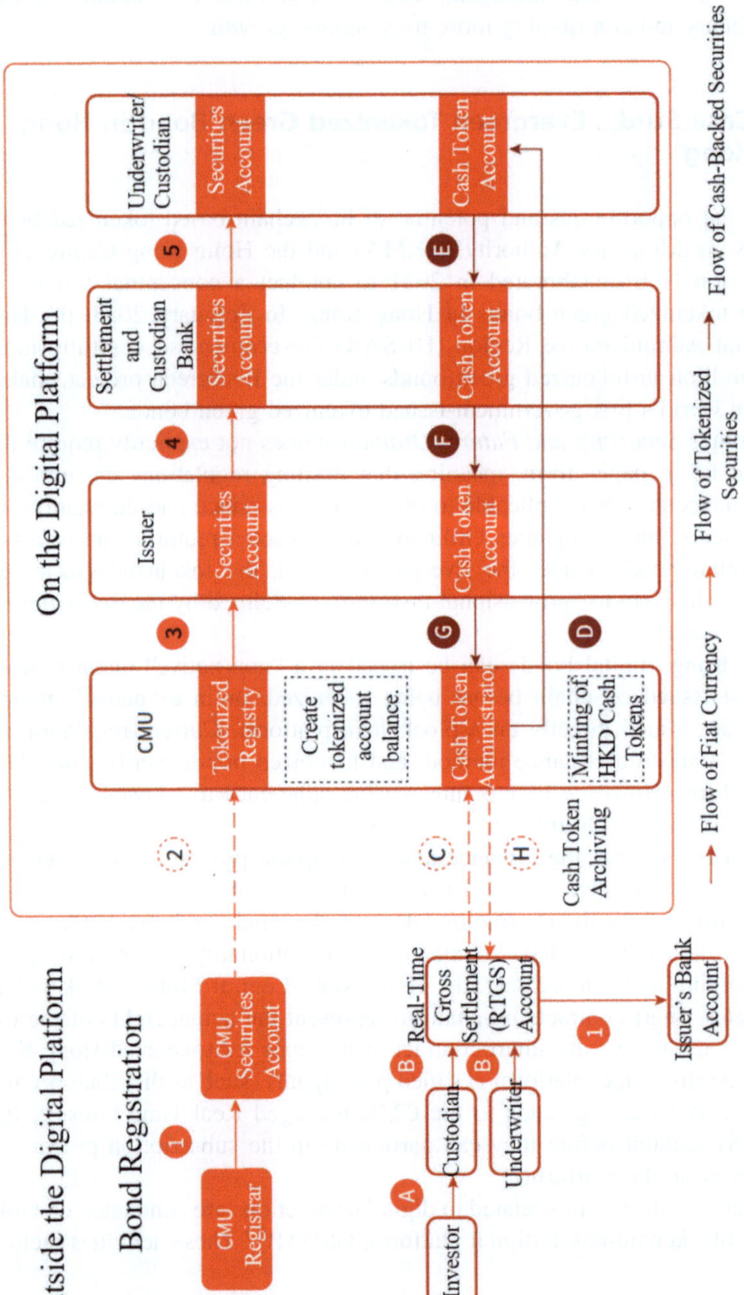

Fig. 5.3 Workflow for the release of the evergreen project (*Source* Hong Kong Monetary Authority)

but are not limited to, fund transfers, bond subscriptions, and secondary market transactions. The platform is accessible only to designated participants, including the issuer of the tokenized green bond (the Hong Kong Special Administrative Region Government), Hong Kong's central securities depository (CMU), the issuer's paying agent, the issuer's agent, distributors, custodians, and secondary market dealers. Each participant is assigned specific roles and responsibilities within the digital platform. Non-direct platform participants (such as clients who have already undergone KYC procedures with banks) hold their entitlements through custodians.

In this project, the digital platform utilizes Hyperledger Besu, an Ethereum-based permissioned blockchain, as the Layer 1 blockchain for node-to-node communication and consensus ledger maintenance. Additionally, the privacy-enabled, interoperable Canton Network serves as the Layer 2 blockchain, ensuring consistent execution efficiency among participating nodes. The visibility of certain smart contracts to different participants depends on whether they are signatories or observers of the relevant contracts.

Finally, all payment and settlement activities throughout the bond's lifecycle—such as interest payments and principal redemptions—are executed via the digital platform using tokenized Hong Kong dollar cash issued by the Hong Kong Monetary Authority. These operations are automated through smart contracts. Other digital securities transactions are settled using tokens that are not issued by the Monetary Authority or any central bank. These tokens, which may be designed for specific transactions, offer flexibility but pose significant risks in terms of counterparty exposure, operational stability, and liquidity. The adoption of a unified tokenized Hong Kong dollar cash ensured the smooth execution of the entire Evergreen project.

The most distinctive feature of the Evergreen tokenized green bond is its integration of DLT, achieving a high level of digitization and automation in financial business processes. This paperless, efficient, and transparent approach eliminates the need for physical certificates and manual entries during the bond tokenization process, saving time and reducing the risk of manual processing errors.

Through the DLT platform, all parties interact on-chain, enabling real-time verification and improving processing efficiency. Additionally, DLT ensures atomic transactions, allowing bond trading and cash payments to be conducted and settled instantly on the platform, thereby reducing settlement delays and risks. More notably, the tokenization of the Evergreen green bond represents an exploration of cross-platform interoperability, stablecoins, and standardization. It not only enhances connectivity between assets, public blockchains, and DLT platforms but also promotes the standardization of on-chain assets, providing a strong reference for global asset classification and regulatory frameworks.

company Digital Asset. Through its privacy protocol, digital assets ensure that data is shared only with eligible stakeholders while providing the scalability required for globally interconnected assets. In November 2022, the European Investment Bank (EIB) issued a €100 million two-year digital bond using this platform.

5.2 Supply Chain Finance

Small and medium-sized enterprises (SMEs) face numerous challenges in international trade financing, limiting their growth. Barriers such as difficulty in obtaining financing, high interest rates, capital shortages, complex processes, information asymmetry, and supply–demand mismatches make affordable trade financing inaccessible to SMEs. Despite the vast size of the global trade finance market, the financing gap for SMEs still amounts to $1.7 trillion.

Given the urgent financing needs of SMEs, several supply chain finance tokenization projects, such as Polytrade and OpenTrade, have emerged. These projects aim to simplify SME receivables financing through blockchain-based solutions, leveraging crypto assets to create new financing channels that address their trade finance needs.

5.2.1 Polytrade Company Overview

Polytrade was founded in 2021 by an Indian team with the goal of building a blockchain-based trade finance platform to provide funding for SMEs with short-term financial needs. Before transitioning into a blockchain platform, Polytrade was formerly Riqueza Capital, a company established in 2014 and headquartered in Hong Kong. The team has extensive experience in traditional trade finance. By 2020, Riqueza Capital had provided trade financing to 5000 sellers, with direct financing services for 250 of them, amounting to a total transaction value of $500 million. Since its launch in 2021, the Polytrade platform has facilitated over $11 million in loans across various trade sectors, including packing loans (37%), apparel businesses (16%), and leather manufacturers (13%). In March 2023, Polytrade completed its seed funding round, with key investors including Matrix Partners, Polygon Ventures, and Alpha Wave Global.

5.2.2 Polytrade 1.0

5.2.2.1 Platform Model

The most common trade financing gap occurs when suppliers or sellers have to wait an extended period to receive payment for delivered goods. Delayed receivables mean that businesses cannot promptly recover funds that could otherwise be reinvested for additional returns, leading to opportunity costs. As shown in Fig. 5.4, Polytrade plays a crucial role in bridging this gap by providing sellers with funding in a shorter timeframe. As sales increase, a large number of purchase invoices can be automatically converted into funds. Lenders purchase due invoices from suppliers at a discount and later collect the full invoice amount, generating profits or returns.

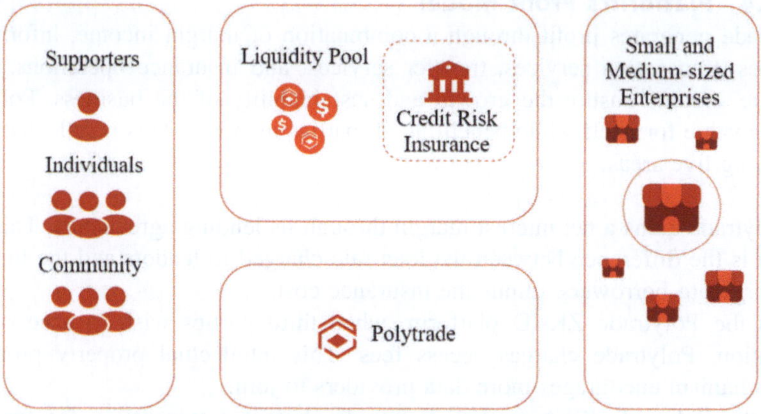

Fig. 5.4 How polytrade connects investors with SME financing

5.2.2.2 Core Aspects of the Platform

Polytrade leverages blockchain technology and algorithms to intelligently optimize assets, borrowers, risk management, and governance, ensuring security and efficiency in trade finance. This is reflected in four key areas:

- Asset Evaluation: Blockchain records asset data and payment history, while algorithmic ratings ensure the quality of underlying assets.
- Borrower Assessment: Blockchain data and submitted materials are analyzed through algorithms to assess borrower creditworthiness and determine loan interest rates.
- Risk Management: The platform prevents excessive concentration of single assets or borrowers by setting concentration limits and adjusting algorithms to ensure risk diversification.
- Governance Model: The governance is based on weighted collateralized voting. The more collateral staked, the greater the voting power. The governance team sets the system rules.

5.2.2.3 Platform Token

TRADE is the token used for governance participation on the Polytrade platform. Holders can vote on protocol upgrade decisions. It is also the utility token used within the platform for paying service fees, rewarding participants, incentivizing the protocol, staking to earn rewards, and facilitating settlements and clearing within the platform. The total supply of TRADE is 1 billion tokens, issued across multiple blockchains, with a reasonable issuance structure. Through the design of the TRADE token, Polytrade achieves unified token payments, governance participation, and fosters organic growth.

5.2.2.4 Platform's Profit Model

Polytrade generates profit through a combination of margin income, information services, transaction services, transfer services, and insurance operations. These revenue streams ensure the growth and sustainability of the business. Polytrade creates value for itself while benefiting all parties involved. This is reflected in the following five areas:

- Polytrade earns a net interest margin through its lending agreements. This margin is the difference between the loan rate charged to lenders and the loan rate charged to borrowers, minus the insurance cost.
- On the Polytrade ZK-ID platform, when third parties wish to access information, Polytrade charges access fees. This intellectual property protection mechanism encourages more data providers to join.
- In the Polytrade RWA market, Polytrade charges a transaction fee for every trade conducted.
- Polytrade also charges service fees when loan assets are transferred.
- Polytrade earns income by providing insurance and guarantee services.

5.2.2.5 Case Example

John runs a furniture manufacturing factory and sells furniture to IKEA with a 3-month credit term. This means that John will not receive payment for the goods until 3 months after shipment. During this period, John needs to pay employee wages, utility bills, purchase raw materials, and cover other costs for preparing future orders. This is where Polytrade comes into play (see Fig. 5.5). Polytrade can directly purchase the invoice and immediately pay 95% of the amount to John. After 3 months, Polytrade recovers the full invoice amount from IKEA. The remaining 5% is Polytrade's income, which compensates for the risk of paying John upfront. In short, Polytrade uses investors' funds to provide financing for SMEs like John. Polytrade uses these funds to finance businesses and regularly pays interest to investors. Through this model, Polytrade helps solve the short-term funding needs of SMEs, enabling fast capital flow and benefiting all parties. This tokenized financing provides new possibilities for the real economy.

5.2.3 Polytrade 2.0

After a year and a half of development, Polytrade launched the Polytrade 2.0 platform in early January 2024. The 2.0 platform extends beyond trade finance and consists of two unique but interconnected business lines: the RWA (Real-World Asset) Market and Institutional Technology. Both lines are based on Polytrade's core trading marketplace, tokenization technology, and ERC-6960 protocol technology, and integrate the rich experience Polytrade has accumulated in both traditional finance and decentralized finance.

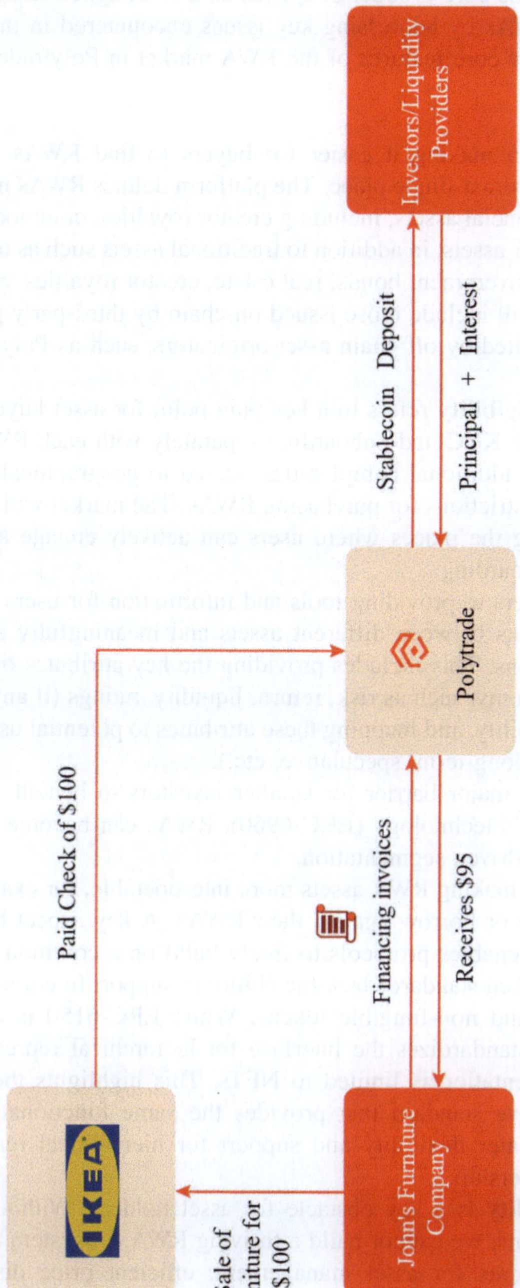

Fig. 5.5 John's process of using polytrade

5.2.3.1 RWA Market

The RWA Market is the core product of Polytrade 2.0, designed to aggregate and integrate on-chain RWAs by addressing key issues encountered in the traditional market ecosystem. The core features of the RWA market in Polytrade 2.0 include the following:

- **Discovery** refers to making it easier for buyers to find RWAs in the ever-growing universe from a single place. The platform defines RWAs more broadly than traditional financial assets, including creator royalties, commodities, physical goods, and other assets, in addition to traditional assets such as trade finance, structured credit, government bonds, real estate, creator royalties, etc. Assets in the RWA market will include those issued on-chain by third-party protocols, as well as assets initiated by off-chain asset originators, such as Polytrade's trade finance assets.
- **Onboarding & Eligibility** refers to a key pain point for asset buyers, which is the need to perform KYC and onboarding separately with each RWA protocol. This also includes additional complexities related to geographical, face value, and certification restrictions for purchasing RWAs. The market will simplify the process by filtering the places where users can actively engage and reducing redundancy in onboarding.
- **Consideration** refers to providing tools and information for users to meaningfully make decisions between different assets and meaningfully achieve their investment intentions. This includes providing the key attributes of RWAs in a standardized taxonomy, such as risk, return, liquidity, ratings (if any), structure, and expected eligibility, and mapping these attributes to potential user intentions (savings, treasury, long-term, speculative, etc.).
- **Ticket Sizes** are a major barrier for smaller investors to benefit from RWAs. Through Polytrade's technology (ERC-6960), RWAs can become more accessible through user-driven segmentation.
- **Usability** refers to making RWA assets more interoperable, for example, allowing users to utilize or borrow against their RWAs. A key aspect here is using ERC-6960, which enables protocols to freely build on a common standard for RWAs. Existing token standards lack the ability to support fractional ownership of both fungible and non-fungible tokens. While ERC-6150 is an extension of ERC-721 that standardizes the interface for hierarchical representations of NFTs, its implementation is limited to NFTs. This highlights the need for a more comprehensive standard that provides the same functionality as ERC-1155 but with greater flexibility and support for hierarchical representations and fractional ownership.
- **Secondary Liquidity** is a key obstacle for asset holders. Without a place to transfer RWA tokens, we cannot build a thriving RWA ecosystem that includes the basic components for asset management, efficient price discovery, and portfolio creation.

Polytrade believes that addressing these core components will lead to demand aggregation, which is crucial for the maturation of the RWA ecosystem. Similar to how OpenSea and Blur created the Art NFT market, a single gateway for RWAs will create a real and thriving market for RWAs.

5.2.3.2 Institutional Technology

The Polytrade team has recognized a surge in interest from other institutions in their core technology, including the ERC-6960 used for tokenizing any physical asset or real-world asset, as well as the Polytrade trading marketplace. Polytrade is part of the Mastercard StartPath Cohort and is also one of the first applications on the Mastercard MTN network.

Polytrade 2.0's institutional technology business line includes collaboration with large banks, institutions, and enterprises, using Polytrade's suite of front-end and back-end technologies to address their challenges. This includes the ERC-6960, market, lender agreements, compliance anti-money laundering (AML) management, lender workflow manager, and lender administrator. Revenue models for the institutional technology business line include platform fees, subscriptions, implementation fees, and service revenues.

5.2.3.3 Evaluation

The Polytrade team has outlined key metrics for evaluating the Polytrade 2.0 platform on their official website, including:

- Total users on the marketplace and loyalty portal
- Total investment in assets through the marketplace (primary or secondary)
- Transaction volume of technology deployed for institutions
- **Total transaction volume**

  This refers to the total sum of all transactions made through the Polytrade platform, including market transactions and institutional deployment transactions.
- **Revenue / Fees**

  1. Market transaction fees, primary fees, channel partner alliance revenue, listing fees, and ecosystem fees;
  2. Airdrop and distribution revenue from partner collaborations distributed to users through the Polytrade portal;
  3. Platform and setup fees for institutional technology.

5.3 Collateralized Credit

Collateralized credit tokenization refers to the transformation of the claims on collateralized loans into digital tokens that are issued and circulated on the blockchain. Tokenization not only enhances the liquidity of these claims and reduces transaction costs, but it also brings greater transparency and efficiency to the collateralized credit market. Currently, there are two main types of projects in the collateralized credit tokenization field: one supports tokenization of fully collateralized credit, such as Centrifuge; the other supports tokenization of under-collateralized credit, such as Goldfinch.

5.3.1 Centrifuge—A Representative Project for Fully Collateralized Credit Tokenization

Centrifuge, founded in 2017, is one of the first projects to explore the tokenization of Real-World Assets (RWA). The project aims to decentralize the process, addressing the liquidity and opacity issues in the collateralized credit market, offering a new solution for financing real-world assets. As of July 4, 2024, Centrifuge has raised over $600 million, with around 1500 projects completing collateralized financing through Centrifuge.

The founding team of Centrifuge has extensive Web 2.0 entrepreneurial experience. The co-founder and CEO, Lucas Vogelsang, founded the e-commerce startup DeinDeal and successfully sold it. Later, Vogelsang moved to Silicon Valley and joined Taulia, where he served as a technical manager. Another co-founder and the current Chief Operating Officer (COO) is Martin Quensel. Quensel started his career at SAP, where he worked as a software developer and architect. Before co-founding Centrifuge, Quensel was also one of the co-founders of Taulia.

Centrifuge transforms RWAs such as real estate loans, invoices, microloans, and consumer finance assets into NFTs and forms asset pools.[16] These asset pools allow liquidity providers to have recourse under legal frameworks, offering DeFi users a relatively stable source of returns. Traditional RWA financing processes require the participation of multiple intermediaries. For example, when a company issues a bond, the process might involve multiple entities like lead arrangers, investment banks, lawyers, payment agents, financial agents, auditors, registrars, transfer agents, calculation agents, listing agents, rating agencies, etc. The involvement of these intermediaries increases the financing costs. By replacing the functions of various intermediaries with smart contracts, the dependency on intermediaries can be greatly reduced, leading to a more cost-effective, open, transparent, and efficient financing method.

[16] Centrifuge's Asset Pool refers to tokenizing a series of RWAs (such as accounts receivable, real estate loans, etc.) and aggregating these RWA tokens into a liquidity pool that can be traded through DeFi mechanisms. This allows investors to trade RWA tokens directly on the blockchain, significantly enhancing asset liquidity.

Centrifuge connects on-chain operations with off-chain asset transactions, eliminating numerous intermediary steps, making the corporate financing process more open, efficient, and cost-effective, and providing small and medium-sized enterprises with financing opportunities equivalent to those available to large corporations.

As shown in Fig. 5.6, Centrifuge has built a complex and sophisticated framework combining financial engineering and digital technologies. At the bottom layer is the P2P information transmission protocol, which serves as the underlying transmission network of the blockchain. The middle layer is the core architecture for tokenizing real-world assets (RWA), where RWA tokenization is completed within the Centrifuge ecosystem, and functions such as token collateralization and lending are carried out. In this middle layer, the Centrifuge Chain, as the underlying blockchain, provides an immutable and unified data source for all participants while handling the creation, transfer, and collateralization of RWA NFTs, as well as cross-chain interactions with Ethereum. NFTs, anchors,[17] and identities[18] on the Centrifuge Chain provide the foundation for RWA tokenization and validation, ensuring that these RWA tokens align with their corresponding real-world assets. The middle layer also includes Tinlake and other DApps. By using Tinlake, RWA holders can collateralize RWA NFTs, convert them into tranches of ERC-20 tokens, and pledge them for stablecoin borrowing. This enables RWA holders to obtain loans based on DeFi, integrating RWA into the broader DeFi ecosystem. In July 2023, Centrifuge officially launched the upgraded Centrifuge App, which integrates all Centrifuge services and gradually replaces Tinlake. However, for the sake of clarity, we will continue to introduce different components separately in the following sections.

Centrifuge believes that using a dedicated blockchain has several advantages when addressing the tokenization of real-world assets (RWA). Therefore, Centrifuge Chain was developed based on the Substrate[19]framework. This is a blockchain built on Polkadot,[20] which offers relatively low gas fees, excellent scalability, and greater flexibility. A key feature is that Centrifuge Chain reserves

[17] An anchor refers to the use of data processing and encryption techniques to convert information about physical assets into a verifiable hash value, which is stored on Centrifuge Chain to ensure the accuracy and security of asset information.

[18] Identities are based on decentralized identity standards (e.g., ERC-725), allowing all participants to have their own on-chain digital identities for identity verification and proof of asset ownership.

[19] Substrate is an open-source, modular, and scalable blockchain development framework designed for building blockchains. Substrate can be used to develop public chains, consortium chains, and private chains, enabling the rapid construction of complete, configurable blockchain systems. Additionally, developers can deploy the blockchain they build as a parachain on the Polkadot network to enable communication, asset trading, and shared security among different chains.

[20] Polkadot is an expandable, heterogeneous multi-chain blockchain composed of a decentralized network of interconnected blockchains. In this network, the relay chain interacts with parallel-running parachains, with all parachains sharing the security of the relay chain. Centrifuge Chain is a parachain on Polkadot.

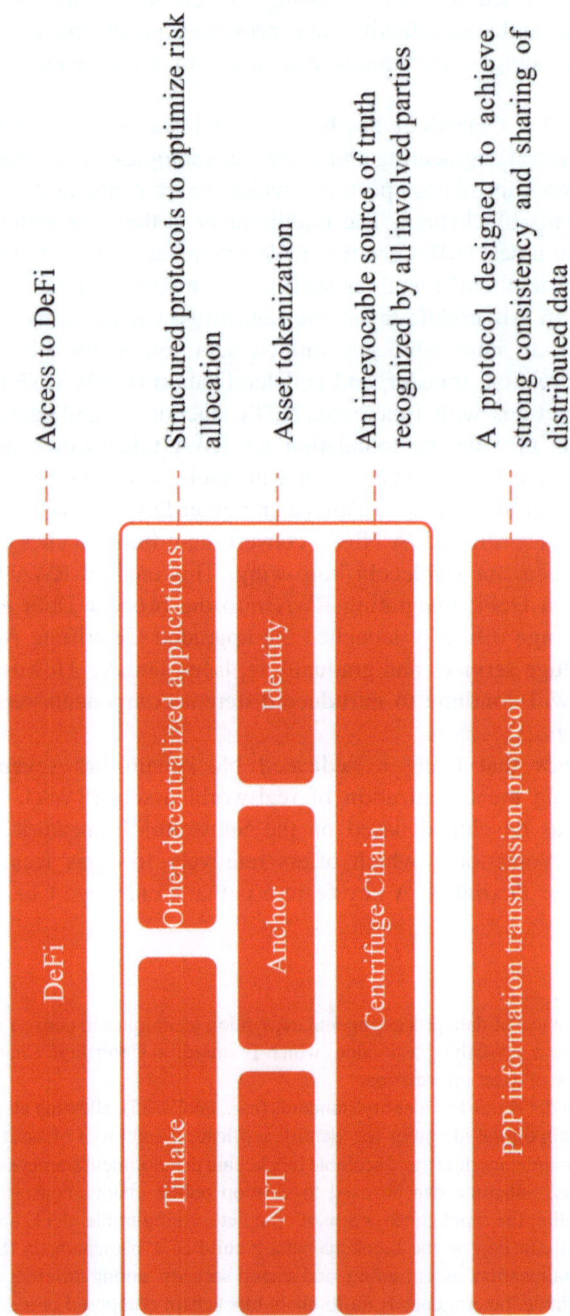

Fig. 5.6 Centrifuge overall architecture and key components

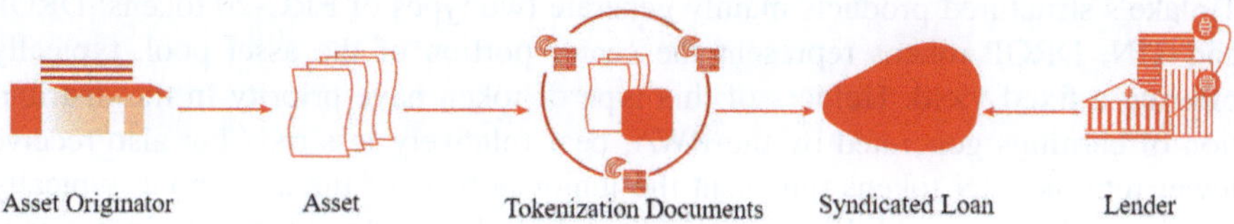

Fig. 5.7 RWA token creation process on centrifuge

dedicated block space[21] to handle transactions related to RWA tokens, ensuring that there is always enough block space for such transactions. Even in extreme cases where blockchain congestion occurs due to a surge in transaction volume, financial activities related to RWA will not be affected. This is particularly attractive to large institutions that need to ensure uninterrupted transaction flow.

Another key component of Centrifuge is Tinlake, a DApp built on Ethereum that converts various RWA NFTs into tokens compliant with the ERC-20 standard. As shown in Fig. 5.7, in order to create RWA tokens on Centrifuge, each asset originator needs to convert the RWA into an NFT. These NFTs contain important information required for asset pricing, financing, and valuation, and embed the relevant legal documents to ensure the authenticity and legality of the asset. At the same time, the asset originator needs to create an asset pool on Tinlake, deposit the RWA NFTs into the pool, and use the RWA tokens as collateral to ultimately secure stablecoin loans. Different types of RWAs correspond to different asset pools. As of November 6, 2023, Centrifuge has 16 asset pools, including those for credit, trade, commercial real estate, voluntary carbon offsets, music streaming, U.S. Treasury bonds, and more.

Tinlake adopts a structured[22] approach, generating multiple tokens with different risk and return profiles based on RWA NFTs to meet the varying risk preferences and return expectations of different types of investors.[23] Specifically,

---

[21] Block space refers to the storage capacity for transaction data within a blockchain. Each block in a blockchain has a maximum capacity limit, which restricts the amount of transaction data it can hold. The larger the block space, the more transactions it can handle at a time, potentially increasing network throughput. However, due to limited space in each block, transaction participants typically need to pay fees to compete for space. In Centrifuge Chain, dedicated block space for RWA token transactions ensures that these transactions are prioritized for processing, even during network congestion, guaranteeing smooth execution.

[22] Infinancial engineering, "structured" refers to the process of creating financial products that meet specific investment or financing needs through the design and combination of financial instruments. Structured products include a wide range of tools such as derivatives, debt, and equity instruments, and can offer investors solutions for yield optimization, risk management, or tax benefits. In structured finance, different capital tranches are usually involved: senior tranches, which are prioritized for cash flow payments and are considered lower risk with lower returns, and subordinate tranches (also known as junior tranches), where investors only receive residual cash flows after senior tranches are fully paid, but they assume higher risk and have the potential for higher returns.

[23] Investors earn rewards by purchasing DROP or TIN tokens from Centrifuge's asset pools, providing funding for asset originators to finance assets and earn returns and CFG token rewards.

Tinlake's structured products mainly generate two types of ERC-20 tokens: DROP and TIN. DROP tokens represent the senior portion of the asset pool, typically offering a fixed yield. Holders of this type of token have priority in the distribution of earnings generated by the RWA, bear relatively less risk, but also receive lower returns. TIN tokens represent the junior portion of the asset pool, typically offering a floating yield. Holders of these tokens have a lower priority in earnings distribution, face greater risk, but have the potential for higher returns. On the Tinlake platform, investors can choose to purchase DROP or TIN tokens based on their risk tolerance and return expectations. TIN tokens have a minimum subscription ratio, and if the subscription ratio for TIN is too low, investors will not be able to increase their holdings of DROP tokens. This design enhances risk management for RWA asset pools.

Over the past four years, Tinlake has made significant contributions to Centrifuge, including creating the world's first RWA asset pool for MakerDAO, launching the RWA market in collaboration with Aave, and partnering with BlockTower to bring the first credit fund's operations on-chain. In May 2024, to provide a better user experience, Centrifuge launched a new, secure, reliable, and simplified upgraded DApp to gradually replace the Tinlake protocol. However, some core functions and business logic of Tinlake, such as asset tokenization, investment structuring, on-chain net asset value (NAV), and revolving liquidity pools, will still be applicable.

In addition, Centrifuge issued its native token, CFG, which has multiple uses. First, it can be used to pay for Gas fees for transactions on Centrifuge Chain. When performing on-chain transactions, such as transfers or executing smart contracts, Gas fees are required, and CFG can be used to pay these fees. Second, CFG is used to participate in governance activities. Centrifuge's upgrades and parameter adjustments require community voting, and users holding CFG tokens can participate in the vote and influence the project's direction. Third, CFG ensures the security of Centrifuge Chain. By staking CFG, nodes can participate in the validation process of Centrifuge Chain. If they act improperly, their staked CFG may be slashed, providing an incentive to maintain the blockchain network's security.

Having understood Centrifuge's multi-layered structure, let's now analyze the RWA financing process on Centrifuge from a legal perspective (see Fig. 5.8). Centrifuge's legal foundation is based on U.S. asset securitization law. If an investor is a U.S. citizen, they must meet the SEC's definition of an accredited investor. Additionally, citizens of countries subject to U.S. sanctions are not permitted to invest in Centrifuge products. Currently, Centrifuge is also developing RWA tokenization product structures for jurisdictions outside the United States.

The entire financing process involves several steps, including off-chain audits, KYC (Know Your Customer) procedures, establishing SPVs (Special Purpose Vehicles), creating on-chain asset pools, and providing liquidity to these pools.

First, the asset originator needs to establish a Special Purpose Vehicle (SPV) for each asset pool they create. The SPV is an independent legal entity established to ensure that the security of the asset pool is not affected by the overall financial condition of the asset originator. Even if the asset originator goes bankrupt, the

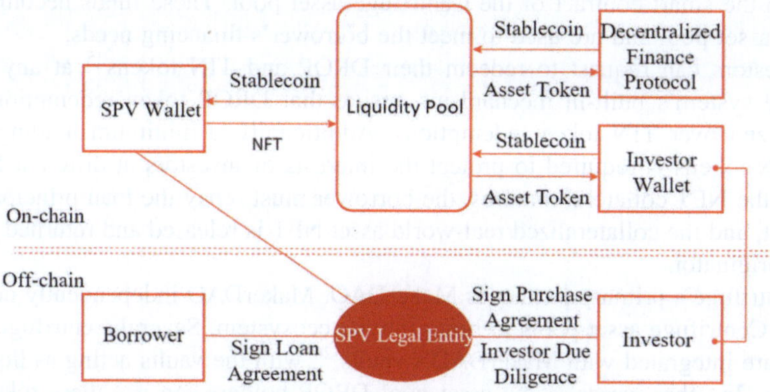

Fig. 5.8 Centrifuge legal framework (*Source* Compiled from documentation on centrifuge.io)

SPV ensures that the asset pool can operate independently and is responsible for handling all legal and financial matters related to the asset pool.

Next, when a borrower[24] wishes to use RWA as collateral to obtain financing, the asset originator steps in to underwrite the asset and may also purchase some TIN tokens as an investor. The asset originator is responsible for converting the borrower's RWA into an NFT. Subsequently, the borrower enters into a financing agreement with the SPV and requests the asset originator to lock the RWA NFT in the asset pool associated with the SPV. Once the NFT is locked, the corresponding DAI is extracted from Centrifuge's asset pool and directly transferred to the borrower's wallet, or it may first be transferred to the SPV's wallet. The SPV then converts the DAI into U.S. dollars and transfers the amount to the borrower's bank account.

At the same time, after completing the KYC and other compliance processes, investors need to read and sign the investment summary for the asset pool and the subscription agreement for the SPV. These documents outline the investment structure, risks, terms, and conditions. The wallet address of the certified investor will be whitelisted by the SPV, and the investor can then use the stablecoin DAI to purchase DROP or TIN tokens on the corresponding asset pool in Centrifuge. This action is known as "providing liquidity to the asset pool." When an investor uses stablecoin DAI to purchase DROP or TIN tokens, they are essentially transferring

[24] On the Centrifuge platform, the borrower is typically the entity that requires funding. It is important to note that the borrower and asset originator are two closely related but distinct roles. The borrower is the party that actually holds the RWA and seeks financing, while the asset originator is involved in creating and managing the asset pool and converting the RWA into on-chain assets. The asset originator is often more deeply involved in the management and financial aspects of the asset pool. In some cases, if the asset originator directly holds the assets requiring financing, they may also act as the borrower.

DAI to the smart contract of the Centrifuge asset pool. These funds become part of the asset pool and are used to meet the borrower's financing needs.

Investors can request to redeem their DROP and TIN tokens[25] at any time, but the system's built-in mechanisms ensure that DROP token redemptions are prioritized over TIN token redemptions. Additionally, a minimum holding ratio for TIN tokens is required to protect the interests of investors at different levels. When the NFT collateral matures, the borrower must repay the loan principal and interest, and the collateralized real-world asset NFT is released and returned to the asset originator.

Centrifuge's primary partner is MakerDAO. MakerDAO independently decides which Centrifuge asset pools to bring into its ecosystem. Several Centrifuge asset pools are integrated with MakerDAO's vaults,[26] with the vaults acting as liquidity sources. In other words, some asset pool DROP holders can use these tokens as collateral to borrow stablecoin DAI on MakerDAO (see Fig. 5.9).

In addition, each asset pool on Centrifuge has a reserve pool, which can be borrowed by the asset originator or redeemed by investors, but it does not accrue interest. Typically, there is no remaining balance in the reserve pool. However, asset pools integrated with Maker vaults can directly use MakerDAO's vault as a source of funds. This means that as long as the debt ceiling of the vault has not been reached, Centrifuge investors can withdraw funds from MakerDAO's vault to complete the redemption process, providing additional liquidity assurance for the asset pool.

Through this cooperation, asset originators on Centrifuge can tokenize RWAs and collateralize DROP tokens on MakerDAO to obtain DAI. This not only provides new financing channels for asset originators and borrowers but also offers diversified investment options for MakerDAO.

For example, in December 2022, MakerDAO, Centrifuge, and BlockTower Credit[27]jointly established a $220 million fund. In this partnership, MakerDAO deployed four vaults, providing $150 million in senior funding, while BlockTower provided $70 million in junior funding. Together, they created a $220 million Centrifuge asset pool to tokenize RWAs and connect them to DeFi. Centrifuge also has several asset pools related to MakerDAO, with the largest pools being BlockTower Series 3 and BlockTower Series 4, where the senior funds primarily come from MakerDAO, and the junior funds are provided by BlockTower.

---

[25] Investors in TIN or DROP tokens can lock their DAI in a Centrifuge asset pool at any time during a period, and then execute investments and redemptions at the end of the period, typically executed every 24 hours.

[26] A Maker Vault is a place where users deposit collateral to generate DAI in the Maker protocol. When users redeem, the Maker Vault will destroy the generated DAI.

[27] BlockTower Capital is a digital asset investment firm and portfolio management company. BlockTower Credit is its subsidiary, primarily investing in real-world credit assets and providing traditional asset-backed securities and structured loan solutions (such as auto loans, trade finance) to fintech originators and non-bank lenders, while using blockchain technology to pursue better risk-adjusted returns.

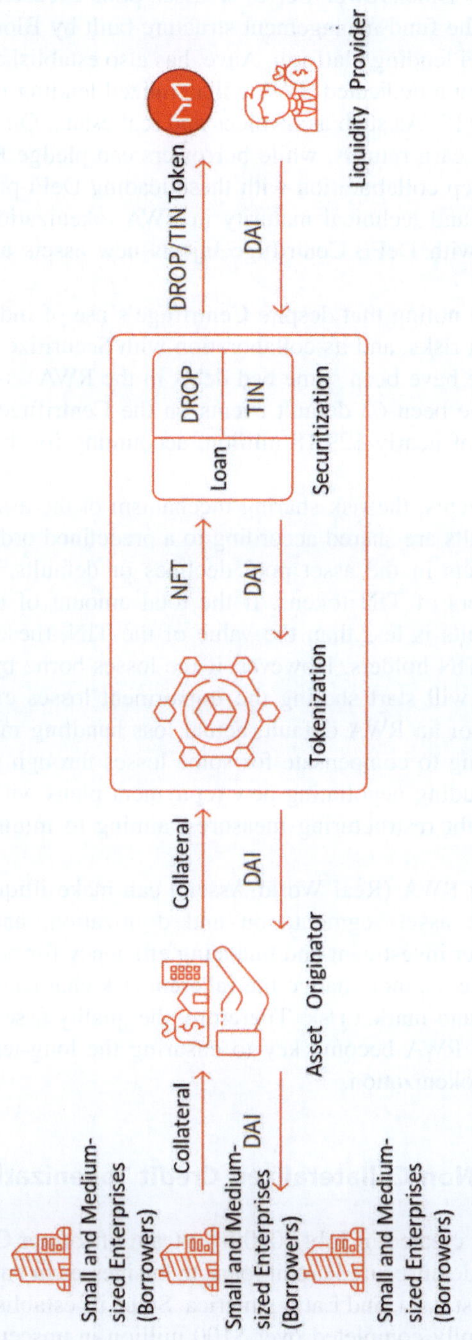

Fig. 5.9 Centrifuge and MakerDAO cooperation mechanism

As of July 4, 2024, the BlockTower Series 3 asset pool has a size of over $99 million, while the BlockTower Series 4 asset pool exceeds $101 million. Figure 5.10 illustrates the fund management structure built by BlockTower.

Another leading DeFi lending platform, Aave, has also established a partnership with Centrifuge, creating a dedicated RWA collateralized lending market platform to provide financing for RWAs such as invoices and real estate. On Aave, investors can deposit USDC and earn returns, while borrowers can pledge RWA to borrow USDC. Centrifuge's deep collaboration with these leading DeFi protocols reflects its pioneering position and technical maturity in RWA tokenization. By bridging traditional enterprises with DeFi, Centrifuge injects new assets and vitality into DeFi.

However, it is worth noting that despite Centrifuge's use of independent SPVs to isolate asset and debt risks, and its collaboration with Securitize for strict KYC/AML verification, there have been some bad debts in the RWA asset pools. As of July 4, 2024, there have been 62 default events on the Centrifuge protocol, with a default loan amount of nearly $29.18 million, accounting for 4.8% of the total loan amount.

Following default events, the risk-sharing mechanism of the asset pool ensures that losses due to defaults are shared according to a predefined order. Specifically, when the value of assets in the asset pool declines or defaults, the first losses are borne by the holders of TIN tokens. If the total amount of the asset pool's value declines or defaults is less than the value of the TIN, these losses will be fully absorbed by the TIN holders. However, if the losses borne by TIN reach its limit, DROP investors will start sharing the impairment losses exceeding TIN's coverage. In the event of an RWA default, actual loss handling may also involve legal procedures, seeking to compensate for some losses through restructuring or other legal means, including negotiating new repayment plans with debtors, asset liquidation, or other debt restructuring measures, aiming to minimize the losses caused by defaults.

Although tokenizing RWA (Real World Assets) can make illiquid assets more easily tradable, enable asset segmentation and digitization, and attract more investors, creating higher investment and financing efficiency for both asset issuers and investors, this model cannot change the inherent risk characteristics of RWA, particularly credit risk and market risk. Therefore, the quality assessment and risk control mechanisms of RWA become key to ensuring the long-term and healthy development of RWA tokenization.

5.3.2 Goldfinch Non-Collateralized Credit Tokenization

Goldfinch is a platform created in July 2020 by a team of former Coinbase executives, designed to provide unsecured credit loans to businesses in emerging markets such as Africa, Southeast Asia, and Latin America. Since its establishment in 2020, Goldfinch has successfully completed over $100 million in unsecured borrowing.

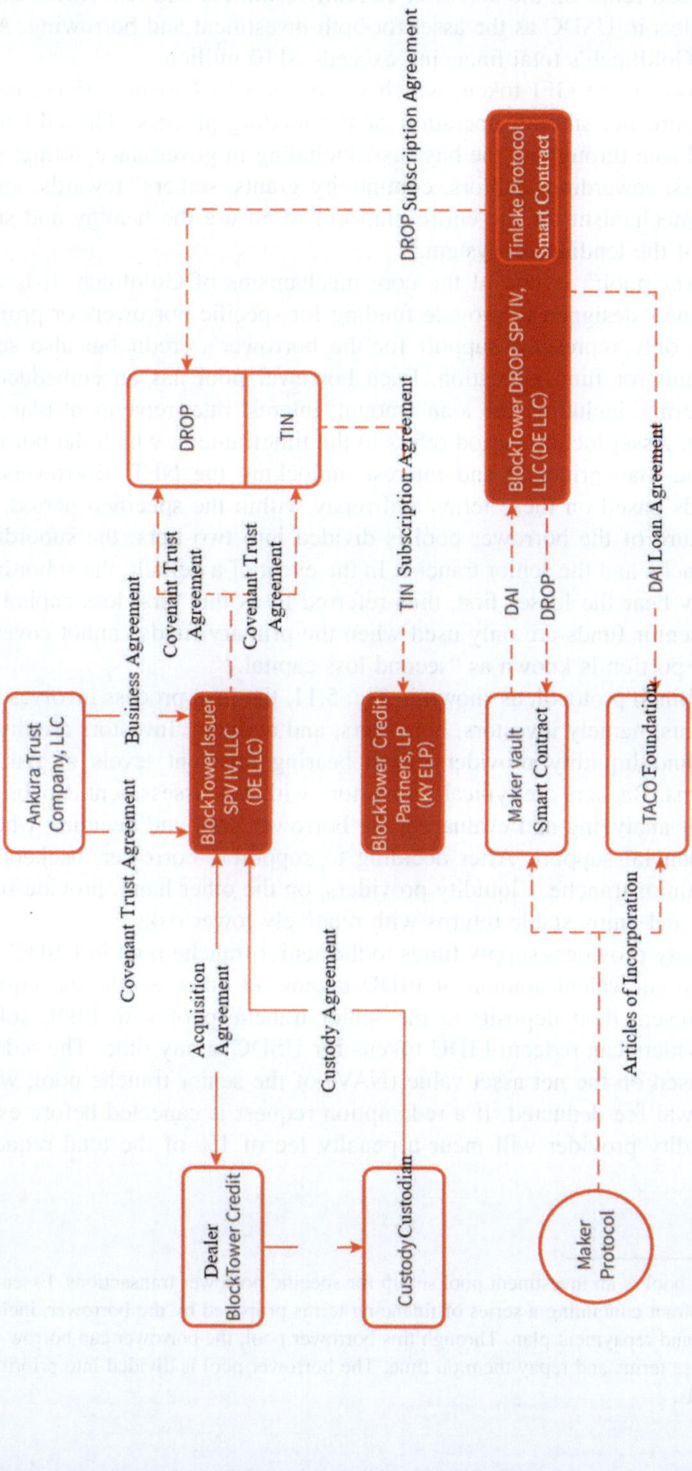

Fig. 5.10 BlockTower's fund management structure

Unlike other lending projects, Goldfinch's tokenized lending is not backed by collateral but instead relies on the borrower's creditworthiness and repayment ability, accepting stablecoin USDC as the asset for both investment and borrowing. As of July 4, 2024, Goldfinch's total financing exceeds $110 million.

Goldfinch issues the GFI token, which serves as a tool to incentivize participants and ensure the smooth operation of the lending process. The GFI token plays a crucial role throughout the business, including in governance voting, staking for auditors, rewarding auditors, community grants, stakers' rewards, and as the incentive mechanism for the entire platform to ensure the healthy and stable development of the lending ecosystem.

The borrower pool[28] is one of the core mechanisms of Goldfinch. It is a set of smart contracts designed to provide funding for specific borrowers or projects. This pool not only represents support for the borrower's credit but also serves as the basic unit for fund allocation. Each borrower pool has an embedded set of financing terms, including the loan amount, interest rate, repayment plan, and collateral term. Asset lockup period refers to the timeframe in which the borrower must repay the loan principal and interest, unlocking the NFT. Borrowers can withdraw funds based on these terms and repay within the specified period. The funding structure of the borrower pool is divided into two tiers: the subordinate (or junior) tranche and the senior tranche. In the event of a default, the subordinate funds typically bear the losses first, thus referred to as the "first loss capital." In contrast, the senior funds are only used when the primary funds cannot cover the losses, so this portion is known as "second loss capital."

In the Goldfinch protocol, as shown in Fig. 5.11, the loan process involves multiple participants, namely investors, borrowers, and auditors. Investors are divided into backers and liquidity providers, each bearing different levels of risk and potential returns. Backers are typically investors with risk assessment capabilities, responsible for analyzing and evaluating the borrower pool and deciding whether to provide financial support. After deciding to support a borrower, backers will invest in the junior tranche. Liquidity providers, on the other hand, provide senior tranche funds and enjoy stable returns with relatively lower risks.

After liquidity providers supply funds to the senior tranche pool in USDC, they will receive an equivalent amount of FIDU tokens. In other words, the liquidity providers represent their deposits in the senior tranche pool with FIDU tokens. Liquidity providers can redeem FIDU tokens for USDC at any time. The redemption rate is based on the net asset value (NAV) of the senior tranche pool, with a 0.5% withdrawal fee deducted. If a redemption request is canceled before execution, the liquidity provider will incur a penalty fee of 1% of the total requested amount.

[28] The borrower pool is an investment pool set up for specific borrower transactions. Essentially, it is a smart contract containing a series of financing terms proposed by the borrower, including the interest rate and repayment plan. Through this borrower pool, the borrower can borrow funds according to these terms and repay them on time. The borrower pool is divided into priority and subordinate pools.

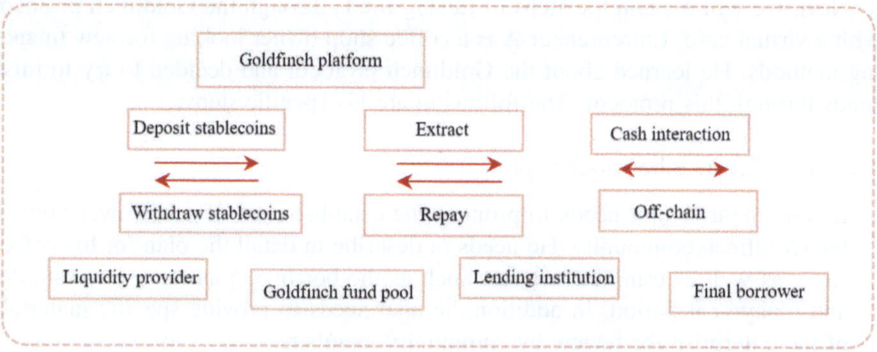

Fig. 5.11 Goldfinch platform participants (*Source* Based on information from the Goldfinch Finance website)

Borrowers are enterprises seeking financing. All borrowers in Goldfinch are real-world entities. They are required to provide detailed information about their enterprises for review by members of the Goldfinch community, so as to minimize the risk of fraud.

In addition, if borrowers want to use the Goldfinch protocol for financing, they need to pay GFI tokens. This is because GFI tokens are not only the governance tokens of the protocol but also the necessary admission tickets for participating in the protocol's ecosystem. By paying GFI tokens, borrowers demonstrate their sincerity in participating in the protocol and provide incentives for other participants in the protocol, such as auditors.

Auditors play a crucial role in the protocol, they are the loan approvers of Goldfinch and are independent third-party entities. The task of auditors is to verify the identity and creditworthiness of borrowers. Once an auditor approves a borrower, the borrower can create their own borrower pool and raise funds from the community's investors. In the specific loan process, auditors need to stake enough GFI tokens. Goldfinch will randomly select auditors for detailed inspections to prevent fraudulent activities and receive corresponding GFI token rewards after verifying the borrower's identity.

Unlike the loan method based on over-collateralization of assets, the assessment of borrowers in Goldfinch relies on the collective judgment of other participants. For example, financiers will also conduct due diligence on borrowers to identify and assess loan risks, and they even have the right to sign independent agreements with borrowers to have legal recourse in case of fraud. Auditors, on the other hand, need to review the borrower's identity and loan details before the borrower submits a loan request. Goldfinch encourages auditors and financiers to conduct their due diligence by directly communicating with borrowers. This real-world direct interaction enhances trust and understanding of borrowers and lays the foundation for creating an immutable credit history on the blockchain.

Next, we will explain the steps of raising funds through the Goldfinch protocol with a virtual case. Entrepreneur A is a coffee shop owner looking for new financing methods. He learned about the Goldfinch protocol and decided to try to raise funds through this protocol. The following are his specific steps:

- Step 1: Create a borrower pool

  Entrepreneur A first needs to propose the establishment of a borrower pool in the Goldfinch community. He needs to describe in detail the plan for his coffee shop, as well as transaction terms such as the borrowing amount, interest rate, and repayment period. In addition, he also needs to provide specific materials of the enterprise for review by community members.
- Step 2: Review the borrower pool

  Goldfinch financiers and auditors start to conduct due diligence on Entrepreneur A's borrower pool. They directly contact Entrepreneur A to discuss and negotiate the borrowing terms. After assessing the enterprise and credit risks of Entrepreneur A, some financiers choose to invest subordinated funds into the borrower pool. The risk of this part of the funds is relatively high. If Entrepreneur A's enterprise is unable to repay the loan, this part of the funds will be written down first.
- Step 3: Allocate senior-level funds

  After the subordinated funds are invested, the senior-level fund pool will automatically allocate capital to the borrower pool. The borrower pool can obtain senior-level funds three times the amount of subordinated funds.
- Step 4: Complete the borrowing

  When the senior-level funds are fully allocated, the borrowing process for Entrepreneur A is completed. He can withdraw USDC from the Goldfinch protocol for the operation of his enterprise. At the same time, he needs to regularly repay the principal and interest of the loan according to the agreed transaction terms. Through the above operations, Entrepreneur A can successfully raise funds through the Goldfinch protocol. This process is decentralized, allowing borrowers to interact directly with fund providers without going through any intermediary institutions. This makes financial services more transparent, efficient, and fair, and also reduces financing costs.
- Step 5: Repay the principal and interest

  When repaying the principal, borrowers need to pay 10% of the interest as a protocol fee. This protocol fee is first used to pay financiers, followed by liquidity providers, and finally for the protocol's revenue.

5.3.3 Sources of Revenue for the Goldfinch Protocol

As shown in Fig. 5.12, Goldfinch has designed a protocol revenue mechanism that can not only generate income but also have a positive guiding effect, enabling the platform to achieve sustainable development. The specific description is as follows:

- When repaying the principal, borrowers are required to pay 10% of the interest as a protocol fee. This protocol fee will be first used to pay senior-level investors, then general investors, and finally contribute to the protocol's earnings.
- When liquidity providers redeem USDC from FIDU, they need to pay a 0.5% withdrawal fee.
- If a redemption request is cancelled before execution, a penalty of 1% of the total requested amount will be charged.
- All the above-mentioned revenues will be deposited into the protocol treasury, and GFI token holders can make decisions on their utilization.

Since its launch, Goldfinch has seen the participation and benefit of many professional lending companies. For example, PayJoy from Mexico, Aspire from Vietnam, and QuickCheck from Nigeria. These three lending enterprises have obtained $1 million through the Goldfinch protocol and distributed it to thousands of final borrowers. With the increase in borrowers, Goldfinch has also started to provide larger-amount loans to enterprises. For instance, Goldfinch has provided a $10-million loan to Float, a cash-management and credit fintech company

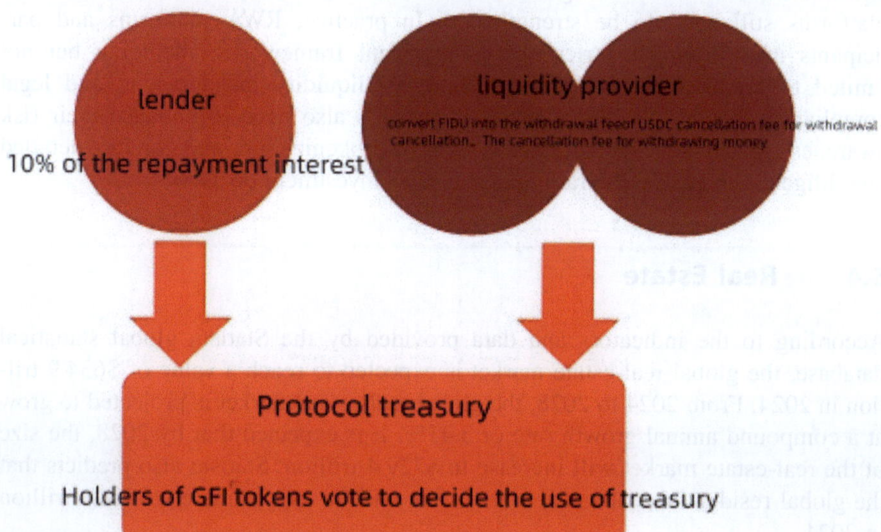

Fig. 5.12 The protocol charging mechanism of Goldfinch

supported by Y Combinator, helping Float complete a $17-million seed-round financing to expand its business of serving African enterprises. It has provided a $5-million credit-borrowing limit to its partner Brex, helping Brex's users obtain working capital to cope with the business challenges brought about by the COVID-19 pandemic. It has also provided $50-million in debt financing to Kavak, a Latin-American car-rental company, to help it expand its business scale in Mexico and Brazil.

However, similar to Centrifuge, this platform has also encountered several serious bad-debt incidents. In October 2021, Tugende, a lending institution from Uganda, obtained a $5-million loan from Goldfinch to expand its business in Kenya. Nevertheless, Tugende failed to repay the loan on time and started to default in June 2023. Although Warbler Labs—the company behind Goldfinch—reached a loan-restructuring agreement with Tugende, and there may be a chance of recovering the $5-million loan in the future, this incident still exposed the platform's shortcomings in risk management. More seriously, in October 2023, a lending pool worth $20 million on Goldfinch showed obvious bad-debt risks, with approximately $7 million at risk of loss. This loan pool was originally guaranteed by the Stratos fund in February 2022 at an annual interest rate of 11%. The Stratos fund's investments in the real-estate technology company REZI and other digital-asset sectors failed to meet expectations, leading to financial losses. Warbler Labs promised to compensate investors for all losses, but this incident still highlighted the high risks that the protocol may face when dealing with RWA (Real-World Assets).

From these incidents, it can be seen that although new sources of funds and lending opportunities are provided, to against the backdrop of frequent financial scandals, the risk management and credit-evaluation mechanisms of RWA platforms still need to be strengthened. In practice, RWA platforms and participants must establish strict risk-management frameworks, including but not limited to credit evaluation, market analysis, liquidity management, and legal compliance checks. At the same time, investors also need to enhance their risk awareness, understand the complexity of RWA tokenization, and conduct detailed due diligence to ensure the rationality of their investment decisions.

5.4 Real Estate

According to the indicators and data provided by the Statista global statistical database, the global real-estate market is expected to reach a value of $634.9 trillion in 2024. From 2024 to 2028, the global real-estate market is projected to grow at a compound annual growth rate of 3.41%. It is expected that by 2028, the size of the real-estate market will increase to $729.4 trillion. Statista also predicts that the global residential real-estate market size will be approximately $518.9 trillion in 2024.

The tokenization of real estate mainly focuses on two directions at present. One is to tokenize real-estate property rights, which can enhance asset liquidity and achieve asset fragmentation. This allows investors to purchase tokens representing partial ownership of real estate, reducing the investment threshold. At the same time, it enables real estate to break through geographical limitations and connect with global investors, aiming to solve problems such as insufficient liquidity and high transaction costs in the traditional real-estate market. The other is to tokenize real-estate financial products. By tokenizing real-estate funds, trusts, rental income, mortgage loans, and other financial products, it can attract more investors to participate and expand financing channels.

5.4.1 Case: Aspen Coin, the First Tokenized Real-Estate Ownership Project

The Aspen (The St. Regis Aspen Resort) is renowned for its elegant decor, first-class facilities, and breathtaking natural environment. In October 2018, the Aspen St. Regis Resort innovatively launched a real-estate tokenization project worth a total of $18 million—Aspen Coin, becoming the world's first case to digitally represent and divide hotel ownership through blockchain technology. This groundbreaking move has opened up entirely new financing channels and investment models for the real-estate industry (see Fig. 5.13).

The tokenized underlying asset is the partial ownership of the Aston Reign Beach Club & Residences. Investors can obtain economic benefits linked to the hotel's operating revenue by purchasing tokens, including income distributions from REIT, but they do not have voting rights. This tokenized property rights design, on the one hand, provides liquidity for real estate assets that were originally difficult to circulate; on the other hand, it greatly lowers the investment threshold, enabling more qualified investors to participate.

The issuance of these tokens strictly adheres to the exemption provisions of Regulation D of *the U.S. Securities Act of 1933* to ensure compliance and investor protection. The issuance and trading processes are handled by two professional institutions: Indiegogo serves as the marketing and promotion partner, providing a purchase channel for tokens to qualified investors; Tempulum Markets acts as the technology provider and trading platform, responsible for the actual issuance and secondary-market trading of tokens. This division-of-labor and collaborative

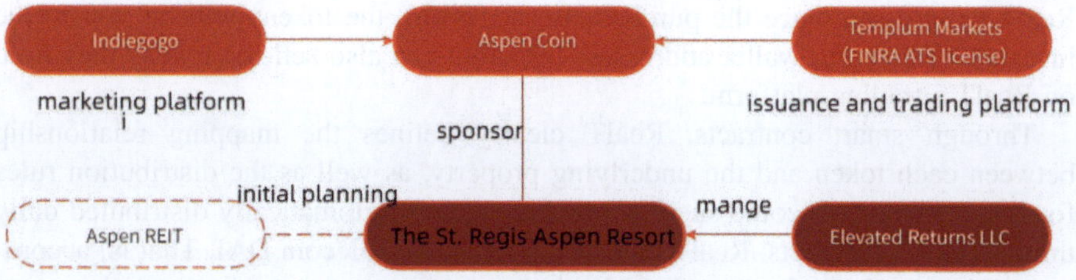

Fig. 5.13 The basic process structure of Aspen Coin

model is similar to the roles of underwriters and stock exchanges in traditional IPO.

In terms of technology selection, Tempulum Markets initially used the Ethereum blockchain and later migrated to the Tezos system to improve performance. Token trading is currently limited to the platform operated by Tempulum Markets to comply with U.S. securities regulatory requirements. In August 2020, the tZERO platform also began to offer trading services for Aspen Coin.

The introduction of Aspen Coin is of milestone significance for the real estate industry. By combining the financial innovation tool of digital tokens with traditional real estate, Aspen Coin has initiated a new model for real estate investment and ownership management. For issuers, tokenization activated assets that were originally difficult to liquidate and broadened the financing channels; for investors, the lower investment threshold and flexible trading methods have increased their participation and return rates. From a macro perspective, Aspen Coin attempts to inject the vitality of the digital economy into the real economy, promoting the coordinated development of the financial system and the real estate industry. It also provides a valuable innovation case for regulatory authorities.

5.4.2 Case: RealT, a Real Estate Tokenization Platform

RealT was founded in 2019 and is a platform dedicated to the tokenization of real estate. On this platform, investors only need to invest $50 to purchase partial ownership of U.S. real estate. RealT, launched in 2019, which has now established a vibrant and highly engaged investor community. As of March 2024, RealT has approximately 16,100 active investors from 154 countries. It has tokenized around 535 properties worth $101 million, including various types such as single-family homes and large-scale residential properties.

Based on the Ethereum blockchain, RealT issues tokens backed by physical real estate, allowing investors to buy and trade property ownership with relatively small amounts of money. For example, the *9943 Marlowe Street* project launched by RealT at the end of 2019. The underlying asset of this project is a single-family home located in Detroit, the United States, with a total value of $63,000. RealT divided the property ownership into 1000 shares, with each share priced at $63. Investors only need to pay $63 to purchase 1/1000 of the ownership of this property. Investors can purchase tokens with digital assets or fiat currency on RealT's platform. Once the purchase is successful, the tokens will be sent to the investors' Ethereum wallet addresses. Investors can also sell the tokens they hold on RealT's trading platform.

Through smart contracts, RealT clearly defines the mapping relationship between each token and the underlying property, as well as the distribution rules for rental income. Income such as property rent is automatically distributed daily through smart contracts. RealT chooses to use the stablecoin DAI. That is, according to the number of tokens held by investors, the corresponding rental income will be automatically sent to the investors' wallet addresses in the form of DAI.

RealT adopts a series of limited liability company (LLC) legal structures. Each LLC independently holds a real estate asset and formulates its own management strategies, enabling investors to directly participate in governance and achieve asset isolation and risk diversification.

Real estate tokenization also faces many complex issues. Firstly, after tokenization, there is still a certain degree of fragmentation between on-chain and off-chain information, increasing the uncertainty in transactions and leases. Moreover, high-quality properties are not difficult to sell offline, and the complexity of the tokenization process even reduces transaction efficiency to a certain extent, resulting in a scarcity of cases of tokenizing high-quality assets. Due to issues such as property leasing and management, such as unexpected situations like tenant defaults, the actual returns obtained by token holders may be far lower than expected. Secondly, in some cases, the liquidity of the fragmented ownership of tokenized properties may be relatively weak. Thirdly, the current business model of real estate tokenization platforms is still relatively traditional, lacking the native approaches of Web 3.0 such as token empowerment. Finally, the platform is overly reliant on the leasing services of outsourcing companies and regional resources. As a result, 90% of existing real-estate tokenization projects are concentrated in the United States, and real-estate token projects in other countries and regions rarely attract attention. In the future, with the gradual maturity and diversification of the business models of real-estate tokenization, models such as crowdfunded real-estate projects and shared housing will be further implemented. The functions and liquidity of real-estate tokens are expected to be enhanced, and ultimately the value of real-estate tokenization will be fully manifested.

5.4.3 Case: Taiji Capital, Hong Kong's First Real-Estate STO

On September 10, 2023, Hong Kong Taiji Capital Group Limited (hereinafter referred to as "Taiji Capital") announced the launch of the PRINCE token. This became Hong Kong's first real-estate STO targeted at professional investors. This STO is the first fund tokenization fundraising model approved by the SFC, completed through the relevant virtual asset licenses held by Taiji Capital's subsidiaries, as well as its technological advantages in Web 3.0 and a team with rich experience in the capital market and operations. This marks an important step taken by Hong Kong in the field of digital assets and financial technology, laying the foundation for more innovations and developments in the future.

By leveraging blockchain technology and smart contracts, Taiji Capital aims to bring transformation to the traditional financial industry, improve efficiency, reduce costs, and provide investors with more choices and opportunities. The funds raised from this STO will be used to acquire five retail properties located at the Prince tourist attraction in the Kowloon area. These properties are in the core business district, which have high investment value and appreciation potential.

The PRINCE token is a security-type token issued by a closed-end fund managed by Pioneer Asset Management Co., Ltd. (hereinafter referred to as the

"Pioneer Company"), a subsidiary of Taiji Capital engaged in capital market and wealth management businesses. Different from traditional real-estate funds, the entry fee for the PRINCE token is only HK$1000, which greatly lowers the investment threshold, enabling more investors to participate in real-estate investment and share the rental income and capital appreciation brought by the properties. This innovative investment model helps to lower the real-estate investment threshold and allows more investors to get involved. To safeguard the rights and interests of investors, Taiji Capital has taken a series of measures to ensure the security and compliance of the PRINCE token. After the subscription agreement is completed, the Pioneer Company will arrange for relevant investors to open a digital wallet account with ON1ON Custody for the distribution and storage of PRINCE tokens. ON1ON Custody is another subsidiary of Taiji Capital. It holds a Hong Kong trust or company service provider license and has obtained the SOC 2 certification from the American Institute of Certified Public Accountants (AICPA). It is a trustworthy virtual asset custodian institution.The PRINCE tokens stored in ON1ON Custody will also be protected by a virtual asset insurance provided by a local insurance company, which further enhances investors' confidence.

Unlike traditional funds, which are recorded in the ledgers by fund administrators, the PRINCE token is finally settled on the public Ethereum blockchain. This innovative application of technology not only improves the transparency and efficiency of transactions but also provides greater flexibility for investors. Through blockchain technology, investors can access the over-the-counter secondary market immediately after subscribing to the PRINCE token, greatly increasing the liquidity of assets.

In addition, if approved by the regulatory authorities, the Pioneer Company also plans to list the PRINCE token on the HKbitEX platform of a subsidiary of Taiji Capital that operates virtual asset trading business. With 24-h automated trading, it will further enhance liquidity. This will provide investors with more trading options and help establish a more active and healthy secondary market.

Apart from bringing new opportunities to investors, the issuance model of the PRINCE token has also opened up a new financing channel for real-estate investors and developers. In the current environment of high interest rates, raising funds through token issuance can help investors and developers offset the high bank loan interest rates and effectively reduce financing costs.

Dr. Gao Han, Chairman of Taiji Capital Group, said, "*We are delighted to launch Hong Kong's first STO, which brings a revolutionary change to the fundraising model in the real - estate industry. Through Taiji Capital's regulated Web 3.0 financial infrastructure, we offer one - stop solutions covering product structure design for STO, tokenization, custody, and token management. Meanwhile, we will also provide a secondary market, bringing new opportunities to both asset owners and investors in all aspects. We are pleased to see the positive responses from the capital market and the real - estate industry to Hong Kong's first real - estate STO project, which indicates that the market has a strong demand for and confidence in this innovative financing model.*"

The launch of the PRINCE token comes at an opportune time, benefiting from the current favorable macro-environment in Hong Kong. In terms of the local property market, since the full resumption of cross-border travel between the Chinese mainland and Hong Kong in February 2024, the number of mainland tourists visiting Hong Kong has increased significantly. Coupled with the rise in tourists' consumption willingness, retail sales have grown. These positive factors are all conducive to the revival of Hong Kong's retail property market, which can also bring better rental income and appreciation prospect of the property which invested for PRINCE tokens.

Overall, the issuance of the PRINCE token is a groundbreaking fund tokenization project, it enables investors to participate in real-estate investment with a relatively low entry threshold and offers the prospect of benefiting from short- to medium-term investment returns and capital appreciation opportunities. With the gradual emergence of regulated Web 3.0 infrastructure, investors will have the opportunity to use the 24-hour automated trading platform to increase asset liquidity, truly enabling investment and trading anytime and anywhere. For some developers constrained by their balance sheets or with a relatively small scale, the tokenization model also provides a new way to carry out capital-intensive projects such as urban area development. By raising part of the funds through token issuance, developers can hold a relatively small share in the early stage of the project while retaining project management rights, and then decide whether to buy out the development project later. This flexible equity structure helps developers optimize capital allocation and improves the feasibility and rate of return of the project.

Wu Xiaochuan, CTO of HKBitEX Co. under Taiji Capital, stated that the development of data elements goes through stages such as resource utilization, assetization, and capitalization. STO encompasses these important stages. In the future, the data elements market is expected to reach a trillion-dollar scale. It is anticipated that data assets will further expand their financial attributes, driving financial innovation. Wu Xiaochuan introduced that Hong Kong has been researching STO for a long time. This case is inspiring for the industry and also has reference value from a regulatory perspective.

Looking ahead, Dr. Gao Han said, "*Starting with real estate, we will continue to support the financing needs of more industries closely related to the economy of the Greater China region and vertical industries, and promote the development of digital finance. Through continuous innovation and exploration, Taiji Capital hopes to become a leader in the fields of digital assets and financial technology, bringing more opportunities and value to investors and industrial development.*"

5.5 Private Equity

Private equity funds have always been regarded as an investment option with relatively high returns. In recent years, global data shows that the average return rate of private equity funds is far higher than that of traditional public market investments.

For example, the strategic return expectations for global stocks, global bonds, private equity, and real estate over the next 10 years by the global asset allocation team of Citi Wealth Management Platform are 10%, 5.1%, 18.6%, and 10.6% respectively. In fact, the long-term nature of private equity funds and professional fund management methods enable them to achieve relatively low risks in complex market environments. These funds often achieve deeper value excavation through direct investment in unlisted companies, thus bringing considerable returns.

Such funds generally have high investment thresholds. Investors need to invest at least $500,000 or more to have the opportunity to participate in investing in such funds. This leads to low liquidity of such funds and is not conducive to investors' diversified asset allocation. However, through tokenization, private equity funds can be divided into relatively small units, enabling more investors to enjoy the benefits of private equity investment.

5.5.1 Case: SPiCE Venture Capital, a Typical Tokenized Private Equity Fund

SPiCE Venture Capital (hereinafter referred to as SPiCE VC) is a venture capital fund focusing on investing in blockchain and technology start-ups, with its headquarters in Israel. In October 2018, SPiCE VC successfully raised $15 million by issuing security-type tokens, becoming the world's first fully tokenized venture capital fund (see Fig. 5.14). This innovative move has opened a new chapter in the venture capital industry and injected the vitality of the digital economy into traditional investment and financing models.

SPiCE VC tokens are currently listed and traded on the Malaysian digital asset exchange Fusang Exchange and the US digital asset exchange Open Finance Network, providing investors with unprecedented liquidity. Different from the rights and interests of traditional venture capital and private equity funds, SPiCE VC

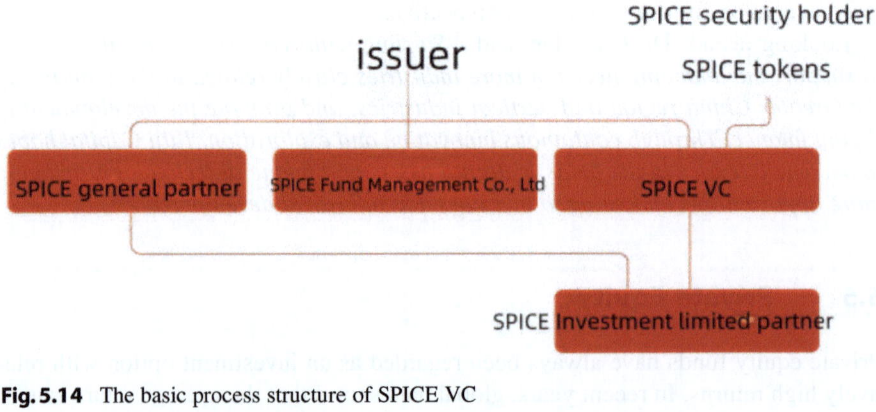

Fig. 5.14 The basic process structure of SPICE VC

token holders do not need to commit to long-term capital contributions and lock-up periods. Instead, they can freely buy and sell on the secondary market, realizing investment returns and exits more quickly. This flexibility and convenience greatly enhance investors' participation and confidence.

The underlying asset of SPiCE VC's tokenization is the limited partnership (LP) interests of the fund, and investors can share in the distribution of the net proceeds from the fund's investment projects in proportion. Currently, these tokens are only issued to professional investors.During the token issuance process, SPiCE VC engaged international law firms to assist in preparing the issuance memorandum and to provide global regulatory compliance advice to ensure the legality of the project and the protection of investors.

In terms of technology selection, SPiCE VC uses the Ethereum public blockchain system to achieve the fungibility and standardization of tokens. Since SPiCE VC tokens are listed and traded on the Open Finance Network and Fusang Exchange, they are simultaneously regulated by the securities laws and regulations of the United States and Malaysia. This multi-regulatory framework provides more comprehensive protection for token holders.

The tokenization solution of SPiCE VC makes full use of the advantages of blockchain technology and simplifies the traditional securities issuance and trading processes. By combining the verification of investors' identities with personalized encryption keys, the tokenization solution eliminates intermediate links, improves transaction efficiency, and effectively reduces the risk of human operational errors. At the same time, the round-the-clock market access and $T + 0$ instant settlement mechanism of virtual asset exchanges greatly enhance the liquidity and trading convenience of tokens.

The successful practice of SPiCE VC has set a benchmark for the venture capital industry. Through tokenization, SPiCE VC has revitalized the fund interests that were originally difficult to circulate, creating more choices and opportunities for investors. Looking ahead, SPiCE VC plans to conduct a second-round financing with a target amount as high as $100 million. This ambitious vision highlights the market's recognition and anticipation of the tokenized venture capital model. With the further improvement of the regulatory environment and the continuous upgrading of the technical architecture, tokenization is expected to become the mainstream trend in the fields of venture capital and private equity, injecting new impetus into the industry's development.

The innovative move of SPiCE VC not only expands the new frontiers of venture capital but also provides valuable experience and inspiration for the digital transformation of the entire financial industry. By combining blockchain technology with traditional financial instruments, SPiCE VC has explored a development path that integrates innovation and compliance, building a bridge connecting the digital economy and the real economy for more institutions and investors. As more and more excellent projects and institutions join the tokenization wave, this brand-new financial ecosystem is bound to embrace a more prosperous and diverse future.

5.5.2 Case: Hamilton Lane and Securitize Collaborate to Achieve Tokenization of Private Equity Funds

The cooperation between Hamilton Lane and Securitize is a typical example of the tokenization of private equity funds. Founded in 2014, Securitize aims to tokenize various Real-World Assets (RWA) through blockchain technology, focusing on transforming traditional financial products and services (such as bonds, stocks, real-estate investments, etc.) into tokens on the blockchain to further enhance the value, liquidity, transparency, and inclusiveness of these assets. Securitize provides a complete set of tools for enterprises to create, issue, and manage their own tokens on the blockchain. In addition, Securitize also provides a compliance framework to ensure that tokens can meet relevant laws and regulations, but this also means that certain transactions may be restricted. For example, some security-type tokens can only be sold in the primary market, and investors can only hold them until maturity.

Securitize also provides investors with a technology called DS Protocol, which allows token holders to directly receive dividends in their digital wallets without going through traditional banks or other financial institutions. This greatly simplifies the dividend-distribution process and improves efficiency. Securitize's platform also supports a redemption mechanism. When the token issuer decides to repurchase tokens, token holders can quickly sell their tokens to the project party.

Securitize has transformed the way assets are traded through blockchain technology, enabling a broader range of investors to access top-tier financial products. Its representative projects include: collaborating with Fidelity Investments Group[29] to tokenize a private real-estate fund with an amount of $500 million, which is issued on the Algorand[30] public blockchain; working with Franklin Templeton Fund Management Company[31] to tokenize a government bond fund on the Stellar[32] public blockchain, with an amount of $150 million; partnering with Sequoia Capital China Fund to tokenize its investment portfolio in China, involving more than 20 unlisted technology companies; and cooperating with the asset management company P10 to tokenize private equity and venture capital funds on the Ethereum blockchain.

Hamilton Lane is a large-scale private equity fund. It not only ranks among the top globally in terms of asset size but is also widely regarded as an industry leader

[29] Founded in 1946, Fidelity Investments Group is one of the world's largest asset management companies. As of December 2022, the assets under its management reached $10.3 trillion.

[30] Algorand is a blockchain project initiated by Silvio Micali, a professor at the Massachusetts Institute of Technology and a Turing Award laureate, in 2017, and its mainnet was officially launched in June 2019.

[31] Franklin Templeton Fund Management Company is a global investment management organization that serves clients in over 155 countries. As of March 31, 2023, the assets under its management amounted to $1.4 trillion.

[32] Stellar is a decentralized, fast, and scalable payment-oriented open-source financial product and blockchain network. It is both a cross-currency trading system and a digital asset issuance platform, aiming to connect the world's financial infrastructure. Global financial institutions have settled payments on the Stellar network, and this network already has over 700 million accounts.

and benchmark in the field of private equity investment. As of June 30, 2023, the assets under its management included a total of $117.3 billion in discretionary assets and $700.7 billion in non-discretionary assets. Hamilton Lane mainly raises funds from institutional investors and high-net-worth individuals. Through customized fund structures, it invests in the equity of non-listed enterprises. The return on such equity investments is relatively high, but the traditional fund model has issues such as high entry barriers and poor liquidity. In 2021, Hamilton Lane tokenized a real-estate fund worth $100 million on the Ethereum testnet.[33] In June 2022, Hamilton Lane, in partnership with Securitize, completed the tokenization of a private equity fund worth as much as $2.1 billion on the Polygon[34] blockchain. This fund is named the Hamilton Lane Polygon Fund and mainly invests in hundreds of top-tier, high-growth unlisted companies under Hamilton Lane. The fund is divided proportionally into 21million tokens, and each token represents a certain share of funds but it's only worth 100 dollars. Investors only need to invest a minimum of $20,000 to participate in purchasing these tokens, which is far lower than the $500,000 investment threshold of traditional private equity funds.

The cooperation case between Hamilton Lane and Securitize shows that tokenization can enhance the liquidity and tradability of private equity funds, enabling this previously scarce asset to be fractioned. It lowers the investment threshold of traditional private equity funds, allowing them to be issued and traded to a broader range of investors, expanding the fundraising channels. It also provides ordinary investors with a rare opportunity to participate in top-tier private equity funds (investors only need to buy some tokens worth a few hundred dollars to enjoy the corresponding value growth), and helps investors achieve better asset allocation. Meanwhile, the immutability of blockchain technology also improves the transparency and audit efficiency of private equity funds, reduces repetitive work in book-keeping, cuts down labor costs, and enhances the liquidity of fund shares and the security of transactions, enabling blockchain to be fully integrated with DeFi (Decentralized Finance) businesses in the future.

As Victor Jung, the digital asset manager of Hamilton Lane, commented: "Since the company's establishment, we have been committed to serving our clients and providing enhanced financial benefits to those who rely on us. The cooperation with Securitize is our latest initiative to further enable a new generation of

[33] The Ethereum testnet is an imitation environment of the mainnet for the Ethereum blockchain, which provides a developer-friendly platform for testing new applications or smart contracts under real-world blockchain conditions without consuming actual funds.

[34] Polygon, formerly known as the Matic Network, is a multi-chain scalable platform that provides a framework for Ethereum-compatible blockchain networks to achieve faster, lower-cost, and more reliable transactions. The advantages of Polygon lie in: it uses a variety of network verification and security mechanisms, enabling the applications built on it to achieve near-real-time transaction confirmation speeds while greatly reducing transaction costs. Choosing Polygon is because of its high-speed and low-cost advantages, which are very suitable for the tokenization of assets of this scale and type. The high throughput of Polygon enables a large number of small-value transactions to be carried out efficiently and economically, making the tokenization process of the Hamilton Lane Polygon Fund smoother and more efficient.

investors to access the strong returns and performance opportunities in the private equity market. The use of blockchain technology has also improved usability and transparency.

5.6 Carbon Credit

Recently, extreme weather events have occurred frequently around the world, once again drawing widespread attention to climate change. The assessment report released by the Inter-governmental Panel on Climate Change (IPCC) in February 2022 pointed out that if global warming exceeds 1.5°C in the next 20 years, the world will inevitably face various climate disasters. More heatwaves, droughts, and floods will exceed the tolerance limits of plants and animals, leading to large-scale species die-offs. Extreme weather will also expose millions of people to serious food and water insecurity issues, and pose significant risks to infrastructure and coastal low-lying residential areas. The IPCC's report in April 2022 showed that although the growth rate of global greenhouse gas emissions slowed down during 2010–2019, the total emissions remained at a very high level, and carbon emissions increased by 5.5% in 2021. To keep the temperature, rise within 1.5°C, the Earth has only a remaining emission quota of 500 billion tons, which means that emissions must peak and decline before 2025.

Against this backdrop, carbon credit has become a core topic of global concern. Carbon credit, also known as carbon emission rights or carbon emission reduction quotas, represents the right to reduce or avoid the emission of 1 ton of carbon-dioxide-equivalent greenhouse gases into the atmosphere. In simple terms, a carbon credit is a certificate that quantifies and verifies the amount of carbon dioxide emissions reduced or absorbed by an entity (such as an enterprise or a country), and this certificate is quantifiable and tradable in the global carbon trading market. The global carbon trading market aims to encourage enterprises and individuals to reduce greenhouse gas emissions through economic means, and the basic principle of carbon trading is to price greenhouse gas emissions through market mechanisms. In specific implementation, the government or other regulatory authorities set a carbon emission cap for each industry or enterprise. Enterprises that exceed this cap need to purchase additional carbon credits, while those with lower emissions can sell their surplus carbon credits to obtain additional revenue. This creates an economic incentive for enterprises to adopt clean technologies and implement energy-saving measures. In the actual operation of carbon trading, enterprises or projects that achieve emissions reduction through clean energy projects, afforestation, high-efficiency energy-saving technologies, etc., can generate carbon credits. These carbon credits can then be traded in compliance or voluntary carbon markets. The compliance carbon market is usually established by the government or transnational organizations, such as the European Union Emissions Trading System (EU ETS), while the voluntary carbon market is participated in voluntarily by entities not bound by mandatory carbon emission reduction regulations.

Through blockchain technology, the transparency and efficiency of the carbon trading market have been greatly improved, thus ensuring the authenticity and immutability of the credit. This also helps to combat those who want to obtain additional carbon credits through fraud or incorrect reporting. As the tipping point of climate change approaches, achieving carbon neutrality will inevitably become an important issue that the Web 3.0 industry needs to address. The blockchain industry should also take more actions in response to climate change. In recent years, some emerging blockchain projects (such as Toucan and Klima) have been exploring how to more effectively utilize blockchain technology to enhance the transparency and security of the carbon market. In this way, blockchain technology not only helps to address the global climate crisis but also provides new growth opportunities for Web 3.0 and other digital industries.

5.6.1 Case: Toucan, a Carbon Credit Token Platform

Launched in October 2021, Toucan is dedicated to tokenizing carbon credits and integrating them into the decentralized digital financial system. Since its launch, the number of tokenized carbon credit projects on Toucan has exceeded 50, covering multiple fields such as wind power and renewable energy, greatly enriching environmental digital assets. The total amount of tokenized carbon credits on this platform has exceeded 20 million, and the total volume of carbon trading has exceeded $4 billion, injecting new liquidity into the carbon market. The cumulative offset of carbon credits has reached 300 tons.[35]

The process of transferring traditional carbon credits on-chain through the Toucan Protocol can be generally understood as follows: First, users can purchase a batch of registered carbon credits for specific projects and years from carbon credit standard institutions such as Verra[36] and Gold Standard.[37] Second, transfer these credits to the chain through the Toucan platform's carbon credit bridge (toucan carbon bridge), and allow anyone to transfer their carbon credit amounts from the traditional registration system to Toucan's blockchain smart contract system, the Open Climate Registry, to achieve tokenization.Trusted members in the Toucan community are called "toucan verifiers". They will audit the carbon credit amounts to ensure that only carbon credits from reliable sources can become NFT supported by BatchNFT. Each NFT contains detailed information such as the type

[35] This is equivalent to reducing 300 tons of carbon dioxide emissions.

[36] Verra is a non-profit organization used for registering carbon credits. After an enterprise is certified through Verra's verification carbon standards, it achieves carbon emission reduction or offset quantities. It is similar to the voluntary emission reduction volume (CCER) in China's carbon trading system.

[37] Gold Standard is a recognized non-profit carbon credit certification institution, jointly established by multiple non-governmental organizations in 2003. It provides standards for emission-reduction projects, ensuring that these projects genuinely and verifiably contribute to the environment while bringing about positive social and economic changes.

of carbon, year, location, and carbon tonnage. The types may involve different emission-reduction projects, such as reforestation, renewable energy projects, or waste treatment, etc. The year refers to the time when the project is implemented or the carbon credits are registered, that is, the actual occurrence time of carbon emission reduction or neutralization. Due to the characteristics of NFT, TCO2 (the general term for fungible tokenized carbon credits) can ensure the transparency and authenticity of each carbon credit. To enhance liquidity, BatchNFT will also be subdivided into fungible TCO2 tokens. One TCO2 token represents one ton of carbon credit (representing 1tCO2e, i.e., one ton of carbon dioxide equivalent). After being converted into TCO2 tokens, institutions like Verra will cancel the corresponding carbon credit records. Enterprises in need of carbon credits can directly use these TCO2 tokens to offset their own carbon emissions, just as in traditional registration institutions. When a carbon token is offset, it will be permanently removed from the circulating market.

Users can deposit TCO2 tokens into Toucan's carbon pool. When TCO2 tokens are deposited into the carbon pool, a carbon pool token will be created and issued to the user. The carbon pool solves a long-standing problem in the voluntary carbon market regarding carbon credits: buying or selling carbon credits can be difficult and time-consuming. By pooling similar carbon credits together and creating a homogeneous, interchangeable carbon pool token for each deposited carbon credit, the liquidity of carbon assets can be effectively enhanced.

Currently, there are two carbon pools, namely the base carbon pool and the nature carbon pool. The base carbon pool is designed by Klima DAO,[38] and its carbon pool token is called BCT (base carbon tonne). The relationship between Klima DAO and Toucan is that of a partnership. Each BCT token represents one ton of carbon dioxide equivalent certified by Verra. Users can deposit TCO2 tokens into the base carbon pool to obtain BCT tokens, and BCT tokens can also be exchanged back for TCO2 tokens. BCT tokens can not only be used as an asset for investors to conduct asset allocation but also serve as a new type of collateral in DeFi. In addition, based on BCT tokens, financial institutions can also convert carbon credits into interest-generating assets and even issue green stablecoins based on carbon credits. Artists can also integrate carbon credits into green NFT projects.

The nature carbon pool only accepts TCO2 tokens related to nature-based projects,[39] and the token of this carbon pool is named NCT. The Toucan platform is collaborating with experts and organizations in the carbon and tokenization fields

[38] Klima DAO supports its actions with real carbon assets by purchasing and accumulating carbon credits in the market, locking these credits in a treasury. This is aimed at driving up the price of carbon credits in the voluntary carbon market (VCM), thereby encouraging more individuals or groups to take action to reduce emissions.

[39] Refers primarily to projects related to ecosystem protection, restoration, and management. These projects directly target the natural environment, such as reforestation, wetland restoration, wildlife conservation, etc.

to design more types of carbon pools, which can satisfy the needs of different people and organizations who want to make contributions to the world.

Overall, through tokenization, Toucan establishes a connection between the carbon market and the digital financial system. It retains the authentic attributes of carbon credits and, by converting them into homogeneous tokens in the carbon pool, provides liquidity to the carbon credit market. This also makes it possible for enterprises to participate in carbon neutrality in a more convenient way.

5.7 New Energy Assets

Against the backdrop of global energy transition, the integration of emerging technologies such as blockchain, big data, artificial intelligence, and the Internet of Things is bringing new vitality to traditional industries. In August 2024, with the support of the *Ensemble* project by Ant Group and the Hong Kong Monetary Authority, Xindiantu, under Langxin Technology (a new energy company listed on the Chinese mainland), served as the operator and service provider of the new energy digital platform. Xindiantu used some of the charging piles operated on the platform as the underlying assets for Real-World Asset (RWA) tokenization and successfully obtained the first cross-border financing through real-world asset tokenization in Hong Kong, with an amount of approximately 100 million yuan. This financing will be used for the energy storage and charging pile industries in the new energy sector. This transaction not only injects new capital into the new energy field but also has significant innovative practical significance, fully demonstrating the huge potential of using blockchain to manage the risks of physical assets and enhance the efficiency of the capital market. Ant Chain provided comprehensive technical support for this tokenization process. The secure, transparent, and tamper-proof data characteristics of Ant Chain help enterprises address various risks they face when bringing real-world assets onto the blockchain. Through the blockchain technology of Ant Chain, the operational status of physical assets can be recorded in real-time, and the data can be securely uploaded to the blockchain. This technology increases the asset valuation of enterprises and enables all participants to assess asset values and jointly manage risks, ultimately improving the financing efficiency and accessibility of enterprises.

By using some charging piles as the underlying assets for RWA, the Xindiantu platform under the Langxin Group issued "charging pile" digital assets on the blockchain using trusted data, so that each digital asset represents the partial revenue rights of the corresponding charging pile. This innovative asset management approach not only improves efficiency but also provides investors with a transparent and trustworthy green investment environment (see Fig. 5.15).

In China, the new energy industry has huge market potential. However, many small and medium-sized operators are still facing financing difficulties. According

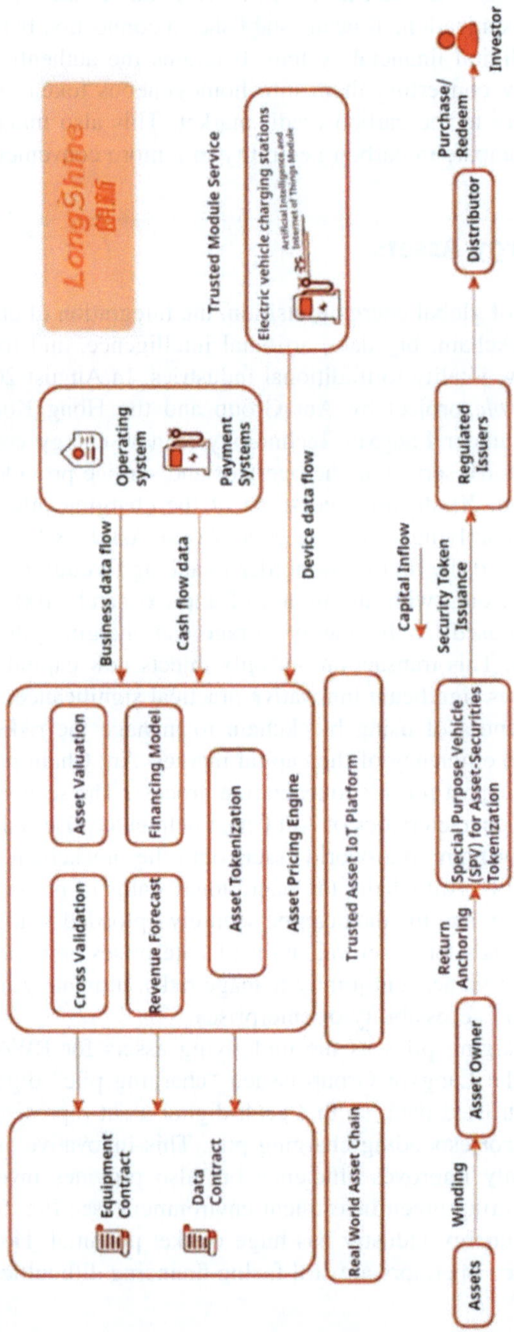

Fig. 5.15 The issuance process of Langxin Company's charge pile digital assets

to statistics,[40] currently 85% of public charging services are provided by private enterprises. Among them, more than 82% of the operators own less than 10 charging stations, and over 50% have an investment of less than 1 million yuan. These operators mainly focus on localized services. Although they can access regional resources, due to the lack of financing channels, a large amount of financing needs has not been effectively met. The RWA (Real-World Assets) on-chain financing model not only applies a variety of modern technologies but also provides a unique and extensive financing channel for investors and operators of new energy assets. This new approach has opened a new door to the Chinese new energy market for global investors, especially those outside China, and has formed an effective link between assets and funds.

Xu Changjun, Chairman of Langxin Group, stated that under the guidance of the dual-wheel strategy of "energy digitization and energy internet", Langxin Group can better apply emerging technologies to the digital construction and operation practices of new energy. "*In the scenarios of energy storage and charging stations, we provide users with intelligent and convenient services, continuously create revenue and value for our partners, and also contribute to building a clean, low - carbon, safe and efficient energy system.*"

Through this innovative practice, the RWA financing method for new energy will help revitalize the high-quality assets of small and medium-sized energy storage and charging pile operators, improve the liquidity of heavy assets, promote a virtuous cycle of investment and financing, and accelerate the transformation of China's green energy structure. The introduction of new capital will not only drive the new energy industry towards intelligence and green development but also strongly support the development of China's new energy industry. The implementation of the first new energy real-world assets RWA project means that Ant Financial Technology has used blockchain verification technology to facilitate the trusted data flow of real-world assets. By digitizing real-world assets and then opening up new financing channels, the industrial Web 3.0 represented by RWA is entering a turning point where it truly empowers real-world enterprises.

5.8 Precious Metals

The tokenization of precious metals has multiple advantages. Taking gold as an example, it provides a new and efficient way to invest in physical gold without having to deal with the actual physical gold. Firstly, compared with traditional gold investments, tokenization avoids the hassle and costs associated with storing, insuring, and transporting physical gold. Secondly, the tokenization of gold can offer higher liquidity, as tokens can be freely bought and sold on the digital asset market. Thirdly, the tokenization of gold can also bring greater financial inclusivity, as it allows investors to purchase a portion of gold at a lower price, which is more

[40] The information is sourced from the Langxin Company's official website.

accessible to many people than buying a whole bar of gold. Finally, by using blockchain technology, the tokenization of gold can provide higher transparency and security, as every transaction will be permanently recorded on the blockchain, and the ownership of tokens can also be verified through digital signatures.

5.8.1 Case: Paxos Gold, the Gold Token

Paxos Trust, established in 2015, is a company that actively explores the application of blockchain technology and digital asset services. It holds a trust license issued by the New York State Department of Financial Services in the United States. The gold token issued by this company is called PAXG, which is an ERC-20 token based on the Ethereum blockchain.

Each PAXG token represents the ownership of 1 troy ounce of London Good Delivery[41] gold stored in the warehouse. The quality of these gold bars is managed and defined by the London Bullion Market Association (LBMA). As of July 31, 2023, the number of gold tokens issued by Paxos Trust was 248,343 troy ounces, with a market value of approximately $476 million.

The gold token PAXG has the following characteristics:

- Traceability: The issuance and storage of PAXG tokens are based on the Ethereum blockchain, which means that the transaction record of each PAXG token will be permanently written into the blockchain, and is public, transparent, and immutable. When issuing PAXG tokens, the specific information of each troy ounce of gold (such as the gold bar's serial number, weight, purity, etc.) will be encoded onto the corresponding token. This mechanism ensures that each PAXG token can be directly traced back to its corresponding physical gold.
- Redeemable: PAXG tokens can be exchanged for physical gold in various forms. For example, PAXG tokens can be exchanged for a complete London Good Delivery gold bar, or small-denomination PAXG tokens can be exchanged for physical gold through designated gold retailers. They can also be exchanged for non-physical gold rights[42] or legal tender.
- Regulated: Since it holds a financial license, the products issued by Paxos Trust Company (including PAXG tokens) are supervised by the New York State Department of Financial Services, which has high requirements for customer

[41] A series of specifications and standards set by the London Bullion Market Association to ensure that gold bars or silver bars can be publicly recognized and easily traded worldwide. Gold bars or silver bars certified as "*Good Delivery*" meet specific standards for purity, weight, and size.

[42] Non-physical gold rights usually refer to gold derivatives in the financial market, such as paper gold, gold ETF, or gold futures. This means that investors own the economic value of gold rather than the actual physical gold. Exchanging for legal tender means that investors can sell the held PAXG tokens to obtain the corresponding currency.

asset protection and operational standards. The entrusted assets are strictly separated from the company's assets. Even if Paxos Trust Company goes bankrupt, the physical gold corresponding to PAXG tokens will not be liquidated as part of the company's property. In addition, Paxos undergoes monthly audits to ensure that the inventory of physical gold is sufficient to support the tokens in circulation. The circulation and trading of PAXG tokens are also monitored to prevent fraud or money laundering.

- Inclusive: The investment threshold for PAXG tokens (0.01PAXG, equivalent to approximately $15–$20 at the current price) is relatively low, making it relatively easy for ordinary people to invest in gold.
- Low Fees: Compared with traditional gold investment products, the fees related to PAXG are relatively low. For transactions on the blockchain, the Paxos transaction fee rate is only 0.02%.[43] There are no storage fees, and the creation or destruction fees are graded based on trading volume.
- High Liquidity: Paxos tokens are issued on the Ethereum blockchain, so instant transfers or transactions can be realized 24 h a day, 7 days a week globally, making gold trading easier and faster.
- Programmability: Based on the digital and programmable features of smart contracts, PAXG tokens are more easily exchangeable, tradable, mortgageable, or usable in other ways. Smart contracts and oracles link the redemption value of PAXG tokens 1:1 to the price per troy ounce of gold.

Therefore, compared with directly holding traditional gold ETF, gold futures, London Good Delivery gold bars, or gold products such as paper gold,[44] investing in the gold market through Paxos tokens has certain advantages (see Table 5.3).

5.8.2 HSBC Hong Kong Gold Token

On March 27, 2024, HSBC announced the launch of its first gold token for Hong Kong retail investors in Hong Kong, China. This product is not only a significant milestone for HSBC in the digital asset field but also the first retail gold token product recognized by the Securities and Futures Commission (SFC) in Hong Kong. This marks a crucial step for Hong Kong in promoting the digitization and popularization of physical assets, providing ordinary investors with a more convenient and flexible channel for gold investment.

[43] Traders also need to pay the Gas fees of the Ethereum blockchain.

[44] A gold ETF is a financial instrument that allows investors to indirectly invest in gold. Compared with directly purchasing and holding physical gold, a gold ETF provides a more convenient and cost-effective investment method. Gold futures are contracts traded on a futures exchange, allowing both the buyer and the seller to conduct gold transactions at a pre-agreed price and date. London Bullion Market gold bars refer to gold bars that meet the Good Delivery standards of the LBMA. Paper gold is a derivative in the financial market, allowing investors to invest in gold without holding physical gold.

Table 5.3 The similarities and differences between Paxos gold tokens and other gold investment products

Itemization	Paxos gold token	Gold ETF	Gold futures	London bullion market gold bullion	Paper gold
Custody fees	None	Annual rate of 0.19–0.4%	None	Annual rate of 0.05–0.25%	Annual rate 0–0.1%
Minimum purchase amount	0.01 troy ounces of gold ($15–$20)	1 share ETF (about $200)	1 contract (about $2000)	Usually the equivalent of $700,000 in gold bars	Agencies have different requirements
Delivery time	Immediate	$T + 2$	Contract expiration date	$T + 2$	$T + 2$
Can storage be split	Yes	Uncertain	No	Yes	No
Can be exchanged in kind Gold	Yes	No	No	Yes	No
Regulatory agencies	New York state finance service bureau	SEC and other institutions	S. Commodity futures trading commission	None	None

The HSBC gold token is supported by the digital asset platform HSBC Orion, which is independently developed by the bank, providing technical support and operational assurance. Hong Kong customers of HSBC can now trade gold tokens anytime and anywhere through the "HSBC HK App" mobile application and the online wealth-management platform. This seamless digital experience makes gold investments unprecedently easy and efficiency.

The HSBC gold token is an innovative digital product launched by HSBC as the issuer. It uses blockchain technology to record and store the ownership of physical gold in digital form. Each HSBC gold token represents 0.001 troy ounces of London-sourced gold, certified by the London Bullion Market Association (LBMA). When investors trade gold tokens, there is no physical delivery of the actual gold. All the physical gold corresponding to the gold tokens is held by HSBC and securely stored in vaults located in England and Wales to ensure the safety and reliability of the assets.

Gold transactions must comply with the requirements of weight, dimensions, purity, etc., as stipulated by the London Bullion Market Association. The ownership of a gold bar can be divided among multiple investors, and the trading unit is troy ounces. A typical London-sourced gold bar weighs between 350 and 430 troy ounces, and its purity is not lower than 99.5%. Gold is priced in US dollars.

To facilitate trading in the Hong Kong market, HSBC converts the gold price into Hong Kong dollars.

The HSBC gold token has a relatively low trading threshold in the Hong Kong market. The minimum transaction amount is only 1 token, equivalent to 0.001 troy ounces of gold. This significantly lowers the investment entry barrier for gold, allowing more ordinary investors to participate in the gold market. The maximum single-order trading volume can reach 50,000 tokens, that is, 50 troy ounces of gold, to meet the needs of high-net-worth individuals and institutional investors. The HSBC gold token is priced in Hong Kong dollars, and the trading hours cover 24 hours a day, 7 days a week, providing investors with ample flexibility and convenience. However, the actual settlement of gold still takes place during the business days in London and Hong Kong, China.

All HSBC gold tokens will be recorded in HSBC's distributed ledger. Purchasing a gold token essentially means buying a share of the corresponding gold ownership. The token itself has no other rights or value except representing the gold ownership. HSBC is the issuer and platform operator of this product and is responsible for its settlement. The product is subject to product terms and conditions, as well as the constraints of the sales agreement. According to Hong Kong laws, this product is regarded as a collective investment scheme and is regulated under Part IV of *the Securities and Futures Ordinance*. Figure 5.16 illustrates the settlement and purchase process of the HSBC gold token.

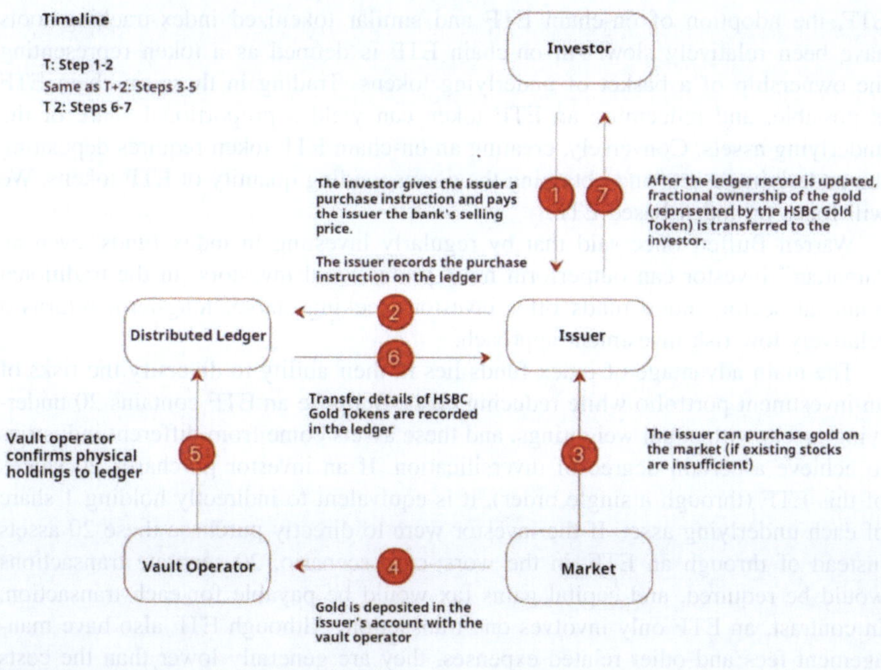

Fig. 5.16 Settlement purchase instruction

Overall, the launch of the HSBC gold token is a significant milestone in Hong Kong's financial innovation, marking the acceleration of the tokenization process of Real-World Assets (RWA). With the joint efforts of regulatory authorities and the industry, Hong Kong is expected to become a pioneer and demonstration zone for the tokenization of precious metal assets globally. This will bring a more diverse and convenient investment experience to investors and inject new vitality into the development of the industry.

5.9 Index Fund

An ETF (Exchange-Traded Fund) is a type of index fund traded on a securities exchange, enabling investors to participate in the performance of an index. An ETF tracks the changes of an underlying index and is traded on a securities exchange just like stocks. Investors can buy and sell ETF in the same way as they trade stocks on the exchange, with the trading prices being determined by the market. According to a report released by a securities exchange in January 2024, the global ETF industry's assets under management increased from $9.2 trillion at the end of December 2022 to $11.1 trillion at the end of December 2023. This growth is not only a quantitative milestone but also indicates the market's dynamic development and the substantial influence of ETF. Typically, ETF play a stabilizing role during market volatility. Additionally, their high-tax-efficiency structure provides investors with more favorable after-tax returns. Despite the success of traditional ETF, the adoption of on-chain ETF and similar tokenized index-tracking tools have been relatively slow. An on-chain ETF is defined as a token representing the ownership of a basket of underlying tokens. Trading in these on-chain ETF is possible, and redeeming an ETF token can yield a proportional share of the underlying assets. Conversely, creating an on-chain ETF token requires depositing the underlying assets and obtaining the corresponding quantity of ETF tokens. We will focus on index-based ETF.

Warren Buffett once said that by regularly investing in index funds, even an "amateur" investor can outperform most professional investors. In the traditional financial sector, index funds offer investors seeking stable, long-term returns a relatively low-risk investment approach.

The main advantage of index funds lies in their ability to diversify the risks of an investment portfolio while reducing costs. Suppose an ETF contains 20 underlying assets with equal weightings, and these assets come from different industries to achieve a certain degree of diversification. If an investor purchases 20 shares of this ETF (through a single order), it is equivalent to indirectly holding 1 share of each underlying asset. If the investor were to directly purchase these 20 assets instead of through an ETF, in the worst-case scenario, 20 separate transactions would be required, and capital gains tax would be payable for each transaction. In contrast, an ETF only involves one transaction. Although ETF also have management fees and other related expenses, they are generally lower than the costs generated by multiple transactions.

Tokenized index funds began to gain traction in 2017. Invictus Capital launched one of the first tokenized index funds, using seed capital to purchase underlying assets. Here, we will analyze tokenized index funds ecosystem's 3 core project: Index Cope, Alongside and infinix finance, and compare them with traditional index cope.

5.9.1 Index Coop

Index Coop was launched as a DAO by Set Labs in 2020, aiming to issue and maintain the best-performing index funds in the digital asset field. Its products were initially built on the *Set Protocol*, but since the beginning of 2023, Index Coop has become the main platform for issuing products. This move enables Index Coop to control the products on its platform, which helps meet potential regulatory requirements that may be imposed on the index-providing protocol in the future. In November 2021, during the previous bull market in the cryptocurrency market, Index Coop achieved its highest-ever TVL, exceeding $500 million. As of July 4, 2024, Index Coop has 6 on-chain ETF products, with a total TVL reaching $78 million. Next, we will focus on analyzing their flagship product, the Defi-Pulse Index (DPI), launched in cooperation with Defi-Pulse, and some of the key mechanisms behind it.

DPI is a market-capitalization-weighted index that tracks the performance of some of the largest protocols in the DeFi field. The index is weighted according to the value of the circulating supply of each cryptocurrency, aiming to track projects in DeFi that have significant usage and are committed to continuous maintenance and development. As of July 4, 2024, the composition of the DPI index is shown in Fig. 5.17.

The method for calculating DPI is to weight the cryptocurrencies in the index according to the market value of their circulating supply. To avoid over-concentration, the maximum allocation limit for index components is 25%. Any overweight exceeding 25% will be re-allocated proportionally to the remaining components of DPI. DPI takes into account a wide range of features that can be divided into four dimensions. Among them, two dimensions are used to evaluate the characteristics of cryptocurrencies, and one dimension is used to evaluate the project, the other dimension is used to evaluate the protocol. The characteristic of the project, and one dimension is used to evaluate the characteristics of the protocol. The inclusion criteria form the basis for selecting which cryptocurrencies will be included in the index. In terms of the descriptive characteristics of cryptocurrencies, the cryptocurrency must be available on the Ethereum blockchain, not be considered a security by the relevant authorities in the relevant judicial jurisdiction, and must be a bearer instrument. The index does not include wrapped cryptocurrencies, cryptocurrency derivatives, synthetic assets, cryptocurrencies linked to physical assets, and cryptocurrencies representing rights to other cryptocurrencies. Regarding the supply characteristics of cryptocurrencies, it must be possible to reasonably predict the supply of the cryptocurrency over the next 5 years, and at

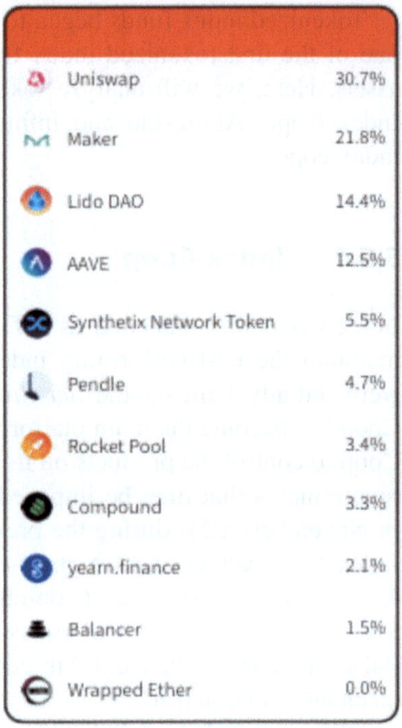

Fig. 5.17 The composition of DPI index (as of 2024.7.4).

least 7.5% of the 5-year supply must already be in circulation. The economics of the cryptocurrency should not have significant locking, minting, or other models that are significantly unfavorable to passive holders.

In terms of the attractiveness characteristics of the project, the project must be widely recognized as building a useful protocol or product, excluding projects that focus on competitive trading / holding, have Ponzi-scheme characteristics, or are mainly used for entertainment. The protocol of the project must have significant usage, and the protocol or product must have been launched for at least 180 days before being eligible for inclusion in the index. In addition, the protocol or project must not be insolvent.

In terms of the user-security characteristics of the protocol, security professionals must have reviewed the protocol to ensure that security best practices are followed in different situations to safeguard the security of user assets. Alternatively, the protocol must have been in operation for a long enough time to reach a consensus on its security in the DeFi space. In the event of a security incident, the team must respond promptly and handle the incident responsibly after the fact, providing reliable solutions for protocol users and providing sufficient documentation for DeFi to ensure transparency about the incident. In addition, the selected cryptocurrencies must have sufficient liquidity on various trading platforms.

To ensure that DPI complies with index norms, the project currently undergoes rebalancing once a quarter (in January, April, July, and October). The rebalancing proposal (including key parameters such as the target weights of the index) must be submitted by Set's managers. Once submitted, the grace period begins, allowing Set cryptocurrency holders to decide whether to exit or continue holding if they are satisfied with the proposal. This alleviates some of the trust issues between the managers and Set cryptocurrency holders mentioned earlier. The rebalancing is maintained in two phases:

- Determination phase

  The determination phase takes place in the third week of the rebalancing month. This phase determines the changes required for the next restructuring. Circulating supply determination: DPI currently refers to the circulating supply data from CoinGecko. The circulating supply is also determined in the last week of the quarter and announced before the restructuring. Additions and deletions: The cryptocurrencies to be added to and deleted from the index calculation are determined in the last week of the quarter and announced before the restructuring.
- Restructuring phase

  Adjust, add, and delete the index components according to the instructions announced at the end of the determination phase. The new index weights, additions, and deletions are incorporated into the index during the monthly restructuring, which takes place on the first working day of each month. As the assets tracked by the index grow, the restructuring window will be extended to more than one day to reduce the impact of restructuring on the market.

Based on the DPI rebalancing situation in May 2023 (see Table 5.4), we can understand the costs for on-chain ETF to comply with index norms.

On June 19, 2024, Index Coop announced a collaboration with Fortunafi to launch a new RWA index token, namely Fortunafi RWA, providing non-US

Table 5.4 The rebalancing status of DPI (2023.5)

Token	Pre-balance weight	Target weight	Weight change
UNI	24.91	24.97	0.03
AAVE	19.65	16.59	–3.06
SNX	14.87	12.63	–2.24
MKR	12.32	10.31	–2.01
LDO	0	10.03	10.03
LRC	8.79	7.34	–1.45
RPL	0	4.99	4.99
COMP	5.46	4.57	–0.89
YFI	5.33	4.48	–0.85
BAL	4.68	4.09	–0.59
SUSHI	3.96	0	–3.96

The source of the information: Scalar

Table 5.5 The index of Fortunafi RWA (as of 2024.5.22)

Project name	Token	Market value (in US$ billion)	Introduce	Weight (%)
MakerDAO	MKR	2.72	On-chain RWA loans	25
Ohdo	ONDO	1.12	RWA fund infrastructure	25
Ethena	ENA	1.27	On-chain native revenue	25
Centrifuge	CFG	0.34	On-chain RWA loans	11.5
Canto	CANTO	0.07	First layer blockchain	6.8
Maple Finance	MPL	0.06	On-chain RWA loans	6.7
RWA	—	—	—	100

investors with a new way to access RWA-related tokens. This product includes projects such as Maker, Ondo Finance, and Ethena, covering various investments such as real-estate tokenization and US Treasury bonds. To attract early-stage investors, Index Coop uses Product Revenue Tokens (PRT), and holders can share the income of the RWA index.

As of May 22, 2024, the potential issuance portfolio of the Fortunafi RWA index is shown in Table 5.5.

The Fortunafi RWA index methodology is provided and managed by Fortunafi. Restructuring and rebalancing will be carried out quarterly, and assets must meet the following criteria: The underlying protocol must be listed on DeFiLlama; the 90-day moving average of TVL (Total Value Locked) must exceed $30 million; the 90-day moving average of the daily trading volume of tokens must exceed $500,000; according to the decision of the methodology developers, the protocol must be centered around RWA; both the protocol and tokens must pass a manual review process to determine their suitability; the protocol must undergo a public audit; tokens must be available on the Ethereum mainnet, and wrapped or bridged tokens can be considered for inclusion.

The weights of the Fortunafi RWA index will be directly proportional to the market capitalization of the underlying tokens. The maximum weight of a single component will be limited to 25%; the excess weight will be evenly distributed among tokens with weights less than 25%. Fortunafi, the developer of the methodology, has the right to add or remove components based on subjective factors, including but not limited to the active development of the project and its commitment to the RWA field. Investors can view comments on the monthly and quarterly performance of the index in Fortunafi's monthly RWA and stablecoin review reports, as well as quarterly industry status reports.

5.9.2 Alongside

Alongside is a crypto index platform that allows investors to invest in cryptocurrencies through indices. It was co-founded in October 2021 by Austin Diamond and Jun Ho Hong. The company's team previously built products used by millions of people at companies such as Google, Omni (acquired by Coinbase), and Maze. In February 2023, Alongside raised $1.1 million in funding led by a16z. Coinbase Ventures, Franklin Templeton Investments, Village Globa, Not Boring Capital, and some angel investors also participated in this round of financing.

In January 2023, Alongside launched its first tokenized index, the Alongside Crypto Market Index (AMKT), enabling people to gain broad exposure to the entire crypto-asset market through a single token. Similar to Index Coop, AMKT is also an index managed by a DAO (Decentralized Autonomous Organization), constructing index-based tokenized ETF products for investors. The main difference between the two lies in the underlying implementation of their products, which is a feature that Alongside hopes will provide a highly diversified index. Currently, the DAO has only approved AMKT to invest in and track 16 on-chain tokens. The AMKT index is chain-agnostic, while Index Coop's DPI is limited to assets available on Ethereum and bridged assets (such as wBTC), which restricts the diversity of the index. Alongside uses a similar market-share-weighted method to determine the weights of assets in the index. The key difference is that there is no upper limit for crypto assets with a relatively high market share (such as Bitcoin).

5.9.3 AMKT Index Token Component Requirements

The AMKT index must only include exposure to the top 15 crypto tokens by circulating supply market capitalization. Only assets that meet the following requirements can be added to the Alongside network:

- Assets must be traded on multiple trusted exchanges / trading venues. The assets on the supported trading venues must have been in operation for more than 30 days. This ensures smooth trading and liquidity when issuing and redeeming component shares, which helps promote token liquidity.
- Stablecoins do not meet the criteria for inclusion in AMKT.
- Assets must not have known vulnerabilities and must meet the industry-safety standards determined by the DAO. This ensures that AMKT token holders will not be exposed to critical errors with prior knowledge.
- An asset must not be determined to be illegal in judicial or other final government proceedings, either in the judicial jurisdiction where the asset is issued or in the judicial jurisdictions where the relevant parties in the AMKT network are located.

Figure 5.18 shows the latest components and proportions of the AMKT index.

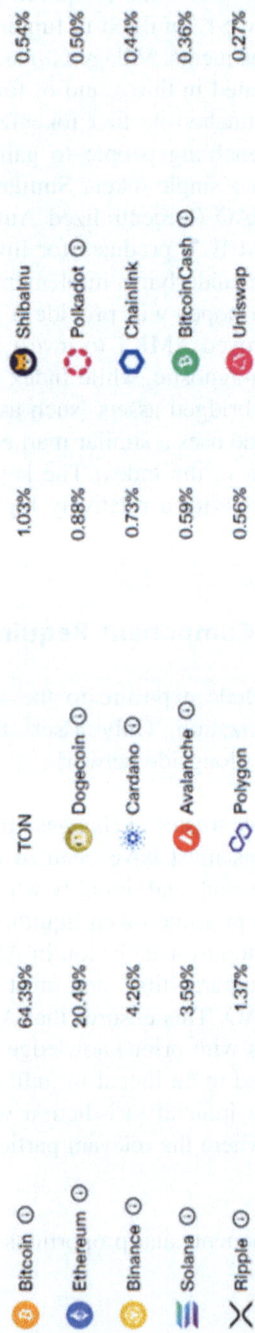

Fig. 5.18 The latest components and proportions of the AMKT index (as of 2024.7.4)

5.9.4 AMKT Token Mechanism

The circulating supply of AMKT tokens is determined by the market. The issuance and destruction of index tokens are decided by the AMKT DAO. The destruction method is to exchange AMKT index tokens for digital assets. Currently, this index token supports wallets such as Coinbase, Metamask, Rainbow, and BitGo, and is listed for trading on multiple DEX (Decentralized Exchanges) like Uniswap, SushiSwap, and exchanges such as Gate.io. These assets (excluding Bitcoin and ETH) are held by the custody service (Coinbase Prime) and monitored by Chainlink's Proof of Reserve (PoR) to ensure that AMKT is fully backed. Obviously, compared with DPI, AMKT makes some compromises in terms of trust, but this is a necessary trade-off for tracking an index of a broader crypto ecosystem. Unlike DPI, redeeming or creating AMKT does not require permission. In fact, it is the same as traditional ETF, where only merchants (equivalent to AP) have the right to redeem or create tokens. So far, a single address has minted more than 99% of the circulating supply of AMKT. Therefore, the arbitrage price difference is limited to the merchants listed by the Alongside DAO.

5.9.5 AMKT Token Redemption

Only merchant addresses can initiate the redemption of index tokens. To achieve this, the "burn" function needs to be called in the contract, which contains the number of tokens to be burned. After that, the amount will be deducted from the merchant's index token balance (on-chain), reducing the supply of index tokens. The merchant creates a burn transaction instruction and then randomly burns n index tokens. The network observes that the index tokens are burned and instructs the custodian to release the underlying assets to the merchant. The custodian then distributes the underlying assets of the corresponding amount to the merchant.

5.9.6 AMKT Token Restructuring

The restructuring is managed by the DAO. The DAO is expected to announce an updated list of components in the index, as well as the expected weights of the underlying assets in the on-chain index. The restructuring frequency may vary for different indices, but AMKT undergoes restructuring quarterly. During the reconstruction of index tokens, the issuance or redemption of new tokens may have to be temporarily suspended. The DAO publishes an updated list of underlying assets and the new weights of each asset in the on-chain index. The custodian executes underlying asset transactions to achieve the desired weights. The network verifies that the custodian now holds the correct weights of the underlying assets.

5.9.7 AMKT Token System Operation

Each index token is supported by a certain proportion of assets held by Coinbase Prime. The AMKT index tokens are designed to measure the market performance of digital assets available on crypto exchanges. These indices are composed based on attributes such as supply, availability, and liquidity. Alongside's indices are constructed by a network of participants, who mint or burn tokens by depositing collateral into a treasury. This provides some special features for Alongside indices, such as full collateralization (each token is fully backed by the assets it represents), redeemability (each token can be redeemed for index component shares), and programmability (tokens are distributed as ERC-20 tokens, allowing them to be fully integrated with DeFi applications).

5.9.8 AMKT Token Governance

AMKT is managed by the AMKT DAO. Each AMKT token grants its holder voting rights (users must undergo KYC before exercising their AMKT DAO governance voting rights) to establish a truly neutral benchmark. The DAO consists of two entities: the holders of the first implementation of the benchmark (AMKT tokens); and a group of AMKT governance administrators. AMKT governance administrators are a group of individuals from across the crypto ecosystem with aligned values. Their responsibilities include owning the smart contract that first implements the AMKT benchmark (i.e., AMKT tokens), working with AMKT token holders to determine whether assets are suitable for the AMKT asset universe, and collaborating with AMKT token holders to draft and adopt the benchmark charter.

In terms of the compliance framework, Alongside selects a service entity to perform tasks that require a legal entity. The AMKT DAO has chosen Battery Labs, which acts on behalf of the Alongside DAO to perform the following index-related sample functions: KYC-related activities, holding institutional custody accounts, operating the front-end, and coordinating audit functions. The AMKT network needs to promptly fulfill its issuance, redemption, and restructuring responsibilities. In addition, merchants and custodians must complete KYC (Know Your Customer) and AML (Anti-Money Laundering) checks in accordance with local laws and regulations. Battery Labs Limited must fulfill its duties to ensure the safety of merchant deposits and management. The laws in relevant judicial jurisdictions may prohibit the transfer of tokens to certain addresses. As part of managing smart contracts, administrators can restrict AMKT from entering or leaving these addresses to comply with the laws and regulations of the relevant regions.

5.9.9 Infinix Finance

Infinix finance (hereinafter referred to as infinix) was established in 2023 and is a fully decentralized on-chain index token trading platform. On infinix, 1 index token equals 1 basket of on-chain thematic / industry tokens (such as GameFi, SocialFi, AI, RWA, etc.). Infinix allows both ordinary and professional users to generate unique indices and adjust parameters. On the infinix platform, users only need to hold one token to easily enter the cryptocurrency investment field. Infinix aggregates the dispersed liquidity of RWA tokens and provides a unique secondary market trading platform for all real-yield tokens, maximizing capital efficiency and enabling users to achieve the best real yields in the cryptocurrency market.

In June 2024, infinix launched its first index token on the Solana public chain and aggregated multiple decentralized protocols within the Solana ecosystem, such as Raydium. Raydium is the first AMM (Automated Market Maker) and liquidity provider built on Solana, and its core product is the Raydium DEX. The uniqueness of Raydium lies in its integration with the Serum order book, which enables market participants to trade digital assets more flexibly. Moreover, Raydium's liquidity pool contributes to the Serum order book, enhancing overall liquidity. This integration ensures that anyone on Serum can trade orders on Raydium, and vice versa. In such a situation, competing AMMs (Automated Market Makers) usually choose to have a cancellation period, and traders bear the gas fees and trading losses. Raydium executes traders' orders at the so-called "optimal price" and cancels the remaining parts.

By aggregating liquidity, infinix attracts investors from traditional sectors, ensuring that users can trade seamlessly and achieve better price discovery. This method of aggregating multi-protocol liquidity not only improves the efficiency of the platform but also provides users with a better trading experience. An important goal of infinix is to attract traditional stock-investing users into the DeFi (Decentralized Finance) field. The platform offers a simple and user-friendly interface, allowing users to easily enter the on-chain market. By using index tokens, users can capture diversified thematic or industry Betas with a single click, without the need for extensive research on individual tokens. In addition, users can trade specific index tokens in a timely manner according to market changes to obtain the best Alpha returns. By reducing the number of transactions, infinix helps users minimize trading costs and increase investment returns. By investing in a basket of tokens, users can effectively diversify risks and achieve a more stable investment portfolio.

In addition to aggregating liquidity, infinix is also committed to improving the accessibility and interoperability of RWA (real-world assets). Users can directly access various RWA from Solana on the platform, or transfer RWA from other chains to Solana via cross-chain bridges. This high level of accessibility, combined with the high liquidity and capital efficiency provided by the platform, has led more and more RWA issuers to choose to tokenize their assets through infinix and trade them on Solana.

Although the prospects of index tokens are still in their infancy, they are developing rapidly under the leadership of institutions such as infinix. From the perspective of investor demand, as of now, index tokens are far less popular than traditional ETF (Exchange-Traded Funds). This may be because native crypto investors believe they can outperform the market by continuously selecting the right assets, or the relatively high correlation among crypto assets reduces the attractiveness of indices that focus on diversification.

With the continuous popularization of cryptocurrencies, on-chain ETF are expected to attract more mainstream investors to enter this field. On-chain ETF have several unique advantages, such as a lower entry barrier, higher liquidity, greater transparency, a wider investment scope, and lower costs. Investors do not need to understand the complexity of individual crypto assets; they can participate in the market by simply purchasing an ETF that covers multiple assets. Index tokens are automatically executed by smart contracts, making transactions and settlements more efficient and providing better liquidity. In addition, the holding, trading, and fee data of index tokens are all publicly transparent, allowing investors to keep track of their investment status at any time. Index tokens can also cover more innovative niche areas (such as DeFi, NFT, Web 3.0, etc.) to meet the needs of different investors. Based on a decentralized architecture, index tokens can significantly reduce management and trading fees, enabling investors to obtain higher net returns.

Currently, although the scale and influence of index tokens cannot be compared with traditional ETF, with the continuous development of the crypto market and the increasing maturity of the regulatory environment, their attractiveness to on-chain investors are growing. The value proposition of diversified index tokens may become increasingly appealing, rewarding those who have laid the foundation for them today.

Stablecoin—The Bridge Between the Real World and Digital Assets

6

Stablecoins play an indispensable role in the Web 3.0 world. As a pioneer and one of the most successful areas in the digitalization of Real-World Assets (RWA), stablecoins skillfully combine the convenience of digital assets with the stability of traditional financial assets. They not only serve as a measure of value for digital asset transactions, providing digital asset investors with a convenient "entrance channel" and a safe "safe - haven", but also play an increasingly important role in the international payment system of the real world. Moreover, stablecoins are not only the key foundation for RWA digitalization, but as the digitalization process of RWA advances, stablecoins will also obtain more diversified value support and reserve sources. Therefore, stablecoins have become an important bridge connecting digital assets and the traditional financial system. The earliest stablecoin, BitUSD, was issued in July 2014. According to the issuance methods and value underpinnings of stablecoins, they can be classified into the following three categories: centralized stablecoins, decentralized stablecoins, and algorithmic stablecoins. With the continuous development of the digital economy, stablecoins will play an increasingly important role in the popularization and application of digital assets, becoming an essential and important component of the digital economy era.

In the financial system, the five major functions of money are: measure of value, medium of exchange, store of value, means of payment, and world currency. Currently, digital assets such as Bitcoin and Ethereum have gradually been recognized for their characteristics of value storage and safe-haven assets. Therefore, many institutions use them as tools for portfolio diversification to improve the Sharpe ratio of investment portfolios. However, the prices of these digital assets are extremely volatile and cannot fulfill the functions of money such as measure of value, medium of exchange, and means of payment, so they are hardly suitable for payment scenarios. Imagine if there is a digital asset that not only has the advantages of digital assets such as programmability and decentralization, but

S. Ba et al., *RWA Tokenisation in Web 3.0 Era*, Management for Professionals,
https://doi.org/10.1007/978-981-96-7663-7_6

also has more solid value support to make the market price more stable. Can such a digital asset play the role of money in the digital world? Thus, a digital asset with stable value came into being, namely the stablecoin. A stablecoin refers to a digital asset issued on the blockchain, existing in the form of a token, whose price is pegged to a certain (or a basket of) fiat currency. Compared with general digital assets, stablecoins are issued with assets as collateral and maintain a stable exchange rate with a certain fiat currency, thus possessing a certain degree of monetary attributes while also having the technological advantages of digital assets. Therefore, they can play a significant role in scenarios such as international payments. Stablecoins do not require users to open a bank account; they only need to have Internet-connected devices to make payments, which can serve groups that traditional finance cannot reach,[1] greatly improving the inclusiveness of financial services. In addition, based on blockchain infrastructure, stablecoin can achieve peer-to-peer payment which enables payment and settlement simultaneously, featuring high efficiency and low cost. These advantages also make the popularization of stablecoins inevitable.

The earliest stablecoin was BitUSD, which was issued in July 2014. BitUSD is a stablecoin generated by pledging the original token BTS on the BitShares platform. However, due to some flaws in the design of its price-stabilization mechanism, BitUSD did not become a powerful stablecoin system. From 2014 to 2016, the stablecoin market was in the early exploration stage. USDT, as a trading medium between Bitcoin and other digital assets, began to gain popularity on major trading platforms. After 2017, in addition to USDT, other centralized stablecoins such as USDC, PAX, and GUSD emerged and captured a small portion of the market. Other categories, such as the decentralized stablecoin DAI and the algorithmic stablecoin AMPL, also began to come into the public eye. In 2019, the market size of stablecoins began to expand rapidly and gradually increased after 2020 (see Fig. 6.1). Data shows that the total market capitalization of stablecoins once exceeded 180 billion US dollars at its peak in May 2022, and as of July 4, 2024, the total market capitalization exceeded 160 billion US dollars.

Based on the issuance methods and value underpinnings, we can divide stablecoin into 3 kinds:

- **Centralized Stablecoins**

  These stablecoins are issued by centralized institutions, with low-risk Real-World Assets (RWA) such as fiat currency deposits, bonds, and bills as reserve assets. The market value of the reserve assets of these stablecoins is generally

[1] According to data from the World Bank, as of 2018, there were 1.7 billion adults globally without bank accounts. The three countries with the highest proportion of the population without bank accounts in the world are all located in Asia-China (13%, 225 million people), India (11%, 190 million people), and Indonesia (6%, 96 million people). In the Asia-Pacific region, the market size for individuals and enterprises that have not yet opened bank accounts and non-bank accounts are estimated to be between $550 billion and $1.15 trillion for Web 3.0.

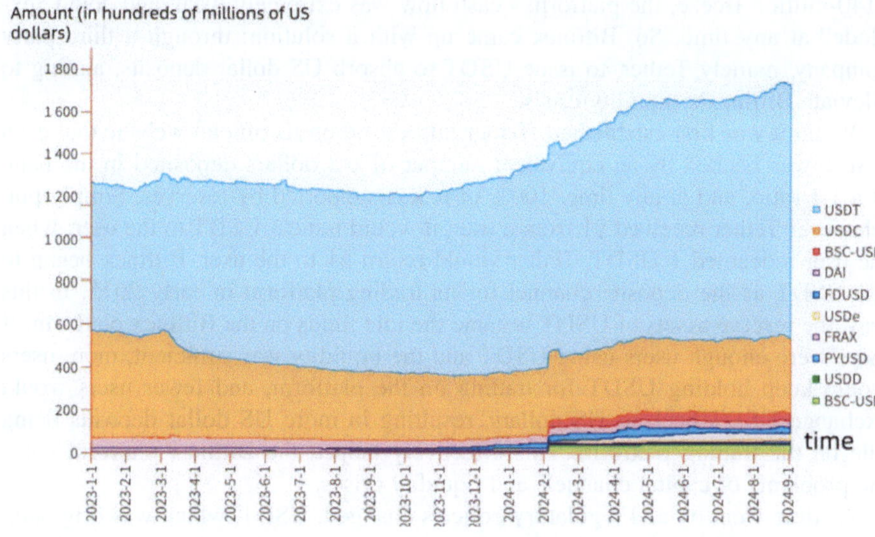

Fig. 6.1 The market capitalization changes of the top seven stablecoins (as of 2023.9.16)

close to or even exceeds the issuance scale of the stablecoins, including USDT, USDC, TUSD, BUSD, USDP, GUSD, etc.

- **Decentralized Stablecoins**

  These stablecoins are based on the collateralization of digital assets (including native digital tokens, RWA tokens, and even other stablecoins) on decentralized smart contracts of the blockchain, and issue digital assets pegged to the price of fiat currency, such as DAI.

- **Algorithmic Stablecoins**

  These stablecoins automatically adjust their circulation volume through the algorithm mechanism embedded in smart contracts, so as to maintain stability against the price (exchange rate) of a certain fiat currency. Such stablecoins include USDD, UST, FRAX, etc.

6.1 The Foundation of Stablecoins: Neutral Stablecoins

In 2014, Tether, a company under Bitfinex, launched USDT, a stablecoin pegged to the US dollar. USDT was initially introduced to help Bitfinex solve its capital channel and liquidity issues. Bitfinex was one of the most active cryptocurrency trading platforms as of 2012. In 2014, Bitfinex's $140-million deposit at Wells Fargo Bank was frozen. At that time, when users purchased digital assets on the trading platform, they generally used fiat currency for direct purchase, and also used fiat currency for settlement when selling digital assets. Therefore, after the

$140-million freeze, the platform's cash flow was extremely weak and could "explode" at any time. So, Bitfinex came up with a solution: through a third-party company, namely Tether, to issue USDT to absorb US dollar deposits, aiming to alleviate Bitfinex's liquidity crisis.

When it was first established, Tether introduced on its official website that each USDT was backed by an equivalent number of US dollars deposited in the bank at a 1:1 ratio, and at any time, 100% of it was supported by reserves. Simply put, whenever Tether received $1 from a user, it would issue 1 USDT to the user; when the user redeemed 1 USDT, Tether would return $1 to the user. Bitfinex began to use USDT as the deposit[2] channel for its trading platform in early 2015. In this way, the reserve assets of USDT became the idle funds on the Bitfinex platform. If there were enough users using USDT and the liquidity was sufficient, more users would keep holding USDT for trading on the platform, and fewer users would exchange USDT back to US dollars, resulting in more US dollar deposits being idle on the trading platform. This effectively helped the Bitfinex platform solve the problems of capital channels and liquidity crises.

As time went by and regulatory policies changed, USDT, which was originally a product to address the crisis, started to be used more widely. Since no regulatory authorities in any country or region supervised Tether, and in the early days, not even accounting firms audited its reserve assets, it had always been a mystery whether USDT corresponded to sufficient US dollar reserves and who exactly held these reserves. It was not until September 2017 that Tether first announced the audit by the US accounting firm Friedman LLP (now merged by Marcum LLP) The audit report indicated that as of September 15, 2017, Tether had corresponding funds of $443 million to back USDT. In March 2019, Tether quietly revised the description of its reserves on its official website. It changed from promising "1:1 US-dollar reserves" to "each USDT corresponds to corresponding reserve assets, which include traditional currencies, cash equivalents, other assets, and accounts receivable from loans to third parties".

In April 2019, the Attorney General of New York State issued a statement, having obtained a court order to sue Bitfinex and Tether's parent company, iFinex. The reason was that Bitfinex had used the reserves of USDT issued by Tether to cover up a loss of $850 million. According to a report in *The Wall Street Journal*, the New York State Attorney General said that in 2018, Bitfinex had given $850 million to Crypto Capital, a third-party payment processing company based in Panama, to handle customers' withdrawal requests. In the following months, Crypto Capital did not fulfill the withdrawal demands. According to Bitfinex, Crypto Capital refused to process customers' withdrawal requests and also refused to return the funds, leaving Bitfinex unable to meet customers' withdrawal needs. To address the liquidity crisis, Bitfinex began considering using Tether's USDT

[2] Deposit refers to the act of transferring users' funds from bank cards to trading accounts. USDT fiat-currency deposit means purchasing USDT with fiat currency and transferring the funds to the trading platform's account.

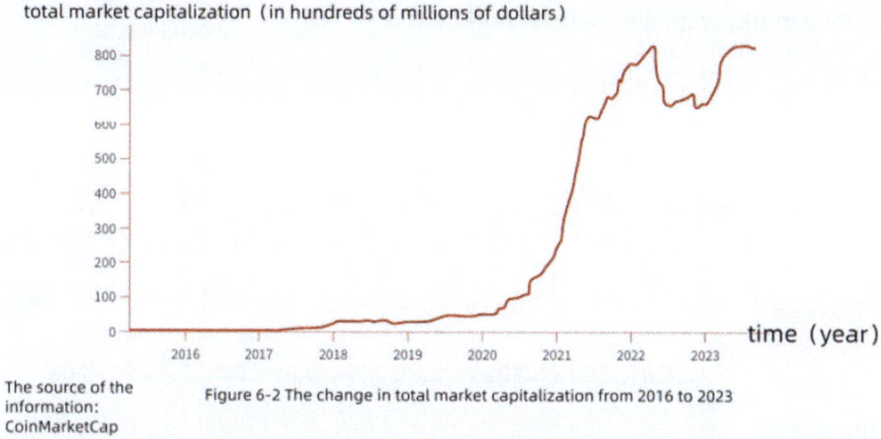

Fig. 6.2 The change in total market capitalization from 2016 to 2023 (The source of the information: CoinMarketCap)

cash reserves to pay for users' withdrawals. Later, Bitfinex reached an agreement with Tether. Under the agreement, Bitfinex obtained a credit line of up to $900 million from Tether with a three-year repayment period and an interest rate of 6.5%. The transaction was completed around March 19, 2019. This is the reason why Tether modified the sources of its reserve assets on its official website to include "accounts receivable from loans to third parties". It was not until February 23, 2021, that Bitfinex and Tether reached a settlement with the New York State Attorney General's Office. One of the settlement conditions was that the two companies had to pay a fine of $18.5 million to the New York State Attorney General's Office.

Since 2017, USDT has embarked on its path of aggressive issuance. On January 1, 2017, the total market capitalization of USDT was only $9.95 million. By the end of 2017, the total market capitalization of USDT had soared from $9.95 million at the beginning of the year to $1.378 billion. As of July 4, 2023, the total market capitalization of USDT had exceeded $111.7 billion, accounting for 70% of the total stablecoin market (see Fig. 6.2).

These stablecoins are issued on more than 10 blockchain protocols, such as Omni,[3] Ethereum, and Tron. (See Fig. 6.3). Among them, the USDT issued on the Ethereum and Tron public blockchains has the largest amount of assets. The USDT based on TRC-20 exceeds $48.2 billion, while the USDT based on ERC-20 is approximately $39 billion.

[3] Omni refers to the Omni LaMPSyver protocol on the Bitcoin blockchain. The Omni-USDT, which is based on the Bitcoin network, has a recharge address that is a BTC address. Withdrawals are processed via the BTC network, and the address starts with 1.

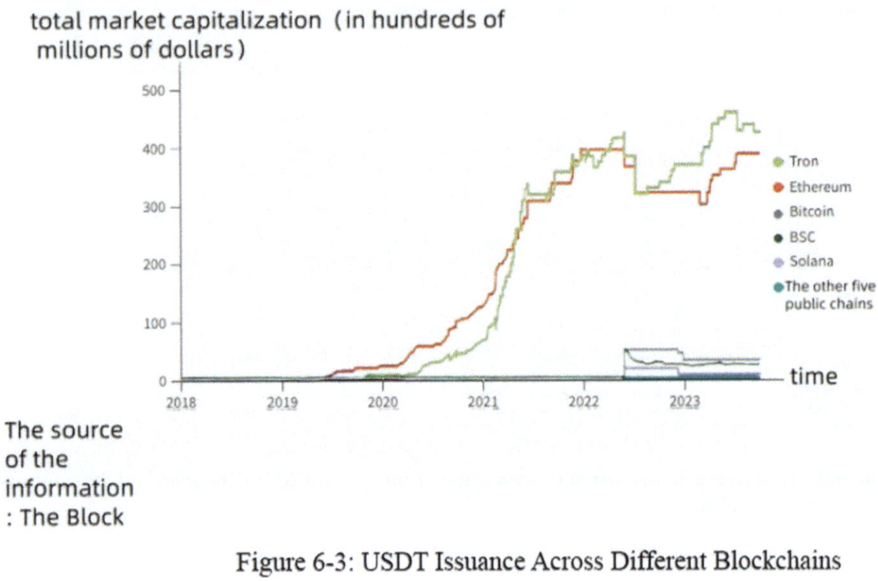

Fig. 6.3 USDT issuance across different blockchains (The source of the information: The Block)

Looking back on the long-standing development of USDT, we can divide it into three key periods. The first key period was from 2014 to 2017, which can be regarded as the incubation period of USDT. During this period, USDT mainly functioned within the exchanges it belonged to, providing users with a stable value-pegging tool. Stablecoins, similar to traditional currencies, showcased the blockchain world to users, enabling new entrants to more easily adapt to the digital asset ecosystem and manage their positions in a way they were familiar with. At that time, USDT was almost the only option in the stablecoin market, offering a platform for value storage and trading for numerous digital asset investors. The second key period was from 2017 to 2019, which can be considered the development period of USDT. During this time, with the boom in the digital asset market and the surge in trading volume, USDT gradually became the preferred medium for digital asset trading. It was not only active on its own trading platform but also played a crucial trading role in major exchanges globally. Meanwhile, although other stablecoins subject to stricter regulation also began to emerge, USDT still maintained its dominant position in the market. Since 2020, as the Federal Reserve implemented loose monetary policies and significantly increased the money supply, USDT and other centralized stablecoins also accelerated their issuance following suit. This not only further pushed up the total market capitalization of the digital asset market but also brought its total market capitalization to an all-time high. The third key period was from May 2022 to July 2024. The total market capitalization of stablecoins dropped from a peak of $180 billion to $160 billion, with a decline of over 10%, while USDT continued to rise after a slight correction. This divergence in development trends helps us gain a deeper understanding of the market dynamics and changing demands behind USDT. Despite the fluctuations in the total market capitalization of the digital asset market, the issuance volume of USDT has shown a continuous growth trend, indicating that its payment function outside of exchanges has started to emerge, gradually evolving from a primary trading medium to a more diversified payment tool. In 2024, this payment function was particularly evident in certain specific fields. Although the continuous growth of USDT is rarely openly discussed, it has indeed left an indelible mark on the market.

In 2024, USDT not only became the absolute leader in the stablecoin market but also achieved an astonishing level of profitability. According to officially disclosed information, Tether experienced rapid growth in the first quarter of 2024. The value of USDT increased by $22.5 billion, with its scale exceeding $110 billion, and it achieved a record-breaking net profit of $4.52 billion in the first quarter. In 2022, Tether reduced its commercial paper holdings to zero and began purchasing U.S. Treasury bonds as its reserves. As of the first quarter of 2024, Tether's direct holdings of U.S. Treasury bonds reached an all-time high, exceeding $73.8 billion, accounting for more than 67% of its total reserves. In fact, if all countries and companies in the world were ranked by their holdings of U.S. Treasury bonds, Tether would be second only to Mexico. The continuously rising yields of U.S. Treasury bonds have also brought Tether substantial returns. Judging from the data, although Tether has only been established for 10 years, the profit it generated in the first quarter of 2023 exceeded, for the first time, that of BlackRock, the world's largest asset management company which has been in operation for more than 30 years, by over $300 million. Moreover, the profit it reported was higher than that of companies such as Nestlé, Starbucks, PayPal, and many other S&P 500 companies.

Despite the rapid expansion of USDT's issuance scale, there have been continuous skepticism regarding the compliance of USDT's reserve assets. On October 15, 2021, the CFTC (Commodity Futures Trading Commission) fined Tether $41 million, stating that during 2016–2019, it had misled investors. The statement that "each stablecoin USDT is backed by $1" was not "100% accurate". In fact, the issuance of USDT relies on the credit of Tether.

The usage scope of USDT in the international market is not limited to legal trading fields. In April 2022, at an official press conference held by the Ministry of Public Security of China, it was stated that, from the perspective of capital channels, the proportion of money-laundering through traditional third-party payment and corporate accounts has decreased. A large amount of money-laundering activities involve using fund-splitting platform in combination with digital currencies, and among them, the harm caused by the use of USDT is the most severe. As the digital asset market continues to expand and the economic activities behind it increase day by day, the calls for the regularization of stablecoins like USDT are also growing louder.

In fact, it is precisely because of the prevalence of this unregulated form of currency in illegal activities that the governments and regulatory authorities of many countries and regions have adopted a more cautious attitude towards digital assets. This also reflects an undeniable fact: in the current economic environment, the regularization of stablecoins is extremely urgent. To ensure the healthy and stable development of the digital asset market, all parties need to take measures to strengthen the supervision of stablecoins and their related transactions, so as to ensure that they play a positive role in economic development while minimizing the potential risks they bring.

Tether has also been constantly striving to address regulatory compliance issues. In May 2022, Tether released the audit report on its reserve assets for the first quarter of 2022. The report showed that the company's total reserve assets exceeded $82.4 billion, of which 86% was cash or cash equivalents, totaling $70.59 billion. The remaining part consisted of corporate bonds ($3.73 billion), guaranteed loans ($3.15 billion), and investments such as digital assets worth $4.96 billion. As of the first quarter of 2024, Tether's total assets were approximately $110.2 billion, total liabilities were approximately $104 billion, reserve funds were approximately $6.2 billion, and the profit reached a record-breaking $4.52 billion. All Tether-issued stablecoins are correspondingly pegged to the relevant fiat currency at a 1:1 ratio and 100% supported by Tether's reserves. Among these reserves, cash, cash equivalents, and other short-term deposits account for 84.05%, and the rest are guaranteed loans (4.29%), precious metals (3.31%), other investments (3.45%), Bitcoin (4.87%), and corporate bonds (0.02%) respectively. In the 84.05% of cash and cash equivalents, U.S. Treasury bills account for 79.88%, overnight reverse repurchase agreements account for 12.2%, and money market funds account for 6.77%. Others such as term reverse repurchase agreements (0.9%), other investments (0.11%), and non-U.S. Treasury bills (0.13%) are also sources of its reserve assets (see Fig. 6.4).In addition, Tether has cooperated with law-enforcement agencies on multiple occasions to freeze problematic USDT addresses. Once these addresses are locked, they cannot receive or transfer funds. Data shows that since November 2017, Tether has blacklisted 692 addresses on the Ethereum blockchain.

In June 2020, the Centre alliance, the entity behind USDC, activated the blacklist function for the first time and added an address holding 100,000 USDC to the blacklist. An address on the blacklist is unable to execute transactions (receive or send) through the USDC smart contract. According to the feedback from the CENTRE alliance, they froze the assets of this address at the request of relevant authorities, but they have never responded to which department or person made the request for freezing, nor have they provided the legal basis. On April 23, 2021, the Centre alliance froze 7 more addresses. The largest among them held over 1700 ETH. Issues such as opaque audits have restricted the development of USDT to a certain extent and foreshadowed the emergence of compliant stablecoins.

In September 2018, USDC, a US-dollar-compliant stablecoin jointly issued by Circle and Coinbase, came into being. Circle is a financial service provider holding

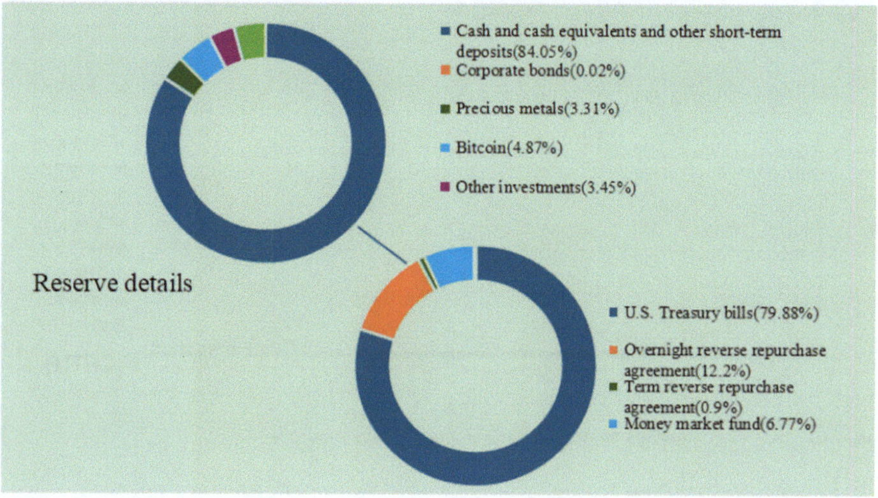

Fig. 6.4 Details of USDT reserve funds (as of the first quarter of 2024) (The source of the information: USDT official website)

a full-fledged US financial license and is also one of the first digital asset institutions to obtain a BitLicense.[4] Circle complies with the laws and regulations of the US government and is supervised by the Financial Crimes Enforcement Network (FinCEN) of the United States. Different from USDT, the operation of the stablecoin USDC relies on the CENTRE alliance, and its reserve assets are entrusted to banks. The third-party audit firm, Grant Thornton, publicly audits the financial status of USDC every month to ensure the safety of customers' funds as much as possible.

In April 2020, Jeremy Allaire, the co-founder and CEO of Circle, the issuer of USDC, stated that through cooperation with Coinbase, USDC had experienced explosive growth. New users came from e-commerce markets, advertising networks, luxury goods manufacturers, recruitment platforms, digital content markets, peer-to-peer lending platforms, payment companies, etc. In December of the same year, payment giant Visa announced its plan to connect 6 million of its merchants with USDC. Visa itself will not custody USDC, but it can help select Visa credit card issuers to integrate the USDC software into their platforms, enabling the sending and receiving of USDC.

On July 14, 2022, the detailed monthly report of USDC released by Circle showed that as of June 30 of that year, the circulation volume of USDC was approximately $55.569 billion. The total value of its reserve assets in the form

[4] The BitLicense is issued by the New York State Department of Financial Services in the United States and is a business license for digital asset activities. These regulations are limited to activities involving New York or New York residents. Due to the stringent requirements, it is extremely difficult to apply for a BitLicense.

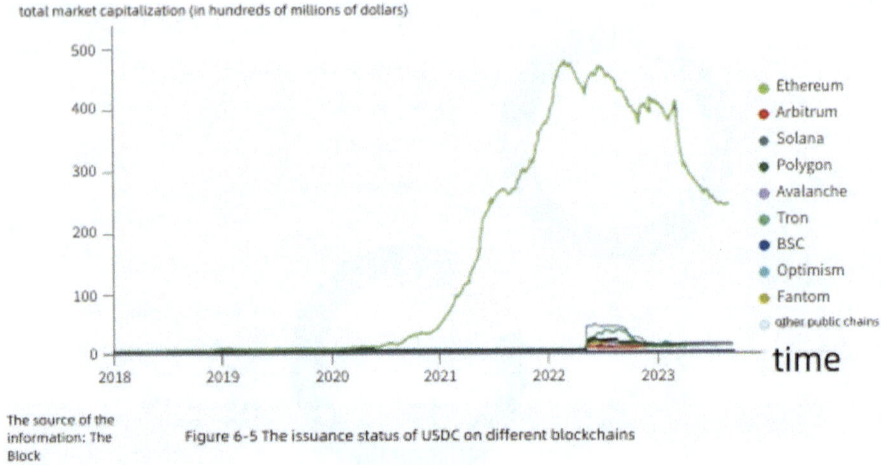

Fig. 6.5 The issuance status of USDC on different blockchains (The source of the information: The Block)

of cash and treasury bonds was $55.7 billion. The reserve funds included $13.58 billion in cash, which was deposited in a total of 8 banks, such as Signature Bank, New York Community Bank, and the U.S. Allianz Bank. Meanwhile, Circle also disclosed information about all the 3-month U.S. Treasury bonds it held. The 19 treasury bond securities it held from July 5, 2022, to September 29, 2022, were all worth approximately $42.122 billion in total.

There is a significant gap between the issuance volume of USDC and that of USDT. Due to the need to comply with laws, regulations, and supervision, USDC has made great efforts in terms of transparency, security, stability, and adaptation to DeFi. An increasing number of users have begun to recognize and use it. After 2021, the issuance volume of USDC has been on the rise, soaring from $4 billion in January 2021 to $55.8 billion in June 2022 (see Fig. 6.5). However, after that, the issuance volume of USDC has been on a downward trend, dropping below $30 billion and returning to the level of August 2021. As of July 4, 2024, the circulation volume of USDC was only $29.3 billion, which is related to the impact USDC suffered during the series of bank failures in the United States in 2023.

On March 10, 2023, Silicon Valley Bank[5] applied for bankruptcy after suffering a bank run, becoming the second-largest bank failure in U.S. history. As the main issuer of USDC, Circle held $3.3 billion in cash reserves in Silicon Valley Bank. This bankruptcy event led to a sharp decline in investors' confidence in USDC, triggering an unexpected bank run. In the chaos, the price of USDC plummeted

[5] Silicon Valley Bank is a small-to-medium-sized bank specializing in private equity investment, venture capital, and financing for technology-based enterprises, with an asset scale that once reached $200 billion.

from $1 to $0.878, and the values of other mainstream stablecoins such as DAI and BUSD also showed significant differences. This crisis not only demonstrated the vulnerability of the banking system but also revealed that, even in the digital asset field, so-called "stablecoins" can be affected by fluctuations in the traditional financial system. Subsequently, many users and investors began to re-evaluate their asset allocation strategies, causing USDC to be abandoned by some.

In addition to USDC, there are many stablecoins subject to regulatory compliance. In September 2018, the New York State Department of Financial Services authorized the digital asset trading platform and custodian Gemini Trust and the financial technology company Paxos Trust (hereinafter referred to as Paxos) to issue their respective U.S. dollar-pegged stablecoins, GUSD and PAX. The two companies are required to ensure compliance with regulatory standards such as anti-money laundering regulations in the state and to carry out processes for mitigating risks. Currently, they no longer hold a dominant position in the stablecoin market. Instead, the two stablecoin projects BUSD and PYUSD, which are operated in cooperation between Paxos and other institutions, have successively become the focus of market attention. However, their fates are quite different; one has been successfully recognized by the market, while the other has been forced to stop operations due to regulatory reasons.

On August 8, 2023, PayPal, a U.S. fintech company, officially launched the stablecoin PYUSD, marking it as the first mainstream financial services company to adopt digital assets for payments and transfers. The value of PYUSD will be pegged to the U.S. dollar, backed by cash deposits, U.S. short-term public debt, and other equivalent cash reserves at a 1:1 ratio. To enhance transparency and credibility, PayPal stated that it would start releasing public monthly reserve reports on PYUSD from September, providing detailed information on the assets that make up its reserves. In addition, Paxos will commission an independent third-party accounting firm to conduct a public attestation of the value of PYUSD's reserve assets, in accordance with the attestation standards set by the American Institute of Certified Public Accountants (AICPA) to ensure its accuracy and reliability. On September 13, 2023, Paxos released the first PYUSD transparency report, which disclosed the relevant unaudited data as of August 31, Eastern Standard Time in the United States. This included a total tokens outstanding of approximately $4.437 million; the current market value of the collateral in U.S. Treasury-backed repurchase agreements was $4.386 million, with a notional value of $4.3 million; the current market value of the collateral in other cash deposits held at insured depository institutions was approximately $1.5 million; the current market value of the collateral in total assets was $4.536 million, with a notional value of $4.45 million. It is worth noting that PYUSD and its reserve assets will be strictly regulated by the New York State Department of Financial Services. This means that even in the event of Paxos' bankruptcy, customer assets will not be used to repay Paxos' debts.

The goal of PYUSD is to be convertible into U.S. dollars at any time, and also into other digital assets provided by PayPal. To achieve this goal, PayPal has integrated PYUSD into its payment application Venmo, allowing users to freely send and receive tokens between PayPal and Venmo wallets. In addition, as an ERC-20 token based on the Ethereum blockchain, PYUSD can also be transferred to third-party wallets that are compatible with PayPal, providing users with a wider range of choices and flexibility. Information on the GitHub page shows that the PYUSD smart contract also includes operations for freezing or pausing functions on specific addresses on the chain, such as freezing the transfer function of a certain address, and can offer more control over the behavior of the smart contract. On September 11, 2023, PayPal officially launched new entry and exit channels for Web 3.0 payments, allowing U.S. users to directly convert digital assets from their wallets into U.S. dollars through MetaMask and deposit them into their PayPal balances. With 430 million users worldwide, PayPal has an advantage that could potentially make PYUSD a true "digital U.S. dollar" and enable its widespread use globally.

The launch of PYUSD came at a time when Paxos was in a standoff with regulatory authorities, which meant that PayPal was in no hurry to introduce PYUSD due to regulatory risks. Regulatory authorities have increasingly high requirements for the compliance of digital assets. For stablecoins to circulate on a large scale in mainstream commercial scenarios, actively embracing regulation is an inevitable choice. The launch of PYUSD is an important step for PayPal to deepen its digital asset business. In fact, issuing stablecoins is not PayPal's first foray into the digital asset field. As early as 2014, PayPal enabled Bitcoin payment functionality through cooperation with digital asset exchanges. Over the years, PayPal has been continuously exploring the digital asset field. Besides creating products and services that enhance the practicality of digital currencies, PayPal is also committed to improving consumers' and merchants' understanding of digital assets, stablecoins, and central bank digital currencies (CBDC), and helps users understand relevant knowledge and risks by providing educational content. The issuance of PYUSD will help PayPal build Web 3.0-based commercial scenarios and simplify the payment experience in the digital environment. Perhaps PYUSD will also prompt regulatory authorities to accelerate the introduction of a policy framework for stablecoins, and its role in the global popularization of digital assets is also worth looking forward to.

6.2 The Important Experiment of Stablecoins: Decentralized Stablecoins

The pioneer and representative of decentralized stablecoins is DAI issued by MakerDAO. Since 2015, the MakerDAO team and developers from around the world began planning to develop a smart contract based on the Ethereum blockchain to issue stablecoins by collateralizing digital assets. After two years of efforts, MakerDAO released its first white paper in December 2017, marking the birth of the stablecoin DAI.

The issuance process of DAI is completely decentralized. Anyone can generate DAI on the MakerDao platform by collateralizing digital assets. The specific operation is achieved through MakerDao's smart contract CDP (Collateralized Debt Position). The CDP stores the digital assets collateralized by users and allows users to generate a corresponding number of DAI based on this. However, generating DAI also means incurring corresponding debt. Only when the borrowed DAI is repaid can users redeem the collateralized assets.

To ensure the stability of DAI, the value of the collateral assets in the CDP must be significantly higher than the value of the borrowed DAI, that is, the collateralization ratio must be much greater than 100%. Taking a collateralization ratio of 150% as an example, if a user wants to generate 100 DAI, they need to collateralize ETH or other digital assets worth at least $150. In specific operations, users need to send a transaction to the MakerDao platform to create a CDP and specify the type and quantity of collateral assets. Then, they can withdraw a specified number of DAI from the CDP. The CDP records the number of DAI borrowed by the user and locks the equivalent collateral assets.

When users repay their debts, in addition to returning the principal of the borrowed DAI, they also need to pay a certain proportion of stability fees. The stability fee rate is usually calculated based on the annual interest rate. As of July 2024, the stability fee rate for ERC-20 tokens on the MakerDao platform is approximately 8%. Therefore, assuming a user wants to redeem the collateral corresponding to 100 DAI after one year, they need to return 100 DAI of principal plus 8 DAI of interest. After the repayment is completed, all the assets locked in the CDP will be released to the user.

Despite the requirement for over-collateralization of assets, MakerDao's model has still attracted a large number of users. The main reason is that users can use the generated DAI for leveraged trading, thereby magnifying investment returns. Without selling ETH, users can collateralize ETH to generate DAI and then use DAI to purchase more digital assets, which effectively expands the investment scope.

MakerDAO initially launched a single-collateral DAI system that only accepted ETH as collateral. Although this solution was simple and transparent, it had limited scalability and flexibility. To enable more users holding other types of digital assets to use the system, MakerDAO introduced a multi-collateral DAI system in 2019. The new system allows various digital assets other than ETH to be used for collateralizing to generate DAI, which has effectively expanded the supply scale of DAI and attracted more users to join.

The design of DAI cleverly utilizes the characteristics of feedback mechanisms and smart contracts to achieve stability without the need for a central authority. Its core mechanism is as follows: The target price of DAI is set to be pegged to the U.S. dollar at a 1:1 ratio, which establishes a benchmark in the market. This target price not only provides a basis for the debt-collateral ratio but also determines the value of collateral assets that DAI holders should receive during system-wide liquidation. However, relying solely on this setting is insufficient to ensure that

DAI always maintains a 1:1 ratio with the U.S. dollar. Therefore, when the market price of DAI deviates from the target price, the system activates a mechanism called the "Target Price Change Rate Feedback Mechanism". This feedback mechanism operates automatically through the CDP. When changes in market demand cause the price of DAI to deviate from the target price, the mechanism automatically adjusts the growth rate of the target price to guide market forces to regulate the supply and demand of DAI.

Specifically, when the market price of DAI is lower than the target price, the system automatically increases the growth rate of the target price. This makes generating DAI more expensive. Meanwhile, due to the increase in the target price, holding DAI becomes more profitable. The combination of these two effects leads to a decrease in the supply of DAI and an increase in demand, thus driving the market price of DAI up and back to around the target price. Conversely, when the market price of DAI exceeds the target price, the system automatically reduces the growth rate of the target price. This makes generating DAI cheaper and weakens the attractiveness of holding DAI. Eventually, it leads to an increase in the supply of DAI and a decrease in demand, causing the market price to fall back to around the target price. Through this self-regulating mechanism, DAI achieves a soft peg to the U.S. dollar, and all of this is accomplished through an automatically operating CDP without the need for human intervention.

Although DAI is issued through the CDP on the blockchain and has achieved a certain degree of distributed governance, this does not mean that DAI is risk-free. The risks of DAI mainly stem from hacker attacks and flaws in the CDP. For example, malicious developers may take advantage of CDP vulnerabilities to cause damage or theft before the vulnerabilities are fixed.

What should be done if the prices of ETH or other digital assets plummet, causing the value of the assets locked in the CDP by users to be lower than the borrowed DAI? Considering the high volatility of digital assets, MakerDAO has set a liquidation threshold. Each CDP type has its unique liquidation threshold, which is determined by MKR holders and based on the specific risk of the collateral assets of this CDP type. When the CDP is below its liquidation threshold, the liquidation process is initiated. After the liquidation is triggered, liquidators in the system (usually arbitrage robots on the chain, and some users also profit from liquidation) will start monitoring these positions with insufficient collateral and send requests to the contract to trigger the liquidation process. The liquidated collateral will be transferred to the auction module of MakerDAO, and an automatic auction process will begin to ensure that the debts within the system can be effectively repaid. Liquidators can use the DAI in their hands to participate in the auction and purchase these collateral assets. During the entire liquidation process, positions with insufficient collateral not only need to repay the original debt and stability fees but also need to pay additional liquidation penalties. Taking ETH as an example, the liquidation penalty is 13%, of which 3% is rewarded to the liquidators participating in the liquidation, and the remaining 10% goes to the MakerDao system as compensation for the system's stability. If the funds in the MakerDao system are insufficient to complete the purchase, the system will enter a special "debt fire - sale" mode, by issuing additional MKR and selling them publicly to raise enough DAI. Then, these raised DAI will be used to purchase and sell those liquidated collateral. In this way, the MakerDao system ensures its own capital liquidity and can continue to operate. When the auction ends, if the DAI obtained in the system is sufficient to repay all debts and liquidation penalties, the remaining collateral will be returned to the original position holders through a reverse auction. This means that although the collateral of users may be insufficient to support their debts at a certain moment, through this liquidation mechanism, the system ensures capital liquidity and stability, and also safeguards users' rights and interests to a certain extent.

This approach also has certain problems and risks. The prices of digital assets often experience sharp fluctuations, and price changes can occur within a short time. The collateralization ratio may drop below 100% within a few minutes, and there may not be enough time for liquidation. To address this issue, the MakerDao team issued the governance token MKR, giving MKR holders certain smart contract management rights. For example, the collateralization ratio in the CDP is determined by a vote of MKR holders. Holders need to lock MKR in the voting contract, and each MKR corresponds to one voting right, allowing holders to participate in governance through voting. As a reward for managing the system, MKR holders will receive transaction fee income. However, if holders do not exercise their governance rights carefully and fail to meticulously design various parameters such as the collateralization ratio of DAI in CDP, the liquidation threshold, and the stability fee, causing the system to malfunction and "go bankrupt", then it is ultimately the MKR holders who will suffer losses.

MakerDAO is not only a pioneer in exploring new Web 3.0 models such as stablecoins, DeFi, and DAO governance but also one of the first institutions to attempt to introduce RWA (Real-World Assets) tokens into DeFi. In September 2020, MakerDAO began to experiment with using real-estate project tokens as collateral to generate DAI. MakerDAO collaborated with Centrifuge to tokenize the 6s Capital real-estate development secured loan project and accepted the tokens of this real-estate development secured loan as part of the collateral for DAI. In December 2020, MakerDAO conducted research with the U.S. real-estate company UPRETS on the model and feasibility of RWA tokenization and secured lending. In April 2021, MakerDAO started issuing DAI loans collateralized by RWA tokens to New Silver, a loan service provider for real-estate investors, with a credit limit of $5 million. For New Silver, this cooperation enables it to raise funds more simply and quickly by obtaining DAI and carry out related businesses efficiently. Figure 6.6 shows the status of DAI in September 2023.

In May 2022, MakerDAO launched the Endgame plan, clearly stating that incorporating RWA (Real-World Assets) into the collateral framework is a key step in building a reserve asset portfolio. SG-Forge, a subsidiary of Societe Generale in France, has also extended an olive branch to MakerDAO twice. In October 2021, the institution submitted a proposal on the refinancing of security-type tokens to MakerDAO, aiming to refinance the OFH tokens (digital secured bonds supported by euro-denominated secured bonds of Societe Generale) issued on Ethereum in

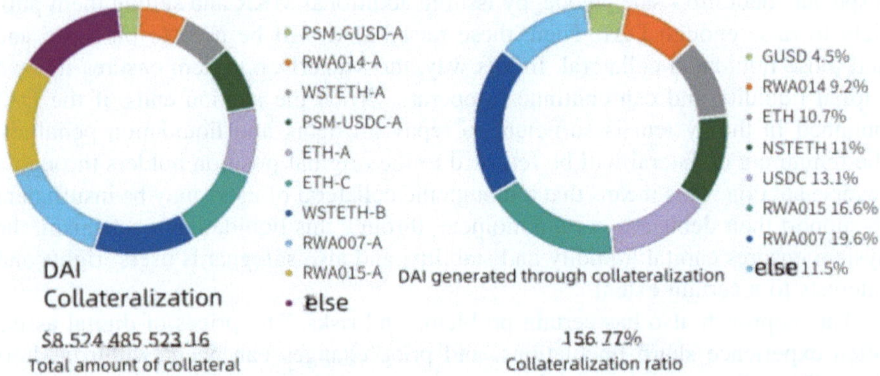

Fig. 6.6 The situation of DAI on 2023.9.12 (The source of the information: MakerBum)

2020. In July 2022, it made a debt financing request for 30 million DAI to MakerDAO. Subsequently, the MakerDAO community voted to accept OFH tokens as an RWA collateral type for the MakerDao protocol, and it was successfully launched on August 2, 2022. Societe Generale once described its attempt in MakerDAO as "a social experiment at the crossroads of regulation and open-source initiatives". Currently, the composition of DAI's collateral has become relatively diversified, including ETH, some RWA, and various stablecoins (see Fig. 6.7). According to data from MakerBurn,[6] as of July 4, 2024, there were 11 RWA token projects, and RWA tokens with a total value of over $3 billion could be used as collateral for DAI. According to Dune's data, these RWA assets have significantly increased MakerDAO's profits. As of July 4, 2024, RWA accounted for about 37% of MakerDAO's total assets and contributed more than 23% of the earnings.

MakerDAO not only has a close partnership with Centrifuge but also signed a trust agreement with the Wilmington Savings Fund Society (WSFS). The aim is to explore how the value of RWA (real-world assets) can be brought into the blockchain ecosystem. WSFS acts as a trustee in this cooperation to ensure the trustworthiness of RWA on the blockchain. To achieve this goal, MakerDAO established an RWA foundation in the Cayman Islands as a client of WSFS. With WSFS serving as the RWA guarantor and auditor, it manages multiple RWA. For new RWA, they only need to be placed in the Special Purpose Vehicle (SPV) established by the RWA foundation. In this framework, the RWA foundation itself does not directly hold any RWA but owns the SPV that actually hold RWA. MakerDAO, after decision-making through the DAO (Decentralized Autonomous Organization), sets up RWA foundations for various projects. The foundations are responsible for managing the corresponding SPV they establish. Each type

[6] MakerBurn is a platform that provides real-time tracking of MakerDAO's CDP (Collateralized Debt Position) projects, observing changes in collateralized debt and stability fee rates.

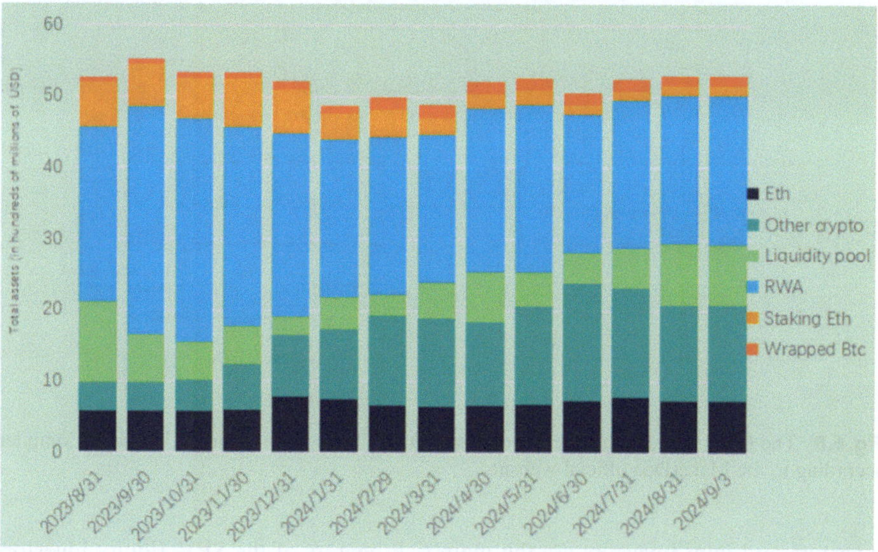

Fig. 6.7 The asset composition of MakerDAO (as of 2023.9.1) (The source of the information: Dune.com)

of collateral can have a foundation, but each type of collateral (or any mixed combination) can also be an SPV. This means that MakerDAO can select the correct jurisdiction/legal structure for each SPV and define a set of rules for it. For example, MakerDao's investments in the United States can be made through a limited liability company established in Delaware and managed by its members (with the RWA foundation as the sole member), or through a statutory trust established in Delaware (with the RWA foundation as the trust initiator). MakerDAO will lend DAI to the RWA foundation, and the foundation will then lend DAI to the SPV to invest in RWA assets (see Fig. 6.8).

SPV (Special Purpose Vehicle) is an independent legal entity specifically designed to hold certain assets, helping companies achieve the goal of isolating assets and liabilities from other business operations. In the investment logic based on the SPV framework, the SPV plays a central role in managing assets and interacting with various stakeholders (see Fig. 6.9). As a key participant in this framework, the asset holder is responsible for managing the SPV, bringing in transactions, and overseeing various types of loans. To ensure the stability of the entire system and effectively control risks, asset holders need to ensure they are in good financial condition and free from major legal risks. Especially when an asset holder manages multiple SPV that may hold the same type of assets, it is crucial to ensure an even distribution of assets among these SPV to avoid unequal resource allocation. In addition, the token issuance platform also plays a vital role in the entire system. It is mainly responsible for bridging the gap between SPV debts and debt tokens (such as the DROP tokens in the Centrifuge model). Equity

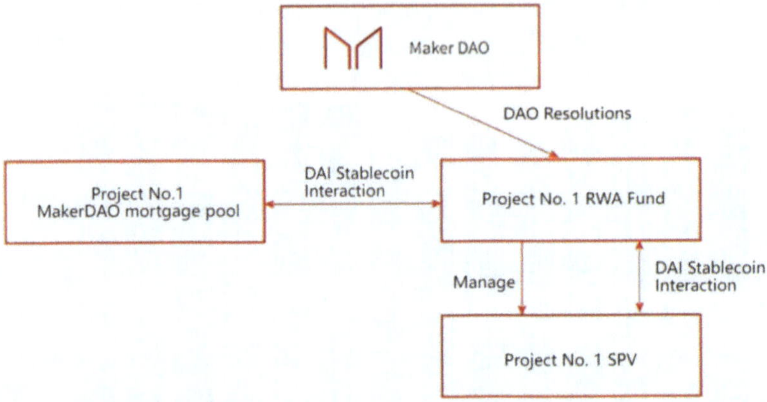

Fig. 6.8 The RWA investment structure of MakerDAO (The source of the information: Compiled according to the MakerDao official website)

investors and joint investors are the main risk-bearers of the SPV. Equity investors are the first group to bear losses. In models like Centrifuge, asset holders need to own a certain amount of equity to participate, ensuring that they can enforce relevant contracts and clauses in case of defaults or other risk events. Through the SPV framework, enterprises can divide RWA (Real-World Assets) into multiple small-sized shares and then issue them as tokens. However, unlike traditional asset securitization, in MakerDAO's SPV, there is no role for settlement and fund custody. Instead, a token issuance platform is added. This is also a significant feature of blockchain technology, which can automatically handle asset issuance, transfer, and settlement without the need for third-party institutions.

Meanwhile, each SPV (Special Purpose Vehicle) can adopt the management model of ABS (Asset-Backed Securities). Under this model, MakerDAO can choose to invest in senior-class assets, which have priority in receiving profit distributions. Other investors, on the other hand, can choose to invest in junior-class assets. These junior-class assets can only participate in profit distributions when the return rate of senior-class assets reach the expected level. For example, in the management of music industry copyrights, creators can price their music based on estimated asset revenues. When the data of these assets is transmitted to the Centrifuge platform, it will be converted into different NFT (Non-Fungible Tokens). This NFT can then be used as collateral, giving rise to two different classes of assets: DROP and TIN. DROP is regarded as senior-class assets and enjoys priority in cashing out and interest payments, but its interest rates are relatively conservative. In contrast, as junior-class assets, TIN has a higher potential return, but it has to wait for DROP assets to be paid first when repaying interest. Both types of assets offer interest, and investors can use DAI to purchase them. For the already-sold DROP and TIN, the issuers are responsible for completing the repurchase within the specified time limit. Through this model, music creators can obtain funds in advance to support their continued creation, while investors

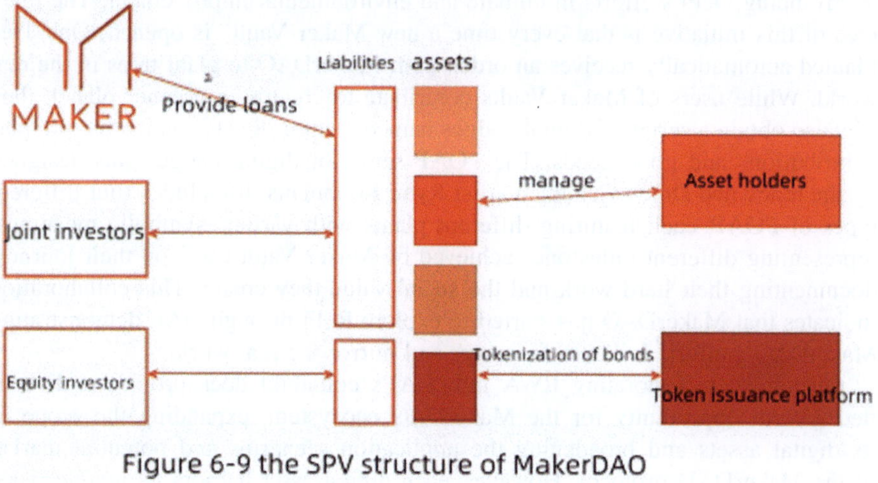

Fig. 6.9 The SPV structure of MakerDAO (*Source* Compiled based on content from the MakerDAO official website)

can also receive a share of copyright returns, further promoting the prosperity of the music-creation field.

Through this series of measures, MakerDAO has diversified its collateral, reducing the risks associated with using native digital assets with high price volatility, such as ETH, as collateral. It has strengthened the connection between DeFi (Decentralized Finance) and CeFi (Centralized Finance), gradually making MakerDAO an important bridge for RWA (Real-World Assets) to enter the DeFi world. By empowering the real economy through the digital economy, it is conducive to the long-term development of MakerDAO.

Through this series of measures, MakerDAO has diversified its collateral, reducing the risks associated with relying on native digital assets with high price volatility, such as ETH. It has strengthened the connection between DeFi (Decentralized Finance) and CeFi (Centralized Finance), gradually positioning MakerDAO as an important bridge for RWA (Real-World Assets) to enter the DeFi world. By empowering the real economy through the digital economy, it is beneficial to the long-term development of MakerDAO.

In addition, MakerDAO is leveraging its own characteristics to build a "Regenerative Finance (ReFi)[7] ecosystem, mirroring the real world. In June 2022, MakerDAO collaborated with One Tree Planted, a global non-profit organization dedicated to tree planting and forestation, to plan and launch an initiative aimed

[7] ReFi aims to reverse the trend of climate change through Web 3.0 technologies. That is, by leveraging the transparency mechanism of blockchain technology, it brings real-world natural assets onto the blockchain. At the same time, it introduces an incentive mechanism to reward behaviors that contribute to green development, thereby promoting sustainable development.

at advancing DeFi's efforts in climate and environmental improvement. The main idea of this initiative is that every time a new Maker Vault[8] is opened, One Tree Planted automatically receives an order from MakerDAO to plant trees in the real world. While users of Maker Vaults contribute to creating a greener planet, they can also obtain a series of digital badges named Nature POAP,[9] which record their contributions and good deeds. The POAP series of digital badges was designed by the renowned Dutch-Canadian artist Ryan Koopmans. It includes four different types of POAP, each featuring different plants with various symbolic meanings, representing different milestones achieved by Maker Vault users on their journey, documenting their hard work and the social value they create. This collaboration indicates that MakerDAO has started to explore ReFi through DAI, demonstrating MakerDAO's efforts to better empower and mirror the real world.

Of course, incorporating RWA into DAI's collateral does provide a diversified growth opportunity for the MakerDAO ecosystem, expanding the scope of its digital assets and broadening the application scenarios and potential market of the MakerDAD protocol. However, each digital asset harbors its unique risks, and RWA are no exception. On one hand, the introduction of RWA adds a new dimension of risk to MakerDAO. Compared with traditional digital assets, RWA are often relatively decentralized, making them more vulnerable to external economic and political factors. RWA may face various sanctions, asset freezes, or other macro-economic issues. On the other hand, although RWA may bring certain stable returns to MakerDAO, their liquidity characteristics are relatively weak. Considering DAI's positioning in the financial market, in the event of large-scale liquidity pressure or a run-on the bank, the liquidity constraints of RWA may lead to extended redemption times and increased transaction costs, thus posing a challenge to the overall stability of the MakerDAO system.

6.3 Algorithmic Stablecoins: The "Lehman Moment" that Ignited the Cryptocurrency Industry

When it comes to algorithmic stablecoins, it is necessary to mention a Nobel laureate in economics, Friedrich August von Hayek. Facing the increasingly severe inflation in various countries around the world since the 1950s, Hayek put forward the idea of the denationalization of money in his last economic treatise *The Denationalization of Money* in his later years, starting from the stance of economic liberalism and based on further research.

Ferdinando Ametrano, a professor at the Polytechnic University of Milan who once served as the project director of the Bitcoin Developers Conference, wrote a paper titled *Hayek Money: The Cryptocurrency Price Stability Solution* in 2014,

[8] The place where users deposit collateral and generate DAI.

[9] POAP (proof of attendance protocol), an attendance-proof agreement, is a digital certificate verifying that someone has participated in an event. It can be regarded as an NFT badge or digital badge.

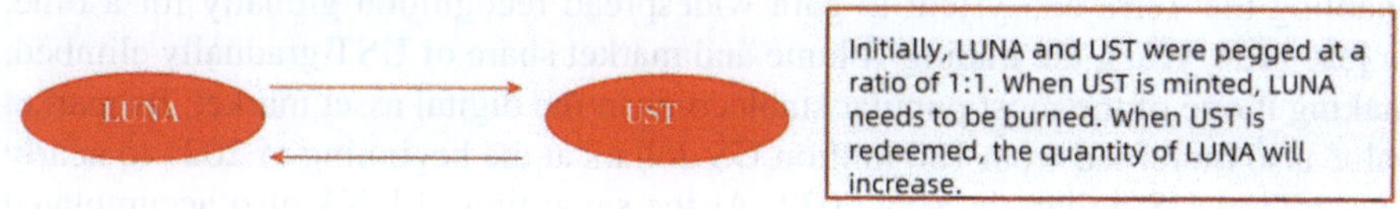

Fig. 6.10 The UST is closely connected to the LUMA

based on Hayek's theories and ideas about money. In the paper, Ametrano stated that due to its deflationary nature, Bitcoin can no longer fully perform the function of money as a measure of value. He then proposed a digital asset established on rules with elastic supply, which can "readjust the supply" according to demand. This is the Rebase mechanism, such as proportionally changing the quantity of stablecoins held by stablecoin holders. Algorithmic stablecoins are digital assets that are almost completely in line with the concept of "Hayek Money".

UST proposed by Terraform Labs is a typical example of algorithmic stablecoins, and Terra is a blockchain ecosystem customized for algorithmic stablecoins. This ecosystem relies on two core tokens, UST and LUNA, to operate. As the algorithmic stablecoin of this ecosystem, UST maintains a stable exchange rate with the US dollar. LUNA plays the role of an ecological governance token and is also the key to ensuring the price stability of UST.

Specifically, the stability of 1 UST is closely related to LUNA worth 1 US dollar (see Fig. 6.10). This is not a simple 1:1 pegging but a dynamic equilibrium mechanism. When UST is minted or burned, the corresponding value of LUNA will also be burned or generated. The operation principle of this mechanism is that whenever 1 UST needs to be minted, the system will require users to burn LUNA of the corresponding value according to the current market price. Conversely, when users burn UST, they will receive LUNA of the corresponding value.

When the price of UST is higher than 1 US dollar, it indicates an increase in market demand for UST. To make a profit, users can burn the LUNA in their hands to generate UST of equivalent value. These newly-generated UST are released into the market, which helps to lower the price of UST and bring it back to the standard of 1 US dollar. When the price of UST drops below 1 US dollar, to balance the market, users can buy UST at a low price and burn it to obtain LUNA of equivalent value. These newly-generated LUNA can then be sold on the market. Users can not only profit from this but also drive the price of UST back up. Under this mechanism, the more people want to buy UST, the more LUNA will be consumed, thus pushing up the price of LUNA.

This unique mechanism of UST and LUNA has won a great deal of attention for the Terra ecosystem. Meanwhile, to further create usage scenarios for UST, encourage users to hold UST, and reduce the quantity of UST in circulation in the market, Terra also established a decentralized fixed-interest-rate lending protocol named Anchor Protocol. The annualized yield for depositing UST on the Anchor platform is approximately 19.5%, far exceeding that of other decentralized lending protocols. This protocol successfully attracted a large amount of liquid capital, enabling the Terra ecosystem to gain widespread recognition globally for a time. In just a few years, the trading volume and market share of UST gradually climbed, making it one of the most popular stablecoins in the digital asset market. Its market value also increased from 180 million US dollars at the beginning of 2021 to nearly 18.8 billion US dollars in May 2022. At the same time, LUNA also accumulated a large amount of community support. The market value of LUNA grew from 320 million US dollars at the beginning of 2021 to nearly 40 billion US dollars in April 2022, and it ranked among the top five in the market-value ranking of digital assets several times, fully demonstrating its ecological value and users' trust.

However, behind the rapid and huge success of UST lies a profound crisis. The key to the UST price-stabilization mechanism is that users can exchange UST and LUNA of equivalent value at any time, and the market supply and demand relationship can remain relatively balanced, allowing the price of UST to quickly return to 1 US dollar. But if the price of UST remains below 1 US dollar for a long time, there will be more and more conversions of UST into LUNA in the market, leading to a significant increase in the supply of LUNA and further causing the price of LUNA to decline rapidly. Once the price of LUNA drops, the number of LUNA that each UST can be exchanged for will increase, which will further intensify the selling pressure on LUNA in the market and accelerate the decline in the price of LUNA. If the price of LUNA keeps falling, investors' confidence will decline sharply. This will lead to users being reluctant to buy UST from the market and exchange it for LUNA to maintain the price of UST. They may even sell the UST and LUNA in their hands all at once, ultimately causing the prices of both LUNA and UST to plummet or even collapse. This process is the so-called "death spiral" (see Fig. 6.11).

In addition, although the high fixed-deposit interest rate strategy of the Anchor Protocol created a huge demand for UST, it also introduced significant instability

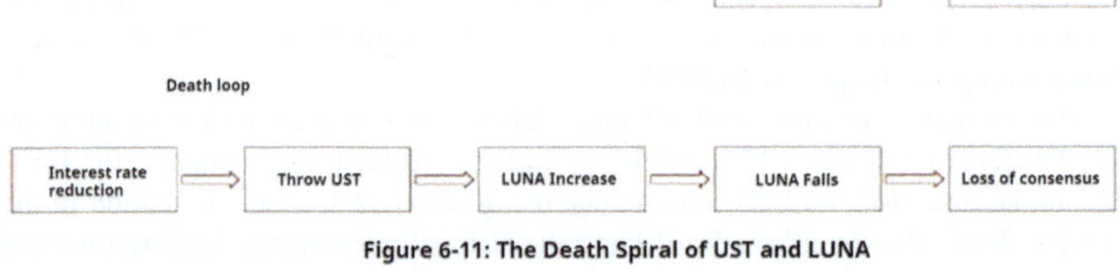

Fig. 6.11 The death spiral of UST and LUNA

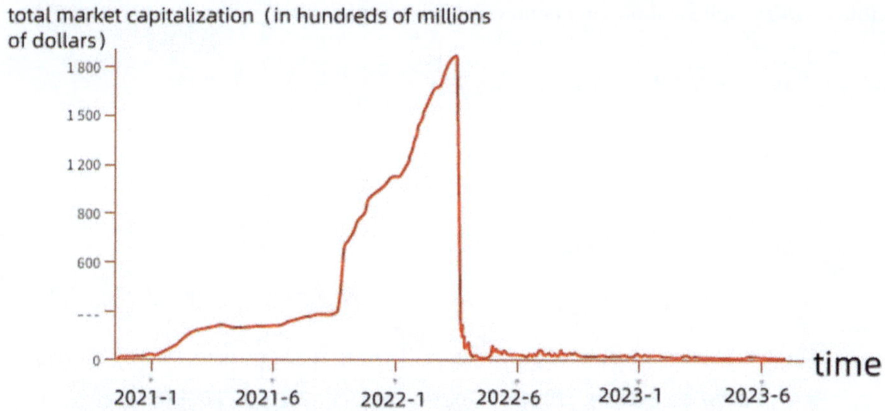

Fig. 6.12 The change of UST's total market capitalization from 2021 to 2023 (The source of the information: CoinMakerCap)

risks. When market confidence was challenged and combined with external economic pressures, the vulnerability of the entire UST stablecoin system was fully exposed, thus exacerbating the collapse of the Terra ecosystem.

In May 2022, affected by the decline in the overall financial market, the digital asset market faced a huge test. On May 8, signs of the collapse of the prices of UST and LUNA began to emerge. By May 15, the unit price of UST rapidly dropped from 0.995 US dollars to 0.133 US dollars, and the unit price of LUNA also dropped from 68.5 US dollars to a minimum of 0.00017 US dollars. Their rapid decline (see Figs. 6.12 and 6.13) led to liquidity problems for institutional investors with large positions in UST and LUNA. Affected by this event, the prices of many other digital assets also experienced significant corrections, causing institutions to encounter a "domino - style" liquidation and margin call. The collapse of UST triggered the "Lehman moment" in the digital asset market in 2022.

After the failure of the LUNA project, Terra launched the "Terra Ecosystem Restoration Plan", which involved creating a new Terra blockchain without algorithmic stablecoins. The old blockchain is called Terra Classic (with the token being Luna Classic, LUNC), and the new blockchain is called Terra (with the token being LUNA). Meanwhile, the restoration plan would also distribute new tokens to LUNA Classic stakers, LUNA Classic holders, remaining UST holders, and important developers of Terra Classic, in order to compensate investors for their losses.

However, this ecosystem restoration plan was also unsuccessful. On September 14, 2022, the South Korean police officially issued an arrest warrant for Do Kwon, the founder of Terraform Labs, and the International Criminal Police Organization (INTERPOL) also issued a Red Notice for him. On October 5, South Korea announced an order for the return of Do Kwon's passport. According to Article 13 of South Korea's *Passport Act*, Do Kwon's passport would lose its validity 14 days

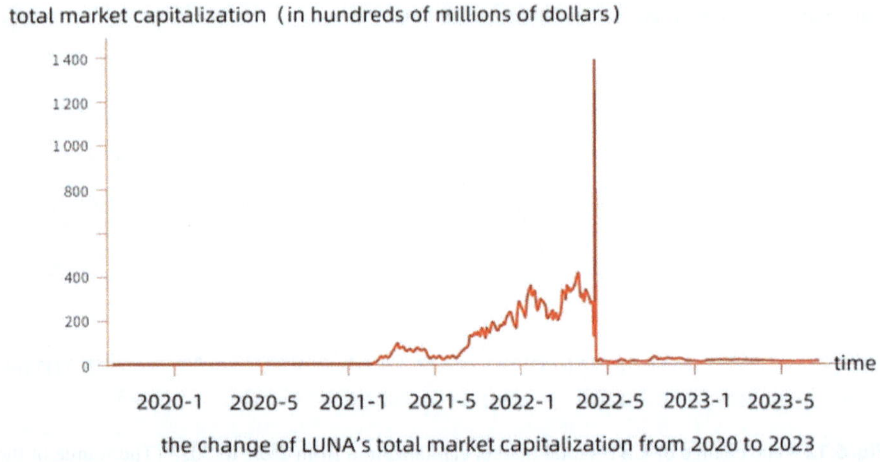

Fig. 6.13 The change of LUNA's total market capitalization from 2020 to 2023 (The source of the information: CoinMakerCap)

after the announcement of the order. In other words, Do Kwon would become an illegal alien, and the Singapore government could deport him.

On February 17, 2023, the SEC (Securities and Exchange Commission) filed a lawsuit in the United States District Court for the Southern District of New York, accusing Terraform Labs, headquartered in Singapore, and its founder Do Kwon of orchestrating a digital asset securities fraud worth billions of dollars, involving algorithmic stablecoins and other digital asset securities, which violated the registration and anti-fraud provisions of the U.S. *Securities Act* and *Exchange Act*. On March 23, Filip Adzic, the Minister of the Interior of Montenegro, announced that Do Kwon was detained by the police at Podgorica Airport in Montenegro for forged documents, and South Korean officials later confirmed that Do Kwon had indeed been arrested in Montenegro. A few hours after the Montenegrin police arrested Do Kwon, federal prosecutors in the Southern District of New York filed criminal fraud charges against him. According to the indictment, Do Kwon was charged with conspiracy to commit fraud, commodities fraud, securities fraud, wire fraud, and conspiracy to manipulate the market. According to estimates by the South Korean prosecution, the criminal proceeds of those involved in the Terra case were at least 414.5 billion South Korean won (approximately 2.18 billion yuan), of which Do Kwon's criminal proceeds were estimated to reach 91.4 billion South Korean won (approximately 480 million yuan). However, Do Kwon had almost no property in South Korea. He seemed to have converted a large part of his property into Bitcoin. In June 2023, Do Kwon was sentenced to four months in prison in Montenegro for passport forgery and was later extradited to the United States. On April 5, 2024, a U.S. jury found Do Kwon and Terraform Labs liable for fraud.

The story of Do Kwon and his UST is truly lamentable. In fact, in addition to stablecoins completely controlled by algorithms, stablecoin designs that combine asset collateral and algorithmic regulation, such as FRAX, have also emerged in the market. In the FRAX system, there are two types of tokens: FRAX and FXS. FRAX is a stablecoin pegged to the U.S. dollar, while FXS is its corresponding governance token. There is a specific indicator in the FRAX system, namely the collateral ratio R (with a value range of 0–1). This collateral ratio is adjusted once every hour according to a preset algorithm, and the adjustment range each time is 0.25%. When the system first starts running, the collateral ratio is set to 1. In other words, at this time, if a user wants to mint 1 FRAX, they need to provide assets that equivalent to 1 U.S. dollar and full collateral. However, as time goes by, this collateral ratio may decrease. When the collateral ratio drops to 0.5, the user only needs to pledge 0.5 US dollars' worth of other stablecoins to mint 1 FRAX. When the collateral ratio is 0, FRAX becomes a pure algorithmic stablecoin and requires no collateral of any form. The unique feature of FRAX's design lies in its arbitrage incentive mechanism. When the market price of FRAX exceeds 1 US dollar, people can mint and sell it at a cost of 1 US dollar to make a profit. This mechanism encourages more FRAX to be minted, thus driving its price back down to 1 US dollar. Conversely, if the price of FRAX is lower than 1 US dollar, users can obtain an asset portfolio equivalent to 1 US dollar in value by burning FRAX, including the pledged tokens and FXS. This mechanism provides users with the incentive to buy and burn FRAX, which helps to stabilize its price. Meanwhile, such a design also ensures that the price of FRAX can be stabilized at around 1 US dollar.

In addition to UST and FRAX, representatives of algorithmic stablecoins also include AMPL based on the Rebase mechanism, Basis Cash which adopts a multi-asset solution similar to UST, and Empty Set Dollar (ESD) which adopts a collateralized lock-up mechanism. However, almost all of these algorithmic stablecoin projects have failed so far. Although different algorithmic stablecoins have some differences in their design mechanisms, the overall design concepts are consistent.

6.4 Regional Development and Regulation of Global Stablecoins

In the Web 3.0 era, stablecoins are of great significance for bridging digital assets into the traditional asset management field. They have increasingly become an important part of the global financial payment system and have even started to pose a substantial challenge to SWIFT. In 2024, the circulation volume of stablecoins exceeded 158 billion US dollars, and the average monthly trading volume reached 1.38 trillion US dollars. Stablecoins have extremely low remittance costs, extremely high remittance efficiency, and a more controllable and secure process. In June 2020, the European blockchain bank Bank Frick began to experiment with using the stablecoin USDC to replace SWIFT for cross-border transfers.

Stablecoins are not beyond the reach of the law. Although the regulatory policies for stablecoins in various countries around the world are still not perfect, with the rapid expansion of the issuance scale and usage scenarios of stablecoins, as well as the gradual clarification of the underlying risk factors, the compliance issues of stablecoins have become increasingly prominent. Financial regulatory authorities and law-enforcement agencies in various countries have also begun to gradually bring stablecoin issuers within the scope of regulation. Generally speaking, the regulatory stances of major countries and regional regulatory authorities around the world towards stablecoins are not identical, and the corresponding regulatory frameworks and legislation are also at different stages.

6.4.1 The United States' Exploration of Stablecoin Regulation and Legislation

In August 2022, the Office of Foreign Assets Control (OFAC) of the US Department of the Treasury added Ethereum addresses related to the decentralized privacy protocol Tornado Cash to its sanctions list, resulting in the freezing of some USDC. This was the first time the agency-imposed sanctions on a smart contract application. This event triggered debates within the industry regarding privacy security, decentralization, and compliance, and also led people to start worrying that this incident could spread to DeFi. In particular, DAI, as the largest-market-cap decentralized stablecoin currently, has a relatively high proportion of USDC in its asset reserves. If regulatory authorities expand the scope of USDC freezes in the future, it will severely impact its collateralized lending business and users' rights and interests.

In November 2021, the President's Working Group on Financial Markets, the Federal Deposit Insurance Corporation, and the Office of the Comptroller of the Currency jointly issued a report titled *Report on Stablecoins*. To address the risks of payment-type stablecoins, the report recommended that the US Congress promptly enact legislation to ensure that payment-type stablecoins and their related arrangements are regulated under a unified and comprehensive US government framework, filling the current legislative gaps in aspects such as market credibility, investor protection, and illegal transactions for stablecoins.

On March 31, 2022, US Senator Bill Hagerty introduced *The Stablecoin Transparency Act*. This bill aims to enhance the transparency of the stablecoin market and establish standards for reserve assets. On April 6, 2022, Pat Toomey, a member of the US Senate Banking Committee, announced the discussion draft of *The Stablecoin TRUST Act*. The draft intends to restrict the issuers of payment-type stablecoins to the following three major categories of institutions: (1) money transmitters registered with a state in the US; (2) entities holding a new federal license specifically designed for stablecoin issuers; (3) insured depository institutions. At the same time, it requires payment stablecoin issuers to disclose their reserve assets, formulate redemption policies, and undergo regular audits by certified public accounting firms. In May 2022, Gary Gensler, Chair of the US Securities and

Exchange Commission, told the Subcommittee on Financial Services of the US House of Representatives that digital asset trading platforms should also pay attention to examining whether stablecoins will be deemed as securities. In April 2023, the US Congress successively introduced two stablecoin-related legislative bills, namely the "American Coinage Bill". After the hearings held later, a revised version of the bill was announced, hoping to gain the support of both the Republican and Democratic parties and be officially passed. During the hearings, several US congressmen emphasized that the US and the US dollar may lose their leading position in the digital asset field, which represents the future trend. Therefore, the urgency of related legislative work is self-evident.

On April 17, 2024, US Senators Kirsten Gillibrand and Cynthia Lummis introduced *The Lummis—Gillibrand Payment Stablecoin Act*. This bill requires stablecoin issuers to hold cash or cash-equivalent reserves equal to the value of their tokens to support their tokens. According to the official statement, the bill prohibits algorithmic stablecoins without cash or cash-equivalent support and stipulates that issuers and users shall not use stablecoins for illegal or unauthorized purposes, such as money laundering. Generally speaking, the bill aims to create an "accountable" innovation framework and points out the beneficial use cases of stablecoins in international fast-track transactions, cost reduction, and providing digital advantages for new projects and applications. The statement also indicates that the bill aims to establish a "US government and state regulatory system" for stablecoin issuers to safeguard the dual banking system.

The dual banking system in the United States refers to the existence of different regulatory authorities for national banks and state banks. The Office of the Comptroller of the Currency (OCC) oversees national banks, while state regulatory agencies supervise state banks. However, a bank can be subject to regulation by both state and federal authorities. The *Lummis-Gillibrand Payment Stablecoin Act* would grant both the federal government and state entities authority over the issuance and enforcement of stablecoins.

In a statement, Gillibrand said: "A regulatory framework for stablecoins is essential to fostering responsible innovation, protecting consumers, and combating money laundering and illicit financial activities. It safeguards consumers by mandating one-to-one reserves, prohibiting algorithmic stablecoins, and requiring stablecoin issuers to comply with U.S. anti-money laundering and sanctions regulations. To draft the strongest possible legislation, our office has worked closely with relevant federal and state agencies. I am confident that this bill will receive the necessary support in both the Senate and the House of Representatives."

In a statement, Lummis stated that the bill also meets "the growing needs of the United States' evolving financial sector," echoing perspectives on the dual banking system and the dominance of the U.S. dollar.

The bill sets a $10 billion cap on the issuance of payment stablecoins by non-depository financial institutions. According to the bill, once the issuance exceeds this amount, the issuer must be a "depository institution authorized as a national payment stablecoin issuer."

Currently, the largest stablecoin issuer in the United States, Circle—whose USDC has a circulation of $33 billion—is not a depository trust institution.

The second-largest stablecoin issuer, Paxos, although its market capitalization is well below the $10 billion threshold, has obtained a limited-purpose trust charter through the New York Department of Financial Services.

A U.S. Senate staffer described the $10 billion cap as roughly the dividing line between small community banks and larger regional financial institutions with potential systemic risk.

Another notable consumer protection measure in the bill is the provision for custodial and resolution mechanisms in the event of a stablecoin issuer's bankruptcy. According to an official statement, the FDIC has established a detailed receivership framework for all payment stablecoin issuers, outlining priority rankings, claim validity, and the classification of payment stablecoins as customer assets rather than issuer assets.

Legislative proposals specific to cryptocurrency, considered the most likely to pass in the United States, have long advocated for stablecoin regulations, but progress has been slow. Patrick McHenry, Chairman of the U.S. House Financial Services Committee, and committee member Maxine Waters have been working on stablecoin legislation for years. In 2023, a bill made progress in the committee, but momentum stalled after then-Speaker of the House Kevin McCarthy was removed from office.

Until early April 2024, stablecoin legislation in the United States had made little progress. However, discussions resumed when Senate Majority Leader Charles met with McHenry and Waters to explore the possibility of attaching stablecoin legislation to the bill reauthorizing the Federal Aviation Administration. On April 16, Senate Banking Committee Chairman Sherrod Brown stated that stablecoin legislation could move forward if it included certain specific safeguards. If the *Lummis-Gillibrand Payment Stablecoin Act* is successfully passed, it will undoubtedly deliver a significant blow to many challengers of Circle, the issuer of USDC.

6.4.2 EU's Stablecoin Regulation and Issuance

Following the Bitcoin bull market of 2017, European investment in digital assets surged, prompting regulators to take notice of the potential risks posed by unregulated virtual assets. By early 2018, European regulatory bodies began assessing the significant threats these assets could pose to retail investors and financial markets, including risks related to money laundering and terrorist financing. In response, the European Union swiftly introduced the *FinTech Action Plan*, granting the European Banking Authority (EBA) and the European Securities and Markets Authority (ESMA) the mandate to review the applicability of the EU's existing financial services regulatory framework to digital assets. The review concluded that most digital assets fell outside the scope of current EU regulations. Consequently, European regulators initiated efforts to develop a new regulatory framework for digital assets.

As early as September 2020, the European Commission adopted a proposal for regulating digital asset markets. Between February and June 2021, the European Central Bank (ECB), the European Economic and Social Committee (EESC), and the European Data Protection Supervisor (EDPS) each provided their opinions on how digital asset markets should be regulated. In June 2022, the European Parliament and representatives of EU member states reached a provisional agreement on the *Markets in Crypto-Assets Regulation (MiCA).* In April 2023, the European Parliament officially voted to approve *MiCA*, making it the first comprehensive regulatory framework for digital assets. *MiCA* is expected to come into effect in January 2025, with stablecoin-related regulations set to take effect on June 30, 2024, following a 12-month transition period. This will make the European Union the first major jurisdiction in the world to introduce a comprehensive regulatory framework for digital assets. *MiCA* is the most substantive digital asset regulatory framework to date, spanning 168 pages. It primarily addresses currently unregulated digital assets, markets, and service providers within the EU, providing them with a legal framework while introducing a single licensing regime for member states. For the first time, the EU has established a comprehensive regulatory mechanism specifically for digital assets, setting clear rules to create market order while ensuring legal clarity. This aims to safeguard the rights of both consumers and investors.

MiCA also includes a comprehensive regulatory framework for stablecoins, outlining specific requirements for their issuance, circulation, capital or own funds regulation, reserve management, disclosure obligations, and consumer protection. Overall, *MiCA* imposes strict regulatory constraints, allowing only the issuance of euro-pegged stablecoins. Furthermore, stablecoins must be issued by regulated EU credit institutions, effectively prohibiting non-bank entities from issuing them. *MiCA* sets additional requirements regarding the composition and scope of reserve assets for stablecoin issuers, while also establishing clear rules on governance, operations, and risk management.

Under *MiCA*, two types of digital assets can be classified as stablecoins. The first type is Asset-Referenced Tokens (ART), which stabilize their value by referencing the value of other fiat currencies, commodities, or digital assets (either individually, in combination, or as a basket of assets). For example, an ART may be backed by an equivalent reserve of gold. The second type is E-Money Tokens (EMT), which stabilize their value by referencing a single fiat currency. The key difference between EMT and ART lies in the composition of the underlying assets supporting the token's price. ART rely on non-cash assets or a basket of currencies, whereas EMT use only a single currency, making them more akin to traditional electronic money. *MiCA* mandates that EMT be backed by 100% reserve assets. For instance, if an issuer creates €100,000 worth of euro-pegged EMT, it must hold an equivalent €100,000 in assets (or euro-denominated assets) stored in a regulated and approved location, such as a vault or a bank account.

On July 2, 2024, the European crypto asset market reached a historic milestone: Circle received official approval under *MiCA* to issue stablecoins in Europe. This decision not only paves the way for the widespread circulation of stablecoins across Europe but also sets a new benchmark for digital asset regulation. Circle, known for issuing the USDC stablecoin, can now offer dollar-pegged stablecoins within Europe following *MiCA* approval. This provides a stable and regulated alternative to more volatile cryptocurrencies like Bitcoin. The approval of Circle under *MiCA* may have significant impacts on the crypto asset market:

6.4.3 More Regulated Market

1. Establishing a Unified Regulatory Framework: *MiCA* provides a unified regulatory framework, ensuring that crypto asset market participants (including issuers, exchanges, and service providers) operate under clear legal and compliance requirements across the EU.
2. Enhancing Transparency and Compliance: By mandating white paper publications, periodic reports, and disclosure requirements, *MiCA* improves market transparency and compliance, helping to reduce fraud and market manipulation.

6.4.4 Strengthening Investor Protection Mechanisms

1. Disclosure Requirements: *MiCA* mandates that crypto asset issuers and service providers publish detailed white papers and periodic reports, ensuring that investors have access to sufficient information to make informed investment decisions.
2. Protecting Investor Rights: Through strict regulatory requirements and complaint mechanisms, *MiCA* effectively safeguards investor rights and reduces investment risks.

6.4.5 Enhancing Market Stability

1. Financial Stability: *MiCA* enforces strict capital requirements and risk management measures to ensure the financial stability of the crypto asset market, reducing market volatility and systemic risks.
2. Risk Control: By imposing strict regulations on high-risk assets such as stablecoins, *MiCA* helps mitigate market risks and protect the stability of the financial system.

6.4.6 Data and Privacy Protection

1. Data Security: *MiCA* requires crypto asset service providers to comply with data protection and privacy regulations, ensuring the security and confidentiality of user data.
2. Transparency in Data Usage: By improving transparency in data usage, *MiCA* enhances user trust and fosters the healthy development of the market.

6.4.7 International Competitiveness

1. Global Competitiveness: *MiCA* establishes a unified regulatory framework, giving the EU a stronger competitive edge in the global crypto asset market. By regulating market behavior and protecting investors, the EU can attract more international businesses and investments.
2. Cross-Border Cooperation: *MiCA* can facilitate cooperation between the EU and other countries and regions in crypto asset regulation, promoting global market connectivity and joint development.

6.4.8 Singapore's Regulatory Framework for Stablecoins

Singapore's regulatory framework for stablecoins has undergone a series of developments. It began with the amendment of the *Payment Services Act* (PSA) in 2019, followed by a public consultation in 2022, and culminated in the finalization of the framework on August 15, 2023. The framework was officially published in the *Response to Public Consultation on Proposed Regulatory Approach for Stablecoin-related Activities.*

MAS stated that when properly regulated and maintaining value stability, stablecoins can serve as a reliable medium of exchange to support innovation, including the buying and selling of digital assets on the blockchain.

Singapore's regulatory framework for stablecoins consists of four main components:

1. Scope of Application. MAS permits stablecoin service providers to issue Single-Currency Stablecoins (SCS), which are pegged to the Singapore dollar or G10 currencies. The G10 currencies include the Australian dollar, Canadian dollar, British pound, Euro, Japanese yen, New Zealand dollar, Norwegian krone, Swedish krona, Swiss franc, and US dollar. However, MAS does not allow the issuance of stablecoins pegged to a basket of currencies, backed by other digital assets, or issued based on algorithmic mechanisms. Stablecoin issuers are categorized into banks and non-bank entities. Non-bank issuers must meet a circulating volume requirement of over SGD 5 million and obtain

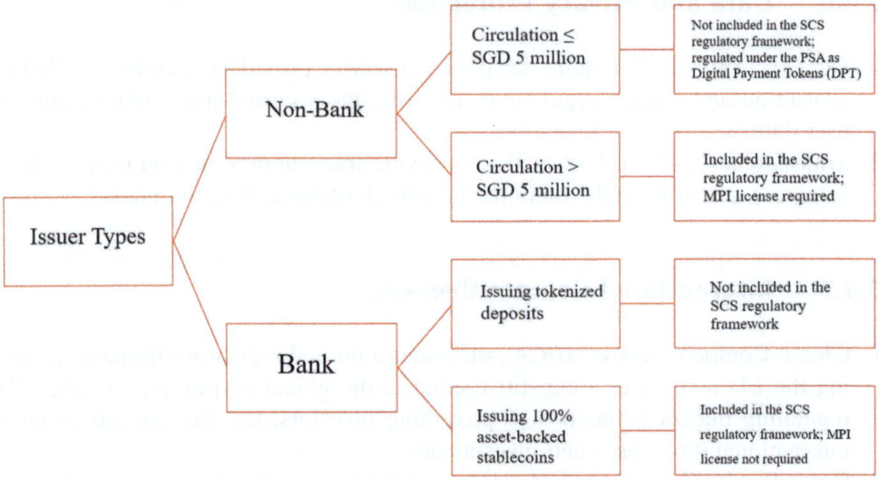

Fig. 6.14 Scope of asset applicability under Singapore's stablecoin regulatory framework

a Major Payment Institution (MPI) license,[10] while banks must issue 100% asset-backed stablecoins (Fig. 6.14).

2. Reserve Management. MAS mandates that stablecoin reserves may only be allocated to cash, cash equivalents, and debt securities with a remaining maturity of up to three months. These securities may only be issued by either the government or central bank of the currency in question or government-backed or international bond-issuing institutions with a minimum credit rating of "AA-".Stablecoin issuers must establish trust structures and open segregated accounts, with custodians required to meet specific qualifications. The daily market value of reserves must exceed the circulating supply of stablecoins, redemption must be completed within five days, and issuers are required to publish monthly audit reports.
3. Licensing Requirements. MAS has set qualifications for stablecoin issuers, including minimum capital requirements, solvency requirements, and operational restrictions. Issuers must maintain at least SGD 1 million or 50% of their annual operating expenses as capital and must hold sufficient liquid assets to meet redemption demands.
4. Business Restrictions. Stablecoin issuers are prohibited from engaging in lending, collateralization, trading, and asset management activities. However, this restriction does not apply to affiliated entities of the issuer. Other companies,

[10] The MPI license is a financial permit issued by MPS. It is a high-level payment institution license designed for handling larger transaction volumes and more complex payment operations. Due to higher capital requirements and stricter regulatory scrutiny, the application process for an MPI license is more complex.

including sister companies in which the stablecoin issuer has no ownership stake, may offer similar services related to stablecoins.

Compared to the EU's *MiCA*, MAS's stablecoin regulatory framework is more open and flexible, allowing multiple major currencies as pegging options. It also permits non-bank entities to issue stablecoins upon approval, and its requirements for reserve asset composition and scope are more flexible and principle-based. However, both frameworks set clear requirements for consumer protection and ensuring the stability of stablecoins themselves.

Issuing stablecoins under Singapore's regulatory framework may also present some challenges. First, MAS imposes restrictions on the types of reserve assets. For example, the reserves for an SGD-pegged stablecoin must be held in SGD-denominated assets, not USD assets. However, the available investment options and market depth for SGD assets are limited, posing challenges to reserve management and potentially restricting the issuance volume of stablecoins. Second, there is the issue of cross-jurisdictional operations. Although MAS proposed two possible solutions, neither could be implemented due to practical constraints. As a result, stablecoin issuers are initially prohibited from issuing stablecoins across jurisdictions. Third, regarding the profitability of stablecoin issuers, issuers are still allowed to invest customer funds used to purchase stablecoins (provided the investments are highly liquid and low-risk). However, MAS does not allow issuers to offer interest or investment returns to stablecoin holders, meaning that issuers retain all investment profits, which reduces their commercial competitiveness. Finally, the difficulty of obtaining regulatory licenses is also worth noting. The cost of issuing compliant stablecoins is relatively high, as issuers must meet strict capital, solvency, and operational requirements. Additionally, non-bank issuers must apply for a PMI license, a process that requires significant time and resources. As a result, under MAS's stablecoin regulatory framework, it is more likely that banks and large corporations will issue stablecoins. Meanwhile, the feasibility of small and medium-sized non-bank enterprises issuing stablecoins under this framework remains uncertain.

In early September 2023, Singapore's DCS Card Centre (DCS) announced the launch of its payment token, DCS Tokens (DUS), with its initial deployment and issuance on the PlatON network. This issuance marks a major breakthrough in the blockchain-based payment settlement sector. DCS also became the first financial institution to propose an initiative aimed at bridging the Web 2.0 and Web 3.0 ecosystems following MAS's introduction of new regulatory guidelines for single-currency stablecoins.

DCS is a financial institution regulated by MAS under Singapore's Banking Act and is licensed to issue credit cards and charge cards. DCS will continue to lead the next-generation digital payment sector, driving innovation and integration across eras.

DUS is an innovative product that integrates digital assets with traditional finance. It is generated through credit card transactions processed by DCS and can only be redeemed as card spending limits and returned to DCS bank accounts.

DUS maintains value stability, with 1 DUS equivalent to 1 USD, serving as a trusted bridge between Web 3.0 and Web 2.0 global card payments. Users can instantly redeem DUS on D-Vault, either to increase their DCS card spending limit or to settle outstanding balances in fiat currency. D-Vault is a feature within the DCS card application, supporting bank transfers and digital asset conversions. It enables users to seamlessly optimize and switch between Web 2.0 and Web 3.0, fully leveraging the convenience and efficiency of both systems.

In early July 2024, Paxos announced that its Singapore subsidiary, Paxos Digital Singapore Pte. Ltd., had received approval from MAS to become a Major Payment Institution, allowing it to provide digital payment token services. This approval enables Paxos to issue stablecoins compliant with local regulations in Singapore.

As of now, 19 companies, including Paxos, Blockchain.com, Circle, and Coinbase, have obtained MPI licenses in Singapore. According to MAS regulations, companies holding an MPI license must have a minimum base capital of SGD 250,000 and maintain a permanent place of business or registered office in Singapore.

Walter Hessert, Head of Strategy at Paxos, stated: "Issuing stablecoins under the approval of a regulator like MAS, which upholds strict regulatory standards, represents a significant step toward the democratization of financial services. Receiving MAS approval is a milestone for Paxos and our global partners, enabling us to provide secure access to the U.S. dollar for more users worldwide."

Additionally, Paxos announced a partnership with DBS Bank Singapore, covering cash management and custody of stablecoin reserve assets. Evy Theunis, Head of Customer Science at DBS Bank, stated: "This collaboration further expands our involvement in the digital asset ecosystem. For years, DBS has been a leader and innovator in this space."

Currently, Paxos has obtained authorization to issue stablecoins in the United States, the United Arab Emirates, and Singapore. Through these partnerships and approvals, Paxos is gradually expanding its presence in the centralized stablecoin market, providing secure and regulatory-compliant stablecoin services to a broader user base.

6.4.9 Hong Kong's Stablecoin Issuer "Sandbox"

On January 12, 2022, the Hong Kong Monetary Authority (HKMA) released a discussion paper aimed at expanding Hong Kong's regulatory framework to include stablecoins. The paper also invited industry participants and the public to provide input on the regulatory approach to digital assets (also referred to as "virtual assets" in Hong Kong) and stablecoins. The discussion paper outlined HKMA's vision for regulating digital assets, particularly stablecoins used as payment instruments. The HKMA acknowledged that stablecoins are increasingly being recognized as a widely accepted means of payment. Their growing usage enhances the possibility of integration into the mainstream financial system but also raises broader concerns regarding monetary and financial stability. As a result, stablecoins have become a key area of focus for regulatory authorities.

In January 2023, HKMA released the *Conclusion of Discussion Paper on Crypto-assets and Stablecoins*, stating that priority will be given to regulating stablecoins that claim to be pegged to fiat currencies. This applies regardless of whether the peg is maintained through algorithmic mechanisms or arbitrage strategies, and whether the stablecoin is primarily used for retail payments, wholesale transactions, or digital asset trading. Any stablecoin claiming to be pegged to fiat currency will be a key focus of regulatory oversight. The HKMA also noted that the mandatory licensing regime for stablecoin activities may overlap with the licensing framework for Virtual Asset Service Providers (VASP), which is currently overseen by the Securities and Futures Commission (SFC). As a result, the HKMA stated that it will further consult with other regulatory authorities to explore ways to prevent regulatory arbitrage in the future.

On March 12, 2024, HKMA officially launched the Stablecoin Issuer Sandbox. The initiative aims to communicate regulatory expectations to institutions interested in issuing fiat-backed stablecoins in Hong Kong while gathering participant feedback on the proposed regulatory requirements.

First, let's understand the concept of a sandbox. A sandbox is an emerging financial regulatory term in recent years, primarily used in the fintech sector. It refers to a regulatory framework where financial institutions are permitted to test new services and products in a controlled-risk and small-scale environment before full deployment. This process allows regulators to collect data and user feedback, helping to accelerate the launch of related products and services while ensuring compliance with regulatory requirements.

The Stablecoin Issuer Sandbox follows a similar concept. Before the stablecoin regulatory framework is fully implemented, HKMA can use the sandbox mechanism to communicate regulatory expectations and provide guidance to institutions planning to issue fiat-backed stablecoins in Hong Kong. At the same time, regulatory authorities can gather feedback from sandbox participants on the proposed regulatory requirements, ensuring that the framework is well-aligned with regulatory objectives.Sandbox participants can test the feasibility of their anticipated business models and engage directly with the HKMA to better understand how to comply with future regulatory requirements.

Next, let's take a closer look at the Hong Kong Stablecoin Issuer Sandbox. For stablecoin issuers, how can they apply to participate in the HKMA's sandbox? The process is actually quite straightforward. Here, we have outlined the application procedure:

- If interested in applying for the sandbox, issuers can express their intent by sending an email to the HKMA.
- During the evaluation process, the HKMA may contact applicants to request additional information. The processing time depends on several factors, including: The complexity of the applicant's business model, The completeness

and adequacy of the submitted information,The speed and thoroughness of responses to follow-up questions and requests from the HKMA

To successfully apply through HKMA, the following conditions must be met:

- The applicant needs to have a real intention and reasonable plan to issue Stablecoin in Hong Kong.
- Applicants need to have specific plans to participate in the sandbox.
- The applicant needs to be able to meet reasonable expectations of the proposed regulatory requirements.

It is important to note that HKMA will assess sandbox applicants based on a range of factors. Successfully becoming a sandbox participant does not imply any form of endorsement from the HKMA or eligibility for current or future regulation by the HKMA or other financial regulatory bodies in Hong Kong. Once the regulatory framework is implemented, sandbox participants intending to apply for a license must submit a separate application in accordance with the requirements of the licensing authority.

HKMA may announce sandbox participation details to the public in various forms, including disclosing approved participants. Before being approved for sandbox participation, no one is allowed to make any public announcement regarding their application status. After approval, if a participant wishes to make an announcement regarding its sandbox participation arrangements, it must first obtain HKMA's approval before publication. Depending on the participant's specific proposal and testing progress, HKMA may adjust sandbox requirements accordingly.

A sandbox participant will be considered to have exited the sandbox under any of the following circumstances:

- If HKMA determines that the participant has failed to operate in accordance with the expected manner specified in the relevant application documents and materials reviewed by HKMA, or if HKMA deems the participant no longer suitable to remain in the sandbox.
- If a sandbox participant decides to withdraw voluntarily, it must exit in an orderly manner and notify HKMA in advance.
- The HKMA may announce the termination of a participant's qualification to the public whenever it deems appropriate.

After HKMA announced the launch of the Stablecoin Issuer Sandbox, RD Technologies, founded by a former HKMA chief executive, welcomed the initiative. The company also plans to launch the HKDR stablecoin, pegged to the Hong Kong dollar, for use in various commercial scenarios both within and outside Hong Kong to support the development of the city's Web 3.0 ecosystem.

The HKMA Stablecoin Issuer Sandbox offers at least three key benefits for the development of the local digital asset market:

- Promoting the Growth of Hong Kong's Stablecoin Market and Enhancing Market Confidence
  The sandbox provides a compliant platform for stablecoin issuers, lowering the entry barriers for the Hong Kong market. This will attract more institutions to participate in stablecoin issuance, fostering the development of the stablecoin market. At the same time, the sandbox will help increase market confidence in stablecoins. Through regulatory oversight of stablecoin issuers, HKMA aims to ensure the stability and security of stablecoins, thereby reducing investor concerns regarding their risks.
- Driving Virtual Asset Transactions and Strengthening Financial Regulation
  Stablecoins serve as a key medium for virtual asset transactions. The growth of the stablecoin market will promote the expansion of digital asset trading, thereby contributing to the overall prosperity of the digital asset sector. The sandbox will also provide HKMA with an opportunity to understand stablecoin issuance practices. By overseeing sandbox operations, HKMA can accumulate regulatory experience and develop a more comprehensive regulatory framework for stablecoins.
- Enhancing Hong Kong's Position as an International Financial Hub and a Global Web 3.0 Center
  The launch of the sandbox demonstrates Hong Kong's open approach to the development of the digital asset market, which will attract more international digital asset companies to establish operations in Hong Kong, thereby reinforcing the city's status as an international financial hub and a global Web 3.0 center.

Overall, the stablecoin market is expected to continue its rapid expansion in the future, but it will also face increasing regulatory challenges. However, the trend toward mainstream adoption, regulatory compliance, and institutionalization of stablecoins is irreversible. The development pace of Web 3.0 differs significantly from that of traditional industries, meaning that existing laws and regulatory frameworks may not be fully applicable to the current state of the Web 3.0 industry and its technological characteristics. In the future, if economies wish to secure a strong position in the stablecoin market, they must accelerate the development of comprehensive legal and regulatory frameworks for stablecoins.

6.5 Stablecoin Applications: Cross-Border Settlement in Global Trade

The cross-border payment system is the infrastructure that underpins the operation of the global economy and financial system, serving as the network channel for international transactions. The primary models of global cross-border payments include the correspondent banking model, interlinked model, single platform model, and peer-to-peer model. Among these, the most common correspondent banking model is the traditional cross-border payment clearing system. Under this model, a commercial bank in one country establishes a clearing account with a correspondent bank abroad and primarily relies on the SWIFT system to transmit cross-border payment messages. The payment and settlement of cross-border funds are conducted through the correspondent bank's clearing system. This model has long been the dominant approach in cross-border transactions.

According to data from the Financial Stability Board (FSB), the volume and value of cross-border payments processed through the SWIFT system have increased annually. However, the number of correspondent banking relationships worldwide declined by approximately 20% between 2011 and 2018, a trend observed across various countries and regions. This indicates that the correspondent banking model is in decline. The international community has expressed concerns about the future capacity of global cross-border payment systems. This decline may lead to an increase in cross-border transactions conducted through underground channels, which could have negative implications for global economic development.

Traditional cross-border payment models often face challenges related to complex multi-party coordination, cumbersome settlement processes, and payment inefficiencies. Cross-border trade involves not only importers and exporters but also banks, regulatory authorities, inspection agencies, customs, audit departments, and transportation companies, requiring extensive coordination. Due to the lack of a trusted technology framework in trade processes, participants are often reluctant to share data and information openly, leading to information gaps, lack of trust, and inefficient process coordination.

- Cumbersome Settlement Process

  The current cross-border payment settlement process is complex, with long payment cycles for export trade. A significant portion of overseas accounts receivable is susceptible to bad debts and defaults. Additionally, small and medium-sized enterprises (SMEs) account for a large share of international trade, but due to their incomplete financial systems, small operational scale, and weak risk resistance, they often face credit assessment difficulties or lack access to credit channels, significantly impacting their financing rates, particularly for SMEs engaged in cross-border trade.
- Payment Methods and Their Challenges

  The cross-border trade payment process varies depending on the jurisdictions involved, requiring third-party payment services, credit cards, and e-commerce platforms for settlement to facilitate international business transactions across different customs territories. Currently, major types of cross-border electronic payments include bank wire transfers, online banking payments, payment gateways, and mobile payments. While these payment methods have improved transaction efficiency, they also present numerous challenges.

In summary, the key pain points of traditional cross-border trade payments can be categorized into the following five aspects: high degree of centralization; high payment costs; lack of transaction transparency; difficulty in establishing a credit system, leading to challenges in factoring and trade financing; limitations of the SWIFT system.

6.5.1 High Degree of Centralization

In traditional cross-border payment systems, every transaction record or invoice must pass through a central gateway and relies on a centralized server for settlement and reconciliation. This means that all transaction and payment records are stored in a large central database, with banks and third-party payment platforms acting as the core hubs of the system.

Imagine a network of cross-border transactions where each transaction node represents a trading activity. These nodes not only contain transaction and payment records but also include privacy-related actions and transaction processes. However, all of this information must be connected to a central server. The central server acts as a "gatekeeper", responsible for verifying, reconciling, recording, and maintaining all transaction information before ultimately facilitating the settlement between both parties.

The centralized cross-border payment model is currently the primary method for cross-border electronic payments and settlements. This centralized transaction clearing model requires all parties involved in a transaction to transmit their transaction information to a third-party server for processing. This inherently increases the time required for transactions and raises both time costs and capital flow costs.

This highly centralized model also impacts the account management system, making it predominantly centralized. In cross-border payments, both fund transfers and transaction data updates must be recorded by central banks and commercial banks. For example, if the payer and payee are customers of the same bank, the bank can internally process balance adjustments to complete the transfer and settlement. However, if the payer and payee belong to different banks, the fund transfer must go through a third party, which typically relies on the central bank's clearing system.

6.5.2 High Transaction Costs

Under the correspondent banking model, cross-border payments must go through multiple stages, including payment processing, correspondent institution clearing, liquidity management, currency exchange, the SWIFT system, system infrastructure, and manual processing. Each of these steps incurs costs, which are ultimately reflected in various fees, such as telegraphic transfer and transaction fees from the remitting bank, intermediary bank transfer fees, and account credit and inquiry fees from the receiving bank. For example, in Q2 2023, the global average cost of a $200 cross-border remittance was 6.2%, far exceeding the G20's goal of reducing cross-border payment costs to 3% by 2030.

6.5.3 High Lack of Transaction Transparency

In a highly centralized cross-border payment system, transaction transparency is often low. The recording and security of cross-border payment transaction data almost entirely rely on banks, intermediaries, and third-party payment platforms. The entire transaction process is only visible to a very limited number of entities and lacks sufficient oversight. This increases the risk of fraudulent transactions, as external parties find it difficult to verify the authenticity of transactions. As a result, transaction credibility is reduced, and the establishment of a reliable credit system becomes challenging.

Moreover, a highly centralized cross-border payment system results in high transaction costs and low efficiency. Third-party institutions must develop complex processes to ensure security, accuracy, and reliability, which inevitably increases costs. Additionally, reliance on third-party institutions creates a barrier between transacting parties, making transactions more difficult, reducing liquidity and efficiency, and increasing both transaction time and associated time costs.

Security risks are also a major concern. During transactions, security threats exist not only for both transacting parties but also for intermediaries. If one party is hacked, leading to transaction data tampering, it can compromise the intermediary's records and storage, ultimately resulting in financial losses. If the third-party institution responsible for transaction security experiences a security breach, such as a cyberattack, it could lead to transaction data manipulation, potentially causing system-wide failures, data breaches, and significant financial losses.

6.5.4 Difficulty in Establishing a Credit System, Leading to Challenges in Factoring and Trade Financing

In this centralized and consolidated billing management model of traditional cross-border payments, transaction information lacks transparency, making regulatory oversight more difficult. This means that the occurrence, recording, regulation, and security of transactions are primarily handled by third parties, posing risks of intentional or unintentional transaction data manipulation and cybersecurity threats such as hacking. Intentional alteration of transaction data can compromise the accuracy of credit records, which hinders the establishment of a reliable credit system and raises security concerns. Currently, the difficulty in establishing a robust credit system has significantly limited the development of factoring and trade financing.

The factoring business of commercial banks is supposed to be a valuable complement to traditional bank loan financing services. However, in cross-border trade, domestic factoring companies find it difficult to establish close integration with overseas e-commerce platforms and must rely on an independent commercial factoring model. Under this model, several issues arise:

First, low efficiency in financing review. Factoring companies with digital information systems need to integrate with overseas e-commerce platforms to obtain supplier order information, while those without such systems must manually retrieve order data. Even after obtaining the orders, additional resources are required to verify their authenticity, leading to high costs and low operational efficiency.

Second, high post-loan risk and difficulty in controlling fund flows. Since each factoring company records financing information independently, data remains isolated, making it difficult to prevent suppliers from using the same order to apply for financing from multiple factoring companies, leading to over-borrowing and excessive financing, which increases the risks for factoring companies.

Finally, lack of flexibility in financing methods. In traditional factoring financing, credit limits cannot be split, meaning that each order can only be financed once, leading to wasted credit capacity. Additionally, suppliers cannot combine their credit limits, making it difficult to meet larger financing needs, resulting in highly inflexible financing options.

6.5.5 Limitations of the SWIFT System

Since its establishment in 1973, the SWIFT system has become the primary channel for transmitting transaction information in global cross-border payments by setting unified communication standards for financial institutions. However, this has also led to certain restrictions. If a country or financial institution is cut off from SWIFT, it is effectively excluded from the international financial settlement system, making it difficult to conduct international trade and other economic activities.Although SWIFT is officially a neutral, non-profit international inter-bank organization, in reality, it remains dominated by Western countries. Particularly after the 9/11 terrorist attacks, the U.S. government leveraged counter-terrorism efforts to turn SWIFT into a tool for financial sanctions and extraterritorial jurisdiction. Amid the Russia-Ukraine conflict, the EU imposed sanctions, prohibiting certain Russian banks from accessing financial messaging services. It can be said that Western countries, led by the U.S., have increasingly normalized the use of SWIFT as a tool for financial sanctions.

With the rapid growth of the global digital asset market, stablecoins have become an indispensable tool in international trade. Stablecoins enhance transaction efficiency, reduce costs, and improve existing payment systems, thereby strengthening the capabilities of financial technology. With stability, free convertibility, high security, and cross-border liquidity, stablecoins provide strong support for global financial innovation.

Globally, policymakers and regulatory authorities are gradually strengthening the oversight of digital assets, reflecting a broad recognition of the potential of stablecoins. These policies not only facilitate the adoption and development of digital assets but also highlight the increasing significance of stablecoins in advancing global trade.

Notably, stablecoins can address several issues present in the traditional financial system within global trade. For instance, they can significantly reduce the time and cost of cross-border transactions by bypassing traditional banking systems and directly leveraging blockchain technology. Additionally, stablecoins serve as a more stable transaction medium, helping to mitigate transaction risks caused by currency fluctuations.

However, despite their numerous advantages, the implementation and widespread adoption of stablecoins face challenges, particularly in terms of regulatory consistency on a global scale. Differences in regulations across countries and regions may hinder the international circulation and acceptance of stablecoins. Additionally, while private entities are capable of issuing stablecoins, these stablecoins may struggle to achieve sufficient market acceptance, which could impact their effectiveness as a tool for global trade.

Therefore, in the field of cross-border payments and transactions, stablecoins should be issued under the leadership of governments or international financial institutions to ensure their widespread acceptance and use. Government-backed stablecoins, such as those supported by national foreign exchange reserves, would offer higher credibility and lower risk, effectively enhancing global trade and financial stability.

Such government-backed or internationally-backed stablecoins would integrate the advantages of blockchain technology—high transparency, low costs, and fast transactions—while operating under a robust legal and regulatory framework to ensure their stability within the global financial system. In this way, stablecoins could not only streamline global trade processes but also enhance the overall efficiency and inclusiveness of financial markets.

So, what advantages do stablecoins offer in the cross-border payment system?

6.5.6 Diversified Cross-Border Payment System

Stablecoins play a significant role in diversifying the global financial market. They can reduce excessive reliance on a single currency, enabling more direct and stable transactions between countries while mitigating the impact of geopolitical instability on trade. Under an appropriate regulatory framework, stablecoins can also reshape a country's international currency strategy and expand adoption to other nations.

6.5.7 Making Cross-Border Trade Logistics and Product Traceability More Efficient

Logistics and transportation form the foundation of cross-border trade. Given the multiple stages involved, this industry presents a wide range of applications for stablecoins. The transparency and traceability of stablecoins help prevent fraud, money laundering, and counterfeiting, connecting all participants in the supply chain, from shippers to customs and banks. Additionally, data monitoring enhances supply chain security and product traceability, strengthening consumer trust.

6.5.8 Providing Additional Liquidity to Support Government and Corporate Financial Projects

Stablecoins backed by the issuing country's credit can supply a significant amount of additional liquidity, enhancing capital flow efficiency and financial market performance. First, these liquid assets can be used to reduce government debt, create more fiscal space for infrastructure and industrial development, and support government financial investment plans to lower project operating costs. Leveraging block-chain's inherent advantages, stablecoins address the lack of transparency and credibility issues in traditional cross-border trade payment systems, thereby reducing the cost and time required for trade authenticity verification. Second, stablecoins can regulate capital flows and ensure proper fund utilization. With interoperability in trade information, stablecoins help prevent projects from applying for multiple financing sources simultaneously. Third, stablecoins support the fractionalization of credit limits, allowing for more flexible financing solutions and lowering the threshold for large-scale financing needs.

6.5.9 Digitizing Trillions of Dollars in Traditional Assets

Stablecoins can help nations and regions digitize traditional assets, thereby expanding the business scope of traditional financial instruments, enhancing liquidity and transparency, and reducing transaction costs.

Digital assets create broader application scenarios, while driving financial service optimization, allowing more people to participate in financial transactions and trading. This transformation not only strengthens regional financial development, increases liquidity and market influence, but also injects new vitality and opportunities into the digital economy.

6.5.10 Easier Supervision and Risk Management

Cross-border trade involves a large number of documents, high operational costs, and poses challenges for customs supervision. Customs authorities primarily focus on the authenticity and legality of transactions, but the lack of reliable data sources and the difficulty of data integration make the regulatory process complex and time-consuming, ultimately reducing trade efficiency. To prevent fraud involving falsified bills of lading and other import documents, mitigate risks, and close regulatory loopholes, customs must verify vast amounts of data, requiring substantial manpower and resources. Despite the need for extensive data verification, only a small portion of processes have been digitized, with most still relying on paper documents, further increasing economic and time costs. Stablecoins can significantly enhance regulatory efficiency and transparency in cross-border trade. First, stablecoins enable real-time recording and automated processing of transaction data, reducing dependency on paper documentation. Second, stablecoin transactions can be tracked and verified in real-time, improving transaction transparency and authenticity while helping customs quickly validate trade information and minimize fraud and counterfeiting. Finally, the digital nature of stablecoins simplifies data integration, facilitating information sharing and collaboration among different regulatory authorities. Governments that directly regulate the issuance and circulation of stablecoins not only enhance the effectiveness of monetary policy but also strengthen regional financial stability and regulatory consistency. Governments can flexibly manage stablecoins based on market conditions and policy needs to maintain price stability. Additionally, they have both the responsibility and capability to protect stablecoin holders' interests and ensure their rights are safeguarded. Compared to private institutions that may face commercial risks, governments are better equipped to combat money laundering and enforce strict financial regulations, ensuring greater oversight of fund flows.

6.5.11 Promoting Financial Innovation

Government backing and regulatory oversight will contribute to the development of stablecoins. Compared to traditional fiat currencies, stablecoins not only inherit their reliability but also incorporate encryption algorithms, block-chain, and distributed ledger technology, while benefiting from the latest research insights from regulatory bodies.

Moreover, compared to traditional cross-border payment systems, stablecoins offer a faster, lower-cost, and more transparent cross-border payment solution, thereby reshaping international trade payment and settlement methods and reducing the complexity and cost of global trade. A stablecoin-supported cross-border payment system can address the challenges of high economic and time costs caused by lengthy cross-border payment processes. First, in terms of economic costs, traditional cross-border payment systems require multiple banks to participate in settlement, and each country's commercial banks have their own technical standards and operational procedures. Additionally, differences in infrastructure development and information accessibility across countries result in high economic costs for cross-border payments. Second, in terms of time costs, cross-border payments typically involve multiple jurisdictions, requiring regulatory reviews to assess risks related to money laundering and terrorist financing, which lengthens the payment process. Furthermore, due to the lack of standardized technical protocols, incompatibility among different national hardware systems further delays cross-border transactions.

Stablecoins, powered by block-chain technology, enable direct peer-to-peer payments, bypassing traditional payment chains, significantly reducing transaction complexity and allowing automated, real-time settlement of payments. The adoption of stablecoins can streamline international trade processes, bringing greater flexibility and efficiency to the global financial market.

In the global cross-border trade landscape, stablecoins can facilitate the internationalization of a country or region's fiat currency, strengthening cooperation between local economies and foreign markets. By establishing interoperability between digital currencies, stablecoins can enhance liquidity, attract block-chain, cryptocurrency, and Web 3.0 enterprises and projects, and provide differentiated, high-quality financial services. Additionally, they can lower transaction and cross-border payment costs for digital assets, delivering more convenient and secure financial services to the real economy.

6.5.12 Supporting Key National Development Strategies

Stablecoins can address trade and investment barriers in international cooperation caused by monetary policies and trade restrictions, offering a simpler, more efficient, and reliable means of capital circulation while improving capital utilization efficiency. Expanding the global adoption of a country's or region's stablecoin can help enhance its role in international trade. The use of stablecoins eliminates redundant steps in traditional transactions, reduces transaction costs, increases transparency and trust, and helps attract international investment.

The development and adoption of stablecoins provide innovative solutions for global trade, addressing efficiency, cost, and fairness issues in traditional financial systems. Today, there is growing demand to fully leverage the advantages of stablecoins and establish a diversified, more efficient, and well-structured payment system for international trade and cross-border payments. As technology advances and regulatory frameworks improve, stablecoins require an environment with strong regulation, close international cooperation, standardized technical protocols, and high interoperability to enhance their role in the global economy and unlock their potential in boosting asset liquidity and expanding international trade.

6.6 Asia RWA Working Group: "Recommendations on the Implementation of Stablecoin Issuance by the Hong Kong Monetary Authority"

Dear Leaders of the Hong Kong Monetary Authority and Relevant Departments,

This letter is respectfully submitted by the Asia RWA Working Group and its members, with the aim of providing professional recommendations on the implementation of stablecoin issuance in Hong Kong, drawing from the development experience of existing centralized stablecoins and related policies in other regions and countries.The RWA Working Group was established in 2023 at Hong Kong Cyberport as a cross-industry autonomous organization dedicated to advancing the RWA ecosystem in Asia, including security tokens and stablecoins. Our mission is to unite industry stakeholders to facilitate the integration of RWAs across Asia and globally, while promoting the healthy and compliant development of Hong Kong's Web 3.0 industry.

Stablecoins are playing an irreplaceable role in the Web 3.0 world. As a pioneer and one of the most successful sectors in the tokenization of real-world assets (RWA), stablecoins have successfully combined the convenience of digital assets with the stability of traditional financial assets. They serve as a unit of value in digital asset transactions, providing investors with both an "entry gateway" and a "safe haven", while also becoming increasingly important in the international payment system of the real world. Furthermore, stablecoins are not only a fundamental pillar for the tokenization of real-world assets, but the advancement of RWA tokenization also enhances the value support and reserve sources for stablecoins. As a result, stablecoins have become the bridge between digital assets and the mainstream financial system. Market data shows that the total market capitalization of stablecoins peaked at over $180 billion in May 2022, and as of February 20, 2024, the total market cap stands at approximately $142.8 billion.

Summary of Recommendations for the Implementation of Stablecoin Issuance in Hong Kong:

- Policy and Regulatory Framework: Establish a clear policy and regulatory framework to ensure that HKD stablecoin issuance and operations comply with international financial standards, while also addressing anti-money laundering (AML) and counter-terrorism financing (CTF) requirements.
- Technical Infrastructure: Adopt advanced blockchain technology to ensure the security, scalability, and interoperability of the HKD stablecoin system. Additionally, consider highly stable and scalable technologies capable of handling large-scale transactions.
- Asset Support and Auditing: Ensure that stablecoins are backed by sufficient HKD reserves or other assets, with regular audits to enhance transparency and credibility.
- Market Adoption and Application: Promote the use of HKD stablecoins in daily transactions through collaboration with financial institutions, payment service providers, and merchants, including applications in cross-border payments, trade finance, and consumer payments.
- Risk Management: Develop effective risk management strategies, covering custody risk, liquidity risk, credit risk, and operational risk, to ensure the stable operation of the system.
- User Privacy and Data Protection: Respect user privacy while ensuring compliance with relevant data protection laws and regulations.
- International Cooperation: Collaborate with central banks of other countries and regions as well as international financial organizations to facilitate cross-border payments and enhance the international influence of the HKD stablecoin.

February 27, 2024.

Signatories:

- Professor Yang Wang, Chair of the Asia RWA Working Group, Vice President of Hong Kong University of Science and Technology, and Chief Scientist of the Hong Kong Web 3.0 Association
- Mr. Tian Gan, Vice Chair of the Asia RWA Working Group, CEO of China AMC (Hong Kong)
- Mr. Haokang Zhu, Founder and Secretary-General of the Asia RWA Working Group, Visiting Scholar at the Digital Asset Think Tank, Hong Kong Polytechnic University FinTech Center
- Mr. Haifeng Bai, Director of the Asset Management Committee, Asia RWA Working Group, Managing Director at CMB International Asset Management
- Ms. YuYi Lao, Chair of the Information Industry Committee, Asia RWA Working Group, Chair of the HK Stocks Top 100 Research Center
- Ms. XiaoQi Hong, Chair of the Venture Capital Committee, Asia RWA Working Group, Partner at Hack VC Asia–Pacific
- Ms. ZheRuan Qiao, Chair of the Legal and Regulatory Committee, Asia RWA Working Group, Partner at JunHe LLP
- Mr. Taoshuo Zhang, Deputy Secretary-General of the Asia RWA Working Group

6.6.1 Recommendations for the Implementation of Stablecoin Issuance in Hong Kong

- **Policy and Regulatory Framework**
  Establishing a clear policy and regulatory framework is essential to ensure the reliability and credibility of Hong Kong stablecoins. This involves the following aspects:
  - Adherence to International Standards: The operation of Hong Kong stablecoins should comply with global financial market rules and standards, including but not limited to the guiding principles of the Bank for International Settlements (BIS) and recommendations from the Financial Action Task Force (FATF).
  - AML and Counter-Terrorism Financing (CFT): The stablecoin framework should incorporate effective AML/CFT measures, enforce KYC procedures, ensure transaction transparency, and prevent illicit financial flows.
  - Regulatory Cooperation: Hong Kong financial regulators should collaborate with other financial regulatory bodies to ensure regulatory consistency and prevent regulatory arbitrage.
  - Policy Transparency: The policy and regulatory framework should be made public to allow market participants to clearly understand the rules, thereby enhancing trust in the system.
- **Technical Infrastructure**
  The development of technical infrastructure must ensure system security and efficiency, covering the following aspects:

- Blockchain Technology Selection: Choose widely recognized and tested blockchain technologies to ensure security and stability. For example, selecting platforms that support smart contracts can enhance automation and reduce human errors.
- Scalability: The technical solution should be able to scale with increasing user adoption and transaction volume, ensuring that the system does not disrupt services due to expansion demands.
- Interoperability: Hong Kong stablecoins should seamlessly integrate with existing financial systems and emerging blockchain networks, ensuring smooth capital flows.

• **Asset Support and Auditing**

Asset support and auditing are critical to the credibility of stablecoins, including the following aspects:

- Asset Reserves: Stablecoins should be fully backed by HKD or other highly liquid assets and segregated in a trusted bank account.
- Regular Audits: Conduct third-party audits regularly to disclose the status of asset reserves, enhancing system transparency and credibility.

• **Market Promotion and Application**

Market promotion and adoption are key to the success of stablecoins, including:

- Partnerships: Collaborate with financial institutions, payment service providers, and merchants to ensure widespread support and adoption of HKD stablecoins.
- Multi-Scenario Applications: Promote the use of HKD stablecoins across various payment scenarios, such as online payments and cross-border remittances.

• **Risk Management**

Effective risk management strategies are essential to ensuring the stability of the system, including:

- Custody Risk: Risks in asset management and custody of HKD stablecoins, including theft, misuse, or mismanagement by custodians. To mitigate this risk, custodians must have high-security protection measures, and regular external audits and transparent asset reports should be conducted to monitor the custodian's operations and asset status.
- Liquidity Risk: Ensure stablecoins can be redeemed for fiat currency at any time to prevent market panic.
- Credit Risk: Manage and assess credit risks associated with stablecoin operations, particularly in asset reserve management.
- Operational Risk: Reduce operational risks by establishing robust operational procedures and training qualified personnel.

6.6.2 User Privacy and Data Protection

In the development of digital currencies, user privacy and data protection are crucial topics, including the following aspects:

- Privacy Protection: The design of Hong Kong stablecoins should ensure that users' transaction privacy is protected while allowing regulatory agencies to conduct reviews when necessary to meet AML/CFT (Anti-Money Laundering/Counter-Terrorist Financing) requirements.
- Data Protection Regulations: Compliance with Hong Kong's data protection laws, such as the *Personal Data (Privacy) Ordinance*, and alignment with international data protection standards.
- Encryption Technology: Utilizing advanced encryption technology to prevent unauthorized third-party access to user data.
- User Authorization: Ensuring that users have full control over the use and sharing of their personal data, following the principle of minimization in data collection and processing.

6.6.3 International Cooperation

International cooperation can enhance the global influence of Hong Kong stablecoins and promote their application in international trade and financial activities, including the following aspects:

- Central Banking Network: The Hong Kong Monetary Authority (HKMA) should establish collaborative relationships with other central banks to explore the use of stablecoins in the global financial system.
- International Financial Organizations: Engaging in cooperation with organizations such as the International Monetary Fund (IMF) and the World Bank to help develop international regulatory standards.
- Cross-Border Payments: Collaborating with different national payment systems to make Hong Kong stablecoins an effective tool for cross-border payments, enhancing transaction efficiency, and reducing costs.
- Regulatory Coordination: Ensuring that the regulatory framework for Hong Kong stablecoins aligns with the regulatory requirements of major countries and regions, facilitating cross-border circulation and regulatory coordination.

Risk Management in RWA and Tokenization

7

7.1 Risks in RWA and Tokenization

The emergence of blockchain technology and tokenization was driven by the pursuit of decentralization, relying on blockchain to ensure the authenticity, immutability, and uniqueness of tokens, thereby maintaining their credibility. The development of tokens has enhanced the low-cost and high-efficiency circulation of assets and rights, injecting revolutionary momentum into the current economic system and initiating a wave of asset digitization. This has led to the creation of a new token-based economic model. The token economy model presents significant challenges to traditional centralized regulation because it adopts a decentralized approach, making traditional regulatory strategies potentially obsolete. While different countries hold varying attitudes toward the token economy, its rapid expansion has drawn close attention from governments, prompting some to adopt more lenient policies while simultaneously increasing research and investment in the sector. New economic models often bring regulatory challenges, as risk management typically lags behind economic innovation. Identifying risks and refining regulatory policies are crucial for better understanding these emerging economic tools. Regulatory reforms can ensure that tokenization contributes positively to national economic development.

7.1.1 Sources of Risks in RWA and Tokenization: Uncertainty in New Technology and Economy

Since the inception of blockchain technology, capital and talent have rapidly flowed into this emerging field. The development of blockchain extends beyond its technology to the construction of blockchain platforms and token economies. Initially, the market was filled with speculative token investments and fraudulent

S. Ba et al., *RWA Tokenisation in Web 3.0 Era*, Management for Professionals,
https://doi.org/10.1007/978-981-96-7663-7_7

projects, but over time, blockchain technology has evolved into a catalyst for economic transformation. Various industries have begun exploring "blockchain + " models to address long-standing industry challenges. They have leveraged tokenization to enable low-cost and high-efficiency operations, fostering the growth of a new economic system.

Governments are actively monitoring the token economy, balancing innovation and regulation to prevent risks while allowing technological advancements. The future of tokenization depends on the ability to integrate compliance mechanisms with decentralized financial models, ensuring that both economic and legal frameworks evolve in tandem.

7.1.2 Technical Risks in RWA and Tokenization

Blockchain technology, as an innovative foundational framework, has injected new vitality into the modern economy through its trust mechanisms and fair value distribution models. As a decentralized medium of circulation, tokenization has witnessed rapid growth on blockchain platforms. blockchain projects rely on tokens to maintain stable operations, and these tokens, based on blockchain's immutable nature, optimize their function as a circulation medium while enhancing security and efficiency. This synergy between blockchain and tokenization expands their potential development space.

However, blockchain's decentralized nature conflicts with traditional regulatory models. The lack of oversight may lead to the misuse of tokens for illicit activities such as money laundering, ransomware payments, and black-market transactions, as seen with Bitcoin. This raises significant concerns for regulatory bodies and poses severe challenges to existing financial regulations.

7.1.3 Economic Model Risks in RWA and Tokenization

The advantages of tokenization include digitalization, fractionalization, and ease of transfer of assets and rights, significantly reducing transaction friction, increasing efficiency, and lowering costs. Through tokenization, economic benefits can be widely distributed, allowing organizations and individuals to issue their own tokens based on resources and services.

Tokenization enables greater inclusivity in financial markets, addressing issues such as low security, lack of creditworthiness, and unfairness in traditional economic systems. The token economy uses tokens as a standardized or non-standardized digital medium to transfer and represent ownership. However, the self-sustaining nature of tokenized economies often creates a disconnect from traditional economic systems, making regulatory integration a challenge. As tokenization gains momentum, understanding and managing these risks will be crucial for its healthy development within the global financial system.

7.1.4 RWA and Tokenization -Induced Risk Mechanism Analysis

Blockchain technology has not only reshaped human behavior but is also gradually altering value systems, significantly enhancing organizational efficiency and value exchange efficiency. However, we must recognize that blockchain technology is still in its early stages of development and remains immature, while the tokenized economy is only just beginning. On the one hand, technological innovation and application require continuous experimentation and exploration, and their far-reaching effects on society are undeniable. On the other hand, government regulatory agencies often lag behind in addressing the societal transformations brought about by technological advancements.

Since blockchain technology and the tokenized economy are still in their infancy, their legal implications remain unclear, making regulation a complex challenge. If regulatory approaches are flawed, untimely, or overly restrictive, they could hinder or even stifle technological innovation. Of course, legal professionals have the responsibility to timely capture risks brought by technological change and economic development, and formulate scientific, reasonable, and precise governance strategies.

7.1.5 The Flow Cycle of "Rights Object → Token → Rights" May not Form

Blockchain technology provides a platform for the tokenization of rights-based assets, while smart contracts automate contractual execution, enhancing transaction security and transparency. In a blockchain network, theoretically, any asset with economic value can be tokenized, leveraging blockchain's traceability and immutability to ensure authenticity and reliability. In a decentralized and intermediary-free network, these tokens can circulate rapidly, enabling value exchange and transformation. Tokens serve as proof of rights and can be redeemed into tangible rights, thus completing the circulation cycle of the token economy.

Although digitizing and assetizing rights-based assets is not technically difficult, the real challenge lies in whether tokens can gain value through circulation and exchange in blockchain networks, and how they can be redeemed for the rights they represent. Tokenization does not guarantee smooth circulation, appreciation, or redemption. To illustrate this issue, examples from movable assets, immovable assets, and intellectual property will be examined to highlight potential governance risks posed by tokenization.

Example: Tokenizing Region-Specific Movable Assets. A movable asset with a single function and regional characteristics may hold inherent value, but its recognition is often limited to local communities. To increase market recognition and value, tokenization could be used to enable wider circulation on a blockchain network. However, since these region-specific assets may fail to achieve broad consensus in an open blockchain network, their circulation and exchange potential is limited, resulting in minimal appreciation opportunities. In simple terms, tokenizing a particular movable asset does not guarantee that other stages such as circulation, appreciation, and redemption will proceed as expected.

In blockchain networks, real estate serves as a rights-based asset, and while its digitization and tokenization are theoretically feasible, there are certain legal and practical obstacles. According to the *Property Law of the People's Republic of China*, the transfer of real estate is restricted due to legal provisions and the inherent characteristics of property. Nevertheless, tokenization allows real estate owners to divide and transfer property ownership into different fractional shares on the blockchain, enabling circulation. A property token holder possesses proof of ownership proportional to their share and jointly owns and manages the property with other holders. However, if there is no clear agreement among property token holders, they may request the partition or sale of the property at any time, potentially leading to a situation where property tokenization loses its intended meaning.

For property usage rights, token holders nominally possess usage rights, but in practice, exercising these rights is difficult. For example, a property token holder with a 1% usage right may struggle to claim actual use of the property based on this proportion. Although the separation of ownership, usage, and income rights provides a theoretical possibility for digital circulation, its real-world application appears to be limited to circulation and value appreciation rather than actual functional use.

Another example is copyright, where tokens play a critical role in ownership verification and revenue distribution. The value of scarce resources can be recognized within blockchain networks and monetized through tokenization, allowing circulation and appreciation.

However, in practice, redeeming tokens for the rights they represent may face difficulties. For instance, a token holder with 1% ownership of a song's copyright may find it challenging to determine how their share should be exercised—whether based on time duration or content contribution. This ambiguity in revenue distribution reveals potential challenges that highly fractionalized rights may face in real-world applications.

7.1.6 Mechanical Incentive Mechanisms May Lead to Dishonest Behavior

Token economy platforms can design carefully crafted incentive mechanisms to increase user engagement and loyalty at different stages. In the early stages of a platform, project developers may adopt a "as long as you join" token reward strategy to rapidly expand market presence and attract consumers. As the platform matures, it may transition to a "as long as you act" model, where users are rewarded for specific behaviors, fostering adaptation to and recognition of platform rules. With further development, platforms may adopt a "as long as you believe" approach, where users vote to identify and reward compliant operators, while simultaneously penalizing violators.

However, token economy platforms driven by economic incentives may encourage dishonest behavior among users, disrupting the existing industry balance and leading to user attrition. Additionally, in pursuit of token rewards, users' actions may negatively impact the credibility of business operators, potentially undermining the integrity of the system.

From the perspective of token economy incentive mechanisms, these platforms leverage the public's profit-driven mindset, using democratic voting to select trustworthy business operators. However, this model also has flaws. For instance, users may fabricate experiences or leave negative reviews solely to earn additional tokens. Some news platforms offer reading rewards to boost article dissemination, but such low-threshold incentive mechanisms may disrupt industry balance, causing truly valuable content to be overlooked.

The incentive mechanisms within token economies provide a foundation for decentralized, tamper-proof, and globally broadcasted trust systems. Users' behavior on the platform is guided by incentives, directly impacting the reputation of business operators. Under this model, every user can participate in evaluations, helping operators build a credibility system. However, both positive and negative reviews are permanently recorded on the distributed ledger.

For business operators, genuine reviews act as feedback, driving them to improve and better meet user needs. For users, reviews serve as critical references for choosing services and products. Yet, the existence of fraudulent reviews can damage an operator's credibility, creating inflated or misleading trust metrics. This not only misguides consumers but also poses serious reputational risks to business operators.

7.1.7 Decentralized Token Economy Models May Lead to Rule Monopolization

The efficient circulation of token economies relies on the automation and strict enforcement of smart contracts. However, despite theoretically flawless blockchain technology, its design, implementation, and usage are ultimately carried out by humans, making the system subject to subjective intentions. Blockchain technology may face risks of self-serving behavior, attacks, and manipulation.

The design of token economy models is determined by developers, including the types of rewarded behaviors, token classifications, rights allocation, and incentive mechanisms. All of these decisions are embedded in the platform through smart contract coding. In essence, developers "implant" their governance philosophy into the platform, using predefined rules to regulate and guide user behavior.

Although community users have the opportunity to vote to amend improper rules, once these rules are encoded into a decentralized distributed platform, blockchain technology and its mechanisms make these rule modifications extremely difficult. For example, in response to a large-scale Ethereum theft incident, the founder proposed a hard fork solution, which invalidated the hacker's transaction records. While 85% of Ethereum participants supported the fork, it caused a division within the community, resulting in the creation of Ethereum (ETH, new chain) and Ethereum Classic (ETC, old chain).

Smart contracts are designed to execute automatically, but they are still essentially similar to contractual clauses since their terms and conditions are predetermined by their creators. In a decentralized business model, where numerous operators and consumers participate, token economy platforms may embed smart contracts with standard form contract clauses to standardize contract flows. According to Article 39 of the *Contract Law of the People's Republic of China*, standard form contract clauses should adhere to the principles of fairness, ensuring that rights and obligations between parties are clearly defined and that reasonable measures are taken to remind parties of potential exemption or limitation of liability clauses.

However, in reality, governance contracts on the internet often use clauses that ultimately allow user agreements and service contracts to override governance mechanisms. These clauses are primarily formulated based on economic benefits, used for managing service software usage, while also indirectly restricting certain behaviors that may threaten these benefits. Even though smart contract code is developed under an open-source model, its core team still retains control, setting rules and guiding project development in a centralized manner.

In the token economy, although it appears that all participants can be incentivized to engage in behavior fairly, in reality, those who control smart contract writing rights may have already established a governance mechanism that subtly dictates the rules. This arrangement may cause participants to be unknowingly manipulated, while developers could potentially use their control to influence the platform's operations and participation mechanisms.

7.1.8 Forms of Risks in the Token Economy

The rise of blockchain technology has undoubtedly led to a new revolution in the digital economy, giving birth to the emerging field of the token economy. The evolution of economic structures and technological advancements pose challenges to existing legal frameworks and regulatory systems. Only by keeping pace with the development trends of the new economy and effectively controlling risks can the sustainable development of new economic models be ensured.

7.1.9 Speculative Trading Leads to the Risk of Artificially Inflated Token Prices

The digital representation of any goods and services can be realized through smart contracts on the blockchain, enabling secure, transparent transactions, achieving low-cost and frictionless circulation. Transforming asset ownership into tokens and ensuring that on-chain token transactions can accurately reflect their fair market value is the core of the token economy.

Assets such as movable properties (e.g., books, artwork) exhibit price volatility and appreciation potential. Tokenizing these assets allows more participants to share in the appreciation space. However, the realization of the asset's appreciation occurs in the market through subsequent transactions, and excessive speculative trading can drive the price of the original asset to artificial highs, deviating from its actual value. Therefore, ensuring that the token price aligns with the value of the underlying asset is crucial to realizing the token's exchange-ability.

7.1.10 The Credit Risk of Tokens Acting as a Medium in Decentralized Circulation

The token economy, born from blockchain technology, is inherently decentralized, yet it does not completely eliminate credit dependency but rather shifts the foundation of trust from centralized institutions to private domains. The value of tokens is ultimately derived from the value of the asset or project itself, forming a unique value system through token-holder relationships, which impacts market and project development. However, as the token economy extends into the realm of term-based agreements, some overly cautious investors may struggle with uncertainties regarding the maturity period of their investments. If the trust system encounters crises, token prices may plummet rapidly, leading to the risk of systemic collapse.

For instance, in real estate, property values are fixed and difficult to transfer, leading to poor liquidity. By tokenizing real estate assets into smaller units, more investors can participate and share in potential appreciation. While investors cannot directly exchange their token holdings for physical assets, they can still benefit from asset appreciation. For example, high-end real estate and early-stage venture capital investments typically have high entry barriers, making it difficult for individual investors to participate. Tokenizing such assets can lower investment thresholds, allowing more investors to share in the opportunity.

However, in the case of tokenized real estate assets, what investors hold is more of a symbolic representation of ownership rather than actual usage rights. Individual investors cannot easily claim usage rights over a property based on their small fractional ownership. Therefore, the core of tokenization lies in the transfer-ability of asset value, and the credit system is essential for maintaining the circulation of tokens. If trust in the system is compromised, investors may engage in panic selling, which could lead to a sharp decline in token value, ultimately triggering financial risks.

7.1.11 The Uncertainty of Tokens with Ample Supply but Insufficient Credit Support

As a market-oriented product, tokens may have an abundant supply, but their credit foundation remains weak. Any organization or individual can issue interest-bearing tokens based on their own resources or service capabilities. In recent years, a large number of asset-backed tokens have flooded the market. While these tokens represent the issuer's commitment, their actual market value remains difficult to determine.

The value of tokens primarily relies on private trust, meaning that market performance is largely dependent on investor confidence in their creditworthiness. If a trust crisis emerges, investors may rapidly sell off their holdings, leading to a quick loss of credit, a sharp decline in token value, or even a liquidity crunch and default risks. Additionally, some tokens' value is closely tied to the success of their associated projects, which inherently come with high uncertainty and risks. Evaluating whether a project's token issuance is backed by sustainable business success requires long-term market validation. In an environment where token supply is abundant but lacks a stable credit foundation, investors need to exercise caution to avoid falling into the trap of speculative or fraudulent projects.

7.1.12 Overly Aggressive Incentive Mechanisms May Lead to Operational Risks

The incentive mechanism is a fundamental feature of a token economy, primarily used to stimulate platform growth. In the early stages of platform development, incentives are mainly designed to attract new users through token-based rewards, which can quickly expand the user base and increase the platform's visibility. As the platform matures, incentives gradually shift toward encouraging sustained user engagement, with the goal of enhancing user participation, promoting content creation, and maintaining an active and vibrant community.

However, the intensity of incentives must be carefully controlled to prevent users from engaging in opportunistic or even harmful behaviors. For instance, if a platform relies too heavily on incentives to drive user activity, it may lead users to manipulate rewards through click farming or fraudulent trust-building activities. Over time, this may drive away genuine users and hinder the long-term healthy development of the platform and its ecosystem.

FCoin's "transaction mining" incentive mechanism is an example. This model indeed increased the exchange's trading volume in the short term. However, as this incentive was based on transaction volume, it lacked long-term sustainability. The revenue distribution of FCoin had structural flaws, and many users engaged in frequent transactions solely to earn more token rewards. This behavior led to a situation where the token economy system was driven by a "holding for trading" logic rather than rational and meaningful transactions. As market enthusiasm faded, rational traders gradually exited, and as rewards became ineffective, the incentive mechanism ultimately struggled to persist.

Furthermore, defining rewards for specific behaviors may lead users to engage in dishonest actions solely to earn incentives. For example, users may leave false reviews on products or services without actual experience just to obtain rewards. Such economic profit-driven incentive models can result in industry development biases. For instance, certain news applications provide incentives for reading news to attract users, but this can lead to lower-quality news content gaining undue attention. When content quality is no longer the core driving force of the news industry, it may ultimately cause the industry to lose its fundamental value.

7.1.13 The Rigidity of Underlying Blockchain Technology Leads to High Costs for Rule Modifications

The token economy relies on blockchain technology and operates in a decentralized manner. In this system, developers play a crucial role—not only as implementers of technology but also as rule makers. They encode rules into smart contracts, which are then strictly executed by the blockchain in an automated manner. This mechanism ensures that transactions in the token economy, as well as interactions and circulation capabilities, are highly transparent, reducing human intervention and prediction errors.

However, although community members can theoretically adjust rules through voting mechanisms, actual operations remain challenging due to the decentralized nature of blockchain. Once a rule is encoded into a smart contract, modifying it requires not only the reuse of complex technology but also incurs high costs. This makes it difficult to modify initially designed rules, which often leads to increased rigidity in practice.

While the design of rule modification aims to ensure system stability and predictability, it simultaneously results in the power to set rules being largely controlled by developers. This type of power structure does not weaken the core concept of decentralization but may instead lead to the virtualization of power and new forms of centralization. In such an environment, having control over the key technology and knowledge behind rule-making becomes extremely important. Additionally, this model may create situations where there is either no legitimate authorization or insufficient community oversight, allowing developers to dominate public affairs. This results in a "recentralization of governance," where a small group of technical elites may have a disproportionate influence over the entire system's implementation.

Furthermore, this model may cause community members to feel marginalized because they lack a sense of control over the platform they are participating in. This not only contradicts the fundamental principle of blockchain technology, which aims to promote openness and enhance participation, but also risks creating dissatisfaction and conflicts within the community, further impacting the platform's stability and development. Therefore, finding a balance between the innovative authority of developers and the participatory rights of community members is crucial to ensuring the sustainable development of the token economy.

7.1.14 Regulatory Lag May Trigger New Risks

Financial technology is redefining the boundaries and operational models of the financial industry through innovation. As an emerging financial technology-driven economic model, the token economy, with its unique business model, processes, and products, has a disruptive impact on traditional financial services. This new financial paradigm not only enhances efficiency and accessibility but also reduces transaction costs, attracting widespread industry attention. Given the rise of such a financial model, it is crucial to explore its development patterns, balance financial technology innovation with security, and promptly identify and mitigate potential financial risks.

The token economy is built on blockchain technology, which is characterized by decentralization, immutability, and pseudonymity. This provides a more efficient and secure alternative to traditional financial transaction systems. blockchain enhances information transmission, transaction speed, and data security in ways that traditional financial systems cannot match. However, blockchain technology is not infallible. When technical flaws or design errors arise in a blockchain-based token economy, they are difficult to correct due to the lack of centralized oversight. The absence of a central authority to intervene exacerbates the rapid spread of risks, making remediation more costly. This increases the likelihood of systemic financial risks, thereby threatening overall financial stability.

During the early development stages of the token economy, a lack of operational and regulatory experience presents significant challenges for regulators. Over regulation may stifle innovation and market activity, hindering the development of the token economy, while insufficient regulation may lead to market failures and increased financial risks. Therefore, establishing a regulatory strategy that fosters healthy token economy development while ensuring overall financial security has become an urgent and complex task. Regulation must remain flexible to adapt to constantly evolving market conditions and technological advancements. It must protect investors while also promoting innovation and maintaining market competitiveness.

The token economy is an important branch of financial technology, with promising prospects for development. However, it also presents numerous challenges. We must understand and manage the potential risks inherent in this new economic model. Through rational regulation and technological innovation, we can expand the accessibility of financial services and ensure more efficient market operations. This is not just a matter of technology or market adaptation but also a responsibility of regulators and policymakers.

The token economy allows global investors to participate in issuance and transactions. However, as the global regulatory framework is still in its early stages, apart from a few countries like the U.S., there are limited legal precedents and enforcement cases for handling violations. This regulatory gap may lead issuers and investors to inadvertently violate local laws. For example, according to U.S. federal law, private securities offerings in the U.S. must undergo data collection, analysis, and filing via the EDGAR system of the Securities and Exchange Commission (SEC). However, among 14 cases labeled as private securities issuances, only five were properly registered. Given the leading position of the U.S. in securities law and enforcement, legal violations in other countries or regions may be even more severe.

In practical contractual terms, the token economy also presents latent risks. Many tokenized products lack clear mechanisms to determine whether issuers should distribute dividends or interest and to ensure fair valuation and due diligence of underlying assets. Some future cash-flow-backed ABS (Asset-Backed Securities) products do not establish Special Purpose Vehicles (SPV). This may result in a lack of separation between asset revenues and issuer liquidity, leading to potential bankruptcy risks for investors. Additionally, products based on alternative assets, such as artworks or gold-backed assets, often face valuation challenges, increasing investor exposure to risk.

Regulatory arbitrage occurs when entities exploit loopholes or inconsistencies in different legal jurisdictions to gain unfair advantages. In the REITs (Real Estate Investment Trusts) sector, the issuance market imposes strict conditions on issuers, requiring clear asset classification and strict investor eligibility requirements. However, some tokenized assets may borrow the terminology and transaction structure of REITs while not adhering to their strict issuance conditions. This could lead to regulatory scrutiny and legal risks.

ReitBZ, issued by BTGPactual, the largest investment bank in Latin America, in May 2019, is an example of a tokenized investment tool. Its underlying assets consist of a portfolio of real estate investments in Brazil. ReitBZ shares some similarities with traditional REITs, such as allowing investors to purchase and hold fractional ownership in real estate investments. This process transforms relatively illiquid real estate assets into tradable financial products, thereby enhancing asset liquidity. However, ReitBZ differs significantly from traditional REITs in aspects such as investor rights, dividend distribution, intermediary operations, and investor protection mechanisms. These differences may introduce regulatory compliance risks.

When examining the differences between ReitBZ and traditional REITs, four key aspects merit detailed analysis: investment objectives, dividend structure, intermediary role, and investor protection mechanisms. Understanding these distinctions helps clarify the unique characteristics of these two investment instruments and their respective market demands.

In terms of investment objectives, traditional REITs typically focus on commercial properties, residential buildings, healthcare facilities, and industrial parks—assets that are strategically located, have stable operations, and can provide investors with steady income. In contrast, ReitBZ's target assets are Brazil's "distressed real estate". These properties often include low-value assets with poor liquidity, which owners sell due to financial difficulties, legal disputes, or unfavorable market conditions. Such assets are generally considered higher-risk investments compared to standard REIT assets, but they may also offer higher returns, thereby attracting a segment of investors willing to take on additional risk. ReitBZ strategically focuses on properties in low-income urban areas, aiming to enhance the value of these distressed assets through active management and market operations.

Regarding the dividend structure, most traditional REITs are legally required in many jurisdictions to distribute a substantial portion of their income as dividends to investors. This regulation ensures that investors receive predictable and stable cash flows. Additionally, many REITs offer tax advantages, such as exemptions or reduced taxation, making them even more attractive to investors. In contrast, ReitBZ does mention dividend distributions in its prospectus, but the structure is loosely defined, and dividends are distributed on a discretionary basis. This uncertainty in cash flow distribution could introduce instability for investors seeking consistent returns.

In terms of the role of intermediaries, traditional REITs rely on a network of financial and real estate management professionals, including fund custodians, fund managers, and property managers, to ensure professional investment management and regulatory compliance. ReitBZ, however, leverages blockchain technology, particularly smart contracts, to automate certain intermediary functions, such as fund custodianship. This approach reduces operational costs and improves efficiency. However, this model requires investors to have a certain level of understanding of blockchain technology to effectively participate in this new investment approach.

In traditional REIT markets, investors are categorized into publicly traded REITs and private REITs, with clear investment thresholds based on investor qualifications and financial standing. Publicly traded REITs are typically accessible to general investors, whereas private REITs are usually restricted to institutional and accredited investors. ReitBZ, in contrast, places higher technical barriers for investors, requiring them to understand blockchain operations and assess related technology and market risks. Additionally, ReitBZ implements KYC (Know Your Customer) and AML (Anti-Money Laundering) policies to ensure the legal compliance and financial security of its investors.

In summary, ReitBZ and traditional REITs differ significantly in their investment objectives, dividend structure, intermediary roles, and investor restrictions. These differences make ReitBZ more suitable for tech-savvy investors who are comfortable taking higher risks in exchange for potentially higher returns, whereas traditional REITs are better suited for mainstream investors seeking stable returns and lower-risk exposure.

7.2 RWA and Tokenization Risk Management Strategies

Blockchain technology and tokenized economies fundamentally aim to address challenges in both the real world and the digital realm, granting individuals greater autonomy. Despite being in its early stages, like all pioneering technologies, it has two aspects: it brings about social and economic progress while also posing risks of misuse. When multiple technologies converge, these risks may not be immediately apparent, but they can have severe consequences. Humanity must not only accept and bear risks but also actively identify and manage them. As society and technology progress, our ability to detect and regulate risks should develop in parallel. This ability does not emerge naturally but requires continuous exploration and refinement. For blockchain and token economy risk management, the following principles should be followed: In market transactions, clear rules and potential incentives should be defined, using strict, unbiased technologies to encourage integrity and limit fraudulent behaviors. Honest participants should benefit from compliance, while dishonest ones should face appropriate restrictions.

Risk management is key to accurately predicting risks, reducing the accumulation of risk factors ("governance"), and eliminating potential trigger points that may lead to sudden financial crises ("control").

7.2.1 Risk Management Theory in Token Economies

As an innovative economic paradigm, token economies are developing rapidly, but at the same time, various latent risks are gradually becoming evident. At this critical moment, timely identification, evaluation, and analysis of these risks, along with the implementation of effective countermeasures, are crucial for the long-term sustainability of token economies.

7.2.2 Internal Risk Management Approaches

Financial risk internal management is crucial for token economy projects. To ensure the healthy development and lasting competitiveness of a project, project owners must proactively identify and effectively manage various potential risks. In this process, adopting self-regulatory management measures becomes critical. First, projects must establish and adhere to industry self-regulatory standards, ensuring that all operations are conducted within legal and ethical frameworks. Additionally, establishing a comprehensive management system and mechanisms is essential, including risk assessment mechanisms, internal auditing procedures, and crisis response strategies. Through the implementation of these necessary commitments and concrete management strategies, token economy projects can operate in a dynamic market environment while ensuring investor protection and fostering the healthy development of the entire industry.

In token economies, the issuance of tokens is often based on the value of tangible assets. While this approach provides an initial value foundation for tokens, the stability and realization of market value are highly susceptible to price volatility and risks. Therefore, ensuring that the market price of tokens aligns with their actual value becomes critical. For payment-type tokens, some countries have begun recognizing cryptocurrency as a legitimate means of payment and have established regulatory frameworks to enhance market accessibility and stability. Although China has previously banned digital currency holding and trading, with the growth of international markets and advancements in domestic technology, it is expected that payment-type tokens may gain legal recognition in the country in the future. Additionally, the value of asset-backed tokens primarily depends on their underlying sources. These tokens typically represent specific ownership or income rights, meaning their valuation is closely tied to the realization of those rights, resulting in relatively high price uncertainty. For asset-based tokens, such as those representing stocks or bonds, their price is relatively easier to determine, leading to greater appreciation potential. However, for art-based assets like paintings, the realization of value may depend heavily on market speculation, increasing the risk of price inflation and deviation from their actual value, which could lead to broader credit issues.

In a token economy, fragmenting ownership into blockchain-based tokens is an innovative asset management approach that significantly improves asset liquidity. For example, tokenizing real estate into fractional ownership allows each share to function as an independent property right while providing investors with opportunities for market circulation and potential value appreciation. This increased liquidity not only promotes economic vitality but also accelerates financial innovation and development.

However, fragmented ownership is rarely convertible back into tangible assets, meaning that the value of tokens depends entirely on real-world transactions to materialize appreciation. For investors, liquidity equates to the ability to realize asset value. Under such a framework, most tokens cannot directly be converted into tangible property or dividends but rather rely on market transactions for appreciation. Consequently, the primary function of token economies lies in strengthening liquidity rather than facilitating real-world asset exchange.

The critical reason for the weakening of the exchange function is that if everyone attempts to simultaneously exchange tokens for physical assets, it may trigger a liquidity crisis, thereby destabilizing the entire economic system. Strengthening liquidity functionality can promote the free trade of tokens in the market, enhance asset liquidity, and prevent excessive demand for exchange, which could lead to potential speculative risks. This strategy not only protects investor interests but also ensures the stable operation of the token economy system.

In conclusion, the development of the token economy should focus on how to enhance asset circulation through an effective market mechanism, increase asset appreciation potential, and ensure efficiency and security in transactions through technology and regulatory measures. By doing so, the token economy can achieve sustainable development while bringing more opportunities and benefits to investors and the broader economic system.

In the token economy, the design and implementation of incentive mechanisms are crucial, as they directly impact the activity and sustainable development of an economic community. Effective incentive mechanisms encourage community members to make meaningful contributions while maintaining the overall stability and growth of projects.

Firstly, an incentive mechanism must align with the long-term goals and core values of a project. This means that incentives should be designed to motivate and mobilize community members, increase user engagement, and promote valuable project-related activities. For instance, rewarding users who contribute content or positively impact the community can encourage broader participation.

Furthermore, the incentive mechanism should be transparent on the platform. Community members must clearly understand what actions will be rewarded, how rewards are determined, and how they can fairly obtain these rewards. This transparency prevents excessive abuse of incentives and reduces the occurrence of fraud and unfair practices.

Additionally, incentive mechanisms should avoid being overly simplistic and solely outcome-driven to prevent community members from engaging only in short-term speculation. Instead, they should prioritize the long-term benefits and sustainable development of the community. A well-designed incentive system should encourage diverse contributions, fostering a more balanced, innovative, and inclusive participation environment.

At the same time, the incentive mechanism should also possess self-adjustment capabilities. As the community grows and the market environment evolves, the incentive methods and standards should be adjusted accordingly. This flexibility ensures that the incentive mechanism can continuously and effectively support the development of the community rather than becoming a hindrance.

Finally, strengthening the supervision and feedback mechanisms of the incentive system is also crucial. Periodic evaluations should be conducted to assess the effectiveness of the incentive mechanism, collect community feedback, and continuously optimize it. This ongoing evaluation and adjustment process ensures that the incentive mechanism remains effective not only in the initial stages but also continues to exert a positive impact over time.

Building a long-term effective incentive mechanism requires a comprehensive consideration of factors such as motivation objectives, fairness, diversity, flexibility, and sustainability. A well-designed incentive mechanism will not only attract and retain active community members but also ensure that the project itself maintains its competitive edge and innovation capabilities in a constantly evolving market.

7.2.3 External Management Methodology

External management of financial risks refers to the risk management measures implemented by external institutions and organizations beyond the core participants of a tokenized economy project. To effectively carry out external risk management, governments should establish and refine legal and regulatory frameworks, and maintain clear oversight and market constraints to uphold market stability and transparency. Regulators play a crucial role in this process. They are not only responsible for developing reasonable regulatory measures but also for providing effective market protection mechanisms. This includes setting up emergency response measures and risk mitigation strategies to address potential market failures and instability factors.

To reduce maintenance costs, enhance system transparency and fairness, and promote open-source platforms as a trend, the tokenized economy should incorporate participatory governance, where the platform and its users share decision-making responsibilities. This means that platform rules should not be determined solely by developers. By involving regulators in co-developing rules, not only can user rights be better protected, but effective oversight can also be implemented at the foundational level, ensuring that all operations comply with legal and ethical frameworks.

The establishment of open-source governance in the tokenized economy is a key regulatory approach. Through open-source mechanisms, regulators can participate in the entire process of defining and executing smart contracts in real time, ensuring transparency throughout. This significantly reduces the likelihood of fraud and unfair practices. At the same time, community participation in rule-making ensures the democratic and rational nature of governance, making the platform more aligned with the expectations and needs of all stakeholders.

Currently, there is still ample room for improvement in China's regulatory policies for the tokenized economy. With the rapid development of tokenized markets, many high-risk speculative projects have emerged, and their disorderly expansion has not only disrupted market stability but also posed significant risks to investors. Therefore, regulators need to participate in platform design and logic from the outset, implementing real-time supervision and dynamic regulatory adjustments to enhance the completeness of the regulatory framework, ensuring the healthy and orderly development of the tokenized economy.

At present, blockchain technology, as an innovative information technology, has attracted widespread attention globally and is experiencing rapid growth. However, this process is far from mature and is still in the stage of continuous exploration and adjustment. The tokenized economy, as a novel economic paradigm based on blockchain technology, faces numerous challenges and risks in its rapid expansion. The advancement of new technology and economic models often outpaces the development of existing legal regulations and policy frameworks, making it challenging for government regulators to adapt to the rapidly changing market environment.

Government regulators play a crucial role in balancing technological development. Excessively strict regulations may stifle innovation and technological applications, thereby hindering further economic progress. Conversely, overly lax regulations may lead to market disorder, risk accumulation, or even systemic financial risks, causing significant harm to the economy and society. Therefore, regulators must strike a balance between promoting innovation and mitigating risks.

To effectively address these challenges, regulators and industry self-regulatory organizations must work together, integrating hard laws with flexible regulatory measures. This means that while establishing necessary legal norms to ensure market compliance, industry participants should also be encouraged to adopt self-regulatory practices for more effective governance. Additionally, regulators should closely monitor the rapid evolution of new technologies to detect potential risks early, formulate proactive response strategies, and establish predictive risk assessment mechanisms, enabling effective preemptive control before risks escalate.

At the same time, relevant government departments should promptly introduce regulatory policies that are tailored to the characteristics of the emerging economy. These policies should fully consider the nature and development trends of the tokenized economy, ensuring a balance between preventing excessive speculation and promoting legal innovation. By implementing these measures, the government can effectively facilitate the standardized development of the tokenized economy, ensuring its healthy and sustainable growth. This dynamic and forward-thinking regulatory strategy will help governments maintain a leading position in global economic competition while protecting consumer rights and interests and maintaining market stability.

7.2.4 Conclusion

The token economy not only accelerates asset circulation through asset fractionalization and the application of blockchain technology but also ensures the fairness and transparency of transactions via smart contracts, significantly reducing transaction costs. This economic model achieves universal benefit by distributing ownership on the chain, allowing more people to participate in the market. At the same time, the public and transparent nature of distributed ledgers ensures that information can be widely shared, which is one of the key advantages of the token economy.

However, the rapid development of the token economy also brings numerous risks, such as regulatory gaps, market speculation, and technological security concerns. Therefore, ensuring the healthy development of the token economy while identifying and managing these risks is of utmost importance. Risk control and the implementation of effective risk management strategies are crucial for its long-term sustainability.

At present, the token economy is still growing at a rapid pace, and regulatory policies are continuously being refined. Although regulators face many challenges and risks, they all follow the general principle of financial technology development. In China, regulatory measures for this new economic model have been relatively inclusive and moderate. This flexible regulatory approach allows the market a certain degree of freedom to explore while enabling regulators to continuously learn and adapt to new developments to formulate more reasonable policies.

In this process, regulatory authorities need to remain proactive, strengthen alignment with international standards, and learn from successful international regulatory experiences. At the same time, they must consider the actual conditions of the domestic market. By implementing scientific risk assessment and regulatory strategies, they can better promote the healthy development of the token economy and prevent systematic financial risks.

Additionally, strengthening public education and understanding of the token economy is essential. Popularizing basic knowledge of blockchain and the token economy can help investors make more informed decisions and enhance their awareness of the risks associated with the token economy, enabling them to better protect themselves and contribute to a healthier and more stable market environment.

In conclusion, the development of the token economy requires not only technological innovation and market vitality but also robust regulation and public education. These factors must work together to ensure that the token economy matures and stabilizes in the future.

7.2.5 Risk Management Strategy One: Utilizing Corporate Governance Mechanisms to Facilitate the Circulation of Rights and Tokens

The token economy provides a resource allocation mechanism different from traditional corporations. It has the potential to break the limitations imposed by a small number of controlling entities, allowing a broader group of participants to share the benefits brought by the token economy. To some extent, we can view the incentive mechanisms of tokenization as an innovative corporate governance approach and leverage governance practices to address risk control issues. Although various rights and assets can theoretically circulate on blockchain networks through tokenization, the differences in the nature of rights associated with tokens may create barriers during circulation. This results in a clear divide between the token economy in the digital world and the real-world economy. To resolve this issue, it is recommended that corporate governance mechanisms be used to promote the integration of the token economy with the real world.

Although, in theory, tokenization technology can be applied to almost any rights-based asset, not all rights-based assets are suitable for tokenization. Tokenization is not merely a marketing tool for commercial goods. In blockchain networks, just like in the real world, the value of an item must be widely recognized to be realized. For goods that hold value only within a specific location or context, their value is built on local perceptions, limiting their liquidity in both the real and digital worlds. Therefore, expecting such goods to achieve widespread circulation and value appreciation through tokenization may not be realistic.

Ultimately, the value of a product must be verified by the market, and its competitiveness is determined by market supply and demand relationships. In simple terms, tokenization is not a guarantee of liquidity and appreciation. The fundamental attributes and market positioning of a product largely determine its value.

The granularity of tokenization can theoretically be refined, but there should be a distinction when holders seek to realize their rights. As mentioned earlier, whether the asset is real estate or intellectual property, tokens can be viewed as divisible units used for liquidity. This approach enables more individuals to hold tokens, and broader participation helps drive liquidity and appreciation—this is the true meaning of tokenization, rather than simply exchanging tokens for actual rights.

In corporate governance, the distinction between major and minor shareholders regarding corporate rights and interests can also apply to the token economy. Those who hold small-denomination tokens can be seen as minor shareholders. Although minor shareholders may not have the right to demand the realization of token-based rights, they do share similar profit distribution, residual claim rights, and benefits from equity appreciation. According to *Article 104 of the Company Law of the People's Republic of China*, minor shareholders can participate in joint decision-making with major shareholders regarding asset transfers and earnings distribution, even though the exercise of rights typically remains in the hands of major shareholders.

In the token economy, there is no strict distinction between "major" and "minor" token holders—all token holders can participate in decision-making on whether tokens can be exchanged for actual property rights. Large-denomination token holders may have a greater impact when their tokens correspond to tangible assets. However, for small-denomination token holders, the practical meaning of converting tokens into actual rights may be minimal; instead, they may focus more on the income generated from token circulation.

When designing token issuance and allocation mechanisms, token economy platform developers must clearly distinguish tokens representing different rights. The design of individual tokens should carefully consider the transferability of rights. Particularly, when a token represents only part of an asset rather than a complete right, it must be clearly defined whether it can be exchanged for actual ownership. This means that different token types should adopt different exchange strategies based on their inherent functions.

For those primarily concerned with whether tokens can generate returns through circulation, tokens serve as symbolic assets. Although the value of tokens is based on the rights they represent, during circulation, tokens and the actual value of the corresponding rights may become disconnected (Fig. 7.1). In such cases, tokens can be designed not to be exchanged for specific rights but only to serve as profit-sharing symbols (e.g., dividends).

However, for those committed to promoting transactions on token economy platforms and ensuring that the rights associated with transactions can be realized through tokenization, even if tokens appreciate in value during circulation, clear conditions should be established for allowing tokens to be exchanged for tangible rights. By doing so, token issuers can prevent token economy platforms from turning into mere speculative marketplaces, ensuring that token economies not only reflect the value of the real world but also maintain a direct connection with it. Whether the goal is to realize income rights or convert tokens into actual ownership rights, issuers must clearly define the issuance and allocation rules during the design phase. At the same time, regulatory authorities must conduct audits and oversight to ensure the healthy and sustainable development of the token economy.

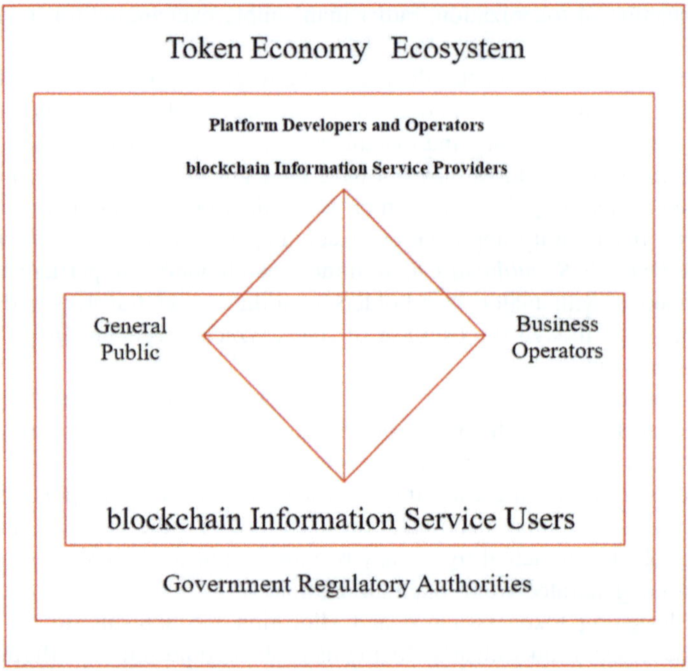

Fig. 7.1 Participants and stakeholders in a token economy platform

7.2.6 Risk Control Strategy Two: Strengthening Incentives for Honest Behavior and Preventing Dishonest Gains

The incentive mechanism in the token economy is designed to allocate rewards based on rational principles, ensuring that individuals who contribute to the platform receive appropriate token rewards. A well-designed incentive mechanism should not only identify and reward high-quality behavior or content on the platform but also effectively avoid actions taken solely for the sake of obtaining rewards. However, in practical operations, incentive mechanisms may sometimes lead participants to exploit dishonest behavior for personal gain. Regardless of whether the designers of the incentive mechanism are platform participants, they may overlook the true meaning of "contribution." A genuine contribution should be about recognizing and supporting quality businesses or projects on the platform, rather than simply selecting economic actors or projects based on superficial criteria.

To prevent participants from exploiting dishonest behavior for personal gain, developers of token economy platforms and government regulatory authorities must take appropriate measures. Developers need to continuously optimize incentive mechanisms to ensure that rewards align with genuine contributions. Meanwhile, regulatory authorities need to strengthen oversight of platform activities to ensure the fairness and transparency of incentive mechanisms.

When designing incentive mechanisms, economic platform developers should ensure that they align with the commercial behaviors of operators or projects. However, any rule design may have loopholes, leading participants to engage in behaviors solely to obtain rewards. To address this issue, developers can set certain "thresholds" for incentive behaviors, but these thresholds should be based on user actions rather than qualifications. Additionally, the value of tokens stems from the rights they represent, so incentive mechanisms should target commercial behaviors that generate actual value. Such mechanisms encourage beneficial behaviors and naturally reduce the profit opportunities for non-credible behaviors. Developers must clearly define which commercial behaviors are worth incentives and the corresponding reward amounts, ensuring that the rewards are attractive enough to users while avoiding excessive rewards that could lead to arbitrage.

When designing distribution rules, developers should encourage broad participation from platform users to ensure the transparency and fairness of the rules. This not only enhances user trust but also promotes the healthy development of the platform.

Government regulatory authorities must avoid relying solely on user evaluations to prevent non-credible behaviors from profiting. Instead, they should use more comprehensive and in-depth methods to assess operators' credibility. Since blockchain technology, as a community technology, profoundly impacts society by altering production relations, traditional regulatory concepts may no longer be fully applicable in the blockchain field. Regulation should be legal and practical, achieving the goals of improving market performance and maintaining social justice.

Token economics builds communities with a high sense of identity through incentive mechanisms. To some extent, the rules governing these communities realize the ultimate value ideal of "self-incentivizing legal systems." The self-incentivizing concept of token economics is inherently positive, but issues may arise from the cumulative effects of user behaviors driven by economic interests.

In addition to continuously revising and improving rules, regulatory authorities should leverage the comprehensive transaction data on blockchain-distributed platforms to conduct more accurate supervision and evaluation of operators. Distributed ledger technology provides regulatory conditions and data support, facilitating more effective oversight.

7.2.7 Risk Control Strategy Three: Utilizing Open-Source Regulation to Break Developers' Rule Monopoly

Token economics combines the concepts of autonomy and exclusivity, emphasizing the realization of individual interests and the sharing of collective benefits. After moving beyond the initial stages of "coin issuance" and "coin speculation," the sustained rapid development of token economics is mainly due to strong national support for technological innovation, with legal incentive mechanisms widely applied across various fields of technology and economic development.

The intrinsic development philosophy of token economics is inherently positive and deserves encouragement. As regulators, governments should fully recognize the positive impact of token economics in reshaping interpersonal relationships and guiding behavioral patterns. However, if token economics platform developers use technical means to implement governance rules and consolidate their rule monopoly through economic incentives, operators and consumers on the platform could be disadvantaged. In the token economics ecosystem where smart contracts are automatically executed, regulatory authorities must effectively oversee the open-source ecosystem, break developers' rule monopoly, promote fair competition, and protect consumer rights.

Open-source regulation is an emerging regulatory model where government regulatory authorities participate in the open-source ecosystem of blockchain, leveraging the public, complete, and immutable characteristics of blockchain technology and traceable distributed ledgers for real-time oversight. This regulatory approach allows regulated entities to conduct economic activities within a legal and compliant framework while ensuring transparency and efficiency in regulation. The core of open-source regulation lies in using technological means to achieve more effective oversight. This regulatory method helps governments better understand and support the operation of token economics but also reflects the consensus reached between various participants in the token economics ecosystem and regulatory authorities, gaining government support. With blockchain technology backing, governments will find it easier to fulfill their supervisory functions.

In implementing open-source regulation, regulatory authorities must first shift their regulatory philosophy. The traditional punitive regulatory model should gradually transition to a model dominated by legal incentive mechanisms. The bidirectional operation of incentive mechanisms can achieve regulatory goals with minimal resistance, quick results, and maximum feasibility. Additionally, the functionalist style in public law aligns with contemporary legal experiences and can mutually reinforce the incentive mechanisms of token economics, working together effectively. The regulatory philosophy dominated by legal incentive mechanisms is essentially a way for regulatory authorities to help token economics communities achieve self-governance. This strategy saves administrative costs and manifests open and progressive governance wisdom, preventing regulatory authorities from becoming stagnant and enabling more effective governance.

Regulatory authorities can address potential rule monopoly issues among token economics developers through open-source regulation by First Participating in the Rule-Making Process. As essential participants in token economics platforms, regulatory authorities can engage in the early stages of developers' incentive rule formulation. Although the technical expertise required for smart contract code may make direct oversight challenging, early intervention before rules are converted into smart contract code can prevent developers from forming monopolies. Secondly, Real-Time Monitoring of Operations: Using distributed ledger technology, regulatory authorities can view all behavioral records within the token economics ecosystem in real-time, overseeing the performance of developers' rules in practice. This real-time oversight helps prevent developers from establishing monopolistic positions.

It is important to note that regulatory authorities' open-source regulation of the token economics ecosystem aims to ensure that all participants can conduct transactions in a secure environment and achieve healthy development within the legal framework. This regulation is not an arbitrary intervention by administrative power over the autonomy of civil entities but a necessary measure to maintain market order and protect consumer rights.

7.3 Global Practice of Tokenization Technology Regulatory Sandbox

Token technology offers advantages such as tamper resistance, strong reliability, and the ability to execute automatically with smart contracts, making it the technical prototype of the next generation of financial infrastructure. However, token financial infrastructure is inherently based on a decentralized organizational structure, which will subject it to triple challenges in technology, governance, and regulation.

To promote the innovative development of token technology in financial fields such as payments, clearing, settlement, and digital asset trading, balance the relationship between risk prevention and technological innovation, and enhance financial regulatory efficiency, regulatory agencies should reform regulatory concepts, innovate regulatory methods, and provide standardized technical and legal frameworks to ensure that token financial infrastructure develops in a more standardized, reliable, and stable manner. The construction of token financial infrastructure involves changes in financial business models, adjustments in departmental structures, and responses to new risks, necessitating the revision of relevant laws and regulations and the establishment of targeted regulatory governance frameworks. When building governance mechanisms, regulatory agencies should balance the dual goals of promoting fintech development and effectively preventing financial risks.

7.3.1 Concept and Principles of Global Tokenization Technology Sandbox Regulation

7.3.1.1 Concept of Sandbox Regulation

With the global development and widespread adoption of tokenization technology, it has become an essential component of the fintech sector. Faced with the challenges and opportunities brought by this emerging technology, regulatory agencies must adopt innovative regulatory methods to ensure the market's healthy development and effective risk management. Sandbox regulation, as a flexible regulatory framework, provides an ideal environment for the testing and iteration of tokenization technology.

Sandbox regulation, also known as a regulatory sandbox, is a specific regulatory framework that allows fintech companies to test innovative financial products, services, or business models in a controlled environment. This regulatory approach enables companies to test new technologies in actual market conditions while ensuring that regulatory agencies can promptly stay informed about technological developments and adjust regulatory strategies.

The main advantages of sandbox regulation lie in its ability to promote innovation, control risks, quickly respond to market and technological changes, and enhance industry transparency. Sandbox regulation provides a safe space for developers of tokenization technology to experiment and innovate and alleviates their concerns about immediately facing stringent regulatory constraints.

At the same time, through the regulatory sandbox, regulatory agencies can better understand the operational mechanisms and potential risks of new technologies, thereby formulating more precise and effective regulatory measures.

Globally, many countries and regions (such as the UK, Singapore, and Hong Kong, China) have already implemented sandbox regulations to address the rapid development of tokenization and other fintech. Regulatory agencies in these regions have successfully run multiple projects within the sandbox environment, providing valuable practical experience for other countries.

However, implementing sandbox regulation also faces numerous challenges, such as balancing promoting innovation with protecting consumer rights and handling data protection issues. Additionally, since tokenization technology often has cross-border characteristics, international regulatory cooperation has become a key factor in ensuring the effectiveness of sandbox regulation.

Sandbox regulation provides an innovative path for global tokenization technology's safe, effective, and sustainable development. Regulatory agencies must continuously evaluate and refine sandbox policies to adapt to changing technological and market environments, thereby promoting technological innovation and the modernization of financial services while ensuring regulatory compliance.

7.3.1.2 Experimental Sandbox Regulation

Experimental sandbox regulation is different from traditional "command and control" regulation. This method emphasizes continuous and in-depth evaluation of regulatory effectiveness during the regulatory process and flexibly adjusts and optimizes regulatory measures based on these evaluations. Compared to traditional financial infrastructure, the business model of token financial infrastructure, as an emerging entity, is not yet clear. Some aspects, such as business processes and responsible entities, are still being explored, with no mature regulatory system. Therefore, the regulation of token financial infrastructure should adopt a "learn-as-you-regulate" strategy.

From a practical perspective, the sandbox regulation introduced by the UK is a typical example of experimental regulatory concepts. Regulatory agencies need to deeply understand the operational mechanisms of token financial infrastructure, providing regulatory guidance while remaining flexible in adjusting regulatory strategies. For example, regulatory agencies should study embedded regulation methods and develop appropriate regulatory rules for developers, operators, and related service providers of token financial infrastructure.

7.3.1.3 Functional Sandbox Regulation

The core concept of functional sandbox regulation is to apply the same regulatory standards to the same risks. Financial regulators in the United States primarily adopt a functional regulation strategy, classifying and regulating token financial infrastructure based on the substance of their business activities. Australian financial regulators share this view, believing that regulatory requirements should be based on the substance of the business rather than the type of institution. European Union financial regulators follow the principle of proportionality in token financial regulation, determining corresponding regulatory requirements based on the size and importance of the risks associated with the business.

Token network service providers, such as big data companies, cloud computing platforms, and algorithm design firms, provide technical support, maintain platform stability, and facilitate transactions. They do not perform the credit enhancement functions traditionally associated with financial intermediaries. Therefore, applying traditional regulatory models that require registered capital and licensing to these service providers may not be appropriate. Instead, based on their risk control capabilities, they can be required to fulfill obligations such as monitoring and reporting abnormal transactions and self-inspecting and correcting algorithm vulnerabilities.

7.3.1.4 Coordinated Sandbox Regulation

In regulating token financial infrastructure, it is necessary to go beyond single-sector regulation and achieve cross-sector coordination. The United States has strengthened the Federal Reserve's macroprudential regulatory functions by integrating existing financial infrastructure operating rules and regulatory frameworks, such as the enactment of the *Dodd-Frank Act*. This coordination is reflected in the Federal Reserve's collaboration with the Securities and Exchange Commission (SEC) and the Commodity Futures Trading Commission (CFTC) to develop risk management standards and enhance information sharing jointly.

In the United Kingdom, the *Financial Services Act 2012* centralized the regulatory authority for financial infrastructure within the Bank of England. The Bank of England further clarified its macro and macroprudential regulatory powers over financial infrastructure in its 2013 publication, "*The Bank of England's Approach to Regulating Financial Infrastructure*." These practices provide valuable references for the regulation of token financial infrastructure. In regulating token financial infrastructure, it may be considered to have the central bank uniformly perform regulatory functions or maintain a sectoral regulatory model while endowing the central bank with macroprudential regulatory powers to ensure effective coordination in regulatory standard setting and information sharing.

7.3.1.5 Cooperative Regulation

The technological innovation and diversity of business models in token financial infrastructure require regulatory agencies to continuously improve their regulatory techniques and strategies to maintain adaptability and flexibility, keeping pace with the rapid development of token technology. However, due to their public nature, traditional financial regulatory agencies may have limitations in creativity and flexibility. At the same time, financial regulation primarily focuses on risk prevention, and the decision-making process is subject to strict constraints and public scrutiny, making it difficult for regulatory measures to adapt to the rapid development of fintech quickly. Additionally, the compensation systems of regulatory departments are constrained by government budgets, leading to a talent shortage in developing and applying regulatory technologies.

To address these issues, regulatory agencies can consider purchasing services from private institutions such as algorithm auditing firms and big data companies to provide technical support. Furthermore, regulatory authorities can encourage industry associations (e.g., banking associations, securities associations) to include fintech firms and promptly formulate and update industry self-regulatory rules to enhance regulatory flexibility. Overall, in the regulation of token financial infrastructure, a public–private cooperative regulatory model can be adopted, establishing a regulatory system led by regulatory authorities with the participation of private enterprises and industry associations.

7.3.2 Innovation in Global Tokenization Technology Sandbox Regulation

7.3.2.1 Adoption of Regulatory Technology (RegTech)

Regulatory technology (RegTech) refers to technological means, including big data, cloud computing, and artificial intelligence (AI), to improve regulatory efficiency and identify and prevent risks. Internationally, the "*Fintech Regulatory Framework*" white paper released by the U.S. National Economic Council (NEC) demonstrates the United States' proactive attitude in advancing the application of AI and big data in securities market regulation. The UK emphasizes interaction between regulatory agencies and financial institutions to promote RegTech's development jointly. The UK Financial Conduct Authority (FCA) is considering converting regulatory rules into machine language to automate regulatory processes, enabling A to enforce regulatory requirements automatically.

Given that token financial infrastructure has enhanced the automation and digitization of financial business processes, exploring big data, cloud computing, and AI to identify potential technical vulnerabilities, alert, and track…Monitoring abnormal transactions becomes particularly important. As relevant technical and regulatory standards are further unified, using regulatory technology (RegTech) to assist in regulation is feasible and helps promote regulatory convergence.

7.3.2.2 Algorithm Auditing

In token finance, algorithm auditing is a critical regulatory tool. It involves reviewing token codes to identify logical vulnerabilities in encryption algorithms and smart contracts. Algorithm auditing can help assess token networks' risks, including hacker attacks, personal information leaks, property losses, fraudulent transactions, terrorist financing, and money laundering.

Internationally, the European Union has recognized algorithm auditing as essential for practical fintech regulation. In April 2019, the European Parliament released the "*Governance Framework for Algorithmic Accountability and Transparency*," emphasizing the importance of algorithm auditing. It believes that algorithm auditing can prevent and correct errors and enhance regulators' understanding of algorithm logic, supporting post-event accountability.

Since the operation of token financial infrastructure largely depends on algorithms, regulatory agencies should consider algorithm auditing as a key basis and tool for market access and ongoing regulation. When implementing algorithm auditing, regulatory agencies can adopt various methods, including organizing internal token algorithm experts for self-audits, purchasing audit services from third-party technical companies, or requiring token financial infrastructure operators to submit algorithm self-inspection reports. For token financial infrastructure found to have technical or financial system risk hazards, regulatory agencies should require operators to make corrections or, if necessary, deny their entry into the financial services sector.

7.3.2.3 Embedded Regulation

The decentralized nature of token technology requires regulatory approaches to innovate accordingly, adopting embedded regulation to adapt to its unique network structure. Token networks can be further classified into public chains, private chains, etc., based on their degree of centralization and openness. For example, the Bitcoin network, as a representative of public chains, relies on technical rules to establish trust. In this model, each node in the network theoretically has equal rights and status, with no single entity controlling the entire token network, and all nodes follow preset consensus mechanisms to maintain network operations.

However, considering the need for risk control and investor protection in financial markets, completely decentralized regulation in token financial infrastructure is unrealistic. Therefore, providing "access points" for regulatory agencies within the token financial infrastructure is necessary to ensure the system's safe operation.

One possible implementation is to introduce super nodes in token networks. These nodes can serve as regulatory nodes and be granted special management permissions. The management permissions of regulatory nodes should be set based on the needs of macro and micro-prudential regulation, fully considering the specific application scenarios of token financial infrastructure, the maturity of the technology, and the specific requirements of regulatory rules. For example, regulatory nodes can have the authority to monitor financial transactions on tokens, ensuring that monitoring agencies can obtain complete, traceable, and real-time transaction data. In emergencies, regulatory nodes can have temporary authority to decide on system solutions, allowing timely remedial measures when technical risks that may induce fraudulent transactions arise. Additionally, regulatory nodes can have the authority to review and decide on the qualifications of ordinary nodes to participate in financial transactions, taking timely measures against nodes suspected of illegal activities.

7.3.2.4 Unified Technical Standards

The cross-border potential of token financial infrastructure requires unified technical standards for token financial software to promote interoperability and seamless integration between different financial businesses. Unified technical standards can reduce participant costs in system construction and learning while facilitating regulatory intervention. They help avoid multiple interfaces between different token systems, reduce "friction" in intermediate links, enhance financial efficiency, and enable regulatory agencies to implement more effective "penetrative" regulation.

However, mainstream token financial applications differ in programming languages, consensus mechanisms, and data structures. For example, Libra uses the Move language and *Byzantine Fault Tolerance (BFT)* consensus mechanism, while other applications may use the GO language and Proof of Stake(PoS) consensus mechanism.

To address these issues, central banks should unify the technical standards for token financial software, fully considering the functional positioning of token financial infrastructure and balancing decentralization, efficiency, and security.

These technical standards should meet the needs of financial transaction speed, throughput, security, and regulatory intervention.

Regulatory agencies play a crucial role in token financial infrastructure. To ensure the healthy development of technology and safeguard public interests, regulatory agencies need to establish clear standards for technology development, maintenance, and testing.

Token networks undertake critical public functions and are closely related to the rights and interests of financial consumers. Establishing full-process operational standards through administrative intervention can provide additional safeguards for the regular operation of token networks and financial software. Currently, there are some departmental standards related to network and software development, testing, and maintenance, such as the "*Securities and Futures Industry Software Testing Standards*," "*Network Key Equipment Safety Testing Implementation Measures*," and "*Internet Information Security Management System Usage and Operation Maintenance Management Measures (Trial).*"

Based on these existing standards, regulatory authorities should develop a comprehensive set of technical and operational standards that cover the entire pre-event, in-event, and post-event regulation process, considering the technical characteristics and operational models of token financial infrastructure. Such standards will help ensure the stable operation of token financial infrastructure and play a key role in safeguarding financial security and consumer rights.

7.3.2.5 Clear Legal Standards

The operational models of token financial infrastructure differ significantly from traditional financial infrastructure, requiring adaptive adjustments to the relevant legal system to clarify the legal attributes of financial activities and establish corresponding regulatory standards. For example, digital asset trading in the United States has been incorporated into the existing securities regulatory framework. Specifically, in the SEC's "*Statement on Digital Asset Securities Issuance and Trading*," the functional test provided by Rule 3b-16 of the *Securities Exchange Act* is used to assess whether a token network platform meets the definition of an exchange under the *Securities Exchange Act of 1934*. If it does, the network platform must register with the SEC as a national securities exchange unless exempted.

The SEC has also issued the "*Statement on Securities Token Issuance*" to impose regulatory requirements on securities token issuance businesses. It is necessary to determine whether specific tokens fall within the scope of *Hong Kong's securities regulations* based on the definition of "securities" in the Securities and Futures Ordinance. Any institution promoting and distributing securities tokens must obtain a license or registration and comply with relevant codes of conduct.

At the legal level, regulatory agencies must accurately define token financial infrastructure's functions and business substance based on existing regulatory norms and formulate new adaptive regulatory requirements for potential new risks. This includes clarifying the legal attributes of tokens, whether leveraged trading of derivatives based on virtual assets is allowed, and the legal status and specific regulatory requirements of virtual asset exchanges based on token technology, such as licensing requirements, reserve amounts, or insurance systems.

Only with clear legal standards can token financial infrastructure better fulfill compliance obligations, and financial consumers can accurately identify transaction risks and promptly obtain rights relief. Additionally, explicit legal provisions help reduce regulatory competition or gaps between different regulatory departments.

7.3.3 Improvement of Subject Responsibility Attribution

Although token financial infrastructure differs in business form from traditional financial institutions, its core financial attributes, risk attributes, and regulatory needs remain unchanged. Therefore, such infrastructure must follow regulatory rules that match its business substance during operation. If these rules are violated, the company will face legal consequences; if consumers are harmed, the company will also bear civil liability.

Given the differences between the participants in token financial infrastructure and traditional financial institutions, regulatory agencies need to reasonably allocate compliance responsibilities based on the characteristics of token technology and each participant's functions, risk control capabilities, benefit compensation, and fault levels. The main participants in token financial infrastructure construction include:

- Technology Provider: Responsible for the design, development, and maintenance of token networks, providing the technical infrastructure, including algorithm design, cloud computing, and big data services.
- Network Operators: Manage and maintain the regular operation of token networks.
- Application Providers: Provide interfaces for end-users to access token networks.
- Other Stakeholders: Provide auxiliary services like digital wallet services and digital currency trading platforms.

Since a single entity may play multiple roles in token financial infrastructure, different entities may complete different functions, and each participant should bear corresponding compliance obligations based on their functional positioning. For example, in token-based payment and remittance services, digital wallets, due to their payment functions, should accept similar regulations as third-party payment institutions and fulfill compliance obligations such as anti-money laundering (AML) and customer identity verification. Algorithm design companies need to comply with algorithm design standards, execute necessary testing procedures, and ensure the accuracy and reliability of token payment services at the algorithm level.

This way, token financial infrastructure can be ensured to provide innovative services, meet regulatory requirements, protect consumer rights, and maintain the stability of financial markets.

7.3.4 Global Tokenization Technology Sandbox Regulation Practice Cases

7.3.4.1 Platform Approach: Practice Cases in Hong Kong, China, and Canada

The Hong Kong Special Administrative Region government is committed to promoting the development of the virtual asset market and issued a policy declaration in 2022, clarifying its support and regulatory framework for virtual asset development. The Hong Kong Monetary Authority (HKM) and the Securities and Futures Commission (SFC) jointly provided clear regulatory guidance to promote the development of asset tokenization. The HKMA also issued regulatory guidelines for digital asset custody services and tokenized products, guiding market participants.

In 2023, the Hong Kong Special Administrative Region government successfully issued the world's first official tokenized green bond, with an issuance size of HKD 800 million, marking Hong Kong's innovation and leadership in tokenized financial products. In 2024, the HKMA launched the Ensemble project, which explores wholesale central bank digital currency (wCBDC) to promote the application of tokenized currency in interbank settlement through innovative financial market infrastructure.

In terms of international cooperation, the Hong Kong Special Administrative Region government actively participates in international exchanges and cooperation, collaborating with institutions such as the Bank for International Settlements Innovation Hub to promote the application of tokenization technology and participating in related exploration work by the European Central Bank and the Bank of France.

Hong Kong's token sandbox regulation primarily targets virtual asset trading platform operators, with a wide range of participants allowed to apply for the sandbox if they provide at least one securities token trading service. The sandbox regulation is divided into two phases:

Phase 1: Qualification Monitoring Phase. The SFC will customize a regulatory framework for platforms within the sandbox based on the standards for licensed securities brokers and automated trading venues and closely monitor their actual operation. The regulatory scope is not limited to token trading services but includes all token and non-token, on-chain and off-chain businesses. The SF will confidentially assess the platforms' willingness to comply, investor protection mechanisms, and impact on financial markets to determine their eligibility for licensing.

Phase 2: Conditional Licensing Phase. Platforms that pass the first monitoring phase will be issued Type 1 (*securities trading*) and Type 7 (*providing automated trading services*) licenses by the SFC under the Securities and Futures Ordinance, with additional licensing conditions. These conditions include but are not limited to restrictions on professional investors, submission of monthly reports, trust segregation of customer assets, insurance requirements for online and offline wallet assets, and prohibition of leveraged trading. After a monitoring period of at least 12 months, platforms can apply to remove or modify licensing conditions and exit the sandbox. The Hong Kong government aims to provide a testing and innovative environment for virtual asset trading platforms through this phased sandbox regulation while ensuring market health and investor protection.

The Canadian Securities Administrators (CSA) published a consultation paper in March 2019 to build a regulatory framework for crypto asset trading platforms and explore their inclusion in the regulatory sandbox. The framework suggests that all platforms providing crypto asset trading services should be included in the regulatory scope, regardless of whether the traded commodities are crypto assets or other types. Exceptionally, hybrid trading platforms with multiple market functions, acting as traders and custodians, will also be a focus of regulation. Key risk areas for regulation include but are not limited to:

- Investor Password Protection: Ensuring the security of investors' trading passwords and assets.
- Platform Trading Rule: Establish clear trading rules to ensure transparency and fairness.
- Internal Risk Control and Supervision: Establishing robust internal control mechanisms to monitor potential risks effectively.
- Investor Asset Segregation: Ensuring the effective segregation of investor assets from platform operating assets to protect investor rights.
- Conflict of Interest Management: Establishing effective mechanisms to address conflicts of interest and maintain market order.
- Prevention of Manipulation and Fraud: Implementing measures to prevent and combat market manipulation and fraudulent activities.

This initiative by the CSA reflects its emphasis on regulating the crypto asset trading sector. It aims to provide space for innovation while ensuring investor interests and market safety. By clarifying regulatory requirements, the CSA hopes to guide the healthy development of crypto asset trading platforms and address potential risks in emerging markets.

7.3.4.2 Business Approach: Practice Cases in Taiwan, China, and the UK

The Financial Supervisory Commission (FSC) under the Executive Yuan of Taiwan, China, announced its regulatory stance on tokens on June 27, 2019, recognizing their attributes as securitie and deciding to introduce a token sandbox regulation system. After comprehensively considering other countries' and regions' regulatory systems and enforcement cases, Taiwan innovatively adopted a tiered management system to regulate toke market activities.

According to the FSC's regulations, tokens with an issuance amount not exceeding NTD 30 million are defined as small-amount tokens. They can be directly regulated under Taiwan's "Securities and Exchange Act." Tokens with an issuance amount exceeding NTD 30 million are classified as large-amount tokens and need to apply for entry into the regulatory sandbox. Tokens that pass the sandbox regulation will be legally issued and traded according to relevant laws and regulations.

Under this tiered management system, Taiwan primarily uses sandbox experiments to regulate large-amount tokens, while small-amount tokens can enjoy regulatory exemptions after meeting certain additional conditions. This model helps concentrate resources on testing and regulating larger-scale token activities. However, existing regulatory rules still need improvement. For example, the FSC recognizes the advantages of token issuance and trading platforms in simplifying intermediary processes and positions them as special securities dealers. However, since the sandbox regulation mechanism does not exclude criminal liability under statutory systems to prevent illegal operations by token platforms, the FSC only allows them to conduct transactions through negotiated pricing models, which differs from decentralized token platforms. This approach is inconsistent with the auction trading model of decentralized token platforms and limits the market price discovery function.

Additionally, for the small-amount exemption category, the FS has set restrictions such as professional investor qualifications, subscription limits per token case, and limits on issuance and trading by a single platform. These restrictions, to some extent, limit the liquidity of the token market. This indicates that managing solely based on issuance amounts cannot fully address the challenges faced by toke regulation.

The UK is actively exploring the tokenization of securities, funds, and deposits, building an ecosystem that supports digital assets and tokenization through policy guidance and regulatory innovation. This demonstrates the UK's open attitude and support for fintech development.

Regarding tokenized securities, in January 2024, the Bank of England and the Financial Conduct Authority (FCA) jointly announced the UK Digital Securities Sandbox Plan, which will run for five years, and launched a public consultation in April. The sandbox aims to relax specific Central Securities Depositories (CSDs) requirements to promote innovation in digital securities trading and subsequent processes, especially in tokenization driven by Distributed Ledger Technology (DLT). The UK has also implemented comprehensive regulations, providing a legal foundation for digital asset innovation and clarifying the scope of activities and participant qualifications allowed within the sandbox.

In terms of tokenized funds, as early as November 2023, the FCA released a roadmap for implementing fund tokenization, allowing eligible funds to adopt tokenization for sales and redemptions within the existing regulatory framework while emphasizing compliance with portfolio composition and traditional settlement procedures. In March 2024, the technical group of the UK Government's

Asset Management Working Group released its second report, delving into practical cases of fund tokenization, particularly the application of fund collateral in money markets and the role of on-chain investment markets. The report highlighted the potential benefits of tokenization for the fund industry and asset management sector, emphasizing the role of the Digital Securities Sandbox Plan in promoting technological innovation.

Regarding tokenized deposits, in April 2024, the UK financial industry organization UK Finance announced the expansion of a pilot project for tokenized deposits, attracting participation from financial institutions such as Barclays, Lloyds Bank, Citigroup, Mastercard, and Visa. This three-year transnational project aims to simplify the procedures for cross-border communication and reduces errors and fraud risks.

7.3.4.3 Infrastructure Approach: Practice Cases in Singapore and the EU

The European Union has been exploring the application of Distributed Ledger Technology (DLT) in financial market settlements. In June 2023, the European Central Bank (ECB) announced plans to begin exploring the use of DL in financial market settlements starting in 2024, aiming to innovate the settlement processes for securities and foreign exchange transactions between financial institutions while simultaneously advancing retail central bank digital currency (CBDC). On May 13, 2024, the European System of Central Banks (ESCB) publicly confirmed that it had partnered with multiple financial entities and central banks to launch a new technology development project based on DLT for wholesale transaction settlements. This marks a significant step for the ECB in adopting innovative technology to handle wholesale transaction settlements of central bank money within the Eurozone. Initial participants in the exploration project include the central banks of Luxembourg, France, Italy, Germany, and Austria, as well as 10 financial institutions and 6 DLT technology operators. According to the ECB's announcement, participants have proposed several business models for transaction settlements using central bank money on DLT platforms. These proposals focus on optimizing different stages of the securities settlement process, such as Delivery versus Payment (DvP), secondary market transaction processing, and securities lifecycle management (including interest payments). Additionally, the announcement revealed that the exploration scope is expanding to other potential scenarios, particularly DvP solutions involving cross-border payments.

The Monetary Authority of Singapore (MAS) is actively expanding its asset tokenization initiatives and advancing the construction of related infrastructure. Since completing the Ubin project in 2016, MAS has explored the potential of tokens and DLT in payments, securities clearing, and settlement. In November 2018, MA collaborated with the Singapore Exchange to develop the Delivery versus Payment (DvP) function, enabling cross-platform settlement of tokenized assets. In May 2022, MAS launched the Project Guardian initiative, partnering with the financial industry to explore the feasibility of asset tokenization and Decentralized Finance (DeFi). The initiative aims to achieve three core objectives:

establishing industry standards for asset tokenization, creating policy guidelines and frameworks to clarify digital asset governance models and accountability, and fostering a healthy and sustainable digital asset ecosystem under these policies and frameworks. Project Guardian focuses on four key areas: open and interoperable networks, trust chains, asset tokenization, and institutional-grade DeFi protocols. Currently, 18 financial institutions are participating in the initiative, covering tokenized financial assets such as fixed income, asset management, and foreign exchange trading. In November 2023, MAS announced the successful pilot of Project Guardian, demonstrating that tokenized financial assets such as fixed income, asset management, and foreign exchange trading can achieve seamless cross-border transactions, distribution, and settlement. MAS subsequently announced further collaboration with the financial industry to expand the asset tokenization plan and develop infrastructure to enhance the potential of the tokenization market.

Notably, MAS is working with institutions such as Bank of New York Mellon, J.P. Morgan, DBS Bank, and Mitsubishi UFJ Financial Group to explore the construction of a digital infrastructure called "Global Layer 1" (GL1). GL1 aims to enable tokenized assets to trade in a global liquidity pool by hosting tokenized financial assets and applications while ensuring compliance with regulatory requirements and guidelines.

7.3.4.4 Attribute-Based Approach: Practice Cases in the United States

The U.S. government has adopted a diversified regulatory framework for tokens, reflecting their multifaceted nature.

- Monetary Business Attribute: In 2013, the Financial Crimes Enforcement Network (FinCEN) of the U.S. Department of the Treasury clarified that Bitcoin and other tokens are not considered legal tender in the United States. However, this does not negate the function of tokens as payment tools. As long as both parties accept using tokens for transactions, the transaction is legal. Token transactions fall under the "money services business" category and must comply with Anti-Money Laundering (AML) regulations. Companies involved must fulfill responsibilities such as recording, preserving transaction information reports, and cooperating with investigations.
- Securities Attribute: The Securities and Exchange Commission (SEC) classifies tokens as securities, meaning that token issuers and exchanges are subject to SEC regulation. Additionally, the Commodity Futures Trading Commission (CFTC) considers tokens commodities and regulates them when necessary.
- Asset Attribute: The Internal Revenue Service (IRS) defines tokens as assets rather than currency for tax purposes. Therefore, investors must promptly report taxable gains from token transactions.
- Regulatory Policy: The U.S. government's regulatory policies on tokens cover four key areas: market access, token transfer, consumer protection, and anti-money laundering.

- Market Access Policy: On May 7, 2015, the New York State Department of Financial Services issued the first token business operating license, known as BitLicense, laying the foundation for the prudential regulation of token businesses in New York State. Consequently, any institution wishing to engage in token transmission, custody, control, management, issuance, trading, and exchange must obtain the appropriate license to conduct business.

Token Transfer Policy: In March 2013, FinCEN issued guidance rules for financial market participants involved in convertible virtual token transactions, clarifying the applicability of the *U.S. Bank Secrecy Act* (BSA).

- Consumer Protection Policy: On July 23, 2013, the SEC's Office of Investor Education and Advocacy issued an investor alert regarding the risks associated with token usage. Subsequently, the SEC and the Consumer Financial Protection Bureau (CFPB) also released related alerts and guidance documents to provide investment advice and guidance to investors and consumers.
- AML Policy: The *USA PATRIOT Act* mandates that businesses establish customer identification mechanisms and maintain data records. This policy has been extended to the token industry, and the Federal Financial Institutions Examination Council (FFIEC) has established a bank anti-money laundering (AML) information database, requiring money service providers and money transmitters to comply with AML procedures.

The regulatory attitudes of U.S. state governments toward tokens vary, with some states issuing warnings about investing in token businesses while others exhibit varying degrees of openness. Despite differing attitudes, all state governments emphasize risk warnings to investors. The U.S. government's token regulatory system has two main characteristics: first, it combines a multi-level regulatory system of federal regulations and state rules; second, it focuses on regulating token businesses' qualifications and transaction processes while strengthening risk education and investor protection. These measures contribute to the token industry's healthy development and prevention of risk.

7.4 Building a Token Financial Sandbox with Chinese Characteristics

A token economy is a new economic model based on token and RWA technology. Its core is leveraging the decentralized, anonymous, and tamper-resistant characteristics of tokens and RWA to establish an economic incentive mechanism that encourages honest behavior. This mechanism aims to stimulate the enthusiasm and creativity of participants and promote high-level financial openness.

Although the token economy is still in its early stages with limited application scenarios, developers are actively exploring ways to integrate it with the real economy to unleash its potential economic driving force.

However, the development of the token economy also faces numerous challenges, particularly in regulation. Currently, China has implemented relatively strict regulatory policies on digital currency. While these strict policies have effectively avoided certain financial risks and ensured the safety and stability of financial markets, they have also caused China to miss out on many opportunities in the digital currency market. The most direct loss includes the power to set the game's rules, which has historically proven long-term importance. For example, the United States dominated the establishment of the TCP/IP protocol in the early days of the Internet, leaving China constrained regarding cybersecurity and technological development.

Additionally, China may lose influence over the pricing of digital currency, which could indirectly affect RMB internationalization. Furthermore, since many digital currency-related projects are established abroad while Chinese users occupy a significant market share, this situation indirectly leads to the loss of domestic fiscal revenue.

Therefore, unlike traditional one-way and passive regulatory strategies, the new regulatory mindset should be open and inclusive. Regulatory authorities should provide room and time for trial and error in the token economy while promoting the effective integration of community autonomy and official regulation. This two-way interactive regulatory model ensures the token economy's legal and compliant operation and promotes efficient and healthy development.

In summary, the future direction of the token economy as a potential tool for transforming socio-economic models remains uncertain. Adopting a tolerant attitude towards the token economy and actively exploring and practicing it will help us better understand its various possibilities and enjoy the convenience and economic benefits it generates.

7.4.1 Risks of Tokens and RWA and the Necessity of Reforming China's Financial Regulatory System

7.4.1.1 Risks and Warnings Brought by Tokens and RWA

Tokens and RWA, emerging models in the fintech sector, rely on token and RWA technologies, ranging from digital currency to smart contracts, bringing profound changes to the financial industry. With its decentralized characteristics, this model enables rapid transaction processing and significant cost reductions, offering major opportunities for improving the efficiency of the global financial industry and lowering transaction costs. However, it also introduces multi-dimensional risk challenges.

As one of the most active countries in internet finance development, tokens and RWA have already occupied an important position in China's financial market and have driven further financial sector development. At the same time, they have also posed unprecedented challenges to traditional finance, with risks gradually emerging alongside development opportunities.

The advantages of token and RWA technologies in simplifying financial transactions, reducing costs, and promoting considerable data utilization are evident. However, the comprehensive impact and hidden dangers of tokens and RWA on financial markets cannot be ignored. Technically, the "disruptive innovation" of tokens and RWA has altered the technological foundation of the financial sector. The security protections of new systems are not yet fully established, posing potential technical risks and security vulnerabilities that could threaten the stability of financial markets. Additionally, the cross-border nature, interconnectedness, and high contagion of tokens and RWA may amplify market operational risks, leading to liquidity or systemic risks.

Regarding consumer protection, the decentralized nature of tokens and RWA increases the difficulty of market participant identity verification, exacerbates information asymmetry, and leaves consumers in a more vulnerable state of protection. Small token and RWA companies have limited capabilities to deal with hacker attacks and protect personal information, increasing the risk of consumer information leaks and rights violations.

In summary, the risks brought by tokens and RWA in technology application, market operation, and consumer protection have unstable the foundation of China's token and RWA ecosystem, making risks increasingly prominent. This requires the Chinese government to actively respond at the institutional design level, engaging in "institutional transactions" to adapt to economic conditions in the financial sector and ensure the healthy and stable development of financial markets.

7.4.2 China's Token and RWA Regulatory Mechanisms Urgently Need Reform

Starting from the basic principles of financial regulation, the core functions of financial regulation are to prevent systemic financial risks, correct market information asymmetry, and maintain market order. To address the risks of tokens and RWA, reforming the current financial regulatory system is a viable path. However, China's current financial regulatory system has shown inadequacies in legislation, regulatory structure, and self-regulation regarding tokens and RWA.

- Limitations of Control-Based Financial Legislation: China's financial legislation is primarily control-based, aiming to achieve transparency in transaction information and credit assurance through strict regulations. However, this legislative approach struggles to cope with tokens and RWA. Tokens and RWA use decentralized systems and "financial disintermediation" to address information asymmetry, effectively bypassing strict legislative controls. While this may help achieve effective market information allocation, in an immature market environment, information asymmetry remains severe, leading to frequent corporate failures and credit crises. Additionally, loopholes in control-based legislation and regulatory gaps for tokens and RWA provide opportunities for regulatory arbitrage, further exacerbating market chaos.

- Inadequacy of Institutional Regulatory Framework: For a long time, China's financial regulatory system has adopted an institutional regulatory model, where specific regulatory agencies are responsible for overseeing different types of financial institutions, following the principle of sectoral regulation. As an emerging financial innovation model, the diverse and ambiguous nature of tokens and RWA makes it challenging to fit into the existing financial business regulatory framework. This results in fragmented or blank regulation, making it challenging to regulate tokens and RWA effectively and increasing the likelihood of financial risks.
- Deficiencies in Self-Regulation: China's financial system lacks effective self-regulation, mainly when dealing with tokens and RWA. The decentralized nature of tokens and RWA, supported by DLT, enhances the independence of payment and credit systems, making relying solely on government administrative power insufficient to regulate their decentralized characteristics. At the same time, self-regulatory mechanisms within industry organizations are underdeveloped, and companies lack enthusiasm for participating in self-regulation, leading to an incomplete regulatory framework and difficulties in conducting effective oversight.
- Limitations of Centralized Regulatory Mechanisms in Tokens and RWA: The current financial regulatory mechanisms are primarily built around traditional financial institutions, making it difficult for existing frameworks to cover cross-border fintech platforms, especially emerging models like tokens and RWA. Under the token and RWA model, the protection of consumer personal information faces challenges, with high risks of information leaks and remote electronic fraud. Due to the decentralized nature of tokens and RWA, traditional centralized regulatory methods struggle to effectively track and identify anonymous accounts of violators, making accountability extremely difficult. As a result, the effectiveness of consumer protection mechanisms is weakened.

Given the inadequacies of the current financial regulatory system in adapting to the token and RWA model, exploring regulatory mechanisms that align with tokens and RWA and promoting regulatory system reforms are crucial for the healthy development of tokens and RWA. International regulatory practices can provide valuable experiences and insights for us.

7.4.3 Practices and Lessons from Financial Regulatory Models

Consumer protection, financial security, and financial efficiency constitute the three pillars of the financial regulatory system. Financial legislation, regulatory goal setting, and regulatory system reform should achieve a balance among these three pillars. Faced with the risks and opportunities brought by new financial models, excellent financial regulators need to learn continuously, keenly identify potential hazards in new products, markets, and services, take timely risk mitigation measures, and, when necessary, halt related activities.

Guided by this principle, many countries have adopted sandbox regulation to balance the innovative vitality of tokens and RWA with their potential risks. Sandbox regulation adjusts the regulatory agency system and strengthens consumer protection. This approach provides valuable lessons for China's regulation of tokens and RWA.

7.4.4 Sandbox Regulation: Balancing Financial Innovation and Risk

The FCA initially proposed the concept of sandbox regulation in 2015. The FCA believes that regulatory sandboxes help shorten the time it takes for innovative ideas to enter the market and promote the development of financial innovation.

This concept inspired countries like the UK, Singapore, and Australia to establish their sandbox regulatory systems. Taking the UK as an example, the implementation of sandbox regulation is based on several core elements: first, establishing the legal foundation for the regulatory sandbox; second, clarifying the role and measures of the FCA in sandbox regulation; third, developing flexible plans for companies to execute within the sandbox; and finally, ensuring that consumer protection measures are effectively implemented.

This regulatory model allows regulatory agencies to provide space for financial innovation while ensuring consumer rights and market stability. This allows companies to explore and validate their innovative ideas in a controlled risk environment, helping to balance innovation and risk and supporting the healthy development of the fintech sector.

The sandbox regulatory standards implemented by the FCA include five key conditions, similar to the requirements for companies seeking support for innovative initiatives. These conditions are:

- Eligibility of the Company: Whether the new proposal in the company's plan falls within the financial services sector.
- Originality: Whether the new proposal is innovative and differs from existing solutions.
- Consumer Benefit: Whether consumers can derive actual benefits during the entire sandbox testing period.
- Necessity of Sandbox Testing: Is sandbox testing genuinely required to validate the new proposal?
- Resources and Regulatory Understanding: Whether the company possesses the necessary resources and understands the relevant regulations and risks.

These five criteria form the foundation for implementing the sandbox regulatory model. The FCA adopts different sandbox regulatory measures for authorized and unauthorized companies to address the distinct challenges they face during the innovation process:

The FCA has established a unique authorization process for unauthorized companies, allowing them to operate within limited scopes solely for testing their innovative ideas. Once a company meets the authorization requirements, these restrictions can be lifted, and the company should apply for full authorization immediately upon meeting the conditions. Companies must meet time and resource requirements before starting testing, and their activities must not exceed the scope of *the Financial Services and Markets Act 2000 (FSMA)*.

For authorized companies, the core of the FCA's sandbox regulatory measures is to provide certainty, ensuring that the FCA will not take enforcement actions against the company's testing activities. Specific measures include:

- No Enforcement Action Letter :It indicates that the FCA will not take enforcement actions against the company's activities.
- Individual Guidance: The FCA clearly explains the rules applicable to the company's testing activities based on guidelines.
- Waiver Statements: When a company's testing activities violate rules, the FCA, as the regulatory authority, will temporarily align the company's behavior with the rules to meet sandbox regulatory needs, but only within the scope of EU legislation.

Although the FCA's sandbox regulatory measures provide significant flexibility for companies, the FCA consistently emphasizes one point: the parameters of sandbox activities must not pose risks to the entire financial system due to ongoing testing. The sandbox regulatory model offers a safe environment for financial innovation, allowing companies to test their innovative products, services, and business models without immediately facing complete regulatory requirements. The FCA establishes its implementation measures and provides flexible execution plans for companies to support their potential role in realizing innovative solutions.

Currently, companies can execute two main types of flexible plans:

The first is the simulated sandbox. Companies can test their new solutions in a virtual environment without entering the real market. The simulated sandbox provided by the FCA has two main advantages:

1. It leverages cloud databases to enable industry-level test data sharing, thereby reducing consumer harm and market risks.
2. All innovative companies, whether authorized or not, can use the simulated sandbox for testing, providing a quick and formal cooperation method for unauthorized companies.

The second is the sandbox umbrella, a non-profit company established within the industry that allows unauthorized innovative companies to provide services under its umbrella. The advantage of the sandbox umbrella is that it simplifies the process for innovative companies to enter the sandbox. However, its limitation is that not all regulated activities, such as insurance and investment management, are applicable and still require restricted authorization.

The sandbox model aims to provide a testing environment that removes regulatory barriers and fully protects participants. It reduces the risk of financial products triggering systemic risks and balances risk control and innovation benefits. Sandbox regulation has become a core regulatory tool for fintech models like tokens and RWA in various countries, occupying a central position in regulatory systems.

7.4.5 Regulatory Mechanisms: Achieving Functional Regulation and "Light-Touch" Decentralized Regulation

The decentralized nature of the RWA model has prompted governments worldwide to gradually shift toward mixed regulation, emphasizing functional regulation over institutional regulation. This regulatory principle leans toward inclusive and principle-based regulation, aiming to safeguard the vitality of financial innovation and enhance overall industry efficiency.

In this field, the UK has introduced the concept of "light-touch" decentralized regulation. A report by the UK Government Office for Science emphasized the importance of strengthening collaboration between government regulatory bodies, industry, and academia. This collaboration helps maintain the government's leading role in regulation and mitigates the risks of "de-governmentalization" in fintech models. The basic idea is that with the deepening application of DLT, governance and regulation should be closely integrated. The government, academia, and industry will jointly become the central bodies for formulating regulatory rules such as personal information privacy protection, distributed ledger content security, and effective authentication of personal and institutional agreements. Together, they will explore solutions to the legal, ethical, and technical risks brought by fintech.

7.4.6 Consumer Protection

Risk warnings and compensation guarantees are key measures to protect consumer rights in financial regulation. The FCA has developed a comprehensive set of consumer protection measures for testing innovative financial products or services to reduce potential harm to consumers participating in fintech activities.

These protection measures mainly include four aspects:

- Risk Warnings: Companies must obtain formal consent from consumers during sandbox testing and inform them of potential risks and compensation mechanisms.
- Individual Agreements: Companies can enter into individual agreements with consumers regarding information disclosure, rights protection, and compensation for damages during testing activities. The FCA ensures that consumers are satisfied with the agreements.

- Equal Consumer Rights: The FCA ensures that consumers participating in sandbox testing enjoy the same rights as regular consumers.
- Compensation Guarantee: Companies must be able to compensate consumers for losses and demonstrate their compensation resources and capital.

These measures form a comprehensive protection system supported by specific rules. Scholars believe that consumer protection, financial security, and financial efficiency are the three pillars of financial regulatory law. A balance among these pillars should be achieved in financial legislation, regulatory goal setting, and regulatory system reform. Faced with the risks and opportunities brought by new financial models, regulators need to continuously learn, identify potential risks, and take adequate measures. Multiple countries have adopted sandbox regulation as a core model for balancing innovation and risk, with corresponding adjustments made to regulatory agency systems and consumer protection mechanisms. This approach provides valuable lessons for China in regulating fintech models such as tokens and RWA.

7.4.7 Feasibility of Building a Token and RWA Regulatory Model Centered on Sandbox Regulation

From the perspective of international regulatory practices, sandbox regulation, as a core regulatory mechanism, shows strong similarities with China's market regarding the current state of financial market operations, the experimental application of related systems, and the construction of financial regulatory models. This demonstrates the feasibility of introducing it into China. This regulatory model's flexibility and innovation-supporting nature provide a significant reference value for the healthy development of China's fintech sector. By drawing on successful international experiences and combining them with China's specific national conditions, sandbox regulation has the potential to become an essential tool for innovation and risk management in China's financial markets.

7.4.8 Mutual Adaptation Between Sandbox Regulation and China's Financial Market Status

In China's current financial market, there are indeed some imperfections. On one hand, the bank-centered indirect financial market has long dominated, leading to structural imbalances between direct and indirect financial markets. The development of the capital market has not yet reached a level where it can autonomously and effectively transfer and disperse risks, increasing the potential risks for banks and other financial institutions. On the other hand, the high degree of monopoly in the financial market makes it impossible for the extensive bank-dominated financial system to ensure an adequate supply of financial services and products or achieve the most efficient allocation of funds. At the same time, the insufficient development of small and medium-sized banks has led to a certain degree of discrimination against small and medium-sized enterprises, causing these enterprises to face financing difficulties generally.

In such a market environment, small and medium-sized enterprises (SMEs) also seek alternative financing channels besides relying on their accumulation. This has spurred the rise of various Internet financing platforms, which have experienced rapid development since the advent of Internet finance in 2012. The RWA model has also become a significant participant in the wave of internet finance. The rise of the RWA model essentially represents an expansion of the traditional financial market's periphery. Given its distance from the conventional financial market, its regulation should transcend conventional boundaries and explore new regulatory models and frameworks. By limiting time and space, the sandbox regulatory model aligns with the position of tokens and RWA in the market and is well-suited to China's current financial market environment.

7.4.9 Institutional Pilot Experience as the Foundation for China-Style Sandbox Regulation

The sandbox regulatory model in China is highly compatible with the domestic financial market environment. Moreover, China's long-standing institutional pilot model provides a solid foundation for promoting sandbox regulation. This model emphasizes achieving institutional innovation and transformation by establishing pilot zones and accumulating rich experience for the broader adoption of sandbox regulation.

Like sandbox regulation, the institutional pilot model allows companies in pilot zones to test innovative products or services within a specific timeframe while enjoying policy incentives and a new transactional environment brought by institutional innovation. If the trials are successful, the relevant industries will be promoted nationwide under government leadership. Although this model resembles sandbox regulation, the influence of administrative power on pilot enterprises is more pronounced.

Taking the Shanghai Free Trade Zone (FTZ) as an example, its establishment aimed to provide a testing ground for Shanghai's goal of becoming an international financial center. The economic and legal innovations in the Shanghai FTZ serve as the overall strategy of Shanghai's economic development and act as a "breeding ground" for a new round of economic construction, offering pioneering experience. The financial legal framework of the Shanghai FTZ follows a "national authorization—ministry support—local legislation" model. Through authorization by the National People's Congress Standing Committee and the State Council, national authority is delegated, and the Shanghai Municipal People's Congress authorizes the suspension of specific local regulations. The municipal government then formulates local government regulations, ultimately creating local rules adapted to the FTZ's institutional experiments. At the same time, rules from State Council ministries support the FTZ's pioneering efforts.

This model confines institutional experiments to the FTZ, allowing bold reform measures to be proposed and applied while enabling risk estimation and prevention. Even if issues arise, their impact is limited, and the valuable experience gained can be quickly promoted nationwide.

This model is similar to sandbox regulation and can serve as the experience and foundation for China-style sandbox regulation.

7.4.10 Compatibility Between Sandbox Regulation and China's Financial Regulatory System

The sandbox regulatory model applies highly to China's current financial regulatory landscape. Regulatory mechanisms are often profoundly influenced by market development and historical traditions. China's institutional regulatory framework is related to the legislative principle of separate operations and the current state of low financial market liberalization, which necessitates administrative intervention.

With the development of financial markets, especially the rise of internet finance forms such as tokens and RWA, the traditional institutional regulatory framework faces challenges. The boundaries of industry segmentation are increasingly difficult to accurately reflect the nature of financial innovation, leading to regulatory gaps, arbitrage opportunities, and insufficient consumer protection. Financial innovations like tokens and RWA must be integrated into the regulatory framework. However, due to entrenched regulatory traditions and administrative controls, this may result in insufficient regulation, rising risk costs, and potential obstacles to financial innovation.

Although academia and industry have long called for a shift from "institutional regulation" to "functional regulation," substantial progress has yet to be made at the legislative level. To some extent, the sandbox regulatory model can break through the existing regulatory framework, promote the development of financial innovation, and maintain the order of financial regulatory mechanisms.

However, introducing the sandbox regulatory model also requires corresponding adjustments to regulatory mechanisms and consumer protection systems to build a complete and adequate regulatory framework for tokens and RWA.

7.4.11 Path to Building China's Token and RWA Regulatory Model

To address the rapid development of tokens and RWA and their demand for institutional reform while considering the compatibility of the sandbox regulatory model with China's financial industry and regulatory system, we can draw on advanced international experiences to explore the construction of a sandbox regulatory model with Chinese characteristics. This institutional innovation aims to provide practical solutions for token and RWA regulation.

China can establish specialized regulatory zones and build the foundational framework for sandbox regulation through the following measures:

- Implement authorized legislation and establish the legal basis for regulation.
- Set enterprise entry standards which make sure that only qualified enterprises can participate in sandbox trials.
- Establish a sandbox exit mechanism to provide a clear exit path for projects when they achieve their goals or identify risks.

Additionally, we need to deeply reconstruct existing consumer protection mechanisms, regulatory systems, and principles to adapt to the characteristics of tokens and RWA. This will help build a comprehensive regulatory blueprint for tokens and RWA, promoting financial innovation while effectively managing and controlling risks.

Through these comprehensive measures, we can ensure the adaptability and effectiveness of the regulatory model, providing a solid institutional foundation for the healthy development of tokens and RWA.

7.4.12 Forming the Basic Framework of China's Sandbox Regulation

The primary task of building a sandbox regulatory model in China is establishing its legal foundation. Since financial regulatory legislation falls under the exclusive authority of the central government, we can draw on the experience of the Shanghai Free Trade Zone (FTZ). The National People's Congress Standing Committee and the State Council can adjust current laws in a timely and localized manner under the *Legislative Law of the People's Republic of China.* This would involve suspending certain administrative approvals for token and RWA activities while granting legislative authority to regulatory bodies within the sandbox zones, enabling them to formulate legal rules that promote financial innovation based on practical conditions.

Updating the existing legal system nationwide is challenging but feasible in pilot zones such as the FTZ. These zones can become "legal special zones" for institutional innovation, leveraging delegated legislation to create institutional advantages and drive innovation in the financial industry.

Despite the rapid development of tokens and RWA, risks such as credit issues, regulatory confusion, and consumer fraud remain. Token and RWA technologies may inherently have features that evade regulation. Therefore, ensuring the qualifications and credibility of participating enterprises is crucial when building a sandbox regulatory platform. In this regard, China can refer to Australia's approach, which allows enterprises with good credit and financial qualifications to expand their business scope and enter the sandbox. At the same time, design registration and approval processes specifically for fintech companies, with regulatory agencies conducting approvals based on standards, providing credit endorsement for enterprises.

Given the sandbox's limited resources, establishing a comprehensive exit mechanism is crucial for the rational allocation of resources. Enterprises should exit the sandbox and enter the market when the testing period ends, the product lacks innovation or feasibility, or the enterprise has matured. Regulatory agencies should specify exit criteria and ensure that the exit process follows legal procedures, treating each enterprise fairly to safeguard market competitiveness.

7.4.13 Strengthening Consumer Protection Mechanisms

As a form of internet finance, RWA, while leveraging advanced token and RWA technologies, also faces common issues in all internet finance activities. There is significant information asymmetry between trading parties, and while online transactions are convenient, they can also lead to the proliferation of false information. Additionally, the varying quality of enterprises engaged in token and RWA businesses makes it difficult to ensure transaction credibility. Consumers are often at a disadvantage in transactions, not only struggling to understand the risks of enterprises and products fully and being easily misled but also finding it difficult to seek compensation for losses due to the virtual nature of transactions.

To protect consumers' legitimate rights and interests in token and RWA transactions and restore balance in transactional legal relationships, China should prioritize consumer protection when implementing the sandbox regulatory model to change consumers' disadvantaged position. During sandbox testing and regulation, the importance of protecting consumer rights should first be emphasized at the legal and regulatory level, with principle-based regulations established, followed by constructing a comprehensive consumer protection system through specific rules.

In terms of institutional design, we can draw on the consumer protection measures implemented in the UK:

- Right to Information: Enterprises must fully disclose the risks of token and RWA products or services and inform consumers that they are in the sandbox testing phase, enabling consumers to make informed decisions.
- Equal Rights Protection: Ensure that consumers enjoy the same rights as other financial consumers, such as protecting consumer rights in contract terms through mandatory regulations.
- Damage Claim Guarantee: Enterprises must demonstrate their debt repayment capability and provide guarantees before entering the sandbox to protect consumer rights.

Through these measures, we can provide more comprehensive consumer protection under the sandbox regulatory model and promote the healthy development of the tokenization and RWA industry.

7.4.14 Reconstructing the Regulatory Framework and Principles for Tokenization and RWA

Reconstructing the regulatory framework and principles is key to effectively regulating tokenization and RWA. Implementing the sandbox regulatory model effectively requires a shift in regulatory thinking and appropriate adjustments and integrations of the regulatory framework and principles.

The sandbox regulation allows enterprises to freely test their products and services in a controlled environment without immediate concern about facing conventional regulatory constraints, effectively providing enterprises with a form of "temporary relaxation" regulation. When implementing sandbox regulation in our country, there should be a greater inclination towards principle-based regulation rather than traditional rule-based regulation. Under the principle-based regulation model, regulatory authorities should be guided by clear principles or high-level strategies, adopt outcome-oriented regulatory methods, and moderately relax control over business operations.

Effective implementation of principle-based regulation requires meeting several conditions: regulatory principles must stand independently as the basis for law enforcement; some necessary rules should be retained; and multiple stakeholders must participate and cooperate.

In pilot areas such as the Shanghai Free Trade Zone, implementing function-based financial system regulation helps to maintain financial security and prevent risks, especially against the backdrop of increasingly integrated financial services. This regulatory approach not only meets the overall regulatory needs of the financial industry but also effectively addresses the limitations of traditional rule-based regulatory models in dealing with new financial forms such as tokenization and RWA.

In the sandbox area, function-based regulation can be a pilot attempt, achieving comprehensive regulation of the entire financial industry through coordination across products, institutions, and industries. This helps fill regulatory gaps, reduce regulatory costs, improve regulatory efficiency, and promote financial innovation.

To adapt to this regulatory approach, the reconstruction of regulatory principles must be accompanied by reorganizing regulatory authorities and redistributing their powers.

Considering the mixed-operation characteristics of token and RWA businesses, it will be necessary to establish a unified financial regulatory agency within the sandbox area to respond quickly and effectively to regulatory needs. Additionally, given the overlapping regulatory issues inside and outside the sandbox, establishing a coordination mechanism among various regulatory agencies is particularly important. This includes optimizing and delineating regulatory functions based on the roles of tokens and RWA and creating a regulatory system with clear divisions of labor and close cooperation. For example, a regulatory coordination mechanism for tokens and RWA could be established at the Central Bank's core in collaboration with the Securities Regulatory Commission and the Banking and Insurance Regulatory Commission.

To enhance data sharing among regulatory agencies, regulatory technology can promote the sharing and utilization of financial regulatory data, thereby improving overall regulatory effectiveness.

Implementing "decentralized regulation" and strengthening industry self-regulation are essential strategies for promoting the development of financial technology related to tokens and RWA. This strategy aims to balance the guiding role of the Central Government with the autonomy of market participants, thereby creating a more flexible and efficient regulatory environment.

In advancing the development of tokens and RWA, the government's role has shifted from traditional regulator to facilitator and coordinator. The government should provide policy support and a flexible regulatory framework for innovation trial and error in the sandbox pilot areas. This support is not limited to policy formulation but includes resource investment and technical assistance when necessary, ensuring financial innovation proceeds in a secure environment.

Industry self-regulation also plays a crucial role. Industry associations and professional institutions should develop and enforce industry standards and self-regulatory rules based on industry expertise and can quickly adapt to market changes and technological advancements. Furthermore, enterprises need to take on greater responsibility by ensuring the safety and compliance of their operations through internal controls, risk management, and enhanced transparency.

Collaboration between the government and enterprises is key to driving regulatory innovation. Both parties should establish closer cooperative relationships to jointly develop and refine regulatory frameworks, promoting innovation while mitigating risks. The government can conduct more effective regulation and risk assessment by leveraging enterprises' technological and data resources. Additionally, establishing a secure data-sharing platform that allows regulatory agencies, financial institutions, and industry associations to access and utilize this data will enable better identification and management of risks.

In summary, promoting the development of tokens and RWA requires a comprehensive strategy beyond adjusting the regulatory framework. It also involves leveraging technological innovation to optimize regulatory processes and strengthen industry self-regulation. Through this multi-dimensional approach, it is possible to foster innovation while ensuring the safety and stability of financial markets.

7.4.15 Regulatory Cooperation: China's Path Selection to Exploring Cross-Border Sandbox Regulation

The decentralized and open nature of token and RWA technologies has triggered significant transformations in the global financial sector while introducing new risks and challenges. In the face of this emerging financial paradigm, China's current financial regulatory mechanisms face challenges in effectively addressing these risks. Drawing on international practical experience, the sandbox regulatory model is compatible with China's market, existing institutions, and regulatory systems.

To construct a sandbox regulatory framework suitable for China, the following measures can be adopted:

- Establish an Authorized Legislative Model: Clarify the legal status and scope of authorization for sandbox regulation through legislation to ensure the legality and effectiveness of regulatory activities.
- Set Sandbox Entry Thresholds for Enterprise: Define clear entry conditions and standards to ensure only qualified enterprises can enter the sandbox for innovation trials. Develop a
- Sandbox Exit Mechanism: Formulate clear exit procedures and standards to ensure that projects within the sandbox can exit promptly upon achieving predetermined goals or identifying unacceptable risks.
- Restructure the Regulatory System and Principles: Adjust the existing regulatory framework to accommodate the characteristics of tokens and RWA while updating regulatory principles to balance innovation and risk control.
- Strengthen Consumer Protection: Enhance the protection of consumer rights within the sandbox regulation to ensure that consumer interests are not compromised during financial innovation processes.

Through these measures, a token and RWA regulatory mechanism centered on a Chinese-style sandbox regulation can be gradually established, supporting the healthy development and risk prevention of China's financial markets.

Summary and Review of RWA and Tokenization and Development Suggestions

8

8.1 Value Creation of RWA and Tokenization

Tokenization and RWA are among the most disruptive and promising applications of blockchain technology, widely regarded as the fourth transformative technology, following steam engines, electricity, and the internet. Blockchain technology initially gained significant attention in the computer field due to its application in financial digital currencies, establishing its importance in this domain. As a widely applicable foundational technology, tokenization and RWA have demonstrated rapid application and dissemination capabilities across various economic and social scenarios, including cross-border finance, tax management, supply chain management, judicial arbitration, and social governance.

8.1.1 The Value Logic of RWA and Tokenization from an Information Economics Perspective

8.1.1.1 Blockchain Technology for RWA and Tokenization

Blockchain technology is a distributed peer-to-peer storage system that uses cryptography to ensure data security. Its core characteristics include decentralization, immutability, trustlessness, transparency, and programmability. These characteristics strongly support blockchain's value creation in tokenization and RWA.

In a decentralized system, blockchain technology enables each node to participate equally in data maintenance and verification. This structure not only enhances the network's resistance to attacks but also provides a secure environment for tokenization.

Immutability is achieved through consensus mechanisms and cryptographic techniques, ensuring that once data is recorded, it cannot be altered or deleted. This is crucial for digitizing and tokenizing physical assets, as it guarantees the

S. Ba et al., *RWA Tokenisation in Web 3.0 Era*, Management for Professionals,
https://doi.org/10.1007/978-981-96-7663-7_8

permanence and transparency of asset histories and ownership information, thereby increasing trust among market participants.

The trustless nature allows blockchain users to conduct transactions without pre-established trust relationships. This is particularly important in tokenizing physical assets, as it enables assets to flow freely globally without the need for traditional financial or legal intermediaries that may require trust.

The transparent nature ensures that all transaction data is visible to network participants (except for specific cases requiring privacy). This facilitates the evaluation and auditing of assets, ensuring the fairness and transparency of transactions.

Finally, the programmability of blockchain, through the application of smart contracts, allows complex financial logic and transaction conditions to be automatically executed during the asset tokenization process. This not only improves transaction efficiency but also reduces operational complexity and costs.

In summary, with its unique attributes, blockchain technology provides an efficient, secure, and transparent platform for the value creation of RWA and tokenization, which is revolutionary in the modern economy.

8.1.2 Information Economics Theoretical Basis for RWA and Tokenization Value Creation

In the theoretical framework of classical economics, the market assumes complete and symmetric information, allowing prices to reflect all relevant information. This enables market participants to make rational decisions based on complete information, theoretically allowing the market to automatically reach general equilibrium and cumulative optimality. However, the widespread phenomenon of information asymmetry in reality breaks this assumption, leading to inefficient resource allocation and market failure. In an environment of incomplete information, individual economic behaviors and decisions are based on subjective predictions of various objective economic factors. Based on incomplete information, such decisions often lead to deviations from optimal resource allocation, causing economic efficiency losses.

In an environment of incomplete information, market participants face costs associated with searching for and judging the authenticity of information. Additionally, data must be transmitted through various signals to facilitate transactions, increasing transmission costs. Information asymmetry exacerbates this issue, as some market participants may possess certain key information that others cannot access.

In the value creation process of RWA and tokenization, the application of blockchain technology may become key to solving these problems. Blockchain provides a decentralized, transparent, and immutable platform for information recording and sharing, effectively reducing the costs associated with information asymmetry and incompleteness. Through tokenization, physical assets can be converted into digital assets, with ownership and transaction history publicly verifiable on the blockchain, thereby reducing information search costs and enhancing market transparency. Furthermore, smart contracts can automate the execution of transactions and contract terms, further reducing information transmission costs and improving transaction efficiency. This makes RWA and tokenization's value creation on the blockchain platform not only enhance market efficiency but may also drive resources toward more optimal allocation.

In economic activities, information asymmetry typically leads to two types of costs: ex-ante costs, which occur before the transaction, where the information-advantaged party may hide critical information due to opportunistic behavior, increasing the costs of contracting and negotiation, and ex-post costs, which occur after the transaction, when the information-disadvantaged party cannot effectively monitor whether the other party fulfills the contract, leading to moral hazard and thereby increasing supervision and default costs. These costs caused by information asymmetry are an essential component of transaction costs.

According to Coase's definition, transaction costs include the negotiation and contracting fees for each transaction in the market and other expenses arising from the reliance on the price mechanism. In the modern economy, where commodity exchange is frequent and production activities are socialized, information costs are significant in transaction costs. Coase pointed out that excessively high transaction costs can hinder the realization of potential transactions, either because the costs of mutual searching, bargaining, and contract signing are too high, preventing resources from being effectively utilized, or because high transaction costs due to information asymmetry reduce the efficiency of market transactions.

In the value-creation process of RWA and tokenization, the application of blockchain technology is critical. Through tokenization, physical assets can be converted into digital assets and recorded and traded on the blockchain, thereby increasing transparency and reducing information asymmetry. This technology reduces search and information costs and simplifies the bargaining and decision-making processes, reducing supervision and default costs. Therefore, the effective management and trading of RWA and tokens can significantly lower transaction costs, improve the efficiency of resource allocation, and promote the realization of more potential transactions. This approach not only optimizes the utilization of assets but also creates more excellent value for market participants.

8.1.3 Economic Mechanisms of RWA and Tokenization Value Creation

Economists such as Coase have recognized the potential of new technologies to alleviate transaction costs. For example, the advent of the internet has greatly facilitated the rapid flow of information, enabling various transaction entities to quickly gather and obtain the necessary information from public networks, significantly reducing transaction costs in situations with high information-gathering expenses.

Against this backdrop of technological evolution, blockchain technology further expands its potential for value creation by introducing RWA and tokens. These blockchain features not only enhance the transparency and accessibility of information but also optimize resource allocation efficiency, thereby fundamentally reducing the phenomenon of incomplete information in the transaction market. (see Fig. 8.1).

Applying RWA and tokenization, blockchain technology significantly improves transaction efficiency and reduces information costs at multiple levels, enhancing market transparency and fairness. All data is recorded on the chain (such as on a public chain), and its "immutable" technical features ensure the authenticity and reliability of on-chain data. This transparency and reliability significantly reduce both parties' time and monetary costs in gathering the necessary transaction information. Tokenization represents assets digitally, making the history and status of each asset easily traceable, thereby reducing the difficulty of finding information.

In blockchain technology, after each transaction is completed, miners package it onto the chain, enabling real-time information transmission. Thus, the time cost of information transmission is reduced, and transmission efficiency is improved. At the same time, blockchain's immutability and public transparency ensure that every individual in the system can access all information promptly, addressing the issue of delayed information transmission in traditional markets and mitigating market failures caused by information asymmetry.

The traceability and immutability of blockchain ensure the authenticity of on-chain data before signing a contract, guaranteeing that the information provided by both parties is reliable and avoiding the problem of adverse selection. The immutability of on-chain data reduces the cost for the information-disadvantaged party to verify the authenticity of information before the transaction. For example, in blockchain-based cross-border financing platforms, duplicate pledging of assets is avoided.

After the contract is signed, smart contracts ensure automatic execution upon meeting the contract conditions, avoiding risks such as unilateral default. The public transparency of on-chain data makes all actions visible, constraining contract execution. Evidence is retained throughout the process, facilitating monitoring and dispute resolution in case of default.

The decentralized, traceable, and immutable characteristics of blockchain technology extensively address the issue of public trust caused by information asymmetry. In scenarios such as public governance and social welfare, these technological features reduce governance costs, improve information transparency, and effectively avoid conflicts of interest and regulatory failures that may arise in centralized systems. In summary, blockchain technology's tokenization and RWA value creation optimize the information circulation mechanism in multiple aspects, enhancing transaction efficiency and improving the overall transparency and trust in the market.

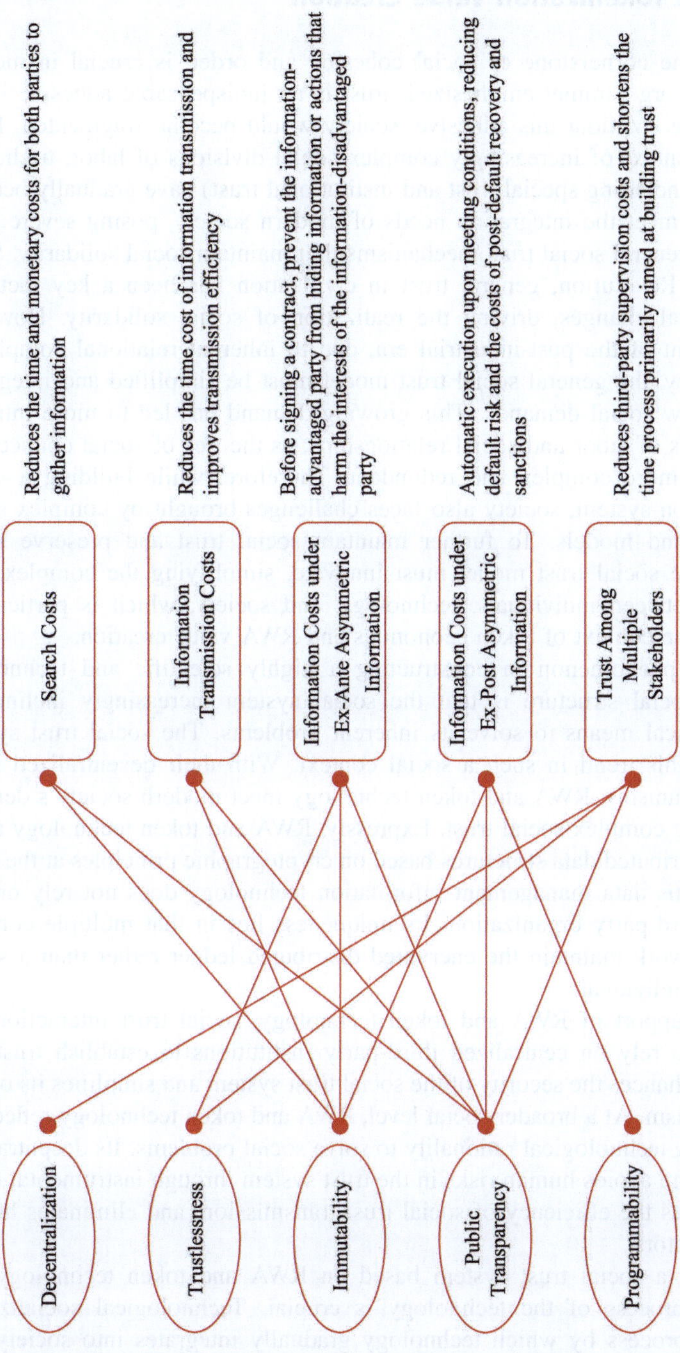

Fig. 8.1 Information economics mechanism of blockchain technology

8.1.4 Social Demand and Socialization Process of RWA and Tokenization Value Creation

Social trust, the cornerstone of social cohesion and order, is crucial in modern society. As Georg Simmel emphasized, trust is an indispensable adhesive in the social structure. Without this adhesive, society would become fragmented. However, in the context of increasingly complex social divisions of labor, traditional trust models (including special trust and institutional trust) have gradually become inadequate to meet the integration needs of modern society, posing severe challenges to the general social trust mechanisms that maintain social solidarity. Since the Industrial Revolution, general trust in civilization has been a key factor in social structural changes, driving the realization of social solidarity. However, with the advent of the post-industrial era, due to inherent relational complexity and redundancy, the general social trust model must be simplified and integrated to adapt to new social demands. This growing demand has led to more intricate social divisions of labor and social relationships, as the ties of social connections have become more complex and redundant. Therefore, while building a social trust civilization system, society also faces challenges brought by complex social relationships and models. To further maintain social trust and preserve social integration, the social trust model must innovate, simplifying the complex trust interactions between individuals, technology, and society, which is particularly important in the context of token economics and RWA value creation.

A notable phenomenon in constructing a highly scientific and technological modern social structure is that the social system increasingly inclined to use technological means to solve its inherent problems. The social trust system also exhibits this trend in such a social context. With their decentralized trust-building mechanisms, RWA and token technology meet modern society's demand for simplifying complex social trust. Expressly, RWA and token technology adopt innovative distributed data structures based on cryptographic principles at the technical level. This data management information technology does not rely on any centralized third-party organization. Its uniqueness lies in that multiple computers in the network maintain the encrypted distributed ledger rather than a single institution or individual.

With the support of RWA and token technology, social trust interactions no longer need to rely on centralized third-party institutions to establish trust and credit. This enhances the security of the social trust system and simplifies its operational mechanism. At a broader social level, RWA and token technology reflect the vision of using technological rationality to solve social problems. Its decentralized trust mechanism avoids human risks in the trust system through instrumental rationality, improves the efficiency of social trust transmission, and eliminates human uncertainty factors.

In building a social trust system based on RWA and token technology, the socialization process of the technology is crucial. Technological socialization refers to the process by which technology gradually integrates into society and forms social attributes under the influence of social integration and adaptation. In this process, technology not only exists as a tool but also plays a specific social role. Technological socialization can be divided into three stages: technological invention, technological promotion and application, and technological transformation. These three stages are closely linked to the early, mature, and declining phases of the technology lifecycle, collectively driving the functional realization of RWA and token technology in social trust construction.

In this process, the socialization of RWA and token technology promotes its popularization and application and provides new solutions for building social trust through decentralized characteristics. This technological socialization helps realize the value creation of tokens and RWA, as it allows the technology to better adapt to social needs, enhancing its role in promoting social trust and value exchange.

In the early development stage of RWA and token cryptocurrency, known as the Technology 1.0 stack period, the technology acquired trust attributes. It gradually established its role in the socialization process. This period marks the invention stage of RWA and token technology and the beginning of its lifecycle. In this stage, through its initial application in digital currency transactions, RWA and token technology began demonstrating its potential as a trust-based payment tool. They also started to be endowed with the attributes of social trust.

In 2008, Satoshi Nakamoto proposed a peer-to-peer electronic cash system based on proof-of-work, laying the foundation for RWA and token technology. This technology, with its characteristics such as a shared ledger, economic incentive mechanisms, traceability, and tamper resistance, allowed the establishment of a new technical trust system that does not rely on P2P trust relationships, drawing widespread social attention to RWA and token technology.

However, as an emerging technology, blockchain was still a relatively new concept during this period, with a limited scope of application. The social trust attributes of RWA and token technology had not yet fully emerged, and the technological maturity needed improvement, accompanied by certain risks. Therefore, during the socialization process, RWA and token technology faced skepticism and restrictions from legal and institutional levels, posing challenges to further development and application.

With the advancement of RWA and token innovative contract technology, we entered the Technology 2.0 era, characterized by establishing decentralized markets, significantly enhancing and perfecting the technology's trust attributes. In the socialization stage of technological promotion and application, RWA and token technology overcame the limitations of the 1.0 era through innovation. Its anonymity, openness, decentralized characteristics, and ability to meet the demand for simplified social trust drove further development and popularization of the technology.

The implementation of smart contracts programmed the complex interactions between human relationships, legal norms, and the virtual world, ensuring the clarity and immutability of contract content. In a reliable network environment formed by RWA and tokens, digital asset transactions and interactions with digital space entities can be conducted safely and efficiently. The perfection of these technical trust attributes enriched technological products and gained recognition from technological and legal systems, increasing social acceptance of the technology.

The integrated application of RWA and token technology played a key role in driving new technological innovations and industrial transformations, with its importance in token economics and RWA value creation becoming increasingly prominent. As the technological socialization process deepened, RWA and token technology established their position as a decentralized technical trust mechanism in broader social spaces and fields, providing a solid foundation for building a more open, transparent, and efficient market environment.

As "RWA and Token Technology + " enters the comprehensive popularization phase of Technology 3.0, its technical trust attributes exhibit exponential growth. The societal demand for effective trust simplification mechanisms continues to exist, and the widespread application of RWA and token technology is driving technological progress and popularization in the 3.0 era. Currently, RWA and token technology are at the peak of their lifecycle, and the socialization stage of their promotion and social application has arrived.

With the further development of internet foundational technologies, especially with the advent of the 5G + era, the ability of RWA and token smart contracts to connect the digital and physical worlds will be significantly enhanced. This indicates that social trust models will face more profound impacts, integration, and reconstruction and that technical trust functions will bring significant economic benefits. These benefits include economic gains within the RWA and token technology industry community, reducing social structure operational costs, and avoiding ineffective social operating costs through technical trust models.

However, this stage is accompanied by comprehensive changes in social trust models, which increase the difficulty of social integration and adaptation and may lead to widespread social anomie and concerns about social integration. In the context of token economics and RWA value creation, the development of RWA and token technology requires technological innovation and a deep understanding and adaptation to social impacts.

8.1.5 The Significance and Role of RWA and Tokenization Value Creation

Reducing financing costs is a core advantage of token economics, and this is particularly evident in the popularization of RWA and tokenization models. The driving forces behind this are mainly two aspects: first, the community effect stimulated by blockchain technology, and second, its decentralized payment network. Since its inception, blockchain technology has fostered a self-organizing community that has expanded from technology enthusiasts to commercial investors. Globally, numerous believers in blockchain technology have become blockchain projects' primary consumers and investors. The decentralized nature and transparency of blockchain payment networks allow users, once they overcome the initial learning barriers, to experience unprecedented satisfaction and control, which psychologically significantly promotes consumption and investment behaviors. Additionally, the market-oriented characteristics of blockchain payments provide convenience for RWA and tokenization financing, effectively reducing related costs.

The principle of token simplification of settlement and taxation is not unique to blockchain technology. Long before the advent of blockchain technology, casino chips demonstrated the prototype of a token model. In this model, transactions between customers and the casino require only one settlement, and taxes are calculated simultaneously. Similarly, in the modern token economy, individuals holding tokens may engage in multiple transactions in commercial scenarios, but tax payments occur only when tokens are exchanged for fiat currency. This mechanism significantly simplifies the tax process and improves efficiency.

Within the framework of the token economy, in addition to acquiring tokens through secondary market trading and control processes, issuers can distribute tokens to community members for free during the project launch phase, a process known as an "airdrop." When users receive these free tokens in their digital wallets, they often become interested in the project and consume them, providing a vital user base for new projects. This is similar to new merchants' strategy to attract customers by distributing coupons and trial cards. However, token airdrops based on blockchain technology are particularly beneficial for startup project teams due to their almost zero operational costs. If users holding tokens expect the value of the tokens to decrease, they may quickly use the tokens for consumption; if they expect the value to rise, they may support the project's market promotion by holding the tokens, similar to sharing voting and like links in social groups.

In the blockchain token economy, the core strategy is to stimulate and activate the internal ecosystem through tokens, enabling newly established enterprises to operate as mature ecosystem enterprises from the outset, which is a significant challenge for management. However, blockchain technology provides a decentralized, self-organizing management system and tools and tokens for internal circulation and incentives within the ecosystem, making this relatively simple. Combining RWA with tokenization to raise funds, from a commercial perspective, can be seen as a "pre-sale" of the company's products rather than "equity crowdfunding." The combination of RWA and tokenization does not distribute company shares to equity investors in the form of cryptocurrency but provides the expected products or product usage rights to early investors or potential consumers through pre-sales.

8.2 The Impact of RWA and Tokenization on the Economic System and Social Structure

RWA and tokenization, as a new way of "manufacturing" social trust, are overturning the social construction of traditional social trust relationships. Through the technological socialization integration of traditional social trust, from the cryptocurrency system under the RWA and token 1.0 technology model to the programmable financial system under the 2.0 technology model and further to the programmable society under the 3.0 model, technical trust—distinct from traditional trust and institutional trust—is transitioning from prophecy to reality. RWA and tokenization strongly intervene in the social trust system through science and technology, making implicit human social relationships and social system structures producible via technology. On the one hand, this represents a further expansion of the practical limits of technology acting on nature and society; on the other hand, during the socialization process of RWA and tokenization, it is necessary to remain vigilant about the negative social structural impacts caused by the transformation of social trust models and to provide timely social warnings and adjustments.

Consequently, the relevant technological actors not only need to establish a necessary sense of responsibility during code writing and technology application but also need to possess a deep epistemological understanding—that the technological activities of information technology actors are not merely one-dimensional technological product development but also the compilation and construction of existing social structures. Information technology products' research and development activities must not be mechanically reduced to writing non-socially meaningful data codes. The technological socialization of any information technology product, including RWA and tokenization products, is a complex, organic integration and construction of social structures. Therefore, the relevant technological actors are responsible for the quality, functionality, and economic value of technological products and the social relationships and structures that the products can influence.

8.2.1 The Impact of RWA and Tokenization on the Economic System

The tokenization of digital assets through blockchain technology demonstrates technological innovation and supplements and optimizes the existing economic model. Introducing this technology does not aim to overturn the existing economic operating model but rather to improve and optimize the existing production relations, forming a new economic model. This model further optimizes and upgrades the existing financial system by supplementing and extending it.

The tokenization process of digital assets involves identifying, creating, transmitting, and realizing digital asset value. This process transforms digital assets from simple binary code into production factors with real economic value. Through tokenization, each digital asset is endowed with apparent value and ownership, enabling it to be traded and circulated in broader markets. This transformation allows digital assets to be more effectively integrated into various economic activities, becoming an essential component of innovation and production. For example, blockchain data can be used in supply chain management to enhance transparency and efficiency; digital art can achieve clear ownership and value circulation through tokenization; smart contracts can automatically execute transactions, reducing transaction costs and time.

The value identification of digital assets provides new financial opportunities for small, medium, and micro enterprises (SMEs) and individual businesses. In traditional monetary systems, the banking-dominated system often relies on liquid collateral to build a credit system. This model usually excludes SMEs and individual companies that lack high-quality assets as "backing," making it difficult for them to obtain necessary financing support, which affects their business development and expansion. However, introducing blockchain technology, mainly distributed ledger technology, offers an innovative solution to this problem. Blockchain platforms, with the assistance of third-party professional service institutions, can conduct in-depth investigations, ratings, evaluations, and information disclosure of underlying assets, enhancing the transparency and authenticity of assets. In this way, even assets previously unrecognized by traditional financial systems as "stagnant" can receive effective value recognition and credit enhancement.

The decentralized nature of blockchain allows these assets to break away from the traditional financial institution credit system and gain value through independent credit mechanisms. After being tokenized, these assets are transformed into digital asset tokens with authority and uniqueness. These tokenized digital assets can be freely traded on blockchain platforms and included in broader financial market asset categories.

For SMEs and individual businesses, tokenization means that their held assets can be converted into tradable digital assets, but, more importantly, the liquidity premium obtained through tokenization can release more excellent economic value. This released value can help enterprises solve cash flow problems and, to some extent, enhance their market competitiveness and sustainable development capabilities. The role of blockchain technology in the tokenization transformation of digital assets is not just a technological revolution but also a revaluation of the existing asset value system. By transforming traditional digital assets into tokenized assets with higher liquidity and additional value, digital assets have seen significant growth and accumulation.

Due to the high replicability of digital products, tokenized digital assets can expand their scale through simple replication. For example, once a digital artwork or software product is created, it can be replicated indefinitely without losing value. On the contrary, as more people access and use these assets, their social value and recognition increase. This scale expansion is difficult to achieve with traditional physical assets, as physical assets typically depreciate with use and the passage of time.

Digital assets generate a large amount of user interaction data and evaluation information, known as "soft information. " This data is often tricky to collect and analyze in traditional financial systems. The introduction of blockchain technology allows this data to be effectively recorded, preserved, verified, and processed in real time using tools such as smart contracts.

Blockchain technology allows transparent recording and the use of this information to enhance the trustworthiness and value of digital assets. For example, consumer reviews and usage data can demonstrate a digital product's popularity and recognition, directly influencing its market value.

Blockchain technology allows for deeper analysis and reorganization of various data related to digital assets. This includes transaction records and all interaction data associated with the assets. This data can uncover hidden value in assets, such as optimizing product design by analyzing user behavior patterns or improving supply chain management by tracking asset circulation paths.

Through these mechanisms, tokenized digital assets replicate themselves and achieve value appreciation with each transaction and interaction. This accumulation of value translates into additional asset value, making tokenized digital assets an entirely new asset class with attributes that traditional assets lack, such as high liquidity and transparent value verification mechanisms.

By enabling the tokenization of digital assets, blockchain technology addresses the issue of information asymmetry and enhances the value and utility of the assets themselves through datafication and intelligent processing. The application of this technology provides new momentum and direction for the future development of the digital economy, signaling a fundamental transformation in asset management and financial transactions. Through the introduction of blockchain technology, the tokenization of digital assets represents not only a transformation in asset forms but also in asset forms and an entirely new way of value circulation and exchange in the digital economy.

The core advantage of this technology lies in its ability to ensure the sustainable transfer and value transmission of digital assets, greatly enhancing their liquidity and economic vitality.

First, through its unique design, blockchain technology addresses a significant technical challenge in the digital economy—the double-spending problem, commonly known as the "double-spend" issue. In a decentralized environment, the replicability of data poses significant challenges to the secure transfer of digital property. Traditional digital transaction systems may not effectively verify whether an asset has already been used or transferred by others, leading to the repeated use of assets or fraudulent activities. Blockchain technology ensures the uniqueness and consistency of digital assets within the system by encrypting and publicly recording the details of each transaction. This mechanism effectively prevents the repeated use of assets, guaranteeing transaction authenticity and security.

Second, the establishment of blockchain trading platforms further promotes the circulation and economic linkage of digital assets. Platform, industry, and geographical restrictions often hinder asset circulation in the current digital economy environment. Blockchain platforms provide a decentralized, open trading environment, allowing digital assets to circulate freely across platforms, industries, and regions. This high level of liquidity improves asset utilization efficiency and fosters economic interaction and collaboration among different communities, industries, and regions. Digital assets can be traded through these platforms in a transparent, open, and efficient market, realizing their value.

Finally, blockchain technology and related trading platforms enhance the value and utility of digital assets and provide strong momentum and support for developing the digital economy by creating a more efficient and trustworthy trading environment. Applying these technologies not only solves some existing core technical issues but also opens up new possibilities and directions for the future development of digital assets.

The tokenization of digital assets achieves value appreciation in multiple ways, primarily reflected in reducing financing costs, increasing financing returns, and improving transaction efficiency. First, tokenization significantly lowers the financing costs for digital asset owners, simplifies the financing process, reduces related legal and administrative expenses, and breaks through the limitations of traditional asset categories, enabling assets to circulate in the form of tokens. Second, tokenization increases investors' financing returns. By leveraging blockchain technology, assets are subdivided into smaller shares, lowering the investment threshold while improving the efficiency of asset profit distribution.

Third, introducing innovative contract technology enhances transaction efficiency, automating trading, accounting, clearing, and settlement, thereby reducing the risks of operational errors and fraud. This improves the overall efficiency and security of the digital asset trading system. These enhancements increase the liquidity and usability of digital assets and provide new growth momentum for developing the digital economy.

Tokenization is not only an innovative way of resource allocation but also constructs a new type of inclusive financial ecosystem, propelling the digital economy into a new stage of development. Against the backdrop of the ongoing transformation of data into production factors, blockchain technology has created a new asset category—tokenized digital assets—significantly enhancing the asset financing capabilities of small, medium, and micro enterprises (SMEs) and individual businesses. Additionally, the token economy lowers the entry barriers for investors, optimizes the flow of social capital, and promotes collaboration and linkage among enterprises, investors, and consumers.

Tokenization transforms digital assets through two key steps: asset digitization and data assetization. Asset digitization involves using blockchain technology to convert the virtual property into standardized blockchain-tokenized asset data. Data assetization, on the other hand, enables tokenized asset data to be quantified, trusted, and controllable through blockchain trading platforms, thereby becoming digital assets capable of generating economic benefits.

Furthermore, tokenization enhances digital assets' financing credibility, breaking through global integration bottlenecks. By improving transparency and trust, blockchain technology makes digital assets transparent, tamper-resistant, and trustworthy, enhancing their financing credibility within the blockchain economic ecosystem. The advancement of blockchain technology also standardizes digital assets, enabling tokenized digital assets to circulate rapidly globally and promoting interconnectivity among different communities.

Tokens also change how collaboration occurs in the digital economy, optimizing the distribution of value appreciation in digital assets. Through incentive-compatible mechanisms, blockchain technology motivates participants to pursue economic benefits without harming collective interests, reducing negative externalities in the Internet economy (such as plagiarism and breaches of trust). At the same time, blockchain's token ownership rights provide contributors who actively participate in community activities with a share of value appreciation, promoting the iterative accumulation and value appreciation of digital assets. These changes drive the development of an inclusive financial ecosystem, bringing new vitality to the digital economy system.

8.2.2 The Impact of RWA and Tokenization on Social Structure: The Construction of Social Trust Models

8.2.2.1 Dimensions of Social Trust Construction

In English, both "trust" and "confidence" are related to trust but differ in meaning. Sociologist Niklas Luhmann distinguishes between these two concepts. He points out that "confidence" is related to risk in the face of uncertainty, while "trust" is related to risk and individual subjective choice. Therefore, social trust can be seen as a complex psychological and social phenomenon with two dimensions: first, it is an individual's subjective choice of the object of trust, corresponding to "trust" in English; second, it is the trust relationship formed based on individual trust choices and social interactions, corresponding to "confidence" in English, or what can be described as institutional trust. The transition from "trust" to "confidence" essentially corresponds to the transition from agricultural to industrial society. However, whether under the "trust" dimension or the "confidence" dimension of social trust construction, humans are the main actors in social trust construction activities, with emotions and rationality serving as mediating variables between the two. However, a clear social trend is that, in the process of social structural changes, technological development increasingly pushes human subjective trust choices toward rationality. Luhmann stated that in complex social changes, "familiarity and trust must find a new mutually reinforcing relationship; familiarity is no longer immediately embodied and can no longer be used to guarantee trust relationships. Such relationships can no longer be guaranteed by excluding strangers, enemies, and unfamiliar people from certain boundaries." With the advent of post-industrial society, social changes have once again raised higher demands on the role of technology in social trust.

Looking back at the evolution of social trust models, we can see that in the early stages of primitive society and unique social trust relationships based on blood ties, the relevance of social trust to technology was not significant. A familiarity-based trust mechanism rooted in blood and kinship ties within the family enabled social solidarity. Engels pointed out, "The family is the cell of society." Only when trust relationships, with the participation of technology, extended beyond the scope of family relationships did the construction of general trust relationships—different from special trust—begin to integrate with social and scientific technologies, forming institutional trust models with the participation of social and scientific technologies, thereby constructing the general trust model of human society. The reason for this is that, at the social level, it is the result of continuous social differentiation driven by the expansion of the social division of labor with the participation of technology; at the individual level, as J.D. Bernal stated, "Human needs and desires constantly provide the impetus for exploration and action." Therefore, driven by their own social needs and the expanding social division of labor, humans, with the help of social and scientific-technological driving forces, explored and established a comprehensive social trust civilization on top of the natural system.

8.2.3 The Reconstruction of Social Trust Models by RWA and Tokenization

We are gradually entering the post-industrial society, a process marked most notably by the transformation of the labor structure, where most of the workforce is no longer engaged in agriculture or manufacturing. This shift indicates that the service sector will replace agriculture and manufacturing, leading to profound changes in social interaction patterns. In the post-industrial society, changes in production methods will also drive the evolution of the social trust system, requiring the reintegration of existing social trust models to adapt to new social interaction patterns.

Against this backdrop, the socialization of RWA and tokenization provides the technical foundation for constructing post-industrial social trust models. Around 2008, the rapid development of internet technology provided the necessary technical support for RWA and tokenization. At the same time, the outbreak of the global financial crisis raised questions about the effectiveness of existing institutional trust models, creating conditions for social recognition and demand for RWA and tokenization as technical trust tools during the cryptocurrency phase.

Specifically, the socialization of RWA and tokenization has led to a trust model that is different from traditional familiarity-based and institutional trust—technical trust. This technical trust focuses on science and technology rather than social technology in a broad sense. In the highly heterogeneous social structure of post-industrial society, the scope of effectiveness of institutional trust and familiarity-based trust is gradually shrinking. In contrast, with its technical rationality, the decentralized technical model driven by the socialization of RWA and tokenization meets the credibility and efficiency requirements of trust relationships in post-industrial society, simplifying the complex mechanisms of social trust interactions.

Therefore, the socialization of RWA and tokenization holds revolutionary significance in social trust construction, promoting the technical "manufacturing" of social trust and making it possible. This information technology-driven manufacturing of social trust fosters a close integration of science and technology with social trust. The decisive technical intervention of RWA and tokenization initiates a new trust model integration that aligns with post-industrial society's trust demands, marking the arrival of the era of technologized social trust construction.

Through this approach, we can redefine the construction of social trust and explore new models of social trust within the context of token economics and RWA value creation to meet the needs and challenges of post-industrial society.

In the current construction of social trust, technology's intervention not only alters traditional trust structures but also redefines how trust is generated and maintained. In non-technological participation models, establishing trust primarily relies on individual interactions and socialization processes. This model is commonly found in traditional social structures based on geography and culture, such as families, friend circles, and communities. Here, establishing and maintaining trust depends on long-term interpersonal interactions, word of mouth, and adherence to social norms.

In weak technological participation models, technology plays a supportive role, enhancing traditional trust-building methods. Through means such as email, social media, online reviews, and recommendation systems, technology helps people establish and evaluate trust within expanded social networks. Although technology plays a significant role in this model, direct human interaction remains key to building trust.

In strong technological participation models, technology is not just a tool but the core of trust construction. The application of advanced technologies such as blockchain, smart contracts, and AI recommendation systems enables trust to be established and maintained with little or no direct human intervention. For example, with its immutable ledger properties, blockchain technology provides a new trust mechanism in areas like financial transactions and supply chain management.

Technology intervention has changed the dynamics of trust, bringing numerous impacts. Technology makes information more transparent and traceable, enhancing trust in institutions and individuals. Additionally, technology allows individuals to transcend geographical and cultural boundaries, establishing global trust networks. The application of technology reduces the time required to build trust, especially in financial and commercial transactions. However, while technology provides new tools for trust construction, it also introduces risks such as privacy breaches and data security issues.

Understanding the expanded role of technology in the construction of social trust offers convenience and efficiency to modern society while presenting challenges and prompting a rethinking of traditional social structures and interpersonal interaction models. This is crucial for designing more effective trust-building strategies and technological solutions.

As shown in Table 8.1, trust is primarily based on kinship and geographical relationships in the non-technological participation model of social trust. This model is adapted to the familiar trust of agrarian civilization and agricultural society. At this stage, trust is regarded as a conceptual dimension of "subjective choice," reflecting the most primitive and fundamental state of social trust. This form of trust is based on the mechanical solidarity of a customary society, where social

Table 8.1 Three-phase model of succession and evolution of social trust models

Social trust mode	Non-technological participation	Weak technological participation	Strong technological participation
Social structure basis	Customary society—Mechanical solidarity	Legal society, post-industrial society—Organic solidarity	
Main technology type	——	Social technology	Scientific technology
Human-technology relationship	Minimal technological involvement	Interaction between humans and (humans + technology)	Interaction between humans and (technological products)
Relationship bonds	Blood, Geograph	Law, Institutions	Technological code, law, institutions
Manifestation of trust	Familiar trust	Institutional trust	technological trust
Conceptual dimension of trust	Subjective choice	Institutional trust	——

and scientific technologies are almost absent in the construction of trust. In this model, blood relations serve as important bonds between social actors, and the construction and maintenance of trust mainly rely on individual psychological and emotional factors, displaying strong characteristics of subjective choice.

With the intervention of social technology, the weak technological participation model of social trust becomes possible. In this model, technology assists the activities of social organizations but does not dominate. Professor Carl Mitcham defines social technology as policies, plans, and programs based on social science theories and survey data, which are operational procedures and rules for solving social problems. In this context, the functions of social organizations expand in scale and credibility, gradually replacing traditional trust models based on blood relations, family, and neighborhood.

Upon entering the intense technological participation phase, scientific technology becomes the core of social trust interactions, promoting the emergence of the technological trust dimension and marking the development of social trust models towards the technological trust stage. Society further evolves into a legal and post-industrial society, with more profound organic solidarity becoming the form of social integration during this period. In this stage, scientific technology gradually replaces the role of social technology, and technological products and outcomes become new nodes in the construction of trust relationships.

RWA and tokenization are examples of technologies that emerged with the rapid development of information technologies such as the Internet. Based on decentralized credit mechanisms, they can effectively mitigate the uncertainty risks brought by human participation, thereby replacing traditional trusted professional communities. The social application of these technologies not only meets the need for simplifying complex social trust structures but also drives the direction of social trust structures toward rationalization and technologization.

8.2.4 The Second Impact of RWA and Tokenization on Social Structure: Innovation in Social Organizational Form

Firstly, to deeply understand the essence of technology, it must be placed within its developmental context. As a companion technology to Bitcoin, blockchain technology has its origins and development closely tied to the evolution of currency. Therefore, a comprehensive understanding of blockchain technology must start with the origin and development of money. Secondly, the concept of a "distributed ledger" is central when discussing blockchain technology. Blockchain is a public ledger that records cryptocurrency transactions (such as Bitcoin). The digitization and encryption of the ledger provide new momentum for economic and social transformation. Finally, from the institutional economics perspective, the advancement of blockchain technology heralds the evolution of organizational forms, potentially expanding the existing triple economic system to a quadruple economic system that includes distributed autonomous organizations (DAO). This could fundamentally alter our understanding of monetary forms.

Through blockchain technology, the token economy has risen, and the tokenization of RWA provides new avenues for asset liquidity and opens up new spaces for value creation. By enhancing transaction transparency and reducing trust costs, the distributed ledger technology of blockchain has profoundly impacted the economy and society. As technology advances, we can foresee that new organizational forms like DAO will gradually become part of the economic and social structure. Through smart contracts and token incentive mechanisms, they promote the efficient allocation of resources and the co-creation of value.

As blockchain technology matures, concepts such as digital fiat currency, smart contracts, and DAO continuously drive changes in economic models and organizational forms. In this series of innovations, the linkage between tokens and RWA becomes a key method for creating value.

Digital fiat currency, the 1.0 version of the blockchain economy, achieves currency digitization through decentralization, laying the foundation for the development of the token economy. Smart contracts, the 2.0 version, automate and programmatically handle transactions and contracts and significantly expand their application scenarios by binding with RWA.

For example, by tokenizing real estate, artworks, and other tangible assets through smart contracts, these assets can exist on the blockchain in a divisible and tradable form. This increases asset liquidity and provides investors with new investment channels.

Furthermore, DAO, as the 3.0 version of the blockchain economy, represent an entirely new form of organizational management. In DAO, tokens are not only a medium of exchange but also a symbol of management and voting rights. Members use tokens to vote and make decisions, guiding the organization's operational direction and fund usage. This token-based governance mechanism reduces management costs and enhances decision-making transparency and efficiency. Additionally, by combining tokens with RWA, DAO can achieve broader asset management and value creation, such as real estate development projects or collective investments in artworks within the DAO framework.

These new economic models based on blockchain, especially the diverse applications of tokens and their integration with RWA, not only provide higher liquidity and market accessibility for assets but also drive the transformation of traditional finance and corporate systems. Although challenges such as legal recognition and security remain, the combination of token economics and RWA has already demonstrated its undeniable potential and influence in the future economic structure.

Under the framework of Coase's transaction cost theory, we typically distinguish between state, corporate, and market mechanisms based on the level of transaction costs. However, in the real world, new types of organizations transcend these three traditional economic forms, such as social enterprises in Western countries. These organizations do not fully conform to the definition of a corporation, nor are they equivalent to state institutions; they are more like social entities that combine corporate characteristics, government authorization, and public interests. Central banks like the Federal Reserve are private enterprises and public institutions. Certain economic activities, such as currency issuance, financial transactions, internet infrastructure, and social security funds, may involve public interest, government interest, and social welfare or have global coverage. Relying solely on state mechanisms for these activities could lead to high transaction costs and inefficient resource allocation. Relying on corporate mechanisms might result in a lack of corporate participation due to significant investments, long cycles, and low returns. At the same time, the involvement of monopolistic corporations could lead to market inefficiency and resource misallocation, resulting in high transaction costs. The complexity of these economic activities and the participation of multiple stakeholders keep transaction costs high, affecting the macroeconomic regulation efficiency of corporate, market, and state mechanisms.

DAO may represent the fourth institutional innovation following state, market, and corporate mechanisms. It balances conflicts between the state and the market by reducing transaction costs and optimizing resource allocation. A DAO is a self-operating organization based on open and fair rules that can function without external intervention. These rules typically exist in open-source software, allowing individuals to become shareholders of the organization by purchasing or providing services. Shareholders can participate in the organization's operations and development and share its benefits. Compared to traditional corporate mechanisms, DAO operate more automatically and efficiently, allowing anyone to join or exit anytime. In a DAO, conventional concepts of income and profit are downplayed, and corporate equity is represented as tokens within the system. This structure simplifies corporate operations, retaining only the roles of investors and producers, thereby significantly reducing transaction costs. A DAO's equity (tokens) can circulate as rapidly as the stocks of a publicly traded company, with their value discovery determined by the market from the outset, further reducing transaction costs.

Historically, the emergence of double-entry bookkeeping, corporate systems, and private property protection laid the foundation for the rise of capitalism, becoming the cornerstone of modern commercial society. With the advent of cryptographic digital currencies, distributed ledger technology, and DAO, we have reason to believe that these innovations will profoundly impact the structure and operation of modern commercial society. Particularly in the context of token economics and RWA value creation, these technologies provide new methods for value exchange and resource allocation, opening up new possibilities for economic and social development.

8.2.5 Concerns About the Impact of RWA and Tokenization on Economic Systems and Social Structures

8.2.5.1 Social Efficiency: The Social Benefits of RWA and Tokenization

In modern society, the pursuit of efficiency has become an essential social characteristic. The philosopher of technology, Jacques Ellul, once pointed out that despite the vast differences in technology across different eras and fields, their common characteristic remains the pursuit of efficiency. This efficiency is reflected in improving efficiency within technological systems and is widely manifested in the overall efficiency enhancement of social structures during technological socialization.

Against this backdrop, the tokenization related to RWA, based on its unique technological rationality, plays a revolutionary role in constructing social trust models, promoting the overall improvement of social efficiency. Specifically, the social application of RWA and tokenization introduces a simplified mechanism of technological trust with strong instrumental rationality.

For example, traditional simplification mechanisms such as laws, institutions, seniority, and reputation at the social structure level help regulate interactions between people. However, the involvement of irrational social variables like personal relationships, connections, and face-saving often leads to operational deviations. RWA and tokenization effectively overcome these issues through disintermediated information technology, ensuring data transparency and security, simplifying social interaction mechanisms, and enhancing the efficiency of social operations.

Additionally, the techno-economic paradigm based on RWA and tokenization continuously innovate, further promoting social efficiency. Looking back at the five technological revolutions over the past 200 years, each has brought a new techno-economic paradigm. Compared to traditional techno-economic paradigms, the information technology paradigm provides unprecedented technical means for solving information communication problems in social production and interaction. For instance, programmable financial systems based on RWA and tokenization have established a decentralized trust payment system. This not only revolutionizes transaction methods in traditional financial systems but also significantly reduces transaction costs and eliminates redundancies in personnel, procedures, and documentation. With the social application of RWA and tokenization 3.0 products, this programmable social trust system is rapidly forming and gradually being innovatively applied and promoted in critical social systems such as cultural education, government governance, and healthcare. This extends the improvement of social efficiency from the financial system to the social system.

In summary, driven by RWA and tokenization, all financial and social systems are moving towards greater efficiency by constructing a strong technological trust model. This technology-driven social transformation demonstrates the inherent power of technology and reflects modern society's relentless pursuit of efficiency.

8.2.6 Social Anomie: Social Concerns About the Socialization of RWA and Token Technology

In the current wave of technological development, RWA and token technology have introduced new value-creation models. While reshaping financial and economic structures, these models also profoundly impact social trust and humanistic values. By digitizing assets, tokenization significantly enhances liquidity and transparency, bringing unprecedented efficiency and convenience to capital markets. Simultaneously, the application of RWA allows traditionally illiquid physical assets (such as real estate and artworks) to be easily traded globally, greatly expanding these assets' market and investment potential.

However, while this code- and algorithm-based trust mechanism reduces transaction costs and time, it may also undermine traditional trust structures based on interpersonal relationships and communities.

In this model, direct interactions between individuals decrease, potentially making social relationships more mechanical and indifferent. This change affects the emotional bonds within society and may lead to further social fragmentation, especially as economic values increasingly replace humanistic values.

Moreover, technology's widespread application and reliance reshape social structures and labor markets. The advancement of automation and intelligence poses risks of transformation or even obsolescence for many traditional professions. This causes shifts in economic structures and brings issues of inequality and alienation at the social level. Therefore, while pursuing technological progress and financial efficiency, we must pay more attention to their impact on social justice and humanistic care.

In summary, token and RWA technologies bring significant economic benefits and efficiency improvements to modern society but challenge traditional social trust mechanisms and humanistic values. In response, society and policymakers should take measures to ensure that technological development promotes social integration and harmonious development by establishing comprehensive ethical guidelines and designing inclusive technological solutions. This way, we can ensure that technological progress is not only an economic success but also a social and cultural advancement.

8.2.7 Social Adaptation of RWA and Tokenization

In the context of accelerating globalization and digitalization, the development of RWA and tokenization is rapidly transforming our economic and social structures. To address this trend, we can strengthen systematic support and regulation in four key areas to ensure these technologies are integrated into broader social development healthily and effectively.

First, strengthening the construction of the legal system is crucial to creating a stable development environment for RWA and tokenization. Formulating relevant policies and regulations can promote the social application and commercialization of these technologies and ensure that technological development does not deviate from the path of fairness and justice. Specifically, policymakers should introduce incentives to support innovation in RWA and tokenization by enterprises and research institutions while establishing strict regulatory norms to combat illegal activities exploiting these technologies.

Second, through procurement policies, governments should support the market demand for RWA and tokenization. For example, governments and public sectors can prioritize procuring solutions that use tokenization for asset management and transactions, providing a practical application platform for these technologies and promoting their socialization through real-world cases.

Third, establishing unified technical standards is the cornerstone for promoting the healthy development of RWA and tokenization. Just as Apple Inc. facilitated the widespread adoption of its operating system through ISO standards, RWA and tokenization also require clear standards and norms to ensure interoperability and security. This helps reduce the complexity of technology applications and builds user trust and acceptance.

Finally, defining ethical standards for technology is essential to infuse humanistic care into developing RWA and tokenization. Technological development should serve the overall well-being of human society, not just pursue economic benefits. During technology implementation, it is crucial to cultivate and promote moral norms that align with public interests (such as honesty, transparency, and responsibility). This will guide technological development to place greater emphasis on social responsibility and ethical considerations.

By systematically advancing these four aspects, we can better harness the potential of RWA and tokenization to drive comprehensive economic and social development. At the same time, we can effectively address potential risks and challenges, ensuring a harmonious unity between technological progress and social values.

8.3 RWA and Tokenization in Hong Kong: The Ensemble Project and Digital Hong Kong Dollar+

The Hong Kong Monetary Authority (HKMA) held the sandbox launch ceremony for the Ensemble Project on August 28, 2024. It announced that the trial's first phase would cover four primary use case themes for tokenized assets (see Table 8.2). This marks a significant step forward in applying tokenization technology in the financial industry. The HKMA's Ensemble Project aims to explore the construction of an innovative financial market infrastructure based on blockchain platforms, promoting seamless interbank settlement using tokenized currency through wCBDC (wholesale central bank digital currency). Through the sandbox trials, the HKMA will verify the technical interoperability between tokenized assets, tokenized deposits, and wCBDC while allowing industry participants to conduct end-to-end testing of tokenized asset transactions in real business scenarios.

The Hong Kong Monetary Authority (HKMA) has completed the sandbox construction. It aims to use experimental tokenized currency to promote interbank settlement and focus on studying tokenized asset transactions. The participating banks of the Ensemble Project Architecture Working Group have connected their tokenized deposit platforms to the sandbox, preparing for future experiments in cross-bank payment versus payment (PvP) and delivery versus payment (DvP) settlements.

After thoroughly considering industry intentions, market development trends, and the potential impact of innovation, the first phase of the sandbox trials will cover the tokenization of traditional financial assets and RWA, focusing on four major themes: fixed income and investment funds, liquidity management, green and sustainable finance, and trade and supply chain finance. To consolidate Hong Kong's position as an international financial center and explore new economic areas with an innovative spirit, the HKMA will continue to actively communicate with industry professionals to understand their interest in tokenization development and jointly develop and identify new themes and use cases related to tokenization.

Establishing an appropriate regulatory framework is particularly important to support the continuous development of Hong Kong's tokenized asset market. As one of the key members of the working group, the Securities and Futures Commission (SFC) plays a significant role in formulating a regulatory architecture to support the ongoing development of Hong Kong's tokenized asset market. Additionally, the SFC will collaborate with the HKMA to lead tokenization initiatives related to the asset management industry, promoting the widespread application of tokenization and enhancing Hong Kong's status as a premier asset and wealth management center.

The Ensemble Project Working Group boasts a strong lineup, including Hong Kong's four major banks—HSBC, Standard Chartered, Bank of China (Hong Kong), and Hang Seng Bank—as well as digital asset financial services group HashKey Group, and global leading technology companies such as Ant Digital Technologies and Microsoft Hong Kong. Non-working group participants in

Table 8.2 Four application themes and related use cases to be tested in the ensemble project sandbox

Theme	Proposed use cases	Industry participants	
		Ensemble project architecture working group members (listed in alphabetical order by English name)	Non-Working group members (listed in alphabetical order by English name)
Fixed income and investment funds	(1) Bonds (2) Funds	• Bank of China (Hong Kong) Limited • Hang Seng Bank Limited • HashKey Group • The Hongkong and Shanghai Banking Corporation Limited • Standard Chartered Bank (Hong Kong) Limited	• BlackRock • BOCI-Prudential Asset Management Limited • Central Moneymarkets Unit • China Asset Management (Hong Kong) Limited • CSOP Asset Management Limited • Franklin Templeton
Liquidity management	(3)Repurchase Agreements (4) Financial Management	• Bank of China (Hong Kong) Limited • The Hongkong and Shanghai Banking Corporation Limited	• Ant International
Green and sustainable finance	(5) Carbon Credits (6) Electric Vehicle Charging Stations	• Ant Digital Technologies • Hang Seng Bank Limited • HashKey Group • Standard Chartered Bank (Hong Kong) Limited	• Cyberport• •EVIDENT* • The Hong Kong and China Gas Company Limited • Hong Kong Exchanges and Clearing Limited • Hong Kong Applied Science and Technology Research Institute Company Limited • Innovation Chain Technology** • Hu Chi* • Longshine Group***

(continued)

Table 8.2 (continued)

Theme	Proposed use cases	Industry participants	
		Ensemble project architecture working group members (listed in alphabetical order by English name)	Non-Working group members (listed in alphabetical order by English name)
Trade and supply chain finance	(7) Supply Chain Finance (8) Trade Finance and Payments	• Ant Digital T• Hang Seng Bank Limited technologies • The Hongkong and Shanghai Banking Corporation Limited • Microsoft Hong Kong Limited • Microsoft Hong Kong Limited	• ARTA-Email HK Limited • Global Shipping Business Network* • ICC Digital Standards Initiative

Note "*" represents graduates of the Data Harbor Program, "**" represents graduates of the Hong Kong Applied Science and Technology Research Institute's Incubation Program, and "***" represents partners of Ant Digital Technologies the project include Ant International, Central clearing system for debt instruments, Hong Kong Exchanges and Clearing, Hong Kong Science and Technology Park, Hong Kong Cyberport, and numerous renowned asset management companies such as China Asset Management (Hong Kong), BOCI-Prudential Asset Management, BlackRock, and Franklin Templeton.

At the international level, the HKMA will also explore collaboration opportunities with the Hong Kong Centre of the Bank for International Settlements Innovation Hub on one or more tokenization themes and work with members of the CBDC Expert Group to leverage their expertise to advance the development of the sandbox further.

The Chief Executive of the Hong Kong Monetary Authority (HKMA) stated: "The launch of the Ensemble Project sandbox to test tokenization use cases marks a significant step forward for the HKMA and the industry in exploring the application of tokenization technology in real business scenarios. Since the launch of the Ensemble Project in March this year, the industry has responded positively to developing innovative solutions to reshape the digital finance sector. The HKMA looks forward to collaborating with the Securities and Futures Commission (SFC), other central banking institutions, academia, and various industry participants to drive further the innovative development of Hong Kong's tokenization market."

The CEO of the SFC commented: "The launch of the sandbox today demonstrates that the combination of innovation and regulation can open new paths for our financial markets. As two major builders of Hong Kong's financial markets, the SFC and the HKMA share the same vision and are committed to leading Hong Kong's financial system into the future through innovative market infrastructure."

8.3.1 HKMA Expands "Digital Hong Kong Dollar" Project and Launches Phase Two of the Pilot Program – "Digital Hong Kong Dollar + "

On September 23, 2024, the HKMA launched the second phase of the "Digital Hong Kong Dollar" pilot program (hereinafter referred to as "Phase Two"), further exploring innovative use cases for new digital currencies (including the "Digital Hong Kong Dollar" and tokenized deposits) for both individuals and businesses (see Fig. 8.2). As the research of the "Digital Hong Kong Dollar" project expands from the "Digital Hong Kong Dollar" to a more comprehensive exploration of the digital currency ecosystem, the project has been renamed "Digital Hong Kong Dollar + ," reflecting the HKMA's commitment to keeping pace with the new developments in financial technology and fully realizing the potential of digital currencies.

The "Digital Hong Kong Dollar" pilot program is a key component of the "Digital Hong Kong Dollar + " project. Eleven selected institutions from various industries will explore innovative use cases for the "Digital Hong Kong Dollar" and tokenized deposits across three major themes during Phase Two, including tokenized asset settlement, programmability, and offline payments. In real-world

Use Case Theme	Participating Institutions
Tokenized Asset Settlement	· Hang Seng Bank, Aptos Lab, and Boston Consulting Group
	· HSBC
	· Standard Chartered Bank, BlackRock, Mastercard, and Liberia
	· Visa, ANZ Bank, Fidelity International, and China Asset Management
Programmability	· Bank of China (Hong Kong) and Sun Fook Kong (Construction Management) Company
	· China Construction Bank (Asia)
	· DBS Bank
	· Hang Seng Bank
	· Mastercard, Kasikorn Bank, and Tianxing Bank
Offline Payments	· Bank of Communications (Hong Kong) and China Mobile
	· Industrial and Commercial Bank of China (Asia)

Fig. 8.2 Innovative use cases

scenarios, the selected institutions will also study the commercial feasibility of new digital currencies for individuals and businesses. Selected institutions and cases include Visa, ANZ Bank, and China Asset Management (Hong Kong), which will explore near real-time settlement for interbank transfers and cross-border payments using digital Hong Kong dollars and tokenized deposits, as well as delivery versus payment (DvP), to facilitate Australian corporate investors in purchasing tokenized funds offered by Hong Kong asset management companies. Zhu Haokang, Head of Digital Assets and Family Wealth Management at China Asset Management (Hong Kong), stated: "China Asset Management (Hong Kong) is honored to participate in the 'Digital Hong Kong Dollar' pilot program's second phase. The success of the first phase has demonstrated the digital Hong Kong dollar's application value in numerous fields (see Fig. 8.2). We look forward to collaborating closely with the Hong Kong Monetary Authority and various partners in the future to explore the application of the 'Digital Hong Kong Dollar' and tokenized bank deposits in more areas, such as tokenized funds."

8.4 Recommendations for the Future Development of RWA and Tokenization

Driven by digitalization, RWA (Real World Assets) and tokenization, as innovative financial tools, are transforming our traditional views on asset ownership and transactions. The tokenization of RWA leverages blockchain technology to enhance asset liquidity, lower investment thresholds, and increase market transparency. In terms of traditional financial innovation, future efforts should focus on establishing corresponding regulatory frameworks, strengthening technological infrastructure, improving investor education, promoting cross-industry collaboration, advancing standardization and regulatory improvements, and encouraging technological innovation and platform development. In terms of compliance, ensuring that the origin and ownership of assets can be verified and meet AML (Anti-Money Laundering) and KYC (Know Your Customer) requirements is essential. On the technical front, upgrades to technology platforms, integration of oracles, enhancement of cross-chain interoperability, and data security and privacy protection are necessary. Future efforts should explore new application scenarios and business models for integrating AI.

8.4.1 The Impact of RWA and Tokenization on the Traditional Financial Industry and Future Development Recommendations

As technology advances and the regulatory environment gradually improves, tokenization is expected to become a significant direction for the financial industry, injecting more vitality and growth potential into the global economy.

For the financial industry, tokenization significantly enhances asset liquidity by enabling rapid transactions on the blockchain. This innovative approach allows investors to buy and sell assets almost in real time, breaking the limitations of traditional markets and greatly enhancing asset liquidity. Additionally, tokenization lowers investment thresholds. Since investors can purchase a fraction of high-value assets at a lower cost, it opens doors for ordinary investors to participate in markets that were previously accessible only to a few. The immutability of blockchain technology brings unprecedented transparency to the market. All transaction records are public, and anyone can verify the authenticity of transactions, increasing market trust and enhancing the transparency of the entire transaction process. Finally, tokenization provides vast space for innovative financial products and services. Financial institutions can now develop token-based derivatives and structured products, offering investors more investment options and risk management tools.

Regarding regulation, regulatory agencies in various countries should actively build and improve regulatory systems that adapt to the characteristics of tokenized assets. This requires clear rules to ensure the legality of assets, the protection of investor rights, and establish preventive measures to prevent financial risks.

The regulatory framework should cover the transparency of the tokenization process, the verification of asset entities, and the auditing and monitoring of assets. At the same time, regulatory agencies should collaborate with international organizations to form globally unified regulatory standards to address the challenges of cross-border transactions.

For the future integration of traditional finance with RWA and tokenization, the following recommendations are proposed:

- **Strengthening Blockchain Technology Infrastructure**: To support the widespread application of tokenized assets, it is essential to strengthen the construction of blockchain technology infrastructure. This includes improving network scalability, security, and interoperability. Scalability is key to handling large transactions, while security is the foundation for protecting assets from harm. By developing cross-chain technology, seamless connections between different blockchain platforms can be achieved, promoting the free flow and trading of assets. Additionally, privacy protection technologies (such as zero-knowledge proofs) should be adopted to enhance user trust in the platform.
- **Enhancing Investor Education**: Improving investors' understanding and awareness of the risks associated with tokenized assets is crucial. Education on tokenized assets, market dynamics, and risk management should be provided through various forms, such as online courses, seminars, and university programs. Furthermore, establishing and improving investor protection mechanisms is essential to ensure that investors have adequate channels for complaints and compensation in case of losses, such as setting up investor education funds and insurance mechanisms.
- **Deepening and Expanding Cross-Industry Collaboration**: Exploring collaborations with a broader range of industries (such as energy, agriculture, and healthcare) can unlock the potential of RWA tokenization in these sectors. Such collaborations can help these industries achieve enhanced asset liquidity while bringing new growth opportunities to the financial sector. For example, tokenization can digitize physical assets like land and crops in the agricultural industry, allowing investors to flexibly divide and trade their interests.
- **Promoting Standardization and Regulatory Improvements**: Strengthening cooperation with international standardization organizations to develop unified standards for tokenized assets, including specifications for security, transparency, and compatibility. Simultaneously, collaborating with government agencies to promote the formulation of laws and regulations that support the healthy development of tokenized assets, protecting investor rights and mitigating financial risks.
- **Encouraging Technological Innovation and Platform Development**: Fintech companies should develop more advanced blockchain technologies to improve the efficiency and security of tokenized asset transactions. They should support establishing comprehensive tokenized asset platforms that integrate issuance, trading, and management functions, providing one-stop services for assets. For

example, specialized blockchain networks can be developed to support large-scale tokenized asset transactions while ensuring transparency and traceability.

- **The exploration and promotion of new business models:** Encourage the creation of new financial products based on blockchains, such as tokenized bonds, stocks, and other derivative products. These products can provide investors with new investment channels in traditional and emerging markets. At the same time, explore the application of tokenization combined with AI and big data technology, such as using AI for asset evaluation and risk management, to improve the intelligence and precision of tokenized asset management.

8.4.2 Future Development Suggestions for RWA and Tokenization in the Regulatory Context

Regulative issues play a crucial role in developing RWA and tokenization. A comprehensive regulatory framework should ensure that all related activities comply with applicable legal and regulatory requirements. This framework should cover evaluating, issuing, trading, managing, storing, and auditing assets while verifying their source and ownership rights and meeting AML and KYC requirements.

At the same time, establishing good communication and cooperation with financial regulatory authorities is also extremely important. Through proactive dialogue with regulatory authorities, companies can promptly understand the latest regulatory dynamics and integrate regulatory requirements into tokenization strategies at an early stage. Collaborating with regulatory technology (RegTech) tools can also automate compliance processes, improve compliance efficiency, and reduce labor costs and error rates.

Since tokenized assets often involve cross-border transactions, promoting international cooperation to establish common standards and regulatory frameworks is key. Cooperation with regulatory authorities and industry organizations in different countries can help establish international tokenization standards, simplify the complexity of cross-border transactions, and protect investors' interests.

Furthermore, regular training and education for industry professionals, regulatory officials, and legal advisors are necessary. Education can enhance the industry's awareness and capabilities in compliance, covering the latest tokenization technologies, regulatory changes, and compliance practices.

Enhancing the transparency of tokenized assets and establishing a robust reporting system are key measures to improve compliance.

All transactions and asset flows should be traceable and queryable. Companies should regularly report their operational status to regulatory authorities, including but not limited to transaction records, asset evaluation, and risk management.

Advanced data protection technology should be integrated into the design and operation of tokenization platforms to ensure the security of user data and transaction information while also complying with data protection regulations such as the EU's GDPR.

Finally, a dedicated regulatory change management team should be established to monitor and analyze legal and policy changes related to global tokenization. This would ensure that companies can quickly adapt to legal changes and reduce compliance risks. Through these measures, a solid regulatory foundation can be laid for the healthy development of RWA and tokenization, enhancing investor confidence and promoting broader market acceptance and participation.

8.4.3 Future Development Suggestions for RWA and Tokenization in the Technical Context

Enhancing the construction of RWA and tokenization technology is key to promoting their future development. To achieve this goal, the following specific suggestions are made:

- **Technical Platform Upgrade**: Developing a more secure and efficient blockchain platform is the cornerstone of supporting RWA tokenization. For example, adopting sharding technology and Layer 2 solutions can significantly improve network transaction throughput and reduce transaction costs. This technological advancement not only enables larger-scale RWA tokenization and trading activities but also enhances the performance and scalability of the entire blockchain network. By integrating these technologies, a more robust and efficient blockchain ecosystem can be constructed to provide strong technical support for large-scale asset tokenization.
- **Oracle Integration**: Integrating reliable Oracle services into the blockchain platform ensures that smart contracts can accurately reflect the value and status of assets. Oracles serve as a bridge between on-chain and off-chain data, which is crucial for ensuring the authenticity and reliability of RWA tokenization. They can provide real-time market data, asset valuation, and other key information, ensuring that smart contracts operate based on the most up-to-date and accurate data, thereby enhancing investor confidence and market transparency.
- **Cross-chain Interoperability**: Developing cross-chain technology is essential for achieving asset and data flow between different blockchains. Implementing this technology can give users a broader range of investment options and more flexible asset management methods. Cross-chain interoperability enhances the connectivity between different blockchain ecosystems and allows assets to flow freely between multiple blockchain platforms, opening up a broader global market for investors.
- Data security and privacy protection. Advanced encryption technology (such as zero-knowledge proofs) can verify asset ownership and transaction authenticity without disclosing user privacy. This technology can ensure transaction transparency and security while protecting user privacy and avoiding leaking sensitive information. Through such technological applications, user trust in the platform can be enhanced, promoting more user participation in RWA tokenization.

8.4.4 Core Development Direction of RWA and Tokenization: Integration with AI

The integration of tokenization with AI is at the forefront of developing cutting-edge scientific fields. This technology mainly involves transforming physical or intangible assets into digital tokens, representing real-world assets' ownership or usage rights. With the help of AI, this technology can open up new application scenarios and business models. For example, AI can help design and execute smart contracts based on specific conditions and automatically handle complex decision-making processes, such as purchasing or selling tokenized assets in supply chain management.

Regarding data markets and sharing, tokenization can create secure data-sharing platforms where AI can analyze data from multiple sources. This advantage benefits the medical industry, where personal health data can be tokenized and securely shared with research institutions. AI can improve diagnostic accuracy or predict diseases during this process. In addition, AI can optimize the management of tokenized assets, such as real-time analysis of asset performance and providing investment advice, which is of great value in the financial services sector.

The integration of tokenization with AI can also predict market trends and consumer behavior, providing customized strategies and products for enterprises. By analyzing user interactions with tokenized assets, enterprises can provide more personalized services and improve user experience. With the clarification of technology and regulations, this combination will expand to more industries, such as real estate, art, and intellectual property management.

Integrating blockchain, AI, and the Internet of Things will lead to more intelligent and automated applications in the future. For example, real-time, automatically adjusted innovative city service systems may emerge. At the same time, with the advancement of technology, relevant regulations and standards will be further developed to ensure data security, privacy protection, and transaction transparency. AI's security and privacy protection capabilities will also be enhanced, and it will be capable of identifying and detecting anomalies to prevent fraud and hacker attacks. As AI plays an increasingly important role in the decision-making process, discussions on its ethics and transparency will also deepen, especially when dealing with sensitive assets (such as personal data or large-scale investments). The depth and breadth of this technological integration indicate that we will enter an era of greater intelligence and automation. Still, it also brings new challenges regarding technological governance and ethics.

MIX
Papier aus verantwortungsvollen Quellen
Paper from responsible sources
FSC® C105338

If you have any concerns about our products, you can contact us on
ProductSafety@springernature.com

In case Publisher is established outside the EU, the EU authorized representative is:
Springer Nature Customer Service Center GmbH
Europaplatz 3, 69115 Heidelberg, Germany

Printed by Libri Plureos GmbH
in Hamburg, Germany